DATE DUE

MY 1			
MY 1			

DEMCO 38-296

Re-Imaging Japanese Women

Re-Imaging
Japanese Women

EDITED AND WITH AN INTRODUCTION BY
Anne E. Imamura

UNIVERSITY OF CALIFORNIA PRESS

Berkeley   Los Angeles   London

The publisher gratefully acknowledges the contribution provided by the
General Endowment of the Associates of the University of California Press.

University of California Press
Berkeley and Los Angeles, California
University of California Press, Ltd.
London, England
© 1996 by The Regents of the University of California

Library of Congress Cataloging-in-Publication Data
Re-Imaging Japanese women / edited and with an introduction by Anne E.
   Imamura.
      p.   cm.
   Includes bibliographical references and index.
   ISBN 0-520-20262-7 (alk. paper).—0-520-20263-5 (pbk. : alk. paper)
      1. Women—Japan. 2. Women—Employment—Japan. 3. Housewives—
Japan. I. Imamura, Anne E., 1946–.
HQ1762.R45 1996
305.42′0952—dc20
                                                            95-21416
                                                            CIP

Printed in the United States of America

9 8 7 6 5 4 3 2 1

The paper used in this publication meets the minimum requirements of
American National Standard for Information Sciences—Permanence
of Paper for Printed Library Materials, ANSI Z39.48-1984.

To Chiyo Imamura, my mother-in-law, whose life reflects the changes and continuities in Japanese women's lives from the Meiji period when she was born through the Heisei period of today, in admiration of her strength and dedication to her family and the courage and flexibility that enabled her to cope with the social change her life encompassed. In many ways, my re-imaging of Japanese women began with her.

CONTENTS

LIST OF ILLUSTRATIONS / ix

PREFACE / xi

Introduction
Anne E. Imamura / 1

1. Fragile Resistance, Signs of Status:
Women between State and Media in Japan
Nancy R. Rosenberger / 12

2. The Telerepresentation of Gender in Japan
Andrew A. Painter / 46

3. Centering the Household: The Remaking of Female Maturity in Japan
Margaret Lock / 73

4. Social Relations as Capital: The Story of Yuriko
Robert J. Marra / 104

5. The Traditional Arts as Leisure Activities for
Contemporary Japanese Women
Barbara Lynne Rowland Mori / 117

6. Producing Mothers
Anne Allison / 135

7. Nurturing and Femininity: The Ideal of Caregiving in Postwar Japan
Susan Orpett Long / 156

8. Mother or Mama: The Political Economy of Bar Hostesses in Sapporo
John Mock / 177

9. Marriage, Motherhood, and Career Management
in a Japanese "Counter Culture"
Millie R. Creighton / *192*

10. Careers and Commitment: Azumi's Blue-Collar Women
Glenda S. Roberts / *221*

11. Popular Reading: The Literary World of the Japanese Working Woman
Nobuko Awaya and David P. Phillips / *244*

12. Women Legislators in the Postwar Diet
Sally Ann Hastings / *271*

13. Three Women Who Loved the Left:
Radical Woman Leaders in the Japanese Red Army Movement
Patricia G. Steinhoff / *301*

Afterword
Gail Lee Bernstein / *325*

NOTES ON CONTRIBUTORS / *331*

FURTHER READING / *335*

INDEX / *345*

ILLUSTRATIONS

1. New women's life course / 5

2. Chart of housewife types / 57

3. Opening scene from *Yome, Shūto, Kekkon Sōdō* / 67

4. Closing scene from *Yome, Shūto, Kekkon Sōdō* / 68

5. Map of Yuriko's village / 106

6. Rate of nonworking women desiring to work and the women's labor force participation rate / 225

7. Women's labor force participation by age group / 227

PREFACE

Those wishing to understand more about contemporary Japanese women have found a relatively small number of works in English. Although there is an increasing number of scholarly studies appealing to graduate students or specialists, few of these fit the needs of nonspecialists or upper-level undergraduates. Searching for a collection of essays that would provide such readers with a varied perspective on contemporary Japanese women's lives has proved especially challenging.

The desire to produce such a volume led to two panels on *Re-Imaging Japanese Women* at the Association for Asian Studies meetings in Los Angeles in 1993. Several of the chapters in this volume were presented there, and the rest were in draft form. All chapter authors present at the meetings came together to discuss the project. Included in the panels were Theodore Bestor and Beverly Lee, whose input into this project we gratefully acknowledge.

Throughout the project we benefited from the support of Sheila Levine, editorial director at the University of California Press. Without her commitment, this volume would not have been possible. The sharp editorial pencils of Erika Büky and of Carolyn Hill saved us from many potential miscommunications, and Chris Robyn assisted with logistics. We also benefited from the outside reviewers whose detailed comments played an important role in shaping the final manuscript.

In this book, Japanese names appear in Japanese order (family name first, given name second), and unless otherwise cited, translations are by the author of the chapter in which they appear. Individual acknowledgments appear in the appropriate chapters. Anne E. Imamura, editor of the book and author of the introduction, is required to state that the views expressed in the introduction are her own and do not necessarily represent those of the Department of State, and that the substantive content of all other chapters is the sole responsibility of the respective authors.

We hope this book will be useful to undergraduates and graduates, the general public, specialists on Japan and gender studies, and social scientists from all disciplines. Most of all, we hope that the volume will contribute to a better understanding of the complexities of women's lives.

Introduction

Anne E. Imamura

In 1991, Gail Lee Bernstein's *Recreating Japanese Women, 1600–1945* shattered a number of stereotypes about Japanese women. Among them were the beliefs that in Japan motherhood has "always" been the primary role of women; that women did not work outside the home; and that issues of combining work with family and striving for economic independence emerged only after World War II. The coverage of Bernstein's pathbreaking book ends in 1945. Since that time, the range of opportunities for Japanese women has increased while their supportive and domestic responsibilities to family and society have remained. This volume, *Re-Imaging Japanese Women*, attempts to shed light on the balance Japanese women today strike among the choices available to them.

Many factors combine to produce the range of behaviors available to members of a given society. Among these factors are traditional norms and values, the needs of society at a given historical period, and contemporary values and fashions. Behavioral expectations are frequently exemplified in heroic personalities and role models. Social institutions affect these models, and competing social institutions attempt to control or limit one another's effect. Foreign influences, popular culture, and the impact of the media compete with the goals of the polity and the economy and frequently produce alternative images of appropriate behavior.

Image differs from role in several respects. Role refers to behavioral expectations, whereas image refers to appearance. "Appearance" as I am using it here has two meanings: first, how the behavior, role, or position is seen from the outside, and second, the deliberate projection of an appearance by a person or institution. Image and role may not correspond: a couple may put forth the image of a happy marriage when in reality they live separate lives under the same roof and do not fulfill the roles of husband and wife. Image may mimic role: a young woman may portray herself as domestically inclined when she meets her prospective mother-in-law even though she may have no such interests or talents. Image can invite someone to assume a role: one may be attracted by the "glamour" of being a flight attendant and only after taking the job recognize the hard work it entails. Image may be part of a role: the nurturing daughter-in-law is expected to conceal her frustration at the demands of a senile parent, and the mother is expected to put forth the image of enjoying long hours playing with her small children. Yet another distinction between image and role is that image can refer to the perception held of another. Thus men may have idealized images of their future spouses, foreigners may hold images of Japanese women, and older generations may have images of younger. Even if none of these images correspond to reality, they may shape the way the image holder treats or defines the object of the image and thus produce real consequences.

Throughout history, the importance of image is clear, whether in the humility of a bride-to-be or the ceremonies that surround royalty to keep them larger than life. Today, image production is a recognized industry. Politicians, entertainers, and other public figures employ specialists to develop marketable images. Professionals place importance on first impressions and strive to project appropriate images. Marketing relies on the development of a product image and creates an "ideal consumer" to appear in advertising, associating brand names with age groups and social class. Image is a recognized factor in self-esteem and education. Thus images are recognized as powerful tools by individuals seeking to create them and groups and societies seeking to control or develop them.

In this volume, we examine images of women in contemporary Japanese society. We explore how and by whom these images are put forth, the power of these images to shape Japanese women's lives, the potential for Japanese women to utilize traditional images for contemporary purposes, and the opportunities such images provide Japanese women for expanding their behavioral choices.

JAPANESE WOMEN: FROM 1945 TO THE 1990s

During the latter half of the twentieth century, the range of images of Japanese women has expanded to reflect the social change and new roles for women in Japan.[1] Immediately following the war, Japanese concentrated on rebuilding their country, and men and women worked at whatever jobs were available. In the late 1950s and early sixties, increased industrial production brought with it the "salaryman family".[2] This archetypical nuclear family, headed by a salaried male breadwinner, included two children and lived in relatively small quarters requiring little maintenance. In contrast to women who married into farm or shopkeeping families, where they helped in the family business and were under the supervision of their mothers-in-law, the wife managed her own household and was considered a full-time housewife (sengyō shufu). Although numerically in the minority, the salaryman family became the ideal: boys strove to become and girls to marry salarymen and attain economic security.

The route to this security was education. Thus the "education mother" was born, and the school system and the family counted on her input. The expectations of the education system shaped her role (Allison, this volume): a mother should help her children with homework, find tutors or cram schools when necessary, define which schools are best for her children, and provide moral support and physical presence during years of preparation for college entrance exams. As Brinton points out, in thus developing Japan's human capital, she became an important underpinning of Japan's economic growth.[3] The image of success became the nuclear family living in a modern dwelling with a full-time mother focused on her children's education.

In the 1970s the image of a successful woman expanded to include varied opportunities along the life course: education, work, marriage, community and child-related activities, hobby and study circles, part-time work, and family leisure.

The development of supermarkets, convenience stores, and fast-food chains provided part-time or temporary employment opportunity for married women and mothers during school hours. Other opportunities arose for community service, adult education, personal improvement, and political or consumer activity.[4] Through such activities, women became involved outside their homes and neighborhoods and had opportunities to develop personal interests and networks while defining their dominant roles as wives and mothers.

The 1970s also saw the appearance of the "new family." This term referred to a young couple who married for love or companionship, not merely to build a home and family with a suitable partner. The "new family" expected to share interests, hoping that the husband would spend more leisure time with his family and thus avoid the problems the previous generation faced when father retired to a family that hardly knew him and a house that had no space for him. However, about five or six years into marriage, the new family began to look like the old family. Father worked long hours and mother was busy with the children. Yet, the new family was not entirely the same as the old: in expecting the father to spend leisure time with his family, the family became a unit of leisure, a change that suited Japan's economic development. Family-style hotels, resorts, restaurants, and amusement parks like Tokyo Disneyland became popular as the growth in disposable income encouraged the purchase of a family car, which facilitated and thus increased vacation travel.[5]

The new family's emphasis on companionship between the spouses has affected both the reason for divorce and the desire to remarry. The increase (although small) in the number of divorces among those who have been married at least twenty years is a contemporary response to the lack of companionship. When the husband retires from work, the wife declares that she is retiring from being a homemaker. Her behavior flies in the face of expectations that she will care for her husband and his parents as long as they live. This desire for companionship in marriage is reflected in press reports: the majority of divorced persons indicate they would like to remarry, *if* they can do so for companionship, in contrast to press reports in the 1970s that the majority of divorced women did not want to remarry.

The 1980s added further dimensions to the changing opportunities for women. In response to signing the United Nations Declaration on Women, Japan passed the Equal Employment Opportunity Law to improve women's access to jobs (Creighton and Roberts, this volume). A labor shortage and the high cost of living combined to make work attractive to women and to make women attractive to employers. Women political candidates emerged, exemplified by Doi Takako and the "Madonna" candidates (Hastings, this volume). Media images of Japanese women fluctuated wildly from the successful career woman or politician or *oyaji gyaru* who drinks and plays golf like "one of the boys" to the "new royalty" of the free spending "office ladies" who travel the world in search of adventure (even sex!) and ever greater bargains in designer fashions. Along with these flamboyant images was that of the successful wife and mother who spends her post-childrearing years in "female heaven" as a consummate consumer, traveling with friends or spouse and enjoying the rewards she has earned by caring for her family (Lock, this volume).

This picture changed slightly in the 1990s. The cost of living pushed women into the labor force, but the sluggish domestic economy cut into women's gains in the job market.[6] Women's age at first marriage rose to twenty-six, crossing the magic number of twenty-five, when women—like Christmas cakes—were supposed to become stale. Women were in no hurry to marry, and once married had fewer children. The birthrate fell to 1.53, a reflection not only of the increased costs of raising children, but also the lack of adequate housing, green space, and time working husbands had to participate in caring for their children. This low birthrate, along with the aging of the Japanese population, led the government to call for women to fulfill their nurturing roles (Long and Painter, this volume).

The multiplicity of images remained. The media offered something for every age and economic group, for those domestically oriented and those currently not. The state tried to propagate three slightly contradictory images of women's roles: fulfilled mothers, caregivers for the aged, and capable workers in hitherto "male" occupations who filled the labor shortage that was no longer the crisis it appeared to be in the mid-1980s.

RANGE OF OPTIONS AND DEGREE OF CHOICE

Women's roles also changed. Sumiko Iwao tells us that over the past fifteen years, the range of roles a "typical" thirty-five-year-old housewife

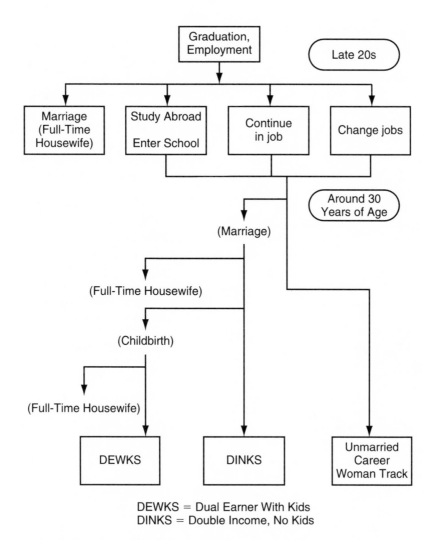

Fig. 1. New Women's Life Course. *Nihon Keizai Shinbun,* January 4, 1993.
Translated by Anne Imamura.

might assume have multiplied. Her options are quite varied, whereas
those of her thirty-five-year-old husband have remained the same and are
quite limited.[7] The *Nihon Keizai Shinbun* illustrated this increased choice in
a diagram (figure 1).

For a variety of reasons, including economic and educational circumstances, not all Japanese women can choose freely among these options.
However, regardless of a given individual's situation, a multiplicity of socially acceptable images of Japanese women have accompanied her expanded roles. In most cases, new images have not replaced old, but have

layered on top of them, each layer having its own appeal as well as its drawbacks. Various interests within Japan can appeal to the appropriate image, and Japanese women can use these images to legitimate a range of behaviors. As women make life choices and develop new images, social institutions employ old images and create new ones to motivate women's choices. In the interaction between these two processes, we see the creative tension between the domestic ideal and the reality of nondomestic life that Bernstein described. The Japanese women whose voices are heard in this volume are nurturers, economic and political actors as well as interactants who choose and develop images to legitimate their own behavior and that of their daughters.

As we listen to the voices of a variety of Japanese women, we strive to appreciate their situations. We examine the relative power of various social institutions and the freedom of the individual to choose. In the first chapter, Nancy Rosenberger points out that, although social institutions in a postindustrial society are noncoercive, they are powerful. She observes that whereas the state is production-oriented, the media tend to be consumption-oriented. Individual women can use the often contradictory images of the media and the state to rationalize their behavior and decrease the control of the state. Thus there is a dialectic between and among competing institutions and the individual actor. This does not produce revolution, but incremental changes that Rosenberger terms "fragile resistances," which affect women's position in society.

The contradiction between the mainstream nurturer role and the image of today's woman trying to cope with new choices is apparent in the chapter by Awaya and Phillips. Awaya and Phillips examine popular literature read by Japanese working women, in which female protagonists deal with divorce, single parenthood, and careers. The problems they face reflect the challenges their readers face, and in many cases they do not have solutions but continue to cope. They may be angry and dissatisfied, confused or hopeful, but they are not submissive or primarily nurturant. They are for the most part strong, goal-oriented individuals whose lives are very different from those of the readers, but whose challenges and questions resonate with young women in Japan today.

The perspective in this literature contrasts with the belief that happiness comes from nurturing. Andrew Painter's study of a television station illustrates how this belief is reflected in the station's gender roles, its programming for the homemaker market, and the theme of a popular "home drama." The female protagonist of the drama finds fulfillment and brings happiness to her family when she ceases to resist the nurturer role and joyously takes on caring for the bedridden mother of her fiancé. This is a route to happiness that would have been recognized by any of the women in Bernstein's volume.

Margaret Lock weaves the threads of image and cultural assumption into the subject of gynecology. She points out that cultural assumptions about the nature of women and their place in society influence how the female body is seen in medical settings, where the recent "discovery" of the menopausal syndrome becomes an argument against individualism and provides "scientific" fuel for the nurturing ideology. Lock argues that Japan's view of women's medical concerns reflects the policy of keeping women healthy to fulfill their nurturing role. The women in her pages show the advantages of capitalizing on the healthy homebody image and the disadvantages of challenging it. Indeed, one way to attain individual goals that might be criticized as selfish is to cast them in the framework of nurturant behavior—legitimizing an exercise class to keep the wife healthy to care for the elderly.

One way to understand Japanese women's lives today is to examine the life of one woman and how it reflects women's choices. Robert J. Marra introduces us to Yuriko, whose great personal sacrifice rehabilitates both her natal family and that of her husband. Now the most respected woman in her village, Yuriko exemplifies the degree to which a woman can build social capital by fulfilling her nurturer role. Clearly, her years of hard work for her family have paid off in her own social status. Indeed, Yuriko is given credit for permitting her daughter-in-law to pursue a career. In caring for her grandchildren while her daughter-in-law is at work, Yuriko—rather than her daughter-in-law—receives praise from the community for her farsighted and liberal behavior.

Just as Yuriko simultaneously advanced the status of both her family and herself, the tea ceremony practitioners Barbara Mori studies find social status and personal fulfillment in the private sphere. These women are for the most part seeking to fulfill their roles in Japanese society while finding personal enjoyment and meaning within them. The tea ceremony provides a socially acceptable outlet and a milieu in which they can attain status, influence, and power. The traditional arts are compatible with the mother's job of passing on culture to her children and fit the image of a desirable, cultured wife. Thus it is difficult for her husband to object to her participation. Yet the traditional arts may provide women with opportunities to work for personal goals that might be defined as selfish in other contexts. Indeed, these traditional arts offer women the chance to attain prestige and status as well as to fulfill their leadership potential without challenging the dominance of their nurturer role.

However, in today's Japan, even the nurturer role contains paradoxes. As Anne Allison points out, the mother is expected to provide her children with the skills to succeed in today's production-oriented economy. A primary goal is to develop independence in one's child. This independence is not individualism, but rather the development of behavior patterns that will enable the child to adapt to and succeed at the tasks of school and work. Because the tasks are rigorous, the adaptation process is difficult, requiring the active participation of the mother. Thus, the school system takes on the task not only of educating children, but of educating mothers to participate; the school sets rigid expectations and high standards for mother and child's school and home behavior. In this sense, her child's school may become one of the most powerful shapers of a woman's behavior.

Although a woman's behavior may conform to the nurturing ideal, Susan Long warns us that we must not confuse the ideal of nurturing with the reality of women's choices or the behavior with the desire of the individual. To do so would mean that we miss both the "stress that accompanies nurturing and the relationship between nurturing and power in Japanese society." Long's study of care of the aged reveals the tension between the state's expectations and the desires of individual women, as well as the impact of the media. Women may carry out their nurturing roles because they perceive no alternative, not because they are truly fulfilled by them. Both the media image and the state encouragement of family care for the aged influence the expectation of husbands and the elderly and produce stress for the wife. Her conformity to traditional expectations is equated with domestic happiness, and nontraditional behavior on her part is blamed for all family ills.

In the public sphere as well as the domestic, there is tension between nurturing and individual goals. Especially since the passage of the Equal Employment Opportunity Law, the media image of the career woman balancing work and home has competed with that of full-time wife and mother. We examine the perspectives of women in three different types of employment that balance work and nurturing.

The bar hostesses John Mock describes are women with few economic and educational resources who fled family hardships in search of independence. They attempted to avoid lives of sacrificial nurturing, yet their only opportunity came as bar hostesses, where they nurture clients rather than spouse and family. This commodification of nurturing sets them apart from the "legitimate" nurturers (wives and mothers) in their neighborhoods. Although their work is, in a sense, a continuation of the nurturing that female office workers and assistants give to male employees, the hostesses lack respectability. Nonetheless, despite this lack and the highly competitive environment in which the hostesses work, they can achieve an independence "legitimate" nurturers cannot. They exemplify yet another way to balance nurturing and independence.

New economic opportunities for women developed in the 1980s after the passage of the Equal Employment Opportunity Law. Yet Millie R. Creighton argues that this law does not reflect an internal shift in Japanese social values as much as a reaction to international pressures. Rather than provide increased opportunity for the majority of women, it provides a small number of qualified women the opportunity for equal employment with men. Creighton examines the situation of department store employees and finds that department stores usually do not promote women beyond low-level managerial positions. More significant, she finds that promoting women to positions of responsibility does not necessarily make them role models for younger women. If women managers are single and childless, they are pitied by younger women, who give more prestige to homemaking than to attaining managerial status. Thus Creighton argues that legal change per se does not equal social change.

In contrast to Creighton's department store workers, Glenda Roberts's blue-collar women work hard to be promoted and value work as much as domestic roles. Although there are many similarities between these blue-collar women's attitudes toward work and those of their department store sisters, two important factors tie blue-collar women to their jobs. First, they are reluctant to give up their permanent, full-time jobs. Second, because they are blue-collar workers, not only do the families need the money, but the women's income comes close to matching their husbands' and thus cannot be considered extra in the same sense as that of the wife of a white-collar worker. As with Yuriko, their mothers-in-law may become the primary caregivers of their children and run the homes in which they live. Although their motivations are primarily economic, they feel strongly that it would be a waste for them to stay home. On the one hand, they have become part of the consumerism ideology because their wages purchase a better life for their families. On the other, they are not challenging the nurturant roles but balancing them with full-time work. The women Roberts describes are survivors. They have a strong commitment to the work ethic and high performance standards. They keep working in the face of disapproval—even of the president of their own company, who thinks women's abandonment of the household is leading Japan on the road to ruin. They work under conditions that give little quarter for pregnancy or nurturing roles. As Roberts points out, the difficulty of their lifestyle suggests that few others will choose it and that those who do choose it must depend on other women to cover their nurturing responsibilities.

Finally, we examine the political arena. During the period Bernstein covered, Japanese women did not have the right to vote. Now there are women at almost all levels of Japanese politics and of all political persuasions. Those familiar with women's entry into politics in the United States will not be surprised that most of the Dietwomen studied by Hastings either worked their way up in "feminine" professions or were related to male politicians whose seats they inherited. In recent years, however, real changes have been made. Younger women do not remember when women could not vote, and women have become important constituents for candidates. Political women have established themselves in the opposition even though, as Hastings argues, the ruling Liberal Democratic Party trivialized women by choosing candidates for their charm or media talent rather than political ability. Women have been elected in large numbers as "clean" candidates after political scandals have toppled male incumbents, but it remains to be seen how women will fare as candidates after the electoral reforms of 1995.

The final chapter by Patricia G. Steinhoff brings us full circle to the competing pulls of nurturance and individualism and to individual versus image. The three radical women she depicts resemble the wives who help run small family businesses in Japan. All are recognized for their ability, but gain formal authority only when their husbands die. None of these women was forced to make a sharp choice between marriage and career; indeed, their public image depends more on their feminine behavior than on their political activity. As Steinhoff illustrates, Shiomi earns great respect for being an exemplary mother and wife, caring for her aged father, and waiting for her husband to be released from prison. Even the police see her as an ideal woman. In contrast, Nagata—who is depicted by the press and the legal system as aggressive and unfeminine—is seen unsympathetically as evil, whereas the beautiful, elusive Shigenobu has become a romantic figure. Thus male media images shape the way these radical women are viewed. In the unlikely sphere of political radicalism, nurturing behavior carries political capital, at least in the view of mainstream society. Yet as Steinhoff takes pains to point out, none of these women is reduced to her media image. Each has a real life whose choices and circumstances reflect the influences at work in the lives of other contemporary Japanese women.

No single book can encompass the full range of Japanese women's lives. This book focuses primarily on urban women who balance domestic and nondomestic responsibilities and opportunities. It attempts to shed light on the forces that influence Japanese women's choices at the end of the twentieth century. The tensions between the society and the individual, between production and consumption, between image and reality are not unique to Japan. How these tensions are resolved, images manipulated, and traditional values incorporated, modified, or discarded is relevant, however, both to our understanding of Japan and to our understanding of gender issues in general. As the women in these pages built on the foundations laid during the time Bernstein studied, so will young women today and tomorrow build on the foundations laid by these women.

NOTES

1. In an extensive review of the American literature on Japanese women over the past 130 years, Yoshi Kuzume finds an interesting dialectic. She argues that

American images reflect more the changing values of American society than changes in Japanese women's roles. At the same time, the American scholarship influenced the image Japanese society had of itself. Hence, the images took on a reality of their own and were developed as one side responded to the images brought forth by the other. See Yoshi Kuzume, "Images of Japanese Women in U.S. Writings and Scholarly Works, 1860–1990," *U.S.-Japan Women's Journal* 1 (1991): 6–50.

2. For a discussion of the salaryman, see Ezra F. Vogel's classic study *Japan's New Middle Class* (Berkeley: University of California Press, 1971).

3. Mary C. Brinton, *Women and the Economic Miracle: Gender and Work in Postwar Japan* (Berkeley: University of California Press, 1993).

4. For a fuller discussion of these developments, see Anne E. Imamura, *Urban Japanese Housewives: At Home and in the Community* (Honolulu: University of Hawaii Press, 1987).

5. David W. Plath discusses the impact of the automobile on Japan in "My-Car-isma: Motorizing the Showa Self," *Daedalus,* Special issue, *Showa: The Japan of Hirohito* (Summer 1990): 229–244.

6. In the spring of 1993, employers cut back on recruitment of all new graduates; however, they cut back more on female recruitment. Nobuko Matsubara, the Director General of the Women's Bureau in the Ministry of Labor, sent a letter of appeal to major economic organizations urging them to comply with the laws guaranteeing equal employment rights for men and women.

7. Sumiko Iwao, *The Japanese Woman: Traditional Image and Changing Reality* (New York: The Free Press, 1993), 6.

ONE

Fragile Resistance, Signs of Status

Women between State and Media in Japan

Nancy R. Rosenberger

Many studies have emphasized that the media help to maintain a stable social order that upholds the legitimacy of the state and the strength of the industrial economy.[1] Less attention has been given to the possibility that images in the popular mainstream press may contradict the social order
informed by government policies and that such contradictions may undercut the power of both the state and the media in people's lives. People are
not merely passive recipients of institutional ideas and practices. While constructing their roles as consumers and citizens, individuals are capable of
"appropriating" institutional messages, making them their own through
reinterpretation and incorporation into their own lives.[2] When powerful institutions such as the state and the media offer social positions and meanings
that are in some ways contradictory to each other, people can expand their
possibilities by playing one set of ideas and practices off against another.

In this chapter I examine institutional representations of women by the
state and the media in Japan and women's use of these representations in
their everyday lives. Both institutions offer women positions and life trajectories that are similar. Yet there are significant differences between the
motivations and images presented to women by government policies and
women's magazines. Japanese government policies channel women into
nurturing positions at home and lower-level positions at work in order to
maintain a societal order that supports high economic growth. Women's
magazines encourage play and the fulfillment of one's desires based on the
ideals of individuality, freedom, and international status in order to sell
consumer goods. The messages of each institution reinforce as well as contradict each other, but two sets of ideas and practices are carved out: one
for women as dutiful switchers between home and work, and one for
women as free, leisured consumers.

The first part of this chapter considers how government policies influence the course of women's lives. The second part shows how women's
magazines influence them. The third part investigates the reactions of a
few young and middle-aged women in Japan as they reinforce, juxtapose,

and reinterpret these institutional messages. By reconstituting media messages in their own lives, some women offset the relations of domination and the tensions that result from the government's expectations that they switch back and forth between home and work.[3] Women's "resistance" is fragile, changing the social order only in small ways and often increasing women's interest in buying things to enhance themselves (instead of "supporting commodification").[4] Moreover, women's individual challenges often rest on economic and cultural capital (education, social background, and so on) that women of lower socioeconomic levels lack. These challenges thus increase the divisions between Japanese women of different socioeconomic positions.

This chapter points to the importance of studying dominant representations in complex society not as a hegemonic whole, but as multiple and competing sets of ideas and practices that vary within and between powerful institutions. This study also suggests that people's reactions to symbolic forms should not be assumed but should be studied on-the-ground, in relation to contradictions among powerful institutions. By juxtaposing contradictory ways of imagining their personal lives, people can switch between alternative positions, investing in neither completely, yet dodging some of the power relations inherent in each.

THE LIFE COURSE ACCORDING TO THE STATE

The Japanese state has gained most of its postwar legitimacy through high economic growth based on export, the hallmark of the Liberal Democratic Party that has ruled Japan for over thirty-five years. Driven to catch up with the West since 1868, Japan has finally surpassed the West in economic terms, though the motivation to be recognized as equal or better remains. Most government policies directly support these central goals of high economic growth and international respect, and none stray far from them.[5]

Government policies influence Japanese women to take a number of different positions, such as full-time worker, economically dependent homemaker, and part-time worker. These policies shape women not as mainstream worker-citizens, but as second-class citizens whose lives have an "irregular" trajectory. At every turning point in a woman's life course, the government has specified the possible positions open to her. Although the postindustrial nation-state frees women to "choose" among these positions, the pervasiveness of state power in the form of government policies is evident; these policies often divide women from one another in sustaining the home/work divide, designing a life course in which women continually leap back and forth from one to the other. In spite of the display of alternatives, each position requires that women fulfill a responsibility that serves a state bent on high economic growth.[6]

Government policies outline the following life course for women. After graduation from high school, junior college, or university, women should work full-time and enjoy leisure on the side, preparing to settle down later. They should marry and have children in their mid to late twenties, and, although they might continue to work, as mothers they must show significant support for their children's education from preschool years on. This support is deemed best given if women become housewives dependent economically on their husbands.[7] After children are in school, preferably junior high, women should return to work with lesser responsibility that allows flexibility to fulfill household functions; part-time work and hobbies appear to fit well. Yet women should also be ready to care for needy elderly in her family and for her husband when he retires. Government policy suggests that a woman should remain married to one man and enjoy half his pension and inheritance after he dies. This smooth exposition masks the struggles and fragmentation that many women feel as they sit now on the work side, now on the home side, then on both sides of a permeating home/work divide.

Full-Time Work

The state encourages women to work full-time through both social welfare policies and recent labor policies. The pension reforms of 1986 motivate individual women to have full-time jobs, since women are required to work full-time for forty years in order to gain maximum individual benefits. The government has discontinued programs that compensate women for shorter working years or that allow women to receive pensions earlier than men. In addition, health benefits stimulate full-time work, since full-time workers get ninety percent of their health care paid through national health insurance whereas dependents receive only seventy percent.

The new pension policy also urges family businesses to pay regular salaries to women workers in the family and indirectly encourages women to seek promotions with salary raises in full-time jobs. In the past, employees of small or family businesses—disproportionately older women— received a lesser pension (*kokumin nenkin*), which was determined only by the length of time they had paid in, not by their salary. Salaried employees at medium to large firms—disproportionately men or unmarried women—received a greater pension (*kōsei nenkin*) based on salary as well as on the length of time paid in. Since 1986, the government has urged small businesses to incorporate, and most businesses are now included in the greater pension. This change encourages women to reach as high a salary level as possible through long-term service at one workplace. Women who are on their own and who work continuously at a job with above-average pay and promotions will have the best chance of being able to enjoy a comfortable old age. Workers who are self-employed or in an unincorporated small business still get the lesser pension, but they too are encouraged to work longer than before. In fact, they must work until age sixty-five to get their pension in full, in contrast to workers earning the greater pension which is available in full at age sixty.[8]

The labor law reform of 1986 also facilitates practices that encourage women to continue working full-time throughout their lives. The Equal Employment Opportunity Laws (EEOL) make it officially illegal for companies to deny opportunities for jobs and promotions to women. In the past, companies regularly kept women out of the managerial track, limiting them to clerical or technical jobs and encouraging them to quit when they married or had a child. The Women's Bureau of the Ministry of Labor issued pamphlets and self-administered questionnaires to companies, urging them to increase women's chances for promotion in managerial-track jobs through equal recruitment, training, transfers, wages, promotions, benefits, and retirement policies.[9] The new labor laws eliminate restrictions on working hours for women in managerial positions. They also extend monetary rewards to companies that rehire women after childbirth or child rearing and give child leave to women workers. Policies require companies to give women eight weeks of leave after childbirth.[10]

Thus, in some ways, government policies create opportunities for women as full-time workers with the possibility of promotions. These policies need to be understood, however, in relation to other policies that encourage homemaking and part-time work, for as Ueno points out, the EEOL has divided elite working women from part-time working housewives.[11]

Homemaking

The government indirectly encourages marriage by registering everyone in Japan as a member of a household rather than as an individual; people must show this household registry at all significant turning points of life. Legally, a woman can now head a household, but strong social custom prefers that a man be the head; thus, most women simply move from their father's to their husband's household registry. Local governments encourage marriage more explicitly, offering to introduce people to each other through "Marriage Consultation Centers," which maintain pictures and information files that prospective partners can choose from. Local governments may even offer gifts if an introduction leads to marriage.

Government pension policies encourage women to be economically dependent housewives. Under the new pension system, the unemployed wives of husbands who receive the greater pension get their pensions paid for them through automatic deductions from their husbands' paychecks. Because more businesses are now included in the greater pension system than in the past, many wives of small businessmen and shopkeepers get their pensions paid by their husbands. Ironically, from 1960 to 1986 these wives of lower-income men were assumed to be economically independent from their husbands to some extent: they were required to pay into the lesser pension plan individually. The wives of salarymen with bigger companies could pay in individually, but this was optional; the government assumed that they could depend on their husbands' pensions. Now the wives of both working-class men and managerial-class men are potential dependents within the pension system. They achieve independence only after divorce or after age sixty, and even then receive low pensions.[12]

Although a divorcée retains the pension paid for her by her former husband prior to divorce, government policies particularly favor widows and disfavor divorcées. Widows get special allowances for each child, tax exemptions, special widow stipends, and widow allowances. Along with half of their husband's inheritance, widows receive half of their husband's pension after the appropriate age. In contrast, divorcées are offered no special allowances or stipends and must go to the welfare office to get their small mother-children stipends, which are about half that allotted to widows. Because child support is low and rarely enforced, divorced women must work even when their children are young, unless they have support from their natal families.

The skewed income pattern between men and women, which the government has done little to change, further encourages women's economic dependence upon husbands. The best insurance of economic stability for the vast majority of women is to marry men whose high income and pension they can share. In 1989, women's incomes were still only 60.2 percent of men's incomes; women's education and length of continual service improved this statistic only slightly.[13] Government policies enforce no affirmative action programs. The government uses persuasion and a few incentives to influence companies to hire and promote women into managerial-track jobs, but it applies penalties only if women successfully appeal to a grievance committee within the company or take the company to court.

Government policies urge women to take positions as mothers, whether or not they work. Maternity leave, an optional year off without pay after the birth of the baby, and breast-feeding time while working encourage working women to give birth. Women's fertility is also protected by policies that allow women to request leaves for menstrual discomfort. These policies are double-edged; they recognize the importance of fertility and motherhood, yet urge women to continue working full-time. Although these policies enable women to continue working, in practice they discourage companies from hiring and promoting women equally with men.

Both men and women employees worry that women with children will not be able to carry their fair burden in the workplace and thus will cause resentment in working groups. Furthermore, without a major curtailment in standard working hours, it is impossible for most women to combine motherhood with a full-fledged managerial career. In response to international pressure, government policies have encouraged employees to work shorter hours and to take vacations. Over half of the medium-to-large businesses now give some Saturdays off, but this work is simply concentrated into fewer days with longer hours.[14] Even if husbands are willing to help with child care, they cannot because of their own long hours. If women have no relatives who can care for young children, finding day care to cover long working hours is difficult. Government day-care centers give preference to government workers of lower income.[15] In combination with unchallenged social practices, government policies encourage women to quit work for a time to raise children and then find different work with lower salary and status, but greater flexibility.

Some officials in the Japanese government are concerned that not enough women are becoming mothers. The youth population is shrinking as the older population is growing; in the future, this will increase workers' economic burden. In 1992, concerned about the low birthrate, the government suggested that women be given monetary encouragement to have children. Women responded negatively and the suggestion has not reemerged. However, the government does pay a certain amount per month to women who have had a third child.[16]

Government education policies encourage mothers to engage intensely in child rearing. The entrance exam system fosters "education mamas." Teachers expect mothers to make school lunches, participate in parent-teacher organizations, and help the child with any problems.[17] Accepted wisdom reinforced by the PTA, teachers, and tutors claims that children will have more success if mothers concentrate on preschool home training and elementary school homework, find good tutors in later years, and provide constant emotional and physical support.

Finally, government policies concerning care for the elderly encourage homemakers to be caregivers of elderly family members. The government's message is that families should take the responsibility for their elderly and that women should be available to undertake this task.[18] These policies assume that women are at home at least part-time or have the flexibility to quit work when necessary. The central government has built few care facilities for the elderly; local facilities tend to offer daytime activities only. Many of the welfare provisions—home bathing trucks, home helpers, haircuts, and one week per year at an approved local hospital—depend on a homemaker who does the main care. Workshops at local government centers train women to care for bedridden elderly. Although some welfare provisions partially reimburse families for full-time elderly care at certain government-approved hospitals or for a care attendant at those hospitals that do not give full-time nursing care, a shortage of nurses, particularly acute at hospitals for the elderly, requires homemakers to help with care. A new system being considered in the Diet would limit the time patients could stay in hospitals approved for long-term care and would leave no other choice but home care.[19] In sum, for continued high economic growth, the state needs homemakers to maintain care for past, present, and future workers.

Part-Time Work

Government policies encourage women to assume part-time work of no more than six hours a day. Firms need a segment of employees whose hours they can vary according to business cycles. Part-time workers provide cheap, flexible labor because they are paid low wages and few or no benefits, with no guarantee of long-term employment.

Tax policy constitutes the main explicit incentive toward part-time work. Women who make under ¥1,000,000 per year (about $11,100 at 1995 exchange rates) do not have to pay taxes on their income. In addition, their husbands can still claim them as dependents for spouse deductions of ¥300,000 per year ($3,300). Women's wages need to be well over $10,400 for them to have an incentive to give up this tax benefit. Even though part-time workers do not get pension and health insurance benefits, many women can work part-time and still build up a small pension fund through the automatic deductions from their husbands' paychecks. If the Ministry of Labor has its way and succeeds in persuading businesses to provide benefits to part-time workers, such work will become even more attractive.

Implicit incentive toward part-time work is supplied by government policies that support women as housewives. Part-time work appears to solve the homemakers' dilemma of home responsibility versus the need for extra money and contact with society. Although it naturalizes their roles as bridgers of the home/work divide, women like part-time work precisely because it helps them fulfill their multiple, even fragmented, roles.

Leisure

The government's position is complicated by policies and white papers that suggest leisure and consumption for women, albeit not with the freedom and abandon that magazines imagine. Central government white papers print statistics and articles that underscore the image of young Japanese women traveling internationally and consuming international goods. To introduce the "Imported Goods Catalog," a government official comments on the importance of young women's consumption in an era of favorable trade surplus that threatens international relations.[20] Local governments provide homemakers with culture centers that offer hobby classes and study groups, some of which receive support from the central government. Deals offered on nationalized airlines and railroads entice young women as well as women with older children to take trips together. In short, government practices and ideas encourage women to play and consume goods, which makes the shift between home and work all the more palatable. In the context of the other positions encouraged by the government, leisure seems to co-opt or undercut women's second-class citizenry at home and work, offering a first-class position as consumers of goods and leisure. It fits with women's responsibilities as citizens because it fuels economic growth and comforts international competitors, yet distances women from economic and political control except as consumers. Nonetheless, government support of leisure shows that state and media discourses about women interact in complex ways.

Powerful but Tension-Producing

Government policies are powerful for several reasons. In an era of debate over women's roles, they legitimize and ease women's "choices" to bridge the home/work divide. Although government policies reproduce the traditional high value placed on nurturing, inner-oriented women who support the state as housewives, they appear to support contemporary discourses urging women to have a life outside of the household.[21] These internal contradictions are themselves a source of power because they seem to resolve these conflicting discourses.

Government policies also reshape these discourses towards goals of high economic growth, although most citizenship positions offered to women are invisible in the "private" sphere and of low status in the "public" sphere. The "good wife, wise mother" role has been reinterpreted so that a woman's household responsibilities support the main productive elements of society: husbands in the workplace and children in the education system preparing to be workers and mothers. Ideas of independence for women have also been reshaped and divided into low-paying jobs with little status or, at the opposite extreme, high-powered jobs with no time for family. When economic growth slows, women can disappear back into households. All too often, women end up as second-class citizens who experience tension on both sides of the home/work divide.

MEDIA: WOMEN'S MAGAZINES

Women's magazines offer alternative images to women. The number of magazines targeting women has burgeoned in Japan throughout the seventies and eighties, growing from four to sixty-two. Compared with earlier women's magazines, new magazines include younger groups, divide the market into narrower age groups, and "create the life of fashion consciousness."[22] This growth is part of a gradual shift among Japanese away from prewar household and community life, toward consciousness of themselves as citizens with needs that deserve state attention and as consumers who can go beyond the *mottainai* philosophy that nothing can be wasted. As we have seen in the last section, government policies are changing in response to the new needs of citizens, but with the needs of productivity well in mind. The Japanese government has stimulated consumption among higher socioeconomic groups where most consumer spending increases have occurred.[23] In contrast, in an effort to create consumers, women's magazines have offered social images of appealingly decorated bodies to women of all socioeconomic levels. Indeed, these social images stimulate women's desires to escape the tensions and subordinations of the home/work dichotomy.

The magazines I have studied both reproduce the social order established by government policies and furnish symbolic forms upon which resistance to the state can be based. Magazines themselves do not explicitly resist government policies; contradictions with government policy have grown out of a desire for profit. Indeed, magazine profit is tightly linked to commercial advertisers and manufacturers whose economic growth depends on government policies. But to view women's magazines as providing only social cement for the status quo is too limiting.[24]

To show the complexity of the situation, before concentrating on the way women's magazines in Japan contradict discourses of citizen responsibility, I will briefly describe some of the ways that they reinforce such discourse. As early as the 1920s, women's magazine publishers reproduced the home/work divide and underlined divisions between managers and manual workers by targeting women of the new middle class who were married to salaried businessmen and government officials. For a brief period after the war, many new women's magazines became political forums for new ideas; however, lacking financial support, these magazines died. Women's magazines from mainstream publishers focused once again on household topics for a growing group of middle-class housewives. Not until the seventies and eighties did women's magazines branch out into "lifestyle magazines" to develop other market niches. But even these markets were groups that had already been standardized in large part by government policies concerning education, work, and marriage: high school students; women students in higher education; young, unmarried working women; and young housewives.[25] Indeed, women's magazines reified government-approved age and sex differences. In the process, they directed citizens' gazes away from inequalities and relations of domination and toward achieving status within a system of commodities.[26] Furthermore, by objectifying and commodifying women's bodies, magazines made it seem natural that biological differences should cause women to center their interests on the house or be subservient in the workplace. In short, the growing consumer discourse has the potential of bringing women under a new form of power.

Yet the social images presented by women's magazines also offer words and images that contradict government policy's discourse of responsibility and productivity. "Culture-makers"—magazine editors and writers, market researchers and advertisers—have infused new meanings into state-crafted positions of students, workers, and housewives by offering carefree, self-oriented "images of sociality" such as freedom, individuality, leisure, international sophistication, high status, and heterosexual attractiveness outside of marriage.[27] Magazine makers try to manage a life course for Japanese women by nurturing tastes for lifestyles represented by fashionable commodities used in fashionable contexts. I will illustrate this life course with examples from magazines published by *Kōdansha* publishing house. These magazines have a wide circulation, cover almost every age group, and target new market niches.

The Life Course According to Magazines

Words and images in women's magazines concentrate on expanding the attitudes and activities of young women into an exciting world outside of school, work, or home responsibilities. The "Stylish High School Girl" bikes, camps, and plays in the sand of Japan and U.S. beaches. Although rebellion is not usually explicit in the magazines, a model who has just cavorted through pages of lively colored photos sits glumly in a black-and-white photo in her school uniform: "Do you like modeling?" "I love it." "Do you like school?" "I hate it."[28] Magazines photograph "typical" girls walking the streets of Tokyo and Osaka on Sundays with their friends only to find they have bought their clothes at expensive boutiques in French casual, Los Angeles, or skater styles.[29] Writers encourage an "individual style" even in high school: "Hating to be all alike, you use your head on little things." The accompanying image suggests ideal characteristics of international sophistication, sexual attractiveness (international and domestic), and the latest fashion consumption: a Japanese girl dressed in an Aloha shirt and shorts sits on a table in a fifties-style Los Angeles diner. She laughs along with a Japanese boy on one side of her, while an American boy on the other side gazes at her through the hole of a donut.[30]

Magazines present the next age group (eighteen to twenty-two) as students and beginning workers, yet they direct their readers' gaze towards becoming sexually attractive adults through consumption. The focus is on the body, with up to two-thirds of magazines filled with ads and ad-articles for fashion and make-up. By adorning themselves in jewelry, young women can "stage an appearance as an adult woman."[31] Work responsibilities are framed by the style needs of after-five leisure: "Superiors also will be convinced by the intellectual mood of a tight silhouette and wrap mini."[32] Magazines feature wealthy girls from leading private schools in Tokyo who model high fashion clothes with a picture of their favorite boutique.[33] Writers urge "individualistic beauty" on one page, but on the next, male students' opinions "keep styles in line."[34] Heterosexual attractiveness becomes more explicit with discussions of "the first time" and "Is Sex Affinity Different from Personality Affinity?" with detail on various ways to have sex.[35]

After their education is finished, the magazines reproduce the idea that young women should work, but not to save money for family, company, or nation. They work so that they can play. In the premarriage (twenty-two to twenty-five) age group, magazines offer freedom through leisure activities. One picture in a magazine that specializes in entertainment spots for young urban women captures a key image: a young Japanese woman sits on tatami at a restaurant decorated in traditional style; she holds out her cup to be served sake by a male employee—just the opposite of the conventional gender relation in this context.[36] Magazines offer cultural products to ensure freedom: beer, golf clubs, cars, and birth control devices. Focus on international sophistication grows with an increase in foreign models, foreign brands (Armani fashion will make you "free and healthy"),[37] and foreign travel—an ad for Singapore pictures a clothes shop floating in a sparkling ocean. In the midst of the fun, however, magazines sustain anxiety about marriage, simultaneously questioning it and reproducing the insistence of its claim. An actress says, "Marriage would make me sad," and another that her "wish for children passed like a fad."[38] An issue of *An-an* begins with the reflections of young divorcées and the conditions women must hold to in marriage, but ends with articles on receptions and wedding dresses.[39] *Sign* features an article entitled "Can I Marry or Not? A Little Worried. . . . Is It True that Happiness Will Never Come to Women Who Continually Stick to Certain Conditions?"[40] The magazines ultimately reinforce government preferences, but by playing on the tension between freedom and marriage, they highlight the individual's struggles and thus appear to champion a woman's point of view.

The volatile twenty-five to thirty-five-year-old age group is difficult for magazine publishers to standardize. The state would prefer that most of these young women take marriage and children as their main focus, but magazine creators are more open to variance because each lifestyle they can capture and standardize gives them another profitable market niche. Magazines targeting young married women with children de-emphasize sexual attractiveness and international sophistication, instead offering prospects of freedom and individuality within the home: "Get privacy and a feeling of emancipation with storage shelves."[41] Training ads for occupations suitable for mothers replace beauty clinic ads, and make-up is now styled to secure a job rather than a man.[42]

Magazines in the late eighties and early nineties have attempted to standardize several new market niches within this age group. One niche follows a continuing trajectory for single women based on self-oriented leisure, sexual attractiveness, and international sophistication. Love and elegance prevail in articles such as "Women's Ideal: One Big Love before Marriage" and "Princess Diana's Cute Scandal."[43] Young women can design their lives around parachuting, travel in Spain, British table settings, and Madonna's views on sex and self.[44] Another niche is pictured as serious-minded. *Nikkei Woman* ignores body adornments, picturing brown-haired foreigners with briefcases in hand and young Japanese women in jobs "that they love," coping with day-care needs or saving money for study abroad.[45] *Crea* focuses women's attentions on good books and contentious issues such as pill liberalization, AIDS, and discrimination within Japan.[46] Finally, young divorcées form an experimental niche in a magazine called *Que Sera* "for Marriage Experienced Lady."[47] Here magazine writers paint divorced women as sexually attractive and successful at work, implying in one article that men and children now accept the unconventional idea of remarriage after divorce.

To middle-aged women, magazines offer images of individuality, leisure, and even international sophistication, but only within the framework of the household. The focus is on cooking, home management, sewing, health, and expensive fashion accessories.[48] Although discussion of work is limited, interviews show women successfully combining career and home care and emphasize the meaning in work rather than the external rewards of profit or high status. In home decorating and design magazines, writers offer middle-aged women self-expression, enjoyment, and satisfying family relations based on emotion rather than obligation. Women with limited incomes can achieve these through their own efforts (imagined as play) as they replace old Japanese styles with Western ones, laying rugs, covering furniture, and taking down walls.[49] Wealthier women can go out and become a "lively working Mrs." by paying companies to update their homes with system kitchens and bathrooms: "It is we who will individualize your spirit."[50] For wives of lower-income men, care of elder family members is never mentioned, but for the wealthy, elders can live in a separate Japanese-style section of a large Westernized home.[51]

Writers assume that middle-aged women are already experiencing the home/work divide and imagine that it is in the framework of the home and the noneconomic side of life that individuality, international sophistication, and pleasure are to be found. These images follow the life course suggested by government policies and even ease women's acceptance of them, but at the same time, they redirect the focus of housewifely duties towards self and do nothing to romanticize the ideal devotion to obligatory relations at home or industriousness at work. Donning these "images of sociality" can also bring women under the power of consumer "needs" throughout the life course. Market researchers ultrasensitive to the newest trends are quick to standardize social changes into new market niches, reducing social movements to a system of commodities.

In the next section, I investigate the sociohistorical contexts in which these images attain broader meanings and encourage actions and attitudes of resistance. When these social images are incorporated and practiced beyond the world of consumption in Japan, they can lead to independent actions that challenge the accepted social order of cooperation with family, school, and work groups. Japan presents the potential for such resistance because most government policies favor a social order that privileges the production and status of the group, rather than the self-oriented status of the individual through consumption.[52]

Magazines' Social Images and Their Meanings

The social image of freedom (*jiyū*) is accompanied by representations of individuality (*kosei*). The word *kodowatta* describes a style that a person gets stuck on and uses to "become herself" (*jibunnari*) or a likeness of herself (*jibunrashisa*). Freedom and individuality are ideas that challenge the conventional social order in Japan. When the ideas of democracy and individualism flooded into Japan after World War II, the popular explanation for *kojinshugi* (individualism) was "do-as-you-like-ism." Although these words have more positive connotations among young Japanese, a person who is seen as free and individualistic can easily be branded as selfish if her actions and thoughts are perceived as harming the welfare and productivity of the group. A person proves her maturity by restraining her spirit and blending it with the spirit of the group, especially in more formal contexts aimed at productivity. This may mean bending her will to the will of the group and taking an inferior place in a hierarchy. Freedom and individuality (rather than individualism) are possible, but acceptable only in relaxed contexts with intimates where one's heart finds expression. The self-oriented images of freedom and individuality found in women's magazines may cause dissension if women expand and assimilate them into various arenas of their lives, so that their heart-felt desires guide activities that present alternatives to, even penetrate into, home and work responsibilities.[53]

A second set of social images used by the magazines includes high status, refinement, and international sophistication. I group these together because the meaning of "international" in Japan is closely related to ideas of status. Japanized English words related to status are used again and again throughout the magazines: "level-up," "one-rank-up," and "high status." They imply that if a woman will only spend enough money to buy quality goods, she will increase her ranking in society. In Japan, where hierarchy and the wish for increased status are well accepted, the association between status and the purchase of particular goods is overt. "Distinction" from lower-level groups is a "natural" wish. International sophistication brings high status and, ironically, reinforces Japanese-ness. As Japanese women buy expensive foreign goods, study abroad, and travel, they reinforce not only their own high status among Japanese but also the high status of Japan relative to Western countries. International travel, study, and consumption need not challenge the social order, but they may if they result in the incorporation of new ideas and practices that affect the demands women bring to the job market, their marriage partners, and their families.

Sexual attractiveness, too, is on offer to young women in these magazines. In the postwar years, many countries have linked consumption to female sexuality outside marriage, and from 1980, Japanese consumer discourse for women has followed suit. In Japan, images of sexual attractiveness focus on heterosexual relationships with men before marriage and basing a marriage on emotion rather than obligation. Foreign models usually pose for the explicitly heterosexual photographs, but Japanese women are described sexually in the back pages. This discourse flies in the face of elite samurai codes for controlling women's sexuality before and after marriage and women's choice in a marriage partner. These samurai customs became law in 1898, and though the law was repealed after the war, the customs had become influential throughout most regions and classes in Japan, prevailing over a looser attitude towards premarital sex and marriage choice that had obtained in villages and lower-class urban areas.[54] Most contemporary young women, raised in an era of middle-class virtues, were trained in the family and at school to be modest and restrained in their personal habits. To them, the magazines' images of heterosexuality and relationships based on sexual attraction appear to resist the status quo, though not as much as such images might in a very puritanical society. The government would prefer to control sexuality before marriage, as is shown by occasional criticism of magazines or comics for young women that become too sexually explicit.[55] Seeking love relationships and "partners" rather than a husband threatens marriage's ability to stabilize the social hierarchy by bringing together two families and obligating the wife to nurture her husband's family members.

Finally, women's magazines offer the image of women enjoying themselves. Women are pictured in carefree, laughing poses in international locations and in places where in the recent past only men found entertainment. A number of words accompany the images: *asobi* (play), *kutsurogi* (relaxation), *kokochiyoi* (comfortable), *tanoshii* (enjoyable), *rirakusu* (relaxing). Such ideas and practices are not foreign to Japan; they have been an important part of Japanese history at festival times, and modern Japanese groups have reinstituted this custom by consciously carving out space and time to relax together. However, presentation of "play" in women's magazines subverts these ideas in several ways. Conventionally, relaxation times are confined to limited parts of life after duties are done. Yet magazines make it look as if women play a great deal of the time, in all sorts of circumstances. Even the workplace and the home are pictured and described as places where women enjoy themselves. Furthermore, social custom has dictated that women's roles in relaxed contexts be more restrained than men's because women entertain or look after the men, who are given license to drink. In magazines, however, young women are shown relaxing at male haunts such as bars, golf courses, and race tracks. They are completely engaged in what they are doing, displaying no concern whatsoever for providing for men's or elders' relaxation. In this sense, women's widespread enjoyment of leisure threatens established gender differences that have been constructed in part through women's facilitation of men's relaxation in intimate contexts. Women's large-scale investment in "enjoyment" challenges the superiority of productive, hierarchical contexts over intimate, relaxed contexts—a superiority that is sustained in the everyday life of schools and work and in the spirit of government policies that expect citizens to be responsible and hardworking.

Women's magazines play on the tensions that the home/work dichotomy causes in women's lives. In 1990, market researchers from Dentsū, the largest market research and advertising firm in Japan, characterized young women's lives between the ages of fifteen and thirty-five with a play on words that reflects the tensions young women feel in facing a life of bridging the home/work divide. Playing on two words using the Japanese sounds *setsuna*, Dentsū characterizes these women as torn between a carefree, live-for-the-moment attitude (*setsuna-teki*) and attachments of a heartrending, emotional character (*setsunai*). The former suggests leisure and consumption, and the latter indicates close relationships with men or children that one cannot turn one's back on, with implications of the ensuing responsibilities. Dentsū describes a trajectory for young women based on this paradox. From fifteen to eighteen years of age, girls express both their emotional ties and their live-for-the-moment attitudes straightforwardly, but between eighteen and twenty-two, women express their feelings of deep emotional attachments only to dissolve them in laughter with gag lines. From twenty-two to twenty-five, women are on a superfast train running from moment to moment, sometimes taken aback at their own impulsiveness, but off again because emotional attachment has a bitter essence. A shift occurs in the characterization of the twenty-five to thirty-five-year-old age group, in which emotional attachment is most important, though they are still attracted to living for the moment.[56] This paradox is the key to understanding the power of the social images offered in these magazines, because the images suggest ways to escape this conflict, however temporarily. Yet this paradox also suggests the possibility for resistance if women incorporate images attached to "live-for-the-moment-ism" into their own lives and use them to first avoid and later lessen the tensions and power relations caused by the emotional attachments of marriage and family.

Despite their complex overlap with government discourse, women's magazines offer rhetoric and images that can lead to attitudes and activities that disagree with the basic intent of government policies. Consumers can use commodities, or the lack of them, as ways to valorize themselves and work toward more than the illusion of freedom. McCracken argues that "goods help the individual contemplate the possession of an emotional condition, a social circumstance, even an entire style of life, by somehow concretizing these things in themselves."[57] Resistance occurs only if readers take the intervening step of reconstituting consumer ideas, elaborating and incorporating them into their own lives, often with encouragement from popular books written by women encouraging other women to broaden their possibilities.

JAPANESE WOMEN IN THEIR EVERYDAY LIVES

The influence of powerful institutions cannot be completely understood by studying the texts of the institutions themselves; only in the context of people's lives can we understand the way institutional messages are perceived and experienced.[58] People actively constitute and reconstitute the cultural products of institutions in a number of different ways according to their socioeconomic positions. In this section, I focus on the words and lives of women at different points in the life course and in different socioeconomic positions, in order to glimpse women's reinterpretations of the state and media messages. I also demonstrate trends toward resistance to the aims of many government policies.

Women's experiences imply that they follow slavishly neither the home/work duties emphasized in government policies nor the freedom and individualities suggested by magazine messages. Instead, women play the ideas and practices of the consumer discourse off against those of the citizen discourse whenever possible. Few women directly rebel against the home/work dichotomy that underlies the national economy. Although fulfilling their traditional roles in form, however, some women undercut

those roles in spirit by extending the meanings of freedom, voluntary relations, or leisure beyond the area of consumption that magazines target.
Although fragile and behind the scenes, this resistance reshapes the general attitudes of the populace and influences a government that must show
some sensitivity to the desires of its second-class citizenry in order to gain
international acceptance.

As we will see from the case studies of women's lives, social background
and economic position affect the extent to which women can or wish to
play media representations of freedom off against state representations of
responsibility. Resistance is complicated because the social images offered
by womens' magazines are part of a system of tastes that women use to attain higher positions within society.[59] Thus, women build on their "cultural capital" by enjoying leisure activities or adding to their international
sophistication. By acquiring these preferences, they improve their "symbolic capital" (prestige, status) in line with the upward economic mobility
of their husbands, fathers, or in a few cases, themselves. Within the limits
of their lives, this use of social images does not discredit their acts as resistance against tensions and asymmetrical power relations. But it is important to realize that these acts of individual resistance elevate social position
and differentiate these higher-status women from those women who cannot afford these preferences except in very limited ways.

College Age

I interviewed twenty Japanese women from a new private, coed university
about their reactions to young women's magazines. These were women of
middle socioeconomic status whose parents could not afford the highest
level private universities for their daughters. At the time of the interview,
they had been in the U.S. for two months as part of a half-year study
abroad program required by their university. Their responses show two
things. First, the magazines made these students recognize their interme-
diate positions in the socioeconomic system, motivating them to find their
own cheaper yet distinctive styles. Second, the students wanted to extend
the magazines' social images into their own lives, enacting these ideas by
many means beyond the purchase of commodities.

These students recognized that they could not afford most of the items
shown in women's magazines. Their response was to deride the elegant
styles and actions of richer women and to attempt to build their own cultural capital through preferences for casual styles and relationships.[60]
Magazines were "for reference only." They differentiated themselves
from students at prestigious women's universities: "We might see a girl
and say, 'Ah, she looks like a JJ girl, doesn't she?' " (*JJ* is a fashion magazine for the eighteen to twenty-two-year-old set.) "At those girls' schools

they always dress up in high heels and skirts, have perms and long hair. They are 'body-conscious' elite girls [*o-jōsan*]." In contrast, even before coming to the U.S., these students wanted a casual style centered on jeans and T-shirts "like you see in *Non-non*." Accordingly, they associated overt sexual attractiveness and sexual relationships with the richer young women, preferring for themselves casual friendships with men.

Although drawn to images of individuality and internationalism, they scorned the magazines' presentations of these images. They thought that individuality disappears when everyone reads the same information, wears the same clothes, and goes to the same places on dates. Individuality itself is "a fad" and "depends on whether you have enough money." Yet they wanted individuality, both in fashions that were "like themselves" (*jibunrashii*)—i.e., found in small stores near their homes—and in the actions of their own lives: "We don't want to conform like some Japanese do." The college students perceived the international images in magazines as "foreign," "a dream world, beautiful, but unattainable." Not only were foreign boutiques too expensive, but the foreign models offered physical images that "don't fit us." Yet these students searched for their own ways to be international, to learn "cool" fashion at reduced prices.

Late Twenties: A Time of Choice

The twenty-five to thirty-five-year-old age group gives the clearest evidence that women reinterpret the meanings of magazine messages, incorporating them into their lives. These women's actions question the standardized roles established for them by government policies and reinforced by magazines that first appeared in the early eighties. By taking a variety of paths, these women have influenced magazines to create new market niches in an attempt to accommodate and manage the freedom and choice that young women have taken to heart.

Women between twenty-five and thirty-five are enjoying the single life—marrying later, divorcing more freely, and having fewer children later. Between 1975 and 1990, the percentage of women between the ages of twenty-five and twenty-nine who had spouses decreased from 80.3 percent (1975) to 74.5 percent (1985) to 57.5 percent (1990).[61] The percentage of women in the thirty to thirty-four-year-old age group without spouses was 20 percent for Tokyo and 10 percent for the country as a whole in 1985.[62] The birth rate for the country as a whole decreased from 1.76 to 1.53 between 1985 and 1990 and in Tokyo from 1.4 to 1.24 over the same period.[63] Between 1980 and 1989, the age-specific birth rate per 1,000 females decreased for women between twenty-five and twenty-nine (181.5 to 146.4) and increased for women between thirty and thirty-four (73.1 to 91.9).[64] Although still low when compared to other countries, divorce rates climbed to a peak of 1.39 in 1985, but dipped to 1.28 in 1990. However, the number of divorced women receiving child allowances rose considerably throughout the seventies and eighties.[65]

What are women who are remaining single, marrying late, or not having children doing? If they are working hard in responsible jobs, then perhaps we cannot claim that they are integrating alternative ideas and practices suggested by magazines' images into their personal lives. A few young women are forgoing marriage or children to work hard in full-time jobs where they get promotions, but most women work as a means toward something else: to pay for leisure, entertainment with friends, and discretionary purchases. Statistics show that clerical employment of women in the late twenties has risen between 1985 and 1991 to such an extent that now almost half of the women in this age group hold such jobs. The other main job areas are sales and specialist or technical work that allows only limited promotion. After the age of thirty, the percentage of women in specialist jobs decreases as women change to less demanding (and lower-paying) jobs or quit working altogether.[66]

The search for freedom and individual choice for many young women involves leisure and consumption rather than jobs that require long hours of devotion within a hierarchy; women recognize that the full-time career role carries as much stress and curtailment of "freedom" as does the full-time housewife role. Seventy-two percent of single women in Tokyo enjoy themselves in the city's entertainment spots.[67] Young single women at home receive a great deal of spending money from their parents; the average allowance for women under thirty living at home in 1989 was ¥65,000 ($720) per month. Women are also using their money to set up their own households—a departure from convention. Between 1984 and 1989, the number of women setting up single households with friends who also work increased 16 percent for those under thirty and 6 percent for those thirty to thirty-nine. Women's consumption in single households rose 12.2 percent from 1984 to 1989. Households headed by people under thirty have the highest rate of owning cars, video decks, and air conditioners.[68] Such statistics are well reported by government agencies, which express concern not about the leisure and consumption of younger single women, but about the deleterious effects on families if this self-centeredness is not controlled.

In sum, enough women have assimilated messages of freedom and individual choice into their lives that marriage, birth, and divorce trends are being significantly affected. These changes create dissension within the social order and challenge power relations. In the next section, I briefly present six individual cases of young women interviewed in Japan in 1990. The first four of the cases illustrate the new trends I have cited, but also show the fine line these women tread between the responsibilities and roles implicit in government policies and the ideas and practices suggested by the women's magazines. Although these people have integrated social images used by women's magazines into their lives in substantial ways, in most cases their resistance is delicate, interlaced with consumption, and hidden behind the rationale that they are simply "putting off" marriage and childbirth. Nonetheless, they bring into serious question the desirability of the tensions and power relations inherent in the home/work dichotomy for married women with children.

The last two cases indicate that young women of lower socioeconomic backgrounds have little taste for the social images of freedom, individuality, international sophistication, and so on promoted by women's magazines. This preference reflects their lower-status social backgrounds and limited economic positions and points out that the forms of resistance suggested by magazines' messages are signs of higher-status backgrounds for the young women who extend them into their lives. These challenges to the conventional social order serve to divide women against one another, reproducing the asymmetrical relations that commodity culture has underlined in Japan.[69]

Case Studies. 1. Ito-*san,* twenty-five years of age and a graduate of a four-year college, works in a market research firm, which she switched to a year ago for a higher salary ($35,000 per year including bonuses) and weekends off. She works until about nine o'clock every night regardless of overtime limits on her nonmanagerial-track work. Because she is on the "specialist track," she can be promoted only within the accounting department. She adjusts to the hierarchy at work, even pouring tea for clients: "I think of pouring tea as part of my account service work. It's not because I am a woman, but because the client feels good if it is done. The men clients tend to see me as soft [*amaku mieru*], but if you adapt, they understand." Despite her long hours, Ito-*san* enjoys her leisure time intensely. Because she lives at home, paying no rent, her salary goes to leisure activities: beer with work friends after work, or skiing, tennis, and ocean sports with university friends. Dressed in trendy, brand-name clothes, she enjoys fashion magazines and is vague about marriage goals.[70] At an age when society says she should be gaining skills and saving for marriage, Ito-*san* is "selfishly" enjoying herself.

2. Shimizu-*san,* also twenty-five and a four-year college graduate, has not achieved such a high salary in her job organizing international shows and conferences. She resists her prescribed role not only by seeking leisure, but by not taking work seriously: "Women have a part of them that is dependent, don't they? So at work, I cheat a bit and say, 'I don't understand,' or, 'Excuse me,' because I don't want to take so much responsibility." Her previous work at various part-time jobs through a job agency al-

lowed her time to travel and study abroad, and she looks forward to more travel. Despite pressure from her mother to consider marriage, she continues to live at home because she could not afford such comfort and convenience otherwise. However, Shimizu-*san* tries to keep her distance from her family, expressing admiration for American independence within families that "see each other as different people, rather than stuck together." She is wary of marriage because she thinks boys "like girls who are 'cute' or ones that don't say their opinions too strongly." But she plays the dating game: "So if you have an opinion, you sort of cover it up."

3. At age twenty-nine, Yasuda-*san* has married, but she is putting off having children despite growing pressure from family elders. A graduate of a prestigious private university, she has an administrative job with advancement possibilities. Because she feels that she was passed over for a promotion after marrying, she is wary of having children, and she consented to a six-week tour of duty away from home to prove her devotion. She enjoys eating at ethnic restaurants in Tokyo, giving wine-tasting parties at home with her husband, traveling abroad, and playing tennis or skiing (both expensive hobbies in Japan). Yasuda-*san* dresses well and reads high-class fashion magazines such as *Cosmopolitan* and *Vinsancans*. Although her determination to work is consistent with the latest labor reforms for women, she has resisted pressure to conform by putting off having children and investing instead in her own pleasure.

4. Otani-*san* is an artist in her mid-thirties, a single woman with her own apartment in Tokyo, despite the fact that her parents also live in that city. She has invested her energy in a continual resistance to marriage and childbirth, not in the interest of a high level of consumption and enjoyment, but in order to pursue her art. Economically independent, she supports herself with part-time research for a journalist. Out of her salary, she pays her own pension and health insurance. She has time to pursue her avocation of metal etching. Part of her three-room apartment is a studio with a press-key for etching. She is not interested in marriage because she feels she would have to adapt to another's needs. "I would only marry if I found a man who would really share the work and had a large space. . . . Life for Japanese women is easy now. We don't have to worry about supporting a family and can be independent if we are outside of company organizations." She wants neither side of the home/work divide.

5. Koumi-*san* is twenty-five years old and hails from a working-class family in downtown Tokyo. With only a high school education, she now works as a bus guide for night tours of the city, including strip shows. She maintains a professional, uniformed posture and offers slightly off-color but not obscene jokes. Although this is not work that a girl from a higher-status family would do, she earns more money than most secretaries because it is evening work. Forgoing leisure activities with friends, she stud-

ies calligraphy and the art of kimono wearing during the day. She will soon have a license so that she can make money by dressing women in kimono for special rituals or festivals. Her plan is to practice this profession out of her home after marriage. She definitely plans on marrying but "later, like other girls my age." Koumi-*san* shows little resistance, satisfied with her practical accomplishments and assets at a lower level of society. Although she will not escape the double burden of home and work, she will have considerable household power and contribute significantly to the family income, a situation that is more acceptable in a lower-class home.

6. Nakagawa-*san*, a twenty-seven-year-old whose parents are small shopkeepers, has married a salaryman whose parents are also from downtown Tokyo. Although she worked for two years as a clerical worker at a large company, she earned only a small salary and was glad to quit "because the men get used to you and things don't go so well . . . ages get mixed up." After marriage to her high school sweetheart, she worked part-time in her parents' shop until she "finally" got pregnant. At home with a baby boy, she is adamant that she does not want to go back to work. She has given up fashion magazines for magazines on cooking and child care. Besides her baby and her small, newly refurbished house, her main entertainment consists of visits with her parents and parents-in-law, occasional meetings with neighborhood mothers, and visits from her husband's old friends. Unlike some young women who aim to marry ambitious men, she does not look forward to the international assignments that her husband may receive. Nakagawa-*san* is predisposed toward home rather than work and is satisfied with her level of cultural capital as proof of her family's solid economic position.

In summary, some young women use messages of freedom and individuality to reshape the expected contours of their lives, at least for a while, but their economic level determines their choices. Some young women desire freedom and international travel, but because they have low-paying jobs, they cannot afford them and begin to think of marriage as a good economic alternative.

Middle Age

Many middle-aged women (ages thirty-five to sixty) are integrating social images offered by women's and home decorating magazines into their lives but still challenge the status quo in different forms than do young women. Already married and responsible for a household and family, most middle-aged women cannot escape the home/work divide, but can only elide the dichotomy, lessening the tension and asymmetrical relationships in their own lives. In the six case studies below, women enact the intent of government policies as they clean, prepare food, and nurture family members on a daily basis. Because their children are grown, most of these women also work, as the government would have them.

Statistically speaking, the most pronounced trend among middle-aged women in the eighties has been their increased movement into the workforce, particularly into part-time work. This is the chief way in which women have been able to gain a modicum of economic strength while still fulfilling the household duties expected of them.[71] In 1980, 19.3 percent of the female workforce was part-time; in 1990, the figure had risen to 27.9 percent, and the vast majority of these women were over age thirty-five.[72] Compared with younger women, middle-aged women hold more sales and crafts or manufacturing jobs, although about a quarter still hold clerical positions. A second statistical trend over the last ten years has been an increase in free time for women, especially those of middle-age.[73] Middle-aged women often spend this time in sports schools and culture centers for hobbies. Spending is up for everyone, but particularly for households headed by people in their fifties, whose spending is particularly high in the area of furniture and house accessories.[74]

As the cases below point out clearly, not all work is equal, nor is free time equally distributed. Depending on its quality, work may be a way of avoiding onerous aspects of the home/work dichotomy, but it may also increase tension and subordination. For women from lower socioeconomic levels, the instability of part-time work is threatening, and their work is often menial, performed within a hierarchy in which women have little say.[75] Although women at this level often desire enjoyment, they have little economic or cultural capital to attain it in the forms suggested by magazines' social images. Women of higher socioeconomic levels, with education and economic support from their husbands or natal families, can afford to be self-employed, work at home, or use hobbies as the basis for their work. In addition, such women not only tend to have more free time, but they also have the money to use it as they wish, in international travel, purchases for the home and self, expensive hobbies, or entertainment with friends. These women of higher socioeconomic status are able to assimilate these social images of freedom, individuality, leisure, attractiveness, and international sophistication into their own lives and play them off against the expectations of government policies and husbands in order to lessen the effects of the home/work divide. But they construct their successful self-images in contrast to women of lower socioeconomic status. The first three cases present women of higher socioeconomic positions, and the last two present women of lower positions.

Case Studies.   1. Tsuji-*san* is in her late forties, wife of a managerial level salaryman in a large company and mother of two university-age children. Her recently refurbished home in the close suburbs of Tokyo is a showcase of sophisticated European-style furniture and the latest in system kitchens and baths. Only her husband continues to sleep in an old-style tatami room. She has used her economic capital to make a workplace for herself at home, while increasing her symbolic capital as a refined, high-status housewife. "My play has become my work," Tsuji-*san* commented. "I try to do all the arts that contribute to the tea ceremony. . . . I employ teachers and recruit women to come and take the lessons with me." At the back of the house is a large tatami room with accoutrements for tea ceremony; the side garage has become a gallery for art displays and large group lessons. Tsuji-san employs a tea teacher from Kyoto once per month, as well as other teachers in pottery, flower arranging, and shell decoration. Her mother teaches haiku in the tatami room. Her husband was against Tsuji-*san*'s idea initially as "in-between" home and work, but she persisted: "It's better than having a stroke. At least I have a meaning in life."

2. Arisawa-*san*, a woman in her late forties, is the wife of a self-employed professional and the mother of two university-age sons who still live at home. She dresses fashionably and decorates her newly built home with large plants and antique Western furniture. A trained pharmacist, Arisawa-*san* worked at a doctor's office after her children were in junior high, but she resented the doctors' high-handed authority over her and the patients.[76] She started a small pharmacy with a friend from university, using money borrowed by her husband and splitting hours with her friend. The flexible work situation allows her to temper both home and work responsibilities with leisure activities; she engages in sports and hobbies, enjoys entertainment spots, and travels internationally with her friends. Her resistance to the tensions and subordination of the home/work divide is summed up best in her own words: "The problem is when you think you're 'one heart, one body' with your husband. You need your own world (*jibun no sekai*)."

3. Fujii-*san* is a woman in her mid-forties whose husband works for an international firm and whose son is in a postsecondary vocational school. Her dress is expensive but casual and sporty, reminding one of her commitment to tennis, which she practices four days a week. Her economic position is evident from her newly built home, with its bay windows, wood floors, and paisley couch; she comfortably houses her mother in a separate tatami room. A computerized heater on the Japanese bath aids her in giving her mother a hot bath when she comes home from work. Her social connections have landed her a part-time job with good pay and working conditions as a medical clerk in a doctor's office. Officially, she stays within the earning limits set by the government so that she pays no taxes, but in fact, she uses the name of a friend to earn twice the legal amount. Fujii-*san* has the economic and cultural capital to mitigate the burden of work and home responsibilities and thus engage in activities that enable freedom and individuality.

4. Mihara-*san*'s life contrasts with the elite life of the previous women. She has neither the economic nor the cultural capital to integrate social images of leisure and freedom into her life and thus lighten the burdens of home and work. Her work as head cook at a government preschool cafeteria is tiring, and her relations with workmates are difficult. She is in her mid-fifties. Her husband is a manual worker, and her three daughters still share their apartment. Mihara-*san*'s income is not high, but it is absolutely necessary to her family's survival, now and after retirement. "I'd quit if I didn't have to work. I get up before six o'clock and work until five. I feel sorry when the train gets there because I have to wake up and get off. . . . Women can't come home from work and collapse. That's the hardest. A person needs some enjoyment in life." Mihara-*san* desires leisure and freedom but must be satisfied with occasional trips to hot springs and hobby classes on Saturday afternoons. Having put one daughter through college, she pins her hopes on the next generation.

5. In her early fifties, Kato-*san* is divorced and works as an insurance saleswoman in a regional city of northeast Japan. Her low-paying, low-status job is an economic necessity. The messages of women's magazines mean little to Fujii-*san;* she did not welcome the independence that her divorce thrust upon her when her two daughters were still young, leaving her with no choice but to fulfill her duties on both sides of the home/work divide. Hers is a line of work where nothing matters but selling. "You have to go out a lot and you get tired. It's a world of numbers. You can't help but worry, and when it all comes at once, physical aches increase." She has little extra money; she dresses in dark, shapeless clothes and lives in a small tatami-style house. Kato-*san* says in a resigned voice that "my work is my hobby," but she dreams of retirement when she can have her "own life" (*jibun no jinsei*) with hobbies she has wished to pursue. With a low-level pension from the country and another from the company, Kato-*san* plans to spend her retirement with her daughter and son-in-law.

The middle-aged women glimpsed here go beyond the narrow range of magazine images offered to them. Although they fulfill their household responsibilities, their lives are much broader, encompassing paid jobs and leisure activities to which magazines give scant attention. Women of higher socioeconomic status reproduce the ideals of freedom, individuality, and attractiveness that the magazines suggest, but they are more creative than the magazines in making or finding jobs that allow them the flexibility to practice these ideals both inside and outside of the house. They resist the magazines' pictorial images of higher status of yore: the ability to stay home. These women's attitudes and actions challenge the authority of husbands and bosses enough to lessen their own feelings of subordination; none break out of their economic dependence, but they use the money available to them to their advantage. Women of lower socioeconomic status have little leeway to follow magazine images, enduring low-status jobs and the tension and fatigue of the home/work dichotomy. Ironically, if they work, they have more leverage with their husbands and more economic independence than higher-status women do. Yet they lack the signs of higher social positions and the ability to live out alternatives to the status quo.

CONCLUSION

This study suggests several important points about the power of institutions and their effect on people's lives. First, in the case of a complex postindustrial society such as Japan, we cannot assume that the media and the state always reinforce each other. Production-oriented government policies contradict in important ways the ideas and images of self-centered consumption conveyed in women's magazines. Although the roles of consumer and citizen sometimes overlap, consumerism and citizenship in Japan prescribe social orders different from one another, each based on different values. Significantly, some representations of women in consumer discourse question the citizenship roles of women in home and work groups. Visions of pleasure, freedom, sexual attractiveness, and international sophistication conflict with female citizens' duties to reproduce and produce on both sides of the home/work divide.

Second, because of the contradictions between the ideas and practices implied by government policies and those of women's magazines, women can take alternative positions by incorporating both into their lives and acting on one or the other at different times. Although most women do fulfill to some extent the positions and trajectories suggested by government policies, they undercut those policies in limited ways by reconstituting magazine images, combining them with other images of freedom and assimilating them into their lives. Their resistance is fragile and momentary, intended to increase options rather than to change the status quo decisively. The strategies of young, single women to delay and avoid marriage are most disruptive to the social order because the youth population is decreasing just as the elderly population is swelling. The tactics of middle-aged women to increase their leisure and freedom outside of the household are effective primarily in decreasing the tension, fatigue, and subordination they experience as they shift back and forth across the home/work divide.

I have claimed that through reinterpretations and assimilation of media messages, women may contest certain aspects of the productive social order that legitimates the state. However, this study has indicated that money, education, and social background can limit the ability to contest that order. Women of higher socioeconomic levels have the means to support the international trips, dinners out with friends, or hobby-based jobs that allow them to assume multiple roles. For many, their enjoyment of luxury is framed within economic dependence on fathers or husbands and the social privileges of their past and present lives. Although their ideas and actions are subtle forms of resistance for themselves as individuals, they are also newly minted signs of their high socioeconomic status, signs that divide them increasingly from women of lower socioeconomic status who cannot afford to develop or have not internalized the desire for these alternate cultural forms. Women with lesser social positions remain caught within the tensions and subordination of the home/work divide, often harboring the more modest hope that they can escape the divide by staying at home.

I am not arguing that Japanese women are making quick or sweeping alterations to the social order envisioned by the production-oriented state. Nonetheless, their fragile resistances are accomplishing some changes, particularly on the level of power relations between women and their parents, husbands, and in some cases, bosses. They are questioning the rigidity of the home/work divide and women's responsibilities to choose sides or leap continually from one side to the other. But the recession in Japan's economy that began in the early nineties tests these fragile resistances as the government calls on people to return to their proper stations for the production battle. Already young women are warning that the bursting of the economic bubble endangers their newfound economic and social freedoms.[77]

NOTES

1. Louis Althusser, *Lenin and Philosophy* (New York: Monthly Review Press, 1971).

2. John Thompson, *Ideology and Modern Culture* (Stanford: Stanford University Press, 1990), 319; Anthony Giddens, *New Rules of Sociological Method* (London: Hutchison, 1976); Cathy Urwin, "Power Relations and the Emergence of Language," in *Changing the Subject*, eds. J. Henriques, W. Hollway, C. Urwin, C. Venn, and V. Walkerdine (New York: Methuen, 1984); Frances Fox Piven, "Ideology and the State: Women, Power and the Welfare State," in *Women, the State, and Welfare*, ed. Linda Gordon (Madison: University of Wisconsin, 1990), 256.

3. As Michel Foucault has shown, social institutions provide many of the ideas that people use to construct a picture of themselves and others. Thus people do reproduce forms of domination. Michel Foucault, *The History of Sexuality*, vol. 1 (New York: Vintage Books, 1980). But as John Thompson argues, the "process of critical self-reflection" enables "individuals to challenge these forms." Thompson, *Ideology and Modern Culture*.

4. Lila Abu-Lughod, "The Romance of Resistance," *American Ethnologist* 17 (1990): 41–55; Judith Okely, "Defiant Moments: Gender, Resistance, and Indi-

viduals," *Man*, n.s., 26 (1991): 3–22; Tamanoi Mariko, "Songs as Weapons: The Culture and History of Komori (Nursemaids) in Modern Japan," *Journal of Asian Studies* 50, no. 4 (1991):793–817.

5. Richard Rose and Rei Shiratori, "Introduction: Welfare in Society: Three Worlds or One," in *The Welfare State East and West*, eds. R. Rose and R. Shiratori (Oxford: Oxford University Press, 1986); Fred Block, "The Ruling Class Does Not Rule: Notes on the Marxist Theory of the State," in *Revising State Theory: Essays in Politics and Postindustrialism*, ed. Fred Block (Philadelphia: Temple, 1987). I agree with Block that state officials are separate from capitalists in important ways, but that the fortunes of the government, its policies, and its officials are dependent on a healthy economy. For more on Japan's continuing motivation to be recognized as equal to the West, see Carol Gluck (speech given at Chautauqua Institution, Chautauqua, N.Y., August 15, 1992). Certain policies such as welfare policies have been influenced by opposition parties and interest groups, but their final form balances the wishes of the Ministry of Finance and the Ministry of Health and Welfare with the blessing of the Liberal Democratic Party and big business leaders. See Kent Calder, *Crisis and Compensation* (Princeton: Princeton University Press, 1988); and Stephen Anderson, "Beyond the Developmental State: Welfare, Wage-earners and Public Pensions in Japan" (paper given at the Association for Asian Studies, New Orleans, April 12, 1991).

6. For the division among women, see Henrietta Moore, *Feminism and Anthropology* (Minneapolis: University of Minnesota Press, 1988), 129. For their responsibility to the state, see Nancy R. Rosenberger, "Gender and the Japanese State: Pension Benefits Creating Difference," *Anthropological Quarterly* 64, no. 4 (1991a): 178–94.

7. Anne Imamura, *Urban Japanese Housewives: At Home and in the Community* (Honolulu: University of Hawaii Press, 1987).

8. Before 1986, the government offered the *kokumin* or national pension to small business people, self-employed professionals, farmers, and so on. An employees' pension or *kōsei* was offered to salaried employees of medium and larger firms, and an even higher *kyōsai* pension went to government employees. This three-tier system is still in place, but now the lower tier is mainly filled by the unemployed such as homemakers and students or by self-employed people. The government has urged small businesses to incorporate and thus pay into the second level of the system. This will not only encourage more people to work longer and earn promotions to get a better pension, but also will bring more money into government coffers. Discussion of the pension system throughout this article has been drawn from the following sources. *Josei o mamoru katei no hōritsu* (Household laws protecting women) (edited by Sugimura Shin). Insert in *Fujin Seikatsu* (Housewife's life) 36 (March 1982); Inoue Eiko, *Manga Nenkin* (Cartoon pension) (Tokyo: Surugadai Publishing Co., 1987); Kashiwagi Takao and Hattori Eizo, *Josei no tame no Zeikin to Nenkin* (Taxes and pension for women) (Tokyo: Jiyū Kokumin Publishing Co., 1986); Kōseishō, *Kōsei Hakusho* (Welfare white paper) (Tokyo: Kōsei Tōkei Kyōkai, 1989); *Nihon Fujin Dantai Rengōkai, Fujin Hakusho* (Women's white paper) (Tokyo: Horupu Shuppan, 1989); and Shimada Tomiko, *Nenkin ga kataru onna no isshō* (A woman's life as depicted in the pension system) (Tokyo: Asahi Shimbunsha, 1988).

9. Rōdōshō Fujinkyoku, *Reberu Appu! Anata no shokuba no Kintōdo* (Level up! The level of equality at your workplace) (Tokyo: Rōdōshō, 1989b); and Rōdōshō, *Rōdō Hakusho* (White paper on work) (Tokyo: Nihon Rōdō Kenkyū Kikō, 1991).

10. For rehiring women after pregnancy, childbirth, or child rearing, small and medium companies are offered ¥300,000 ($3,300 at 1995 exchange rates of ¥90 to the dollar) per rehired employee, and large companies, ¥200,000 ($2,200). For childcare leave, small and medium companies are given ¥600,000 ($6,600) per person the first year and ¥400,000 ($4,400) per person the second year. Big companies are given a corresponding ¥450,000 ($5,000) and ¥350,000 ($3,900). After the third person given child leave, small and medium companies are given ¥200,000 ($2,200) per person and big companies ¥150,000 ($1,700) per person. A woman must indicate her intention to return to the job and cannot receive unemployment compensation. See Rōdōshō Fujinkyoku, *Reberu Appu!*, 18. Women may opt to return to work six weeks after birth, but may take eight weeks of leave if they wish. The company furnishes forty percent of their pay, and sixty percent is paid by social insurance. If they wish, women can also take six weeks off before the birth and cannot be made to work overtime or late at night while pregnant or soon after birth. See Inoue Yoshiki, *Danjo Koyō Kikai Kintōhō Q&A* (Gender employment opportunity equality act Q&A) (Tokyo: Nihon Seisansei Hombu, 1986); and Rōdōshō Fujinkyoku, *Reberu Appu!*.

11. See Takie Sugiyama Lebra, "Gender and Culture in the Japanese Political Economy: Self-Portrayals of Prominent Businesswomen," in *Cultural and Social Dynamics*, vol. 3 of *The Political Economy of Japan*, eds. S. Kumon and H. Rosovsky (Stanford: Stanford University Press, 1992); Ueno Chizuko, "The Japanese Women's Movement: the Counter-values to Industrialism," in *The Japanese Trajectory: Modernization and Beyond*, eds., G. McCormack and Y. Sugimoto (Cambridge: Cambridge University Press, 1988), 179.

12. Pension policy since 1986 makes sure that as many people as possible are paying into the pension coffers, because the government predicts there will be only 2.5 workers supporting every elder person by 2015. See Kōseishō, *Kōsei Hakusho* (Welfare white paper) (Tokyo: Kōsei Tōkei Kyōkai, 1989), 115. Because pension payments are guaranteed only if they are fed through companies, the latest pension policy directs workers in the higher-level pension to pay two extra percentage points of their salary toward a pension account for their wives. See Kōseishō, *Kōsei Hakusho*. Women receive much smaller pensions than men. In 1990, women received 71.4 percent of the lower-level *kokumin* pension, with an average monthly payment of ¥30,000 (about $333 at 1995 exchange rates). In contrast, women received only 32.6 percent of the higher *kōsei* pension; men's average payment was ¥300,000 ($3,333) per month, whereas women's average payment was only ¥170,000 ($1,888) per month. See Nihon Fujin Dantai Rengōkai, *Fujin Hakusho*, 139.

13. This figure rises only to 63.4 percent when controlling for education, to 68.4 percent when controlling for the continuous number of years worked, and to 68.6 percent when controlling for the type of work. See Rōdōshō, *Rōdō Hakusho* (White paper on work) (Tokyo: Rōdōshō, 1991), 13.

14. In 1989, Japanese worked 2,159 hours per year (thirty hours less than a year earlier), as compared to 1,957 hours in the U.S. and 1,638 hours in Germany. See Rōdōshō, *Rōdō Hakusho*, 63.

15. Government day-care centers accommodate about sixty percent of children in day care. If both government and private day-care centers are considered, supply exceeded demand in 1985, and the number has decreased slightly in the nineties. See The Japan Research Institute on Child Welfare, *Graphs and Charts on Japan's Child Welfare Services* (Tokyo: The Japan Research Institute on Child Welfare, 1993), 8, 17.

16. Child allowance for the first and second children is ¥5000 ($56) per month, and for third and subsequent children ¥10,000 ($111) per month. Parents receive this allowance only until the child reaches the age of three, and parents with higher incomes are not eligible (about $40,000 per year for a family of four). See The Japan Research Institute on Child Welfare, *Graphs and Charts*, 32.

17. Anne Allison, "Japanese Mothers and *Obentōs:* The Lunch-Box as Ideological State," *Anthropological Quarterly* 64, no. 4 (1991): 195–208; Imamura, *Urban Japanese Housewives*, 120.

18. Linda Gordon, "The New Feminist Scholarship on the Welfare State," in *Women, the State, and Welfare*, ed. Linda Gordon (Madison: University of Wisconsin, 1990), 13.

19. Nihon Fujin Dantai Rengōkai, *Fujin Hakusho*, 147–9.

20. Bando Mariko, *Nihon no Josei Deeta Banku* (Japanese Women's Data Bank) (Tokyo: Ōkurashō), 1992; *Yūnyū Zakka Katarogu* (Imported goods catalog), no. 1 (1993): 2.

21. Sharon Nolte and Sally Hastings, "The Meiji State's Policy toward Women, 1890–1910," in *Recreating Japanese Women, 1600–1945,* ed. G. Bernstein (Berkeley: University of California Press, 1991).

22. In 1970 there were four main women's magazines, concentrating on homemaking. That number increased to twenty-one women's magazines in 1971 and forty-six in 1982. In 1970, the four women's magazines sold 36,800 copies. In 1981, the circulation of women's magazines reached 1,620,000. See Inoue Teruko, *Masukomi to Josei no Gendai* (Mass communication and women today) in *Josei no Imēji* (The image of women), ed. Joseigaku Kenkyūkai (Tokyo: Keisō Shobo, 1984), 43–5. By 1988, the number of magazines targeting women had grown to sixty-two, with increasing use of visuals and advertising. See Inoue Teruko, *Josei Zasshi o Kaidoku Suru: Comparepolitan Nichi, Bei Mekishiko Hikaku Kenkyū* (Deciphering women's magazines: *Comparepolitan,* Japan, U.S., Mexico comparative research) (Tokyo: Kakiuchi Publishing Company, 1989), 20–1, 55. For the newer magazines, see Inoue *Masukomi to Josei no Gendai*, 43.

23. Rob Steven, *Japan's New Imperialism* (Armonk, N.Y.: M. E. Sharpe, 1990), 43. The "upper class" is estimated to be thirty to forty percent of the population.

24. I am not arguing whether magazines mirror society or mold it, as I think both of these occur. See Karl Rosengren, "Mass Media and Social Change: Some Current Approaches," in *Mass Media and Social Change*, eds. E. Katz and T. Szecsko (Beverly Hills, Calif.: Sage Publishing House, 1981). In "The Image of Women in Canadian Magazines" in *Mass Media and Social Change*, Susannah Wilson argues that magazine editors and writers represent conservative interests in society because of their links with commercial advertising. However, Pierre Bourdieu, in *Distinctions: A Social Critique of the Judgement of Taste* (Cambridge: Harvard University Press, 1984), has suggested that such editors and writers are "culture makers" who

lack in economic power, but gain power through their manipulation of new cultural styles. For arguments that the media provides social cement for the status quo, see Louis Althusser *Lenin and Philosophy;* Nicos Poulantzas, "The Problem of the Capitalist State," in *Ideology in Social Science,* ed. Robin Blackburn (New York: Random House, 1973); Ralph Miliband, *The State in Capitalist Society* (London: Weidenfield and Nicholson, 1969). For arguments that this view is too limiting, see Thompson, *Ideology and Modern Culture,* 96.

25. The base of consumers had broadened precisely because of profits from the high economic growth policies of government and business. Furthermore, increased consumption satisfied international pressure on the Japanese government to ease trade surpluses. The Japanese government did little but allow in high-quality, high-priced goods from abroad.

26. Jean Baudrillard, *For a Critique of the Political Economy of the Sign* (St. Louis: Telos Press, 1981); and Bourdieu, *Distinctions.*

27. Nancy Rosenberger, "Japan's Youth Economy: Messages about Freedom and Status in the Mass Media" (paper given at the Association for Asian Studies, New Orleans, 1991). Arjun Appadurai, "Introduction: Commodities and the Politics of Value," in *The Social Life of Things: Commodities in Cultural Perspective* (Cambridge: Cambridge University Press, 1986), 56. In a comparative study of Japanese and American advertising, Kline found that American ads valued practicality, work, and convenience, whereas Japanese ads valued leisure, beauty, sensuality, and health. "The basic consumerist, rather than industrialist, values seem to be the basis of Japanese advertising." See Stephen Kline, "The Theatre of Consumption: On Comparing American and Japanese Advertising," *Canadian Journal of Political and Social Theory* 12, no. 3 (1988): 101–120. Magazines vary somewhat in the level of style they offer, depending on price and quality, but all emphasize these images. Only in the late eighties and early nineties have such magazines appeared for men, and then only a few. Men are targeted in specialized magazines about cars, sports, and pornography.

28. *McSister* (Tokyo: Fujingahōsha) (July 1991): 85.

29. *McSister,* (July 1992): 54–68.

30. *McSister,* (March 1990): 10.

31. *Vivi* (Tokyo: Kōdansha) 9, no. 8 (1991): 98.

32. Ibid., 60.

33. Ibid., 72–7.

34. *Vivi,* 8, no. 3 (1990): 33–4.

35. *Vivi,* 10, no. 7 (1992): 131.

36. *Hanako* (Tokyo: Magazine House) 2, no. 5 (1989): 53.

37. *With* (Tokyo: Kōdansha) 8, no. 3 (1990): 8–17.

38. Ibid., 21; *With,* 9, no. 8 (1991): 30.

39. *An-an* (Tokyo: Magazine House) 21, no. 5 (1990): 6–84.

40. *Sign* (Tokyo: Gakken) 4, no. 6 (1991): 6–7.

41. *Mine* (Tokyo: Kōdansha) 4, no. 2 (1990): 28.

42. Ibid., 98–107; *Mine,* 5, no. 11 (1991): 40.

43. *Frau* (Tokyo: Kōdansha) 2, no. 11 (1992).

44. These examples are taken from *Fiore* (Tokyo: Takii and Co.) spring 1992; *Classy* (Tokyo: Kobunsha) 10, no. 2 (1993); and *Cosmopolitan Nihonhan* 15, no. 1 (1993).

45. *Nikkei Woman* (Tokyo: Nikkei Home Publishing), no. 23 (1990); and *Nikkei Woman* (Tokyo), no. 55 (1992).

46. *Crea* 3, no. 3 (1991); and *Crea* 4, no. 7 (1992).

47. *Que Sera* (Tokyo: Shodensha) May 1990 supplement to *Bisshe*.

48. *Sophia* (Tokyo: Kōdansha) 7, no. 2 (1990); and *Shufu to Seikatsu* (Tokyo: Shufu to Seikatsusha) 48, no. 1 (1993).

49. *Utsukushii Heya* (Beautiful room) (Tokyo: Shufu to Seikatsusha) 14, no. 72 (1990).

50. "Rifōmu Jitsurei 1000" (Reform, 1000 examples) "Plus One" supplement to *Futari no Heya* (Tokyo: Shufunotomosha, 1990), 102; and *Sumai no Sekkei* (Dwelling plans) (Tokyo: Fuji Sankei Communications Group) 30: 337 (1990), 115.

51. Nancy R. Rosenberger, "Status, Individuality, and Leisure: Messages of Western Styles in Japanese Home Magazines," in *Remade in Japan*, ed. J. Tobin (New Haven, Conn.: Yale University Press, 1992).

52. See Clyde Prestowitz, *Trading Places: How We Allowed Japan to Take the Lead* (New York: Basic Books, 1988).

53. Moeran argues that popular media images of individuality in Japan support the purity of the spontaneous heart. See Brian Moeran, "Individual, Group, and Seishin: Japan's Internal Cultural Debate," in *Japanese Culture and Behavior*, eds. W. Lebra and T. S. Lebra (Honolulu: University of Hawaii, 1986). Tanaka claims that images of individuality simply remain meaningless against the strength of the hierarchical world outside of fashion. See Tanaka Keiko, "Intelligent Elegance: Women in Japanese Advertising," in *Unwrapping Japan*, eds. E. Ben-ari, B. Moeran, and J. Valentine (Honolulu: University of Hawaii Press, 1990). Moeran's interpretation is closer to my own, although I am suggesting an expansion of the spontaneous domain beyond its conventional boundaries for higher-class women.

54. This undercurrent of the acceptability of female sexuality has never disappeared, and television, magazine, and comic book portrayal of sexuality is quite explicit by American standards. In postwar Japan, public displays of sexuality were limited to the entertainment spheres of bars, nightclubs, and bathhouses. In the eighties however, some university coeds have begun to work on the side as bar hostesses.

55. In 1984, government groups complained about magazines for teenage girls that discussed sexual intercourse. Politicians thought the magazines would give girls bad ideas that might undermine their willingness to take on their traditional responsibilities (personal communication, Keiko Aiba). In 1992, government groups and the consumer movement attacked the explicit depiction of sex at increasingly young ages in comics popular throughout Japan (*Nihon Keizai Shimbun*, April 5, 1992). In both cases the uproar was quelled when publishers promised to regulate internally their handling of the topic.

56. Dentsū Advertising Company, "Setsuna sa sedai Seikatsu Jiten" (A life dictionary for the "setsuna" generation), chapter three in marketing report (Tokyo: Dentsū Publishing Company, 1990).

57. M. M. Bakhtin, *Rabelais and His World* (Bloomington: Indiana University Press, 1984); Michel De Certeau, *The Practice of Everyday Life* (Berkeley: University of California Press, 1984); Keith Hart, "On Commoditization," in *From Craft to In-*

dustry, ed. Esther Goody (Cambridge: Cambridge University Press, 1982); Grant McCracken, *Culture and Consumption: New Approaches to the Symbolic Character of Consumer Goods and Activities* (Bloomington: Indiana University Press, 1990), 110.

58. Thompson, *Ideology and Modern Culture*, 306.

59. Bourdieu, *Distinctions*.

60. See Bourdieu, *Distinctions*.

61. Sōmuchō Seishonen Taisaku Honbu, *Seishonen Hakusho* (White paper on youth) (Tokyo: Ōkurashō Insatsukyoku, 1991), 145.

62. Keizai Kikakuchō, *Kokumin Seikatsu Hakusho* (White paper on citizens' life) (Tokyo: Ōkurashō Insatsukyoku, 1991a), 209. For women between twenty and twenty-four, the rate of having spouses decreased from 30.3 percent in 1975 to 13.5 percent in 1990, but the sharp decrease came by 1980. See Sōmuchō Seishonen Taisaku Honbu, *Seishonen Hakusho*, 145. Even in the thirty-five to thirty-nine-year-old age group, about 15 percent were single in Tokyo. Acceptance of the idea that women should have a choice whether to marry has also risen, reducing social pressure on women. About 50 percent of both women and men across the country agree that, because of individual freedom, women should have the choice whether to marry, with higher agreement in the big cities. See Keizai Kikakuchō, *Kokumin Seikatsu Hakusho*, 210.

63. Nihon Fujin Dantai Rengōkai, *Fujin Hakusho* (Women's white paper) (Tokyo: Horupu Shuppan, 1991), 253. Keizai Kikakuchō, *Kokumin Seikatsu Hakusho*, 208.

64. Birthrates per 1,000 women aged thirty-five to thirty-nine also increased from 12.9 to 19.6 between 1980 and 1989. See Health and Welfare Statistics Association, *Health and Welfare Statistics in Japan* (Tokyo: Kōsei Tōkei Kyōkai, 1991), 38.

65. In 1970, 64,923 divorced women received child welfare allowances. This number rose to 300,269 in 1980 and to 503,201 in 1989. See Nihon Fujin Dantai Rengōkai, *Fujin Hakusho* (1991), 277.

66. Mizunoya claims that women work out of a "fashion sense," wanting little responsibility and changing jobs often without any career plan. See Mizunoya Etsuko, *Women's Shindorōmu Kakuteru* (Women's syndrome cocktail) (Tokyo: Wave Shuppan, 1992), 19, 26. In 1991, the type of work held by women in the twenty-five to twenty-nine-year-old age group was as follows: 45.5 percent in clerical; 11.2 percent in sales; and 22.7 percent in specialist and engineering work. The biggest rise since 1985 was in clerical work, with a slight rise in farming, fishing, and forest industries as well as in sales and specialist or technical work. Men of the same age group worked in much higher numbers in manufacturing and craft work or sales. Between 1982 and 1987, there was a slight increase in women university graduates occupying management positions, but most such positions were held by older women with high school educations who headed family firms. Most women educated above high school in 1991 worked in specialist or technical jobs. See Rōdōshō, *Rōdōshō Hakusho*, 112–117.

67. Iwao Sumiko, *Japanese Women: Traditional Image and Changing Reality* (New York: The Free Press, 1993). This rate drops sharply after the birth of one child to fifty-two percent, and to forty-nine percent after that child is in school. In contrast, men's rate of enjoyment of entertainment spots is slightly lower than women's while single, but rises to sixty-four percent after the first child is in school.

68. Keizai Kikakuchō, *Kokumin Seikatsu Hakusho*, 31, 39, 47, 187.

69. Lila Abu-Lughod, "Romance of Resistance," 41–55.

70. She mentioned reading *An-an*, *NonNon*, and *Vinsancans*, the latter of which has particularly high-quality foreign fashion. She also mentioned reading the entertainment magazine *Hanako* and the popular cooking magazine *Orange Page*.

71. In a poll, about fifty percent of Japanese thought that women should do the housework, whereas only fourteen percent of unspecified foreigners agreed with this. See Keizai Kikakuchō, *Kokumin Seikatsu Hakusho*, 162.

72. Nihon Fujin Dantai Rengōkai, *Fujin Hakusho* (1991), 269.

73. In 1991, of women between ages forty and forty-four, 27.9 percent were in clerical, 27 percent in crafts and manufacturing, 15.1 percent in sales, and 9.9 percent in specialists or technical work. See Rōdōshō, *Rōdō Hakusho*, 113–7. In 1991, women in their twenties had fourteen minutes more free time per day than they had in 1981; in their thirties, twenty minutes more; in their forties, twenty-six minutes more; in their fifties, twenty-seven minutes more; and in their sixties, twenty-one minutes more. This was paralleled by a decrease in free time for men. Men in their thirties had fourteen minutes less per day; in their forties, twelve minutes less; and in their fifties, fifteen minutes less. (Keizai Kikakuchō, *Zu de miru Seikatsu Hakusho* (White paper on life as depicted through charts) (Tokyo: Ōkurashō Insatsukyoku, 1991b), 58.

74. Keizai Kikakuchō, *Zu de miru Seikatsu Hakusho*, 58, 31.

75. The flip side of part-time work is its instability. In 1987, a government agency judged that almost half of women workers had unstable employment, and that number was increasing. See Nihon Fujin Dantai Rengōkai, *Fujin Hakusho* (1989), 29. Dorinne Kondo, *Crafting Selves: Power, Gender, and Discourses of Identity in a Japanese Workplace* (Chicago: University of Chicago Press, 1990).

76. Most doctors in Japan mix and sell drugs directly out of their offices, so many employ pharmacists directly. The Ministry of Health and Welfare is working to change this situation by encouraging the establishment of separate drugstores.

77. Yamashita Etsuko, "Josei no Jidai: Ima ya Kadoki," (Women's era: Now a time of excess), in *Asahi Shimbun* (June, 27, 1992): 17.

TWO

The Telerepresentation of Gender in Japan

Andrew A. Painter

Gender was not at the top of my list of topics to investigate when I began my nineteen months of fieldwork (from February 1988 until September 1989) inside the production department of a major Osaka television station. At the beginning of my research on how producers and directors create television in Japan, I envisioned a rather macho sort of political analysis that would identify influential individuals and groups, study factions and schisms, and chart the symbols and strategies that made up everyday life inside the television station (hereafter "ZTV"). However, this approach soon showed gender to be a key feature of company life. Fascinated, I paid close attention to the many ways men and women deployed representations of gender within the television station, and I tried to make sense of Japanese television programming in reference to this ethnographic grounding.

The first part of this chapter examines the cultural and ideological climate of TV production in Japan with particular reference to gender. The second part focuses on how TV planners, researchers, and producers imagine and entertain one type of gendered audience: what they call *shufu* (housewives). Although the overall tone of much that follows is critical, at the same time I want to leave space for ambiguity and change. If my research inside ZTV taught me anything, it is that gender in Japan, both on and off TV, is a far from settled matter.[1]

GENDER AND HIERARCHY INSIDE ZTV

According to a friend in the ZTV research department, the two most important factors that program planners consider when thinking about television audiences are age and sex. A similar perspective can shed light on the situation of women workers within ZTV. At ZTV, men minimize women's power and influence most obviously by outnumbering them. With close to ninety percent of the full-time employees (*shain*) being men, women inside ZTV are marked, both numerically and symbolically, as less significant. Moreover, *shain* women rarely occupy positions of power

46

or even minimal authority. In 1989, none of the seventy-five *shain* women had reached the level of *buchō* (section manager), the lowest managerial position in the company. Meanwhile, the company employed well over one hundred "temporary" women employees. In this category women outnumbered men, though the low status of their work made them (and, in certain ideological extensions, all women at ZTV) second-class citizens within the organization. Produced in such an environment, it is hardly surprising that Japanese TV programs do little to empower women or work for change in the area of gender relations.

To understand how people negotiate gender relationships within the patriarchal and hierarchical organization of ZTV and how women at different levels in the company often adopt differing strategies to deal with their situations, it makes sense first to focus on the sorts of ideologies women in the Japanese TV industry must face. Among the most pernicious, especially among senior ZTV employees, are those that depict women as inherently inferior workers. The president of ZTV is one prominent proponent of this dominant view, and he shared the following opinions with me during a man-to-man talk one afternoon in his spacious office:

I often say that, you know, according to the Japanese constitution, and probably in the American constitution too, it is against the law to discriminate according to sex—they are both equal. Now, that "equal" is based on the law; that is not a realistic equality. . . . Regarding ability, to speak in general terms, of course men's ability is higher. Isn't it the case that in Greek philosophy they said "homo sapiens"? That is, women are not people. And it's the same in China too. . . . And in the case of presidents, while there are great (*erai*) women like Thatcher, speaking in general and statistically, men have to be higher [than women]; if you look at history . . . there are very few cases where women have come out on top in struggles for power. In fact, Japanese people have [the sport] sumo wrestling—now even if a woman tried she couldn't win, could she? Even in the Olympics they divide things up according to male and female. . . . So people think that I am a male chauvinist.

So even my wife bitches [at me]. . . . But basically, compared to men, women are less intelligent, they have less physical strength, even their bodily structures are different—that is the philosophy I hold to—but in order to show that the company president is *not* a male chauvinist, we are also hiring women. They are people too, after all. While they may have certain limitations, there must also be "territories" where they can make use of their abilities, too. [*He acts as if directing the personnel department.*] "Use them in places like that." For example, there wasn't a single female announcer in the company, [so I asked them] "Isn't that a little strange? There are, after all, many female viewers!" [*We laugh.*]. . . .

> So it's not exactly discrimination against women . . . but speaking realis-
> tically, in overall terms, statistically and in terms of number—it is a male-
> dominated society. I think that is the trend in the world.

These discriminatory statements are indicative of the degree to which
women are seen as the inferior sex and thus as inferior employees by the
elite managers of many Japanese corporations. Except in certain limited
"territories" (the ZTV president used the English word), women are at
best anomalies in the company organizational scheme. They are difficult
to fit into regular senior/junior relationships, they do not drink as long or
as well as the men, and they are—in this view at least—generally irra-
tional and emotional.[2]

Recent changes (post-1986) in hiring practices notwithstanding, the
company will probably continue with policies that make women workers
marginal while localizing them in appropriate "territories." As women
workers are sometimes not so subtly reminded upon marriage or the birth
of a child, the most appropriate territory of all is in the domestic sphere.
(As we shall see, Japanese telerepresentations also assign women to appropriate territories, especially the home.)

Despite the confidence with which some men assert their superiority
over women at ZTV, they can only do so by ignoring or rationalizing
away the presence of very talented and successful women workers inside
the station. One is a veteran television producer affectionately called
"OK-*san*" by her workmates. Recruited early on from a publishing company where she wrote a cooking column for housewives, her experience
made her attractive to ZTV where, "in those days" according to OK-*san*,
"male or female, the company needed [talented] people." One of the most
friendly and helpful of my informants, she had this to say about the early
years at the company:

> At that time, you know, the company had just gotten started so . . . the or-
> ganization was still soft. It wasn't like today, some thirty years later, where
> the organization has become so completely systematized. There was still a
> relatively free sort of atmosphere at work. We all started at the same line, so
> to speak—our ages were all about the same—and so there was a strong
> sense of group consciousness [*nakama ishiki*]. So in the beginning we didn't
> feel that we were being mistreated or discriminated against so much—at
> that time. It was still a new medium, you see? . . . And the people [in the
> television station] too, they hadn't yet, how to put it, they weren't yet so
> rigid. There was a feeling that we were all working together. . . . We drank
> together, talked together, and did things as a group, so the atmosphere was
> much better then than now. . . . From print, from the cinema, and from the
> stage and "show business" we took the best things we could use. . . . We
> were sort of groping around in those days. So in a way, we were able to
> work freely. If one said, "I want to do this," you were able to, and sponsors

weren't such trouble, and people didn't complain so much about ratings . . . so in that way it was better before the organization was firmly established.

The image OK-*san* gives of the early years at ZTV is of a flexible and relatively free environment infused with a sense of group consciousness and a shared sense of purpose. Gradually, however, both the organization of the company and many of the people inside it changed from "soft" (*yawarakai*) to "rigid" (*katai*). Freedom decreased as the focus at ZTV shifted from horizontal relationships within the company to vertical, from "group consciousness" to "promotion consciousness," and from participation to competition in many areas of experience. Although OK-*san* did not say it explicitly, the increasingly rigid structure of ZTV may have worked to establish the power and prestige of men within the company.

For women, the growing rigidity proved disadvantageous in many unexpected ways. The sense of community forged during the early days of the company began to give way to routinization and the pressures of profit making. At the same time, women came to be classified as a separate and subordinate category within the company workforce. It became clear that women were not going to be treated equally within the organization, and they could not count on much support from the overwhelmingly male company union in their struggle. Starting a "women's group," ZTV women worked to ensure their fundamental rights within the television industry. OK-*san* was an active union leader for over ten years; she participated in sit-ins and general strikes while also campaigning for women's rights in private broadcasting companies. The successes of women in her generation were fundamental and important: the establishment of equal base pay for men and women; the repeal of unequal mandatory retirement ages for women (which were as low as the mid-twenties in some Japanese stations); the guarantee of the basic right to return to work after having a child. Despite these important victories, real problems remained to trouble almost every woman working in the Japanese television industry.

Another person conveniently ignored by those who would portray women as inferior workers was Ms. Kiyomizu. Now a powerful and respected documentary producer and director, she was originally hired by the television station as an announcer. After getting married, she was told that her popularity with the public was slipping, and she was transferred into the ZTV news production department. She was greeted at her new post by a boss (of course, a middle-aged man) who said, "We don't really expect anything from you." Despite (or perhaps because of) this less than flattering welcome, Ms. Kiyomizu kept on working and became one of the most prestigious of ZTV documentary directors. Her presence, her intelligence, and her obvious success all call into question much of what the company president and second in charge say about women workers.

Although women like OK-*san* and Ms. Kiyomizu should put some strain on patriarchal ideologies of work and gender in the company, most men at ZTV view such women as exceptions that prove the rule, "special cases" (*tokubetsu na keisu*). Because these women do not fit into the prevailing discourses of gender and domination, they are either marginalized or ignored altogether by those who promote ideologies of male superiority in the workplace. These ideologies maintain and reproduce themselves by dissimulating the actual state of affairs within the station.[3] (Analogous processes of dissimulation can also be seen in gendered telerepresentations in Japan.)

The women I got to know best were actively involved in TV production. They worked in what were called *genba* sections, areas where hands-on creation took place. *Genba* workers, including those relatively low on the totem pole, were given much prestige within the TV station.[4] When I began working inside the ZTV production department, there were two female directors: the veteran OK-*san* and a new employee, Ms. Kameoka, who was still in her first year. Because most of the training of new entrants is done by one's immediate superiors (*sugu senpai*), much of the onerous work of teaching me how to become a floor director fell on the shoulders of Ms. Kameoka. Less than five months later, when the next group of annual recruits entered the company, I became the *sugu senpai* of the next female director to enter the production department. I was thus working daily alongside women just beginning their careers inside the television station.[5]

For these women, the most pressing concern was to secure acceptance into the hierarchical groups that made up the production department. Though they were officially already entitled to full membership, they had to prove themselves as workers in order to be seen as one of the team. Inside of the production department, the most important relationships were with those in one's immediate work group. Ms. Kameoka and I were members of the team that produced the "Two O'clock Wideshow," a live talk show broadcast nationwide five days each week. Our group was led by an amiable *buchō*, Mr. Ohira, who told me that he welcomed the coming of young women directors onto his team. Perhaps because of the friendliness of the section leader, women were generally treated well by other members of the department.

Within the work group there are three kinds of colleagues: *senpai* (superiors), *dōki* (same year entrants), and *kōhai* (inferiors). Seniority is the primary determining factor in the company hierarchy. The problem for women in such a system is that they have to juggle two kinds of subordination, whereas men have to only deal with one: although both men and women are defined and ranked according to seniority, women are also ranked (by some) as inferior. Inside the production department the usual official solution was to recognize only seniority; gender was rarely discussed openly by either men or women.

Women workers intent upon being ranked solely by seniority rather than gender attempted to mute gender differences. New women directors deliberately avoided calling attention to gender because it would highlight how they were different from the men in the group. This was made clear, for example, by the way *shain* women dressed. In stark contrast to the temporary workers, who almost always wore skirts or dresses, the *shain* usually wore slacks or blue jeans. When working in the studio, they often wore the navy blue ZTV windbreakers that were used by the (always male) cameramen and program technicians. Despite these attempts, however, women's seniority-based ranking and gender-based ranking were conflated, and the women were viewed as *kohai*, especially when they were found wanting in some way.

As a consequence of their attempts to deflect attention from gender within the production department, the women did not protest the ways in which they were treated inside the station or gender was depicted on TV. Intent on achieving harmony with their male workmates, women directors let many things pass that they probably objected to personally. For example, they suffered quietly the behavior of a chief producer in the production department, whom I will call Mr. Takimoto. Known to touch women in the station whenever possible, he quipped, "I'm harmless because I just touch; I don't do anything more serious!" His exploits were seen as humorous by most men within the department, to the point that being "attacked" by Mr. Takimoto was viewed as a sort of rite of passage for women entering the section.

The fact that women in the production department could not complain about such immediate and personal attacks helps explain their hesitancy to speak up about discrimination against women on TV. I never heard any of the ZTV directors, men or women, object to that discrimination, although once, during new employee training, a young woman in the programming division did give an articulate presentation on the subject of "why TV representations of women and ideas about female audiences are out of date." I was impressed by her talk, but even more by the reaction of her fast-rising section chief, who smiled bemusedly and confided to me man-to-man that "she really has no idea about the business side of television."

The ambiguous position of *shain* women at ZTV was compounded by the presence of low-status, non-*shain* women employees. Women full-timers were outnumbered by pretty, temporary workers who adorned every office, tending the three pseudo-domestic zones of the Japanese workplace: the copy machine, the tea area, and the word processors. Women struggling against the stereotypical image of females as harmonious and decorative "flowers of the workplace" *(shokuba no hana)* faced very real problems in relating to the temporary women in their sections. Solutions varied, but many feared that socializing with the temporaries would hurt their professional image in the company. The resultant distancing was noticed by many men, who often interpreted it as a sign that women employees were "naturally" unable to get along with each other.

The temporary women workers in the production department were kept busy with such tasks as answering telephones, making copies, and sorting postcards from viewers. More unusual duties included helping guide visitors to the various studios and assisting in logistical work when the production staff went on location to film special programs. The women were expected to prepare and serve tea to all the employees in the office several times each day, especially in the morning when work began, after lunch, and during the so-called three o'clock snack time. Having women play the role of waitress several times a day underlined their subservient status while also making men feel important. Expected to dress stylishly and to be pleasant and agreeable at all times, the temporary women played a crucial symbolic function within the station: they provided a nonthreatening other against which men could define and create masculine identities. Although these women probably found many of the ZTV men ridiculous, their *tatemae* (superficial) behavior was respectful, agreeable, and subservient.[6]

Because I was interested in learning more about women working in the company, I tried to stay on good terms with the temporary workers. I felt especially close to Tami-*chan*, whose eight-year career at ZTV was much longer than that of most temporary workers (who usually stayed for only six months to a year). She had come to ZTV from a personnel agency and was now responsible for scheduling and managing audience visits to the various studios. An efficient and respected worker, Tami-*chan* was in many ways the leader of the temporary employees—indeed, at times this energetic woman appeared to be the de facto leader of the entire production department. Her ambiguous position within but outside the company hierarchy allowed her to openly subvert, play with, and parody the system.

For example, after many months of fieldwork, I noticed that in conversation among themselves the temporaries often did not use proper names to refer to various men who worked in our section. When I asked Tami-*chan* about this, she thought a bit before confiding that they had actually compiled a list of nicknames to refer to the men in the office. They called one entire section of the production department "the zoo." "Don't you get it?" Tami-*chan* prodded. "Haven't you noticed that many of the men look like different types of animals?" I had not noticed, but after Tami-*chan* gave me a couple of examples (one poor man was "the giraffe," and another was "panda"), I saw the humor in these well-coined nicknames. One of my friends in the department was labeled "monster-man" (taken from a popular Japanese animated program), and I didn't have the heart to tell him his nickname because it fit only too well. (I never did discover whether or not I had been given a nickname—I was afraid to ask!)

Although the temporary female workers were among the lowest in status at ZTV—or perhaps because of this organizational reality—they managed to make the work enjoyable by creating their own alternative perspective on the company and the people who worked there. These women were free to parody the hierarchies at ZTV in a way no *shain* could, and their irreverent behavior was enjoyed by both women and men inside the company. The famous "elevator incident," graphically related to me by a temporary worker friend, is just one of many Tami-*chan* myths that are told and retold at ZTV. Understanding the myth requires one ethnographic observation about a company elevator that would make a loud buzzing noise when overfull. Almost invariably, the person who got off the elevator to lighten the load at such times was the lowest-ranking employee. Even if this person had gotten on first, he or she was expected to defer and let the higher-ranking workers ride. I was struck by the alacrity with which hierarchies were computed and enacted at such times; figuring out who was lowest on the totem pole was done quickly and automatically. Introducing Tami-*chan* into the picture, however, often resulted in a glitch in the system, as one part-time worker told me in an interview.

> One day Tami-*chan* was riding the elevator up towards the production department. When it stopped at the second floor, our department manager, Mr. Ohira, got on. The elevator sounded BZZZZZ. Before we could decide who was to get off the elevator, Tami-*chan* accused in a loud voice, "Wasn't it you, Mr. Ohira?" [*Ohira-san desho!?*] As if by reflex, the startled *buchō* jumped off the elevator and began the long walk up to the sixth floor. The doors closed and the elevator began to rise in stunned silence until, all together, we burst out in laughter!!

Tami-*chan* made the office more pleasant by poking fun at the hierarchy that threatened to become too powerful. Her energy and humor were infectious. Constantly telling jokes, she often had the people around her in stitches before she would suddenly sit up straight and accuse them of "not working seriously." (This usually made us laugh even harder.) She would straight-facedly say to our *buchō*, "*Domo arigato gozai mammosu*" (roughly, "Thank you very mammoth!"), hoping to get some reaction. Knowing he was outmatched, the boss usually just pretended he didn't notice her joking.

Tami-*chan* and the ZTV temporary workers can help us in thinking about Japanese television and how it addresses and entertains audiences.

First, just as the women temporary workers were paid to agree with men, to compliment them, to serve them, and to add harmony and beauty to the workplace, women are routinely used on Japanese TV in exactly the same way, to listen to and agree with men. Women "introduce harmony" into Japanese telerepresentations with their (presumed) focus on the maintenance of warm human relations (*ningen kankei*). Unlike men who struggle for superiority and dominance, these women in powerless positions are no threat to anyone. Whatever they may actually think, they express only support for the very system that dominates them.

Women on TV, however, are not limited to simply echoing what has already been expressed by men. Like the temporary workers in ZTV, women on TV often make fun of the status quo. As I have argued elsewhere,[7] much of TV in Japan appeals to audiences by representing a world where hierarchies are subverted by spontaneous play and informal interaction. For example, two *manzaishi* (comedian) women whom I got to know well, stage-named Ikuyo and Kuruyo, construct many of their routines by exaggerating and parodying dominant notions of women. Single and in their early forties, they pretend to be preoccupied with getting married "before it gets too late." The ridiculousness of their act cannot but reflect on the ridiculousness of a patriarchal system in which women are said to have an ideal age for getting married (*tekireiki*), after which they apparently spoil like unpurchased fruit.

There was room for play within ZTV (especially for those who had the least to lose), and there was room to play on Japanese TV, where women and men are able to represent themselves in a variety of ways. In both cases, however, the overarching hierarchical structures of the television industry work to ensure that the play and flexibility does not go too far. Tami-*chan* was always careful to show that she was "just joking around" and never really questioning the authority of the men in power. Similarly, Japanese TV performers play with gender and hierarchy, but always within very real (albeit undefined) limits.

CREATING GENDER ON TV: IMAGINARY HOUSEWIVES

Having considered in some detail the various ways in which women and men construct gender in their everyday interactions within ZTV, we are ready to look at how gender is constructed in program planning and production.[8] I focus in particular on the cultural category of *shufu*, (housewives), who watch more television than anyone else in Japan. People at ZTV talked constantly about the characteristics and predilections of the elusive *shufu*—although homemakers themselves never took part in the discussion. (Married women who worked at ZTV did not qualify as housewives. A *shufu*, it seemed clear, was a woman who stayed at home. Just as female ZTV *shain* downplayed their gender, they almost never talked about their private lives, and they never referred to themselves or other working women as *shufu*.)

My experiences working on the housewife-oriented "Two O'clock Wideshow" revealed many times how TV producers look down upon the *shufu*. Particularly memorable was a program planning meeting where a key writer for the show glossed the entire category by saying that "all housewives are interested in" is "voyeurism, gossip, and wife and mother-in-law relations" (*nozoki, uwasa, yome-shūtome kankei*). Looking around the table, I saw the producers and directors nodding in solemn agreement. Nevertheless, TV producers were well aware that they needed to know more about housewives to attract and keep their audience's attention. Whenever the ratings for their show dropped off, they started looking around for ideas. They often turned to the ZTV research division, which provides detailed and "scientific" information about the composition and predilections of various TV audiences. The research division's 1989 *ZTV Data Book* was devoted entirely to housewives, promising to help advertisers "narrow your sights and pursue appropriate housewives." Instead of arguing that all housewives are the same, ZTV researchers pronounced that "housewives now fall into six patterns" (*Ima no Shufu. Mutsu no Pattan ni Wakaremasu.*) Each type was described in a brief paragraph accompanied by a sketch of a faceless woman.

Bannōkatatsu-gata Shufu (Broad-minded, Almighty Housewife): 15%

Socializing widely, I am not worried when meeting someone even for the first time. Even if I am spoken to in English, it is no problem. I also have the power to take on anything actively. I am sensitive to all sorts of information in many areas, including politics and economics. After managing the home, I prefer to do things for myself. Even the relations with relatives are left to me; I am strongly self-assertive. I am a broad-minded, almighty housewife.

Gaikōjizai-gata Shufu (Liberated, Diplomatic Housewife): 14%

Socializing widely, I am pushed into being a leader more often than most. I also like to participate in local activities. Although I prefer to be active, I am relatively uninterested in politics, economics, and international events. I do not assert my personality [*kosei*] much in the home, and I often let my husband help me do the housework. I am a liberated, diplomatic housewife.

Kanaikanpaku-gata Shufu ("Woman of the House" Housewife): 16%

I don't care about the outside world. I am less interested than most in politics, economics, and local activities. Inside the house my leadership is strong, and I put priority on my own ideas. I decide by myself about the children's education and major purchases. I am the "woman of the house" housewife.

Saishokuenman-gata Shufu (Harmonious Wit and Beauty Housewife): 16%

Although I am more sensitive than most to information and events in the world, I am not so very active. I do handle the management of household economics, but the final decision-making power is left to my husband. I take care of things within my range on my own, and I consult with my husband about other things. I am the "harmonious wit and beauty" housewife.

Kenshinnaijo-gata Shufu (Devoted and Helpful Housewife): 17%

Socializing widely, I am eager to take on all sorts of things. But I am yet to reach the level of leading other people and participating in social movements. In the home I concentrate on the housework. Placing my own priorities after those of others, I am the type that works hard for my family. Hating to use money on myself, I am the devoted and helpful housewife.

Heionjichō-gata Shufu (Tranquil and Prudent Housewife): 23%

I do not enjoy socializing. I also don't pay much attention to information and events in the world. Inside the house I do not promote my own ideas, I leave most things to my husband. Passive and pensive, I am the tranquil and prudent housewife.

In this way, the Japanese *shufu* are made into targets and markets for sponsors and television programmers alike. But what are the cultural and ideological suppositions that underlie this high-tech style of TV research? When I asked my research division friend for an explanation of these types, he explained that he had been surprised that the housewives had sorted out into six discrete groups. Looking again at the six types, he added an observation: "In many ways, I guess, this Harmonious Wit and Beauty Type housewife is the most ideal." The ideal wife, it seems, is one who upholds the domestic front (without, of course, being so presumptuous as to make important decisions before asking her husband) while being interested but relatively inactive when it comes to the wider world.

In figure 2, consider the two axes that are the foundation for the entire project. The vertical axis represents the degree to which housewives are or are not "aggressive about domestic life" (*katei seikatsu ni sekkyokuteki*), whereas the horizontal axis indicates the degree to which housewives are "aggressive about social life" (*shakai seikatsu ni sekkyokuteki*). In that these poles are already set before women are asked a single survey question, this research project reifies and reinforces views of gender in which women are defined as fundamentally domestic (*kateiteki*) creatures who are more or less active in the somewhat more ambiguous realm of the public (*shakai*). Completely ignored in this apolitical model are the many ways—symbolic, social, and physical—that men dominate women in everyday life in Japanese society.

Although this dominant view of gender is rapidly changing in Japan, the continuing domination of television programming and production by older males has kept TV firmly on the conservative side in cultural strug-

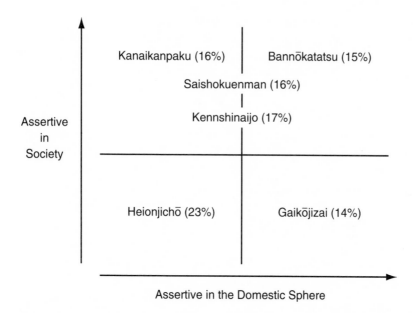

Fig. 2. Plot distribution of housewife types. Adapted from the *ZTV Data Book*, 1989.

gles over gender. Moving from research to production, I want to conclude this chapter with a close reading of how one particular Japanese "home drama" (*hōmu dorama*) represents gender, work, and caring for the elderly in a rapidly aging society.

Katei-*bound Housewives in the Japanese* "Hōmu Dorama"

The "home drama" is a good example of how commonsensical cultural representations of family and social relations, such as filial piety (*oya kōkō*) and obligation (*on*), are combined on television into ideological formations that legitimate and naturalize the inferior and subservient status of women in Japan. Women are portrayed on TV as obsessed with harmonizing human relations. They never rock the boat in the name of social change.

The *hōmu dorama* would not be possible without the active and creative participation of women themselves. Indeed, the particular drama analyzed here was written by a woman. In this sort of drama, women are usually more central to the story than men, and female characters often outnumber males by a wide margin. In some ways, the *hōmu dorama* portrayals of women's lives are realistic—for example, money is less celebrated than on American programs, where characters tend to be fantastically rich— but in the end, Japanese TV dramas slant reality in ways that must be criticized as ideological. The example presented here is perhaps remarkable in its degree of closure, but it is far from atypical in terms of its treatment of gender within the narrative conventions of the home drama genre.

Wife, Mother-in-Law, and a Complicated Engagement (*Yome, Shūto, Kekkon Sōdō*) was first aired on February 21, 1991, and rebroadcast in October 1994. Shown during "Golden Time" (prime time), this drama deals with a motif central to much of Japanese television programming: the strained relations between the wife and her mother-in-law. A secondary topic concerns caring for the aged, a huge social and political problem in rapidly aging Japan. A popular television magazine, *TV Station*, provides the following brief summary of the drama:

> Having watched her mother (Yoshiko) and mother-in-law (Fusae) quarrel and fight a war of words for over twenty years, the daughter Natsuko had firmly resolved that she would never live together with her mother-in-law when she got married. Natsuko got engaged to Kohei, only to find soon after that his older sister's husband had been transferred overseas; thus Natsuko and Kohei would have to live together with Sumi, her [future] mother-in-law. Becoming angry with how things had turned out, Natsuko finally cancels the engagement. Then Fusae [Natsuko's grandmother] is incapacitated by a stroke.[9]

This drama is about a complex nexus of human relationships rather than a single character. Indeed it is difficult to identify who the protagonist is, or if there is one at all. Twenty-four-year-old Natsuko is in a difficult position because she loves Kohei, an eldest son. According to tradition, she is obliged to stay with his parents and take care of them in their old age.[10] (Kohei's father died when he was only three, which makes his feelings of obligation even stronger toward his mother.) Making matters worse for poor Natsuko, her future mother-in-law, Sumi, is slowly recovering from a stroke. Not only must Natsuko get along with her mother-in-law, but she must also take care of her indefinitely.

This situation provides the central tension for the drama and is supplemented by other subplots that deal with related issues of individual, family, obligation, and tradition. The crisis of Natsuko's grandmother's stroke and the way Natsuko's mother selflessly cares for her make Natsuko think twice about her own behavior. In the end she realizes that she has been "selfish" (*jibun katte*) in putting her own comfort above her obligations to Kohei's family. The modern daughter, Natsuko, ends up falling into line with the dominant ideology of family in Japan, a conversion that is portrayed in the drama as a real step toward maturity. The drama speaks in the voice of (patriarchal) common sense, urging women to persevere, to endure, and to sacrifice.

In addition to depicting their subordination to men, the narrative shows how women in Japan are subject to domination by older women, especially their mothers-in-law. The bickering and petty conflicts that go on between women in the family illustrate their inability to cooperate with each other. It is hardly surprising that they are happiest when under the firm control of their betters—that is, men. (The reader may recall a similar logic at work in the explanations from some ZTV men for the strained relations between *shain* and non-*shain* women in the company.) In the opening scene, the women characters are introduced thus:

> [*In the home. Natsuko is getting ready for her* yuinō—*the formal presentation of betrothal gifts from the groom's family. Natsuko's mother, Yoshiko, dressed smartly in a black skirt suit with white accents, is helping her tighten the obi of her kimono. The dialogue begins just before the mother-in-law, dressed in an appropriately demure but elegant kimono, enters the room.*]
>
> YOSHIKO: [*Smoothing out wrinkles on the back of her daughter's pale pink kimono*] Let's try not to get it dirty, okay?! How's that?
>
> NATSUKO: [*Happily studying herself in a mirror*] Umm! [*The mother-in-law hurries into the room and dramatically complains.*]
>
> FUSAE: Why didn't you have her wear the *furisode* [a long-sleeved kimono appropriate for formal occasions]?
>
> YOSHIKO: Well, you see, she says that she doesn't want to overdo it, so . . .
>
> FUSAE: [*Insistently*] The *furisode* kimono is best for the *yuinō!*
>
> YOSHIKO: In this case, mother, they say that the *nakōdo* [go-between] is not even going to be in attendance.
>
> FUSAE: No matter what the case may be, it's not necessary for you to be so restrained. At the *yuinō* of your only daughter, of all things. . . . Look! I even wore my hand-dyed kimono!
>
> NATSUKO: [*Smiling*] You look absolutely wonderful, Grandmother.
>
> FUSAE: [*Flattered, but still complaining*] I can't sit next to her simple *hōmongi* wearing this!
>
> YOSHIKO: It's all right if you don't sit with us during the *yuinō*. No, really! The meeting is arranged to be only for the parents, so that's all right—
>
> FUSAE: It's Natsuko's *yuinō*, isn't it? Then I too will attend. I insist!
>
> YOSHIKO: [*Emphatically*] No, Mother, you can come in when the celebration begins. That's best.
>
> FUSAE: [*The sound of drums starts as background music, like war drums signaling the reopening of a primordial battle between the Japanese wife and her mother-in-law.*] No! I will sit beside Natsuko! After all, I raised her!
>
> NATSUKO: [*As the mother raises her hand to her brow in disgust, the daughter scolds them both.*] Would both of you please stop it? It's not necessary that you continue to fight right up until my *yuinō* ceremony, is it?
>
> FUSAE: [*To the mother*] Is that the case? It is wrong for me to attend the ceremony? I understand then! All right! [*She leaves the room in a huff as the mother and child continue to primp themselves in the mirror.*]

From the outset of the drama it is evident that wives and mothers-in-law will fight over even the smallest details. Both the mother-in-law, Fusae, and the mother, Yoshiko, are agitated throughout the scene. This irrationality is extremely common in telerepresentations of women in Japan.

As the drama progresses, it stresses repeatedly that the major source of conflict between Yoshiko and Fusae is the fact that Yoshiko has maintained a career outside the home, leaving the duties of child rearing to her mother-in-law. Fusae harps upon this, painting herself as the poor, suffering grandmother and Yoshiko as the unfeeling, selfish wife. Fusae's histrionics lead the viewer to empathize with Yoshiko, who is clearly not as negligent as Fusae claims.

The second scene takes place in the guest room of their house. The formalities of the *yuinō* ceremony have been completed, and everyone is eating festive foods and drinking beer and sake. Kohei, the man Natsuko is to marry, sits at one side of a low table along with his older sister and her husband, who are taking the place of his parents. (Kohei's mother is hospitalized.) On the other side of the table sit Yoshiko, her husband, and Natsuko. Between the two groups, sitting at the head of the table, is Fusae, who tries to take credit for raising Natsuko.

FUSAE: So Kohei's mother is in the hospital?

KOHEI'S SISTER: Yes. It's been over a month now. Since Kohei is the youngest in the family, Mother has been greatly looking forward to his marriage to Natsuko. But I don't know whether or not she will be able to attend the ceremony . . .

KOHEI: I've arranged it so that Mom will be able to attend the ceremony in a wheelchair. The most important thing, after all, is for her to get better.

YOSHIKO: [*The camera takes a tight bust shot of Natsuko's mother appraising Kohei.*] My word! Kohei is certainly a very nice man, isn't he?

FUSAE: [*To Natsuko*] Isn't it fortunate that you were able to find such a nice man to marry?

NATSUKO: [*With pride*] *That* is why I chose him! [*Everyone laughs as Kohei pretends to be upset at Natsuko's remark. There is a pause in the dialogue as everyone eats and drinks.*]

SISTER: [*To Yoshiko*] I have heard, Mother,[11] that you work at the domestic affairs court, is that right?

YOSHIKO: Yes.

SISTER: And I hear you are handling the mediation of divorces and the like.

YOSHIKO: Not only divorces, we are also involved in many other sorts of problems.

SISTER: It's so nice for you to have such a good job! Don't you think so, dear? [*Her husband agrees with her, as Yoshiko collects the empty sake containers, places them on a tray, and prepares to go get more.*]

YOSHIKO: [*Modestly*] It's really not so good a job at all. . . . Please excuse me for a moment. [*She leaves carrying the sake containers.*]

NATSUKO: I had wanted to continue my job, but I decided to quit at the end of the month. You see, I don't have enough confidence to handle both outside work and housework like my mother has done.

FATHER: Women are things that are happiest when waiting at home for their husbands to come back.

NATSUKO: So, Father, did you really hope for Mom to stay at home all the time?

FATHER: [*A bit flustered*] In my case I didn't think that way so much because your mother had always been working . . .

FUSAE: And so all of the responsibility was shifted onto *my* shoulders. That is, Yoshiko only had a short vacation when Natsuko was born, and since then she has always been working on the outside.

SISTER: Because Grandmother has been so healthy, you've been able to do that.

FUSAE: Healthy, well it's been twenty-four years, I tell you. . . . Because I had to take care of both Natsuko *and* all of the housework, it was very difficult for me.

[*The camera has shifted to the hallway outside the room where Yoshiko has paused, listening to her mother-in-law accept all the credit for raising her daughter.*]

FUSAE: It's almost as if I raised Natsuko all by myself! [*The husband tries to tell her to change the subject, but she presses on with the relentlessness that only a Japanese mother-in-law, it seems, can muster.*] I think my son, too, has put up with an awful lot. [*She laughs.*] It's tough for those who guard the home, but it's probably even tougher on those who must work outside!

BROTHER-IN-LAW: That's right! You know what they say: "If you take even one step out of the home, then you make one enemy!"

YOSHIKO: [*Entering the room and putting the hot sake containers down on the table*] That's right! More than any other form of support, without the understanding of her husband a woman won't be able to work outside. The credit for my being able to continue working all goes to my husband.

SISTER: That must be the case.

FUSAE: That makes it sound as if *I* wasn't of any use at all, doesn't it?

YOSHIKO: [*Losing her cool and suddenly speaking informally*] That's not at all what I said, Grandma! [*She catches herself and restores a calm* tatemae *formality.*] Of course, I can hardly express in words how much mother has helped.

NATSUKO: Perhaps *I* was the one helped most of all by Grandmother. Grandma always came without fail on the days when parents came to observe classes at school, right Grandma?

FUSAE: And I would do things like bringing your umbrella if it rained, wouldn't I?

KOHEI: So you were a little "grandma's girl," weren't you?

NATSUKO: [*Smiling*] That's right!

FUSAE: Elder sister, if by chance you have any problems with Natsuko, please come to *me* for advice. She is after all the grandchild that *I* raised.

[*Kohei's elder sister nods in agreement as the camera zooms in on an unhappy Yoshiko.*]

Although we are still some distance away from the program's first commercial break, we have already learned much about the characters. Kohei seems like a nice fellow who cares a great deal for his mother. He shows more outward affection for Natsuko than she does for him. Natsuko seems to have a strong sense of self. She says, jokingly, that she "chose" Kohei because he is nice, and she does not back down before her parents or her mother-in-law. Natsuko's father is a down-to-earth man, honest and good-natured. Natsuko's mother, Yoshiko, is an intelligent woman who is elegant and warm at the same time. (Perhaps she is so positively depicted because women of about her age—mid to late forties—make up the target audience for the drama.) Despite her many strong points, however, Yoshiko is given to fighting with her crusty old mother-in-law, Fusae, who is in her late sixties. Both Fusae and Yoshiko behave irrationally when they fight, and the father and daughter routinely treat their constant struggles like the tantrums of spoiled children.

Subsequent scenes show the conflict between Yoshiko and Fusae in more detail and introduce a subplot about an old man who lives alone next door and refuses to let his son and daughter-in-law move into his house. This subplot is an inversion of the main plot of the drama: Natsuko refuses to move in with a sick mother-in-law and thus resists the socially recognized obligations befitting the wife of a firstborn son; the old neighbor refuses to allow his own firstborn son to move in with him and thus resists the model of a typical three-generation, extended family. By the end of the drama, both of these plots will be resolved in favor of common sense and "tradition." In fact, the correctness of the traditional Japanese family system is about the only thing that Yoshiko and Fusae can agree on. The two women are thus avid supporters of the very system that subjugates them.

Although Natsuko has vowed never to live with her mother-in-law, she soon discovers that the sister who planned to live with Kohei's mother must go overseas with her husband. With nobody else available to take care of the mother, Kohei's sister asks Natsuko to move into the main house. Natsuko and Kohei would become the de facto heads of the family home. This is exactly what Natsuko did not want to happen, and she dramatically cancels her engagement with Kohei. A good and loyal son, Kohei is unable to consider putting his mother in an old-person's home, but he is also unwilling to let go of Natsuko. Yet no matter how hard he tries to change her mind, Natsuko will not listen.

Meanwhile, Yoshiko is working on the problem of the cranky old neighbor, Mr. Kotoyama. (As a woman, it seems, she is naturally inclined to fix problems between families—even those that are not her own.) She meets with the son and his wife, who explain that they want to live with the old man because they worry about him in his old age. When old Mr. Kotoyama comes down with a cold one day, Yoshiko calls his daughter-in-law at work and suggests that she drop by to take care of the old man. The relationship between Mr. Kotoyama and his daughter-in-law improves, and finally he consents to let her and his son move in with him.

The main plot involving the canceled engagement between Natsuko and Kohei is less easily resolved. Although Natsuko assumes that the relationship is over, Kohei has yet to tell his mother and sisters that Natsuko has backed out of the wedding. Kohei appears one night at the their door and rushes inside to talk with Natsuko. Telling her that he must decide by the next day whether to cancel the wedding hall reservation, he asks her once again to marry him. Natsuko, however, is still unwilling to live with his mother. She shakes her head "no" without looking up to meet his gaze. Kohei runs from the house.

This crisis is followed by another, pivotal one: Fusae collapses in the hallway. She has had a stroke, just like Kohei's mother. Yoshiko, despite years of fighting with Fusae, unhesitatingly becomes her primary caretaker and even takes a one-year leave of absence from work so that she can stay home with the bedridden old woman. In an emotional scene, the husband bows low to his wife to thank her for taking care of his mother. In yet another scene, Yoshiko and old man Kotoyama are sitting at Fusae's bedside when Fusae gestures to Yoshiko, who moves close to the old woman. Fusae tries to speak, but the sounds that come from her lips are not articulated into words. Nonetheless, Yoshiko nods and answers her, "I understand. I will ask the doctor." When old man Kotoyama comments, "Well, at least she can speak," Yoshiko replies, "No, she can't speak yet. I guess it's because we lived together everyday for so long, but I understand almost everything that she is trying to tell me."

In this way the drama informs us that there is no one better qualified to take care of elderly stroke victims than their own (female) family members. Who else, after all, would be able to read their minds and anticipate their wishes in this way? *Isshin denshin*, the "heart to heart communication" so idealized in Japan, is used here to show how close the connection between these two women is, even though they have often been too busy fighting to realize it. The importance of this connection is made explicit in another scene when Yoshiko addresses the half-conscious Fusae in front of her husband and daughter:

> YOSHIKO: [*Holding onto Fusae's hand*] It's okay, don't worry. It's a matter of course that I will take care of you. [*The camera cuts to a shot of Natsuko watching her mother.*] You, Grandmother, are a very important person to me. So please depend on me as much as you can, Grandmother.

In urging Fusae to depend on her, Yoshiko uses the word *amae*. "Amae" describes a relationship of passive dependence, whose very archetype is the relationship between a mother and child.[12] Fusae has finally become very much like a child, and Yoshiko quite naturally falls into the role of caring mother.

In yet another scene, Natsuko and her mother are taking care of Fusae, who gestures to Yoshiko that she wants to have her back massaged. Yoshiko complies happily, saying:

> YOSHIKO: Lying down all the time makes your shoulders sore, doesn't it, Grandmother?
> NATSUKO: Grandmother is depending on you like a child, Mom!
> YOSHIKO: That's right. Grandmother has become a total baby! Grandma, you are my baby, aren't you?
> [*The feeble grandmother nods and Yoshiko and Natsuko laugh.*]

At this point the implicit logic of the so-called traditional family system becomes clear: housewives endure the pain of living with their mothers-in-law and being treated like children by them, but in later years the tables are turned and it is the mothers-in-law who become the babies. To fail to take care of an elderly relative is akin to abandoning an infant. Yoshiko plays the self-sacrificing mother role to the hilt: she does everything from washing Fusae's hair to cleaning and ironing her diapers. Selfless sacrifice, in this worldview, is what being an ideal mother is all about.

Yoshiko's efforts to care for Fusae have a remarkable effect on Natsuko. Seeing her mother sacrifice so much for another, Natsuko reflects on her own behavior. She comes to realize that she has been selfish in her behavior toward both her family and her fiancé. Natsuko promptly goes to the hospital where Kohei's mother is recovering and asks Kohei's elder sister to teach her how to take care of the woman. Putting on an apron as a sign of her resolve—the feminine equivalent of a man wearing a *hachimaki* or rolling up his sleeves—Natsuko learns to change her future mother-in-law's kimono. Kohei enters the room and is shocked to see Natsuko there. When his sister explains that she came to help take care of his mother, he jumps for joy and runs out to call the wedding hall to reschedule their marriage ceremony. The final happy scenes of the drama take place back in the house:

> [*Yoshiko lies awake on her futon. She is worrying about Natsuko, who is late. Just then, she hears the front door open. Getting up and going into the kitchen, she finds Natsuko sitting at the table drinking a glass of water. (On Japanese television drinking a glass of water often signifies that a character has been drinking alcohol.)*]
> NATSUKO: I'm home!
> YOSHIKO: Weren't you a little bit late?
> NATSUKO: Yep. I just got back from a date with Kohei.
> YOSHIKO: [*Surprised because she thought they had broken up*] What?!
> NATSUKO: Oh, and about this Saturday—Dad is going to come back, isn't he?

YOSHIKO: Yes, but—

NATSUKO: This Sunday Kohei says he is going to come over with the *yuinō*.

YOSHIKO: What do you mean *"yuinō?"*

NATSUKO: I decided to get married to Kohei. [*A piano begins to play the theme song.*]

YOSHIKO: What is this all about? Please explain to me.

NATSUKO: I . . . watching you and Grandmother I came to realize that I was wrong in my thinking. So today I went to the hospital and tended to Kohei's mother, and I apologized.

YOSHIKO: [*Smiling proudly at her daughter*] Congratulations to you Natsuko. That's wonderful news.

NATSUKO: [*Somewhat shyly and hesitantly*] Mother . . . [*Bowing*] I'm sorry. I realized that I have been selfish. And I thought that I want to be gentle and kind to old people . . . Anyway, Kohei says that he's going to come by himself on Sunday, bringing the *yuinō*. Please welcome him. [*Natsuko bows once again to her mother, showing that even the young in Japan still know the rules of filial piety.*] Anyway, good-night.

[*Natsuko gets up and starts to head for her room, but Yoshiko extends her arm to shake hands with her daughter. They shake, and then Natsuko slaps her mother's hand, American style. They both laugh, and Natsuko goes to bed.*]

YOSHIKO: [*To herself*] Wonderful. This is how it should be.

[*Cut to the final scene, which takes place in the same room as the first scene of the drama. It is Sunday, and the* yuinō *ceremony is being held once again. This time it is Yoshiko who is dressed in a demure kimono. Natsuko is wearing a black dress suit with white trim. Kohei presents the gifts and intones some formulaic words appropriate to the* yuinō *ceremony. Natsuko gets up and walks over to show the colorful gifts to Fusae, who is lying half-conscious on a futon next to the others.*]

NATSUKO: Look, Grandma, it's the *yuinō* gifts!

YOSHIKO: Yes. Do you understand, Grandmother? [*Looking at her husband*] You know, perhaps it is Grandma who looked forward to seeing Natsuko's wedding day more than anyone, don't you think?

FATHER: That may be the case . . . [*Sniffing the air with a quizzical expression on his face*] Don't you smell something? There! Can you smell it?

YOSHIKO: [*After looking around for a minute, she squeals.*] It's Grandma! You know . . . [*Everyone realizes that Fusae has defecated in bed.*]

FATHER: Oh my god!

YOSHIKO: Everyone please leave the room for a moment. I'm sorry!

[*As the father gets up to leave, he makes a joke to Kohei.*]

FATHER: You know, Kohei, this time the *yuinō* will definitely not be broken.

KOHEI: Why is that?

FATHER: Because it has been "blessed with luck!"

[*The men laugh uproariously at the pun* "un ga tsuita." *This joke is based on the close resemblance between the word* "luck"—"un"—*and the word for feces, which is colloquially* "unko." *Thus the father's pun can mean both* "blessed with luck" *or* "soiled with feces."]

YOSHIKO: Here we go, Grandma!

As the theme music swells, Yoshiko lifts up the covers of Fusae's bed and makes a face reflecting the foul odor. Natsuko and her mother laugh with joy. Cut to the neighbor's home, where old man Kotoyama and his son are playing the traditional game *shōgi* together on the back porch. They are being served tea by the young wife. The credits begin to roll as we see the final sequence of shots: Fusae sleeping on her futon; Kohei and Natsuko deciding together about where to take their honeymoon (Natsuko sits on the ground while Kohei sits up on a chair, just as Yoshiko often sat below her husband); Yoshiko outside hanging Fusae's diapers. Her husband is trying to help, but he is obviously incompetent at the task—Yoshiko reprimands him playfully. This is a happy ending, Japanese style.

One remarkable feature of this drama is its ideological transparency. The conservative message could hardly be clearer, and the ending ties together all the loose ends into a neat package. I want to unpack this parcel by discussing some of the cultural and ideological representations it contains. The first scene of the drama spun around the appropriateness of particular kinds of dress for particular occasions. Confusion and conflict reigned in the beginning, but by the end of the drama, everyone is wearing appropriate clothes. Sartorial confusion here is symbolic of problems created by people failing to fulfill their proper social roles. Yoshiko's wearing of a demure kimono in the last scene signifies that she has matured to assume the role of the senior woman in the house. Natsuko wears a black and white outfit that is very similar to the one her mother wore at the beginning of the show. She too has matured, and the change in costume informs us that she is ready to play the role of the wife under the auspices of a mother-in-law. Natsuko has learned that it is wrong to be selfish and that true happiness does not come from thinking of one's self before others.

This common cultural emphasis on playing the role appropriate to one's age, even if the role conflicts with one's own personal feelings, is articulated in many areas of Japanese society. Natsuko's new attitude fits very well within such an explicitly nonindividualistic worldview. This hardly explains, however, her previous "selfish" attitude. Upon considering the structure of the narrative, it seems clear that Natsuko's selfishness is subtly linked to her mother's working full-time outside the home. This helps us to understand why Natsuko is so impressed when she sees her mother taking care of Fusae, whom she calls her "baby." Natsuko sees, as if for the first time, the suffering and self-sacrifice that go into taking care of both children and old people. Just as women "naturally" take care of infants, they naturally take care of the aged. Indeed, the drama goes so far as to make it seem that no woman could truly be fulfilled without such experiences.

During the almost surrealistic last scene of the second *yuinō*, two hours of carefully planned melodrama are punctuated by the grandmother's silent defecation and by the strangely overjoyed response of the people in

Fig. 3. Opening scene from *Yome, Shūto, Kekkon Sōdō:* sartorial coding in three generations.

the room, especially the women. While the men leave laughing about the pun told by the father, Natsuko floats into the room, smiling broadly as she carries a bucket and towel to aid in the cleanup. Yoshiko seems deliriously happy to be able to change the old woman's diaper, and even the foul smell is met with laughter and good spirits. It is no coincidence, however, that this drama never shows us the actual work involved in taking care of an elderly or sickly person. By careful editing, even caring for an invalid can be portrayed as joyful, because the tedious and often dirty realities are simply not shown. (Thus, when Natsuko went to her future mother-in-law's hospital and helped to change her kimono, the actual work of doing the job was cut. We are shown instead "before and after" scenes, almost as if the change took place by magic.)

Women on TV are eager and competent to do just the sorts of jobs that men generally will not do. Even when men try to help (as in the very last scene of the drama where the husband is trying to help his wife hang the laundry), they just get in the way of doing what is, naturally it seems, women's work. The drama *Wife, Mother in Law, and a Complicated Engagement* is full of this sort of reification. The unfolding process of the drama, including its crises and commonsensical resolutions, are all portrayed as a common cultural script for human relations and individual conduct. Enacting ideologies of naturalization, women in TV families defer to their

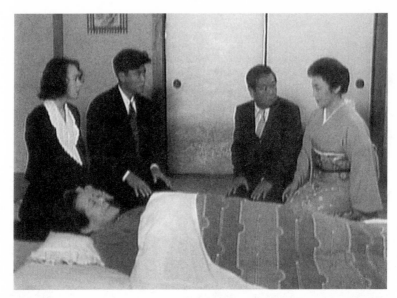

Fig. 4. Closing scene from *Yome, Shūto, Kekkon Sōdō:* Natsuko's clothes echo those worn by her mother in the opening scene, and her mother's echo Natsuko's.

husbands, serve them tea, and clean up after them. Women who work will only be shown sympathetically if they also play their "natural" role as housewives within the home. Indeed, the division of labor inside these TV families seems as old as the earth itself. Dominant ideologies of gender like these display the pattern that Thompson has called reification through "eternalization":

> Social-historical phenomena are deprived of their historical character by being portrayed as permanent, unchanging and ever recurring. Customs, traditions, and institutions which seem to stretch indefinitely into the past, so that any trace of their origin is lost and any question of their end is unimaginable, acquire a rigidity which cannot be easily disrupted. They become embedded in social life and their apparently ahistorical character is re-affirmed by symbolic forms which, in their construction as well as their sheer repetition, eternalize the contingent.[13]

Women's subordination to men, the trials and tribulations of women who marry into eldest son's families only to be dominated by their mothers-in-law, and the entire so-called traditional Japanese family system are all promoted, in politics, in theory, and on television, as eternal features of the national landscape. What is left out is the careful consideration of the actual social-historical factors that shape contemporary social relations in Japan.

Just as telerepresentations of men's lives in Japan often focus on the ne-
gotiation of human relations and hierarchies within companies and other
public organizations, telerepresentations of women's lives often focus on
human relations within the domestic sphere. With the exception of short
scenes in the next-door neighbor's garden and in a hospital room, the entire drama interpreted here takes place inside the home. The limiting of
women's lives to the *katei*, (home) itself an example of dissimulation,
greatly circumscribes the possibilities for dramatic tension. Thus program
creators and producers locate conflicts inside the home. Although husband and wife relations are by no means always harmonious in Japan,
marital discord is rarely portrayed on television. Almost by default, this
leaves wife and mother-in-law relations as the simplest means to introduce
conflict into a drama.[14] The resulting image of women as incompetent in
public and hardly able to get along with each other within the *katei* is anything but empowering. (As we saw in the ethnography of gender inside
ZTV, this formula works against women in the workplace as well.)

Many women in Japan are far ahead of such telerepresentations in
their thinking about society, family, and self. The increasing trend among
women toward "separation from television" (*terebi banare*) has led producers to try new sorts of serial dramas in which women are shown as active
workers, aggressive lovers, and anything but housewives. A pertinent example of this genre is *Selfish Women* (*Wagamama na Onnatachi*), a ten-part
program broadcast in late 1992. The story is about three women: an aggressive single businesswoman who faces discrimination at work, a young
mother who is raising her daughter alone while her photographer husband is living with another woman, and an ex-housewife who decided to
divorce her husband and set out on her own because she found home life
to be empty and unrewarding. In *Selfish Women* there are several male
characters, but all of them (except perhaps one) are depicted as less interesting than the women. The irony contained in the title (women who assert themselves in Japan are often labeled "selfish" by men) is celebrated
by the lead women in the drama, who use the term in a positive way to encourage each other: "*Motto motto wagamama ni naro to!*" (Let's become even
more selfish!). Though dramas like *Selfish Women* are perhaps not revolutionary, they are indicative of the fact that telerepresentations of gender in
Japan are changing, at least in some areas.

I would like to conclude with two points. First, although many telerepresentations of gender on Japanese television can be criticized as ideological forms that legitimize, naturalize, and eternalize the subjugation of
women in that society, it is crucial to remember that TV programs are always built out of variously interpretable and multiply relevant cultural
representations that are not in themselves ideological. Themes of obligation and reciprocity on Japanese TV are not necessarily ideological; they

are as valid as individualism or any other rubric for orienting the self in the social world. Similarly, the many images of romance and love that fill the screen are not always ideological. Only when these elements are systematically combined inside specific narrative telerepresentations do they achieve closure in ways that may be ideological.

Second, there is no strong evidence that viewers in Japan accept all the patriarchal ideologies within telerepresentations. Telerepresentations can be analyzed and reinterpreted—a practice common among viewers as well as so-called media critics—in ways unimagined by TV producers. There is thus always a degree of uncertainty in the operations of ideological production and cultural reproduction. Indeed, to the distress of Japanese television producers and advertisers, women may simply turn off the television and do something else. To understand more fully how television fits into the complex processes of the social construction of gender, we need more ethnographic studies of how Japanese TV viewers themselves interpret and elaborate on what they see and hear on TV. Such research will likely show ideas of gender to be rapidly changing in Japan, and television (whether its producers like it or not) to be inevitably caught up in the ongoing cultural debate.

NOTES

My fieldwork was supported by the anthropology department at the University of Michigan, a Jacob C. Javit Fellowship, and a Fulbright-Hays Training Grant. I would like to thank Conrad Kottak, Aram Yengoyan, Tom Rohlen, Susan Brownell, and Quentin Durning for their advice and support.

1. I want to state early on my opposition to two common views of the relationship between gender and media in Japan: first, models that depict Japanese gender relations as stable and unchanging, and, second, presumptions that Japanese audiences have no power to resist and reinterpret what they see on TV. Just as it would be misleading in the extreme to portray women as always and everywhere dominated by men within the patriarchal structures of the TV station, so too I think that television in Japan does far more than simply reproduce a monolithic "gender system."

2. Women inside the company are very conscious of this kind of discrimination, and they most often deal with it by trying to prove it wrong. A bright young woman in the public relations department explained the situation during an interview:

> Well . . . while I wouldn't say twice as much, there is the fear that if I don't work at least fifty percent harder than the others [i.e., male employees], then I will be let go [transferred to another department]. So, I'm working extremely hard. My immediate superior [a woman old enough to be a section manager], she's worked hard like that for a long time and now, no surprise, she is having health problems. . . . So, I think about that . . . but the problem remains that if you don't work half again as hard [as the others], then you won't get recognition for doing the job."

3. On dissimulation, see John B. Thompson, *Studies in the Theory of Ideology* (Stanford: Stanford University Press, 1988), 370. "Relations of domination may be concealed, denied, or obscured in various ways, for example by describing social processes or events in terms which highlight some features at the expense of others, or by representing or interpreting them in a way which effectively veils the social relations of which they are part."

4. In most Japanese companies, of course, the *genba* is a low-prestige area because it is populated by blue-collar workers. Professor Tom Rohlen pointed out to me that inversions like that at ZTV are also found in the research and development divisions of leading Japanese companies. In both cases workers in the *genba* feel that they are doing the most interesting work in the company, whereas the higher-ups just push paper.

5. Why were women being assigned to the production department again in the late 1980s after some twenty years during which OK-*san* had been the lone female director? Both the company president and the head of the personnel division at ZTV were quite frank in informing me that the decision to assign women to the *genba* was directly related to the 1986 passage of sex discrimination legislation in the Japanese Diet. Their commitment to real change is at best questionable, and it is probably not a good sign for women that after three consecutive years in which women were able to enter the production department as new directors (1987, 1988, and 1989), none have been assigned there since.

6. For an insightful discussion of this phenomenon inside a Tokyo cake shop, see Dorinne Kondo, *Crafting Selves: Power, Gender and Discourses of Identity in a Japanese Workplace* (Chicago: University of Chicago Press, 1990).

7. See Andrew Painter, "Japanese Daytime Television, Popular Culture, and Ideology," *The Journal of Japanese Studies* 19, no. 2 (1993): 26–67.

8. The two areas of the company that are most influential here are the programming and production departments. In theory, the programmers decide what genre of program will work best in a particular time slot (or *waku*), whereas the producers and directors in the production department go about the creative work of making the shows. In practice, senior members in both departments have much more say regarding the form and content of programs than younger ZTV directors would like. The company hierarchy makes it easy for senior men in the company to retain creative control—a situation not unrelated to the highly conservative images of gender on Japanese TV.

9. *TV Station* (February 9, 1991): 39.

10. Although the traditional family system that was structured around primogeniture and nonpartible inheritance was abolished in the postwar constitution, Japanese families still place a special emphasis on the firstborn son and his future family. For this reason, many young women in Japan today say that they do not want to marry a *chōnan* (firstborn son).

11. At this point, the future in-laws begin to use kin terms in reference to Natsuko's family. This is a gesture of closeness that will be reciprocated by her family for the rest of the conversation.

12. Doi, Takeo. *The Anatomy of Dependence* (Tokyo: Kodansha, 1973).

13. Thompson, *Studies in the Theory of Ideology*, 66.

14. There were many television dramas about so-called *kateinai bōryoku* (violence in the home) during the middle to late 1980s in Japan. These dramas almost always dealt with sons who were under pressure from the school system and who exploded violently, almost always at their mothers. These themes attracted large audiences, but their serious subject matter did not fit well with the desire of advertisers to keep television programs upbeat.

THREE

Centering the Household

The Remaking of Female Maturity in Japan

Margaret Lock

Until recently, received wisdom had it that, should they have life to live all over again, virtually all Japanese men and many women would opt to be men. Today this preference seems to be changing. Ono Mikinori, a consultant to the Aging Well Club, a Tokyo-based senior citizens' organization, wants to turn the traditional hierarchical ordering of karmic rebirth on its head: "The next time I want to be born as a woman. Nowadays everyone wants to be reborn as a woman."[1] Ono is alluding to a sentiment shared by many: that middle-aged women in Japan live in *onna tengoku* (women's heaven), where fun and leisure abound, while their husbands and children are worked so hard that some of them are literally worked to death.[2]

How are we to reconcile this image with the results obtained from a recent survey conducted by the *Kokumin Seikatsu Center* (The center for the study of national living conditions), from which it is concluded that "an overwhelming ninety-eight percent of housewives in the larger cities of Japan are dissatisfied or anxious about rising prices, old age, and environmental destruction"?[3] Is it merely the younger women who are anxious about life, while the older generations fill their time contentedly with travel abroad, ballroom dancing, and sewing clubs?

After the formation of the Japanese state at the 1868 Meiji Restoration, the government began efforts to standardize and "normalize" the life of its citizens along certain clear trajectories. As in other technologically advanced societies, enumeration and tabulation of social phenomena allowed what Hacking has termed the "making of people."[4] From the start, in Europe, Japan, and North America, gender difference was apparent, and the "making" of women, in contrast to men, consistently used a rhetoric in which biology figured prominently. Although the relationship between citizens and the state has changed considerably over the past one hundred years, in official discourse the conflation of individual women with female biology remains very evident.

As part of the process of normalization, the course of life from birth to death, and in particular female life cycle transitions, have been the subject of debate and policy making, although the form that this debate takes is dependent upon local knowledge, history, and culture. The experience of maturation is simultaneously a social and a biological process. However, in northern Europe and North America, commencing at approximately the beginning of the last century, life course transitions were subject to increasing medicalization with the result that the focus of attention was gradually confined ever more intently to the body physical.[5] This has meant that, in the case of women, the subjective experience of reproduction and maturation and associated changes in human relationships have been marginalized in medical discourse. This progressive fragmentation of biological maturation from social change, although initially a product of the medical world, is by no means confined to medicine, since there is today a widely shared (but nevertheless contested) belief among the public that a biologically based approach to female maturation and aging is sufficient, appropriate, and rational. For example, middle-aged women have in effect been essentialized and reduced to Menopausal Woman in both medical and popular literature—transformed into a creature understood entirely in terms of her biology and subject to unavoidable decline and decay unless systematically medicated.[6]

Although the Japanese medical profession has shown an interest in the management of the life course since the early part of the twentieth century, clinical gynecology (with the exception of surgery) has yet to achieve the status and power accorded to it in Europe and North America. Medicalization of the female life course, especially its latter phases, has not taken root with the same vigor as in the West. However, this difference cannot be explained by simply examining the structure and power of the respective medical professions.

Inseparable from the process of modernization is the development, institutionalization, and expansion of scientific knowledge, one component of which is biomedicine. It has been assumed until recently that biomedicine is essentially a universal endeavor, at least in terms of knowledge production. Yet a rapidly expanding body of social science research has demonstrated that biomedical knowledge and practice are so riddled with assumptions and values that, to be accurate, we should talk of biomedicines in the plural.[7] Gynecological knowledge, for example, is infused with cultural assumptions about the "nature" of women and their place in society, assumptions that in contemporary life become disguised as scientific facts, with the result that culture influences the way the female body is "seen" and "managed" in medical settings.[8] Similar assumptions influence the state in its efforts to legitimize the position assigned to women in contemporary society, in particular the importance attributed to reproduction and nurturance of the family, together with normative conceptualizations about passage through the female life course.[9] Japanese women, as we will see, are thought of predominantly as biologically destined to be nurturers of their families (see also Long, this volume). Until recently, little attention has been given to their aging bodies and the effects of the end of menstruation on their well-being; instead, the focus has been on their role in the family, particularly from middle age on, as nurturers of the elderly.

Being a potent and malleable signifier, the female body is therefore a forum for the delineation of sex and gender relations. It is the site for determining to what extent women should be granted equity in social life (in reality and not simply in name), together with autonomy over their own lives and bodies. The extent to which medicalization of the life course takes place and the form it takes are not merely manifestations of changing medical knowledge and practice, nor are they simply due to the power base of the medical profession, but are products of potent, never settled, partially disguised political contests intimately linked to surveillance and normalization of the family in late modern and postmodern society. Reciprocally, women's subjective experience of middle age is shaped by their expectations, expectations that are in turn influenced by dominant state and medical ideologies.

On the basis of survey research, narrative accounts given by individual women and health care professionals, and a textual analysis of government documents and professional and popular medical literature, I advance three theses about female middle age in Japan. First, kōnenki, although usually translated as menopause, is not the same concept as menopause, and the subjective experience of kōnenki is different from what is assumed (mistakenly) to be a universal menopausal event. This difference has major implications not only for the subjective experience of this stage of the life cycle but also for the cultural construction of knowledge about the end of menstruation. It also has implications of a different order, namely our general understanding of the relationship of biology to culture.

Second, because menopause in Europe and North America is usually represented as a biological process, any distress that women may experience is interpreted as the result of endocrinological changes and therefore deemed beyond conscious control.[10] In contrast, in Japan the experience of kōnenki is conceptualized as both a social and a biological process in which mind and body are inextricably linked. It also has a moralistic component: certain women are assumed to be more "at risk" for distress because of their leisured lifestyle in onna tengoku. It is assumed that women who live in nuclear families and do not work, and who thus lack clear social responsibilities once their children are raised, will dwell on what are considered to be minor physical changes in their bodies rather than simply "riding over" the midlife transition as do busy and socially productive women.[11]

Third, in response to the pressing concerns of its rapidly increasing population of dependent elderly, the Japanese government seeks to "make" middle-aged women into nurturers and primary caregivers for its "aging society." In North America, by contrast, policymakers focus directly on the bodies of middle-aged women, promoting aggressive medical intervention, in the hope of avoiding medical expense as the baby boomers grow old.[12] It is not surprising to find, therefore, that the narratives of Japanese women reveal great concern about the care of dependent elderly, while, partly in response to the moralistic discourse, they tend to dismiss *kōnenki* as a trivial event.

I certainly do not support the position that women and medicine in Japan are "backward" because the medicalization of female middle age has not taken place there. Over the past two or three years the situation has changed somewhat, and, although the aging society continues to dominate public discourse in Japan, a concern with *kōnenki* is much more apparent in popular literature than before. Despite these changes, I remain of the opinion that routine medicalization of normal aging is inappropriate and, further, that because medical knowledge about this stage of the life cycle is exceedingly unreliable and poorly researched, there can be no justification for systematic medical intervention except in cases of severe distress.[13] The pathological approach to middle age that dominates the picture in the West is the product of research conducted almost exclusively in clinical settings with very small samples of women, most of whom have undergone gynecological surgery and are therefore not representative of the population at large.[14] It is also in part the result of the value placed on youth, combined with a medical approach that defines the young female body as normal and the process of aging as unnatural.[15] Moreover, an exclusive concern with the bodies of individual women tends to eclipse serious discussion about social approaches to health care, together with other concerns common to many women as they reach midlife.

Although the Japanese and the North American views of middle-aged women and their place in society differ, they are both "authentic" in that they are culturally contingent, contested, and subject to debate. However, the Japanese debate takes place in full knowledge of what is customary in North America (the reverse is not true, of course; North Americans still know so little about Japan). Although in the world of economics Japan no longer thinks of itself as "catching up," in some areas of science and medicine this is not the case. The health of middle-aged women is one such area. A good number of feminists and physicians alike are at present working to strip away the moralistic rhetoric associated with *kōnenki*.[16] Ironically, in an effort to make the approach to *kōnenki* more scientific, some seek to medicalize the aging process as has been done in North America, on the misguided assumption that the dominant North American gynecological approach to menopause is value-free, "advanced," and adaptable to any cultural setting.

Because aging in Japan is understood as both a social and a biological process, it is important to consider how postwar changes in household structure and demography relate to both *kōnenki* and individual narratives about aging. The three-generation household, the *ie*, was recognized as the official family unit in Japan for three-quarters of a century, from the formation of the Japanese state at the Meiji Restoration until the end of World War II. In this household are enshrined the ancestors, symbols of moral and spiritual values instilled in younger generations by the adult woman of the household, who is considered the core or center of the family. Whereas feudal Japan exhibited an acute sensitivity to class and occupational difference, the early modern state theoretically obliterated such difference, and Japanese women were appealed to for the first time as a unified body in terms of gendered social roles to be carried out within the household.[17] Modeled on the samurai system of feudal times and laced with a little late-nineteenth-century European sentiment, the "good wife and wise mother" was educated to discipline herself for her role in the family.

Although in feudal Japan women were sometimes described as a "borrowed womb," from the end of the nineteenth century onwards they came to be thought of primarily as nurturers of family members, and their economic contribution to the household was regarded as very important. They retained this role throughout the life cycle, although their specific duties changed as they aged. Obviously reproduction was important, and the bearing of a son particularly so, but the Japanese have through the years been remarkably flexible about the formal adoption into their families of children and even adults, should a couple not produce offspring or the family be faced with the early death or the mental or physical incompetence of an eldest son. The dominant image of a woman in Japan for more than one hundred years has been that of nurturer, a quality with which all females are assumed to be endowed by nature.[18] Emphasis is given in this ideology to dedication to a lifelong gendered role, and reproduction is rendered somewhat less important. Japanese feminists have coined the term *boseishugi* (the doctrine of motherhood) to capture the essence of this ideology.

A woman reaches the prime of life in her fifties and, in theory, enjoys the acme of her responsibility in the *ie*. Although this responsibility gradually wanes, it is never extinguished unless she succumbs to severe senility or some other catastrophe. Some older Japanese women still live in these circumstances (more than twenty percent of households are extended), and their days are filled with monitoring the household economy, care and education of grandchildren, and care and nursing of dependent in-laws. In addition to these duties, many women work part-time outside the home or do piece work inside the home. As we will see, life in the extended family does not always bring the rewards or prestige that the ideology suggests are associated with such a family.

A widely shared sentiment in Japan today is that, although the economic "health" of the country is excellent, the state of the nation itself and the "spiritual health" of its peoples are not.[19] The conservative government and like-minded intellectuals lament what they describe as a loss of traditional values—in particular, the "thinning" of family relationships and the decline of the extended family, which lead to an undue emphasis on the "Western" value of individualism. The Ohira government said the 1980s would be characterized as the "age of culture," a time when the "freedom" and "abundance" produced by unprecedented economic prosperity would be tempered by "restoration of warm human relationships in the family, the workplace, and local regions."[20] This call for a return of "warmth" in the family appears to have been driven not only by a concern about the decline of tradition, but also by an accelerating disquiet produced by the rapidly proliferating aging society with its ever increasing nonproductive and dependent population.

In contrast to the fifty-year life span in prewar days, an eighty-year life span (*jinsei hachijūnen*) is now recognized as the "average" life span in Japan. Plath has pointed out that this newly received "gift of mass longevity" is in some ways disquieting.[21] Although individuals presumably look forward to a ripe old age, planners, politicians, and bureaucrats envision disaster as sixteen percent of the population passes age sixty-five. The "graying of Japan" is particularly disturbing because demographic changes that took eighty-five years in Sweden, one hundred thirty years in France, and seventy years in the United States, have taken only twenty-five years in Japan.[22] Some official estimates calculate that, if present trends continue (that is, fertility remains low, and mortality continues to decline), by the year 2025, people of age sixty-five and over will make up a remarkable twenty-four percent of the Japanese population. Among the elderly, more than fifty-three percent will be over seventy-five years old. Japanese life expectancy is the longest in the world, over seventy-six years for men, and over eighty-two for women, and already well over three thousand people are more than one hundred years old. It is projected that the most dramatic demographic changes will occur when the postwar baby boomers reach old age during the first quarter of the next century. This change in the structure of the population will not only produce a rapidly aging labor force and a major increase in expenditures of all kinds for the elderly, but it will also be accompanied by a decline in economic growth. Ogawa Naohira points out that (again, if present trends continue) there will be more than two and one-quarter million Japanese suffering from senile dementia by 2025, of whom sixty-six percent will be women, and more than two million people will be bedridden, of whom sixty-two percent will be women. Ogawa voices a major government concern when he questions where the "manpower" will come from to take care of this decrepit population, known euphemistically as the "silver" generation. Other Japanese writers ranging from feminists to health care professionals have voiced similar concerns.[23]

Since the 1970s, when the aging society began to capture the serious attention of Japanese policymakers, conservative governments have commented on the dangers of the "English disease," referring to the pre-Thatcher social welfare system of the United Kingdom, which is thought to have been excessive. The ruling Liberal Democratic party set out to create instead what has come to be known as the "Japanese Welfare Society," in which individuals and their families are made responsible to some extent for taking care of and financing their own health and welfare needs. Hence, with reference to the elderly, the "Long-Term Outlook Committee" of the Economic Planning Agency of the Suzuki government stated:

> The home is extremely important to the aged for a secure life of retirement, health, and welfare. In an attempt to form a social environment ideal for future living, it will be necessary to correctly position the home in society. . . . The role of people caring for the aged at home will become more important. . . .
>
> Also, it will be necessary to promote a land policy aimed at pressing for three family generations to live in the same place or for family members to live within easy reach.[24]

Not even the most conservative of policymakers resorts to the prewar term for the household, the *ie,* to describe the kind of family that is being promoted, no doubt because of the term's oppressive symbolic associations. The "new residence system" (*atarashii jūtaku shisutemu*) goes under the less inflammatory tag of "living together in three-generation households" (*san sedai dōkyo*).[25]

Together with an emphasis on extended family life, it is now accepted policy that, if possible, the elderly should not be placed for any length of time in hospitals or even nursing homes, even though more of these institutions are gradually being constructed. Care of the elderly has for the most part been regionalized and is administered through local governments, where it is grounded in the policy that government and families should cooperate so that old people stay at home in the family's bosom. Funds have been set aside as part of what is known as the Gold Plan for care of the elderly. This includes the training of home helpers, public health nurses, and nurses who make home visits to assist middle-aged and elderly women as they care for their parents-in-law and, later in life, their spouses. It is asserted that "the quality of life" of the elderly will be enhanced if families cooperate to keep the elderly at home.[26]

A white paper on women, authored by women, highlights the gap between government policy and the realities of family life. Despite the existence of the Gold Plan, there is an acute lack of professional and even volunteer assistance for those women nursing elderly relatives. The maximum time most people receive help is half a day per week, which in any case has to be paid for. Stays in nursing homes and other facilities are usually limited by local governments to seven days and can only be lengthened under highly extenuating circumstances. The white paper concludes that, given the current social welfare policies in Japan, the burden of care for the elderly is simply dropped into the laps of younger (that is middle-aged) women.[27] Hosoya Tsugiko, a social worker, characterizes the current welfare system in Japan as "private," since it assumes that the family can be made use of for tasks that in contemporary society be should be funded by government, and the social critic Higuchi Keiko states that "hidden behind the superficial glamor [of the modern household] the prewar family system lives grimly on."[28]

A recent study conducted by the Ministry of Labor showed that out of nearly five hundred people nursing the elderly in their Tokyo homes over eighty-one percent were women, whose average age was fifty-six. More than sixty percent of these women had been looking after their relatives single-handedly for three or more years, and over sixteen percent had been caregiving for more than ten years.[29] In another study, a ninety-year-old woman was taking care of her bedridden husband alone, and over fifty-seven percent of the caretakers were daughters-in-law or daughters, many of whom were themselves in their seventies. When middle-aged respondents nursing their relatives were asked about health problems, fifty-three percent complained of lumbago (presumably from lifting immobile people), forty-four percent said they suffered from lack of sleep, and thirty-six percent cited "nervousness" as a major problem.[30] It is further estimated that one in three women have to give up work in order to nurse their relatives, indicating that not only is home care a physical and psychological burden, but it also frequently produces economic hardship.[31]

In trying to promote its position, the government reminds the public of what the upcoming generation of elders have done in the way of nation building: "The people who will retire from their active careers and be included among the aged toward the twenty-first century will be those who have lived in turbulent periods, supported the era of high economic growth in Japan, and helped establish the country's present economic affluence. It is the duty of the succeeding generation to assist these people in building an affluent society in which they can live well."[32] This document goes on to state that the value placed by the Japanese in the family and a united household is fundamentally closer to that of Asia than it is to either Europe or America, and that "it is possible to expect the home to act as a vital force and function positively in supporting society in its care of the elderly." The government report on the proposed "enrichment" of the Japanese family explicitly discusses the role of middle-aged women as a vital force. After stressing the importance of cultivating their own psychological and physical welfare through hobbies, sports, cultural activities, and further education, the document states that women should take a positive attitude toward work, and that with their newly found freedom from child-rearing demands, they should take up suitable part-time employment or consider volunteer work such as assisting other women in the care of the mentally ill or the infirm.[33] This brief interim period, as every Japanese woman knows, is being turned at the government's suggestion into a preparation period for the time when a woman is expected to spend the final years of her life taking full-time care of first her in-laws and then her husband.

THE PATHOLOGY OF MODERNITY

In contrast to the "warm" extended family, the nuclear household in which approximately sixty percent of Japanese live these days is thought by many commentators to be a fragile "pathological" conglomeration because it lacks both enshrined ancestors and the elders and because the juridical powers of the male household head were stripped away at the end of World War II, leaving a vacuum devoid of an authoritative and moral voice.[34] Kelly points out that the New Middle Class (to which over ninety percent of Japanese claim to belong) is a "folk sociology."[35] This core institution of postwar mass society, synonymous in the minds of most with a nuclear family, is generally assumed by those in power to be symbolic of the privatization of life (*shiseikatsushugi*), the fragmentation of a state-controlled value system, and the incursion of personal and family concerns into the running of the country. Visualized as a four-person household composed of working husband, full-time housewife and mother, and two studious children (down to 1.32 according to the latest statistics), this "normalized" family is targeted in government ideology as not being in the best interests of the nation.

A plethora of newly "discovered" syndromes and neuroses said to be of recent origin and intimately associated with a loss of traditional values and the embrace of individualism are thought to abound in the urban centers of modern Japan. Glossed as "diseases of modernization" (*gendaibyō*) or "civilization" (*bunmeibyō*)[36] these diseases are portrayed as a plague to which the whole nuclear family is vulnerable. Their very labels suggest social pathology: apartment neurosis, moving day depression, child-rearing neurosis, the kitchen syndrome, school refusal syndrome, adolescent frustration syndrome, video generation lethargy, salaryman depression, maladjustment-to-the-job syndrome, fear of going to work, and—the latest and most unnerving of all these problems—death from overwork. This wave of distress is accounted for in government, medical, and popular reports by a close relationship postulated between health and well-being—both physical and mental—and individual behavior. It is frequently suggested that rapid postwar changes in both values and the structure of social relationships, in particular in the family, produced transformations in individual behavior that are not conducive to good health.[37] The painful and sometimes fatal symptoms from which victims of *gendaibyō* suffer are often dismissed out of hand by those in power as signs of indolence or willful nonconformity.[38] Alternatively, patients are medicated and monitored by the medical and psychological professions; individual narratives of distress are thus transformed into a medicalized discourse about the sick body, although recently victims and their families have been fighting back in certain instances.[39]

Among the diseases of modernization is "menopausal syndrome," an ailment associated by both physicians and the public alike with the "professional" housewife (as she is known) living in an urban nuclear family. The life of the hypothetical modern housewife has been subject to ridicule as a result of the mechanization and commoditization of housework. Housewives have had their day sardonically described as *san shoku hiru ne tsuki* (three meals provided, with a nap thrown in). The rhetoric associated with them implies that, in contrast to all other Japanese, many are selfish, idle, unsurpassed consumers who fill their endless empty hours with a life of luxury and ease unknown in Japanese society before this time.[40] A conflicting but equally unflattering depiction accuses them of becoming excessively fastidious, withdrawn, nervous, and overly concerned with tidiness and order. In both scenarios the middle-class housewife has departed from the fully occupied, balanced, and correctly disciplined life of the "good wife and wise mother" of the traditional extended household. In a society driven by the work ethic, once this anomalous woman becomes middle-aged, she is believed to be highly vulnerable to distress at *kōnenki* and is singled out as a potential victim of "menopausal syndrome." It is this kind of woman whom policymakers have uppermost in mind when they call for women to undertake voluntary work and for a return to three-generation households, because it is clearly she who is liable to abandon her in-laws and turn them over as so much garbage (*kuzu*) to the care of the state.

When asked what kind of woman is likely to have trouble at *kōnenki*, a Kobe gynecologist replied: "Let me see . . . I guess those who are relatively well off, who have few children and lots of free time, and those whose families don't have much 'communication' with one another. Also those who are introverted. Women who go out a lot or who have lots of hobbies and friends don't have so many symptoms. The ones who have trouble tend to concentrate on their own bodies."

An Osaka gynecologist, asked if he thought that all women experience trouble at *kōnenki*, answered: "Not necessarily. Women who are busy, who don't have much leisure, don't have many complaints. *Kōnenki shōgai* is a sort of luxury disease (*zeitakubyō*), it's high class. Women with lots of free time on their hands are the ones who say it's so bad."

A Tokyo physician responded: "These women have no *ikigai* (purpose in life). They have free time but can't think of anything to do, so they get a psychosomatic reaction; they can't complain openly so they use 'organ language' [said in English]. They find that there is no reward today for all their sacrifice and suppression, and they're lonely. Working women have fewer symptoms and in any case don't notice them; housewives can't control and master their symptoms like they used to."

A physician who specializes in the practice of traditional herbal medicine focused on family dynamics in addition to individual shortcomings: "Being in a nuclear family affects women very much. There's no one to teach life's wisdom to the children and everything falls onto the shoulders of the housewife. She often becomes neurotic, obsessed with trying to create a good child. Her husband doesn't talk to her. Also women have changed, they used to *gaman* (persevere, endure), but they've lost all that since women's lib. They have low self-control now."

And a Yokoyama-based physician stated: "They say that women have become stronger, but I think women may have a mistaken idea about strength. Women must be gentle (*yasashii*), and must be able to take care of and comfort others. Taking care of people does not mean that one is weak. Nowadays women seem to feel that they must really push themselves at *kōnenki*, and instead of just living through it by looking after their health properly, they come for help."

One or two doctors commented on the attitudes of husbands: "The husbands of women with menopausal problems are often only interested in their work, and they may have trouble with sex, either because they are using all their energies in their work, or because they have lost interest in their wives—'She's getting to be a dumpy middle aged woman, no good any more.' In these homes the housewife may be just like a maid." Several physicians pointed out that lower-class women who work, and others who live in extended families and do rural work, never have problems with *kōnenki* because they are "too busy" to notice minor physical ailments.

These physician analyses reveal the extent to which the symptoms associated with *kōnenki* are tagged with a moral discourse, one that centers on a metaphorical association between lack of work and physical distress. Thus the selfish and ailing housewife becomes one piece of an allegorical myth about the supposed waning of solidarity in the modern Japanese family.

The irony of this rhetoric, which is found frequently in popular literature written for women, does not pass unnoticed by feminist commentators.[41] In theory the "homebody" is idealized; she is the standard by which all modern women are measured. Yet it is estimated that less than thirty percent of Japanese women are "professional housewives." Women have systematically been deprived of full participation in the workforce in postwar Japan; nevertheless, the majority are employed, usually as "temporary" blue- or pink-collar workers, classified as part-time but working long hours with few benefits and subject to hiring and firing as the economy waxes and wanes.[42] Aside from the "helping" professions, married women are rarely found in white-collar and professional jobs because of the enormous social pressure placed on them to resign once they become pregnant. Being rehired at a later date in a responsible job is virtually impossible, even though most women express a wish to work. Despite this situation, once their children are raised, homemakers are subject to stigmatization because while the rest of the nation, with the exception only of some of the elderly, is worked to exhaustion, some middle-aged homemakers pass their time by playing tennis and making plastic flowers.

Against this background—this urgency about the pressures the aging society places on the economy, and the ongoing concern about a loss of traditional values—individual Japanese women today are maturing, ending their reproductive years, and becoming middle-aged.

CONTRADICTORY CONSCIOUSNESS: RHETORIC AND REALITY

Because the homebody is taken as exemplary and policies are formed on the basis of this evocative image, it is important to establish the relationship of the lived experience of Japanese women to official ideology about the modern family. A long-standing intellectual tradition in Japan demonstrates a keen awareness of ideology, which is perceived, in Gluck's words, as "two worlds in interaction with one another: the state . . . with its dominant ideology, and society, or the people, with ideologies actively opposed or privately detached."[43] It is now well recognized that political dissent in Japan has been and remains effective in keeping those in power on their toes. However, when it comes to the largely unarticulated practices of everyday life, it is much harder for the "natives" on whom it is practiced (and here Japan is no different from other societies)[44] to articulate resistance. That which is taken to be "natural" in connection with techniques of socialization, gendered behavior, family relationships, the relationship of individuals to society, ideas about human nature, and so on—everyday practices that "civilize" the body and penetrate to the very core of subjectivity—are only dimly grasped for what they are: fables that make society tick.

The dominant Meiji ideology, at least as it is reconstructed today, visualizes the body as immersed in the cycling planetary cosmos, the rhythms of the seasons, the continuity of generations, and the daily round of communal labor and harmonious living. Since the beginning of the Meiji era, segments of this ideology have been legitimized as scientific knowledge, thus making it all the more powerful. The "scientific" concept of human nature (*jinsei*) was invented at that time and became part of official dogma (*shisō*). So too was the idea of a mothering "instinct" (*bosei honno*), which understood women as biologically destined to nurture others and therefore best suited to domestic life. Although this ideology has been increasingly subjected to criticism in recent years by Japanese feminists and others, it nevertheless survives as a reinvented tradition around which politicians and certain intellectuals can spin very effective webs of nostalgia in which the "warm" extended family is contrasted to the "thin" relationships taken to be characteristic of the nuclear family.[45]

However, ideological discourse does not exist in a vacuum. To be successful, it must be actively embraced and reproduced in everyday life. By drawing on over one hundred interviews conducted in 1984 in the households of women who were then aged between forty-five and fifty-five inclusively, I will briefly discuss the reception and reproduction among individual women of ideologies about modern leisured women, their health, and their role in the care of the elderly.[46]

Middle-aged women, perhaps more than anyone else in Japan today, embody a contradictory consciousness. They sit on the cusp, Janus-faced, between early and late modernity, between what is characterized as an integrated traditional society of "warm" extended families and that society's evaporation into one fragmented and driven by consumption. Today's generation of fifty-year-olds, including the cohort whom I interviewed in 1984, were children during the depression and the early years of the war, a period sometimes described as the "dark valley" (*kurai tanima*), particularly when contrasted to the "happy go lucky" days of the Taisho era and the economic "miracle" of the postwar years. They are the generation that is old enough to have suffered but young enough not to have been responsible for the war. Their generation is known as the *shōwa hitoketa* (people, born in the early years of the *Shōwa* reign). Educated in the values of prewar Japan, they have lived out their adult lives in the postwar years of massive social change.

It is generally believed that the women of early *Shōwa* have preserved traditional values, particularly with respect to the household and work. Based on the results of a survey carried out by the Hakuhodo Institute of Life and Living (a major advertising company), analysts point out that "older housewives" (by which they mean women aged forty-five to fifty-five) often do not feel comfortable with the social changes of postwar Japan. Analysts concluded that respondents believed that political rights for women were necessary; however, the married lives of the women are characterized as adhering closely to traditional values:

> When their husbands returned home, sometimes around midnight, they made sure that the bath water was hot enough for their husbands to drain away the stresses and strains of the work day. They took out the kimono their husbands would wear while sipping hot sake and eating dinner.
> They understood their husbands might not want to talk. "If I worked as hard as my husband did at his place of work, I wouldn't want to talk much," they thought. "In fact, I wouldn't want to be bothered much at all."
> They did not bother their husbands with household affairs or the problems they faced each day in raising children. Those were their responsibilities as housewives and mothers. They fully realized that those were the qualities their husbands wanted them to display.[47]

This was the last generation of women explicitly raised to be "good wives and wise mothers," disciplined for a life of devotion to the extended family. When they reflect on the past, a certain ambivalence is evident. They are grateful that they did not have to endure the incredible hardships that they believe dogged their mothers and happy that the poverty of their wartime childhood is long behind them, but they are nevertheless concerned that, *because* their lot is relatively easy, they do not apparently have the endurance or willpower of their mothers. A factory worker agreed that her life had been tough, but immediately added, "It was nothing like as hard as my mother's. She really suffered for us. Thanks to her strict child rearing, though, I can take anything."

A Nagano farmer stated explicitly that it is appropriate for a woman to suppress her feelings inside the family: "I try to suppress my feelings like my mother, although I don't always succeed like she did. If I were always blowing up about things, that would cause fights with my husband, which would be unpleasant for the children. But as long as I just keep quiet and endure, then it's easily forgotten. It doesn't make much difference no matter what I say, so in that case we might as well keep things pleasant."

Statements like these reveal the extent to which women take pride in self-control and endurance, qualities that are highly valued. The majority of women interviewed took a similar position, and then went on to elaborate in more abstract terms about women in general in a manner similar to the gynecologists:

I think that if a woman keeps herself occupied every day and intellectually active, then she might be able to avoid *kōnenki*. It's a disease of housewives who are financially secure and have a lot of spare time and nothing much to worry about. I think they could avoid it by keeping their eyes open to the outside world and doing some volunteer work such as becoming home helpers or helping with people who are mentally ill—by contributing to society instead of being so selfish. Around here we always encourage each other, and someone who might have a difficult *kōnenki* is usually asked to become the leader of our local women's group to keep her mentally active.

A textile factory worker articulated a similar message about people who do not apparently contribute to society: "I've heard from one or two housewives that they have severe headaches [at *kōnenki*]—so much so that they can't keep their heads up. I told them it's because they have so much free time. I think they should get out and do some work, even if their husbands complain about it."

A few women at first sight appear to accept that the ideology about leisured life applies to themselves, as did this Kobe housewife: "My mother had seven children, and the way it was in those days, she had no freedom, in fact she had no self (*jibun ga nai*); she was always suppressing herself and not letting anything show on the surface. I can't do that, I'm a spoiled type, and I had trouble at *kōnenki*. Women who work or have hard lives don't suffer with *kōnenki*." However, her ensuing narrative about married life with a drunken husband clearly revealed that she did not take her own platitudes very seriously. Her statement was rhetorical, a pro forma response (*tatemae*) with which it was assumed, correctly, that her listening friends would heartily disagree.

As with any other myth, when its authenticity is prodded and poked a little, rents and tears become apparent. When talking about themselves, women may flirt self-consciously with negative images, but this is most often deliberate dissembling. In actuality, any distress that they or their friends have at *kōnenki* (which most in any case do not experience) is accounted for in terms of philandering husbands, stress at work, other social problems, or alternatively, in terms of specific biological changes with little or no moral rhetoric attached. An ideology of indolence is simply not entertained, or else firmly rejected. It is usually only when talking about people whom they do not know that women launch into ideological sermonizing. In the abstract, as pure ideology, the majority agree that a distressful *kōnenki* is a luxury-induced illness.

Thus the myth of the leisured housewife is contested in personal life, but nevertheless survives in the abstract largely untrammeled, fueled mostly by the media and popular medicine. It remains a divisive and pernicious narrative, grist to the mill of nostalgia for tradition associated with the *shōwa hitoketa* and all previous generations of Japanese women. When I produced statistical data to show that housewives report fewer symptoms than do working women at *kōnenki*, this information was inevitably greeted with audible gasps. I found very few women who actively dispute the mythology in toto.

SATISFACTION, RESIGNATION, AND REFORM: VICISSITUDES OF MIDDLE AGE

The lives of the women whom I interviewed are, not surprisingly, extremely varied. The majority report that they are happy and fortunate (*shiawase*), but a large number, working or otherwise, are decidedly not content, and many keep up a barrage of "low profile" resistance against the perceived perpetrators of their unhappiness, usually their husbands.[48] Blue-collar women at times expressed hostility about working conditions and a lack of security at work. However, when asked to talk about care of the elders, they expressed little hostility. Although everyone agreed that it was hard work that often demanded considerable sacrifice on the part of many women, almost none disagreed with the view that close female relatives should be primarily responsible. Those women already living with the older generation and those in line to do so, whatever their occupation, assumed—usually without hesitation—that their lives should be restructured and, if necessary, their financial contribution to the household curtailed to take on this task. Yet few women today, when they in turn become infirm, expect to be looked after by their daughters-in-law.

Provided that one's parents-in-law do not become chronically ill and senile, caring for the elderly can be a satisfying and rewarding task. I found many women who had worked out an amicable and even loving relationship with their in-laws over the years, and who did not feel particularly oppressed by their extended family situation. On the contrary, a good number are proud of their achievements on the domestic front. Rather than endure the punishing routines associated with white-collar work in Japan, many middle-class women actively embrace and reinforce the ideology of their worth as a homebody, particularly because care of the family is publicly recognized as a crucial and valued activity. Conflicts usually occur, however, when there is a major health problem in the family (sometimes the daughter-in-law becomes sick in addition to the elderly relative), or when the middle-aged woman has to give up work from which she derives satisfaction or financial security, or when the usual caregiver, the wife of the eldest son, does not step forward to fulfill her designated task. Geography compounds the problem today because urban residents often live far from their elders in the countryside. The following narratives reveal some of the complications middle-aged women face.

Shiba-*san*, fifty-two at the time of the interview, kept the account books for nearly thirty years in the farm co-op in the village where she lives. Two years previously she had resigned from this job in order to take care of both her parents-in-law. Until she became ill, Shiba-*san*'s mother-in-law had done all the housework and cooking while Shiba-*san* put in a full day at the co-op, and her husband worked their land in addition to doing a part-time office job in the nearby town. Two months after she resigned from her job, her mother-in-law died, but Shiba-*san* could not take up outside employment again because her father-in-law was not able to take care of himself.

Her son, married to a nurse and with two small children aged two years and eight months, intimated that now that Shiba-*san* was at home all day, she probably felt rather lonely. He went on to suggest that perhaps his family should move into the "big house." Shiba-*san*'s husband encouraged this idea, with the result that for six months prior to the interview the family had been living with four generations under one roof.

What's your day like?

Well, I get up at 6:30 and make breakfast for everyone. My daughter-in-law helps sometimes, but because she's a nurse she often works at nights, so I pretty much do everything. After everyone leaves for work I do the cleaning and the washing. The washing has increased enormously with all these people in the house. My daughter-in-law does some of the children's things, but I help with the diapers and so on.

How does it feel to be a housewife after working full-time most of your life?

Well, the best part about the work was getting out of the house each day. I really enjoyed it, and I had a lot of friends. I was giving some psychological counseling too, and I particularly liked that. Now, as a hobby, I manage to do Japanese classical dancing once a week. It's good exercise and I feel really fit afterwards. But unfortunately I can't do any practice at home because my father-in-law is here and it would disturb him.

Do you find it constraining to live in an extended family? What was it like when you were first married?

When I came here my mother-in-law was only about forty-six years old. She was a very independent woman and at first it was hard. I was working in the co-op already, but I had to start looking after this huge family as well—my parents-in-law, my husband, and his four brothers.

It's never been my intention that my daughter-in-law should experience the same kind of hardships that I did. My husband knows it's a bit hard on me at present, but he says that if we are to keep the peace in this family, then everything depends on me. So I must stay quiet and try to fit in with the young people's needs. On Sundays, when my daughter-in-law is at home, in order to let her sleep in, I try to stay in bed as long as possible although I really want to get up. In the past, if a mother-in-law got up earlier than her daughter-in-law and fixed breakfast, then the daughter-in-law wouldn't be able to swallow the food from shame. But now young people don't take things that way any more.

Will you live together for a long time?

Well, we have some land. We could build a house on one of the rice fields, but somehow I don't think that will happen for a long time.

How do you feel about taking care of the grandchildren?

They go to a day-care center for a few hours each day so that helps.

[*Here Shiba-san paused, clearly wondering whether she should go on or not. She looked down, sighed, and then continued in one long rush.*]

My daughter-in-law has a good steady job, and she may be an exception, but in general I think that a mother should stay at home for a while and raise her own children, otherwise everyone suffers. Of course, if she stopped her work as a nurse she would probably never find a decent job again. I think the children are much too small to go into day care all day, and anyway there are no facilities around here for full-time care. So it's very hard on me, but I'm still young and so I'm helping her. Sometimes I feel upset, I don't really agree with how things are working out, but I keep that to myself . . .

Do you find it hard to do that?

Yes, but I was trained to suppress my feelings, and I've had plenty of practice living with mother-in-law for so long. When I get older I'll be able to say what I want . . . but not yet.

Shiba-*san* assumes that when she is infirm her daughter-in-law will probably not relinquish her work in order to look after her. When pushed, she admits that she feels caught between the generations, since she expects little recompense for a life devoted to the care of others. In common with virtually all women of her age, Shiba-*san* believes that raising children is a woman's vocation. Men are usually characterized as helpless and passive onlookers at home, and Shiba-*san* has no expectations that her husband can ease her present burden, nor she does call on either him or her son to give even minimal assistance with the children. Shiba-*san* does not mention this, but her family may well have suffered some economic hardship when she gave up her job. In addition to being the pillar of the family, the majority of middle-aged women today *must* work to contribute to the basic necessities of life.

In contrast to Shiba-*san*, Ishida Atsuko has spent her married life in a nuclear family. She is, therefore, a candidate for the label of selfish housewife. Ishida-*san* sat in her cramped high-rise apartment and recounted the highlights of her life for me:

I don't think my husband and I ever had a very good marriage, but when my mother-in-law moved in things started to get worse. She was widowed, and because my husband is the oldest son, she decided that she wanted to come here and live with us. My daughter was living here too then, in this small apartment. *Obāsan* [mother-in-law] had the front room. As you know, I teach the tea ceremony to students here at home, and that front room has the special tatami mat that can be taken up easily so that the tea kettle can be heated in there. It wasn't easy after *obāsan* came because there was always some tension about having to ask her to stay out of her room for a few hours once a week while I met the students. My husband and I slept in the room next to her, with just the sliding doors separating us from her—that was very difficult too. My daughter was in the little single room at the back where I sleep now.

It must have been very crowded for you all.

When she first came it wasn't so bad, although she was quite bossy and tried to make me do everything her way. I changed a lot of my habits about cooking and so on just to keep the peace. But she went out a lot and was involved with various social activities. Then, all of a sudden it seemed, she started to decline quite rapidly and about three years after she'd been living with us I noticed that she was becoming forgetful and doing strange things like hiding food in the closets. Then she had a mild stroke and she was in the hospital for a good number of months. After she came out, things were never the same again. She was taking medication, but she had become really senile, and she was incontinent too. I did all the nursing myself, and of course, the worst part was changing the diapers. She was bedridden and wouldn't do anything for herself.

Did your husband help at all?

No! You know what Japanese men are like. It was my job, naturally, to look after *obāsan,* and he barely talked to her even when he was here. Toward the end she would call him in when he came home at nights and tell him that I was trying to poison her by giving her rotten food. All he did was to tell me to try harder to be nicer to her. I really didn't go out much for about eleven years except to do the shopping. I always had to be here looking after her.

Couldn't you get any outside help? No social services or anything?

Well, the doctor came twice a week, and he was always very kind, but of course there was nothing to be done. He said if things got really bad, I could ask to have a volunteer come round sometimes, but I didn't feel comfortable about that, and *obāsan* wouldn't tolerate the idea for an instant. In fact, we tried a volunteer one time and *obāsan* was so awful to her I didn't dare ask anyone in again. When my daughter got older she was very helpful though, and sometimes, after she came home from school, I could go out for a while.

How did you endure it?

You know, Japanese women still think they are supposed to endure everything and put everyone else first. I decided that I would see the job through until she died. Fortunately it happened almost at the same time as my daughter left home and entered college. I wasn't angry with *obāsan*—she was pitiful—but I decided that I couldn't live with my husband any longer. I asked him to leave. I own this apartment, so I just drove him out. He'd been having an affair for some time anyway, so I just said that he had to go. It was then that I started to look back over my early life and felt some regrets. Not that it could have been any other way I suppose . . . well, maybe it *could* have been different. My mother died when I was thirteen, and I had four young brothers. My father decided to take me out of school and make me into a kind of maid at home. I had to do all the housework for all those men. I think he probably could have afforded a caretaker quite easily, but he didn't want to ask a stranger into the house.

Didn't he ever marry again?

No. So what I really regret now is not having had a proper education. All my brothers went to university, but I didn't even go to high school.

That must have been really hard on you when you had to find a job after your separation.

Well, not too bad considering, because I'd done a lot of reading all those years I was looking after *obāsan*, and I'd started to get interested in interior design as well, so my mind wasn't dead. Anyway, for most ordinary jobs they expect to have to train you more or less from scratch, so they weren't too hesitant, even though I'm getting a bit long in the tooth. I have an exam next week, and I'm rather nervous about that.

So you didn't have to look around a long time to find a job?

No, not really, because I don't want to work full-time. I can manage if I work two or three days a week. They weren't looking for a young, full-time woman, but for someone older like me so that they don't have to pay any benefits. It works out well because I go to study two mornings a week, I work two-and-a-half days a week, and I still have time to teach the tea classes on Saturday afternoons.

Do you feel happy in your new life?

So far it's fine, I'm fairly healthy, and I don't mind commuting too much. I've made some friends at work, but I'm a bit lonely sometimes, especially because my daughter lives in Tokyo now.

Did you have trouble with kōnenki?

Oh no! I don't really recall when it happened with all the other things going on in my life.

I met Watanabe-*san* tucked away diminutively in the corner of the examination room of a Yokohama hospital, looking unusually tired for a Japanese housewife. When asked what she thought caused the shoulder tension and feelings of tiredness and irritability that had brought her to the doctor, she launched tearfully into a long monologue:

My husband does not like me to go out or to make friends, so I feel very irritated and have a lot of stress. . . . He thinks that his wife and children are nothing more than his belongings. . . . It's as though we are his pets. . . . Three or four years ago he started having an affair. He wouldn't come home at all. I started having mental problems and went to a mental hospital. . . . When my younger son quit school I became something like a *haijin* [someone who cannot function as a human being]. . . . I am tortured by that woman. . . . Recently he came home and said: "Let's make it up." . . . That's all right but he has to think of me as a housekeeper and not his wife. . . .

My mother-in-law lived with us, she was in and out of the hospital, but I took care of her at home. When she had a stroke our children were using diapers. I had to use diapers on her too—ten at a time. It was before disposable diapers were cheap so I had to wash diapers for three. I finally collapsed from exhaustion. My mother-in-law said I was weak and not like my mother. Everybody was so cold to me, but I told myself it was my job to take care of everybody in this house I married into; I didn't give up. She finally went into a nursing home. Each night while she was with us, when my husband came home, she would say with tears in her eyes that I was abusing her. She would tell him that she would rather die than be abused by me. She also called her daughters to tell them that she wanted to die by jumping in the river. I finally had a nervous breakdown, but I couldn't escape from the situation. . . . My body was tired like a rag. [Pause]

My husband would abuse me physically. [pause] When he couldn't see his woman, he used me for his sexual desire [pause] it was terrible [pause] I told him in tears that I didn't want any sex and that I would rather die. . . . He eventually stopped abusing me. . . . Now he just accuses me of being a delinquent housewife. . . . He's a Meiji man in a suit. . . .

I'm in *kōnenki* now and all this stress has made it bad. . . . The shoulder tension is bad, so I come for medicine.

Is this *onna tengoku?* Watanabe-*san* told me that when she filled out answers to two lifestyle surveys she responded that life is "generally satisfying" and that she indeed has a very comfortable life as far as material goods are concerned. The kind of misery that these three women have endured is simply filtered out in both survey research and ideological constructions about the homebody.

In many other interviews, the expectations placed on women and unequivocal demands made by family members were very evident. A single woman, for example, had been bullied by her brothers and their wives to give up her lifelong employment with a printing company in order to look after her own parents. This woman, the youngest child in the family and therefore not normally expected to look after her parents, is now at serious risk of becoming impoverished as she grows older. Another woman, Miyata-*san,* is a self-employed architect in order to avoid the discrimination she experienced in the company that formally hired her. While working at home, she keeps an eye on her reasonably active mother-in-law, who lives with the family. Miyata-*san*'s husband is supportive of her work and helped convince his mother that she must allow her daughter-in-law to work uninterrupted, but he plays no part in the running of the household except to do a little cooking on Sundays. Miyata-*san* is hoping that she can persuade her sisters-in-law to help with their mother in the future, because if the full burden of nursing falls entirely into her hands, she will have to give up her work entirely.

At forty-nine Inagaki-*san* looks frail and tired. She lives on a Nagano farm that she used to work almost single-handedly and is at present nursing her mother-in-law. When interviewed, she was recovering from major surgery for breast cancer. During her stay in hospital, Inagaki-*san*'s mother-in-law had also been hospitalized but, at her insistence, was discharged the same day as Inagaki-*san*, who resumed full care of her right away with only a little assistance from her husband and father-in-law. Inagaki-*san*'s wound did not heal well; she had a severe reaction to the chemotherapy and received no psychological counseling of any kind. She struggles on, surrounded by the sad remains of the largely untended farm, receiving occasional help with the housework from her husband and mature children. She is still unable to look at her body in a mirror and is terrified each time she visits the doctor that he will tell her that the disease has returned. Inagaki-*san* made every effort to retain her composure throughout the interview, but several times was reduced to tears as she recounted her story.

Given the realities of daily life, government preaching about "warm" families is clearly out of place. To suggest that women should take up more hobbies or do volunteer service is obviously gratuitous. The stereotyped image of the indolent, middle-class woman taken as representative of middle-aged females in Japan today is not tenable, although there are, of course, a good number who are not "productively" occupied, at least for small portions of their life course. Among those women whose lives are given over in service to the family, outright resistance is rare. On the contrary, many are genuinely content, especially when they compare their situation with that of their own mothers. Others, however, are unhappy with their lot and work towards gaining small changes on the domestic front. Only a very few women are actively engaged in combating the government rhetoric. When it comes to nursing sick elderly, since there are very few realistic alternatives for care, women would need to have a remarkable indifference to the suffering of family members and an ability to surmount numerous social pressures before they could resist what is naturalized as appropriate behavior for middle-aged females.

Until recently, it was the extended family through which the ideology of service to a household was largely perpetrated, as a Nagano woman revealed when she reflected on her life with mother-in-law:

At first when I came to live with this family it was very hard because I didn't know anything. That's natural, it takes a long time to master the customs of a particular household. It took me about seven or ten years. After that it was easy. *Obāsan* was very smart and she was a hard taskmaster, but she was never unreasonable. Because she was so strict, I learned things really well. My husband pretended not to notice any conflict between us. He always said that my troubles were nothing compared to what he had as a soldier. At first I was never confident enough to say what I thought about anything, but after about ten years I got some confidence and began to speak up a bit. Once *obāsan* started to be nicer to me, I began to feel that I wanted to take good care of her when she got older.

I lived with her for twenty-eight years. She was bedridden for her last two months; before that she would sometimes do things for herself, but I always had to help her dress once she got old. I had two sets of *futon* for her, one was always hanging out because there were quite a lot of accidents. It was just like having a baby in the house. She could eat by herself, but I had to carry her on my back to take her outdoors for some fresh air. It was like that for many years until she died last year. She was eighty-eight years old.

Without the backing of the traditional household with its disciplinary rigors, perhaps the government is right to worry about the predicament of the elders of the future, the first of whom will be the *shōwa hitoketa* who surely deserve some kind of recompense for their service to society.

THE JAPANESE LIFE COURSE, MATURATION, AND *KŌNENKI*

Despite a concern about the "graying" of the nation, aging as such is not thought of as an anomaly. On the contrary, Japan is a society exquisitely sensitive to the passing of time and positively wallows in the ephemeral nature of human life. Life cycle transitions of both men and women are formally marked and celebrated as social events; continuity with past generations and the presence of the ancestors in many households still reinforce the notion that each individual is part of a larger cosmically ordained order.[49] The *shōwa hitoketa* were immersed in this ideology as children, and the majority still embrace it.[50] As we have seen in the narratives, movement through the life cycle is subjectively experienced largely in terms of how one's relationships with other people shift through time, and women's lives are expected to become meaningful according to what they accomplish for others rather than for themselves, regardless of their private aspirations or their situation in the work force.[51] Under these circumstances, biological aging and the end of menstruation are not very potent symbols. Whereas a few women feel ambivalence and mourn for lost sexual attractiveness, most emphasize what is described as the inevitable process of aging itself: graying hair, changing eyesight, faulty short-term memory, and so on.[52] Furthermore, these signs of aging, though they obviously represent irretrievable youth, are primarily signifiers for the future—for what may be in store in terms of an enfeebled body as old age approaches, and hence an inability to contribute to the family.

In both the questionnaire survey and follow-up interviews, I devoted a good deal of questions to establishing what meaning *kōnenki* has for Japanese women and what symptoms, if any, they associate with it.[53] Nearly eighty percent of the interview responses were along the following lines:

> I've had no problems at all, no headaches or anything like that. . . . I've heard from other people that their heads felt so heavy that they couldn't get up. A few of my friends complain that they don't exactly have pain, but that they just feel generally bad.

> I started to have trouble sleeping when I was about fifty; that was menopause, I think. Some people have dizziness, headaches, stiff shoulders, and aching joints.

> In my case, my eyesight became weak. Some people get sensitive and have headaches.

> My shoulders feel as if they are pulled and I get tired easily.

> The most common disorders that I've heard about are headaches, shoulder stiffness, and aching joints. Some women get irritable too.

A small number of women, twelve out of the sample of more than one hundred, made statements such as the following:

> The most noticeable thing was that I would suddenly feel hot; it happened every day, three times or so. I didn't go to the doctor or take any medication. I wasn't embarrassed and I didn't feel strange, I just thought that it was my age.

The survey questionnaire included a long, culturally appropriate symptom list of fifty-seven items, not all of them necessarily associated with *kōnenki*. Women were asked if they had experienced any of these symptoms in the previous two weeks. Overall reporting was low and significantly different from comparable North American samples. The most frequently reported symptoms were, in descending order of frequency: shoulder stiffness, headaches, lumbago, constipation, chilliness, irritability, insomnia, aches and pains in the joints, frequent colds, sore throat, feelings of numbness, and then, reported equally, loss of memory and hot flashes (reported by only ten percent of the sample as opposed to thirty-one percent and thirty-five percent in Manitoba and Massachusetts samples, respectively). These were followed closely by "heavy head" (*atama ga omoi*), ringing in the ears, and eventually, almost at the bottom of the list, night sweats (reported by only four percent of the sample as opposed to twenty percent in Manitoba and twelve percent in Massachusetts). The "classical" symptoms of menopause, hot flashes and night sweats, are not reported to anything like the same extent as in comparable North American samples.[54]

Over forty percent of the Japanese women interviewed agreed with the statement made by a Kyoto factory worker: "*Kōnenki* starts at different ages depending on the person. Some start in their late thirties and some never have any symptoms; they don't have *kōnenki* at all." In the survey, twenty-four percent of the subsample who had ceased menstruating for more than one year reported that they had no sign of *kōnenki*, indicating that *kōnenki* implies something different from menopause, associated by most North American women rather closely with the end of menstruation.[55] The term *shōgai* (ill effects) is usually added to *kōnenki* (change of life) to indicate physical distress at this time of life, but some women who experience no signs or symptoms simply state that they have no *kōnenki*.

THE DISCOVERY OF *KŌNENKI*

The end of menstruation has been noted for nearly a thousand years in traditional Japanese medicine as the "seventh" stage in a woman's life, when a quality known as *tenki*, intimately associated with the female reproductive cycle, goes into decline. An overly abrupt decline in *tenki* was recognized as the cause of numerous nonspecific symptoms that often last for a few years, including dizziness, palpitations, headaches, chilliness, stiff shoulders, a dry mouth, and so on, but no specific word was reserved for this time, or for any physical effects associated with this stage of the life cycle.[56]

Toward the end of the nineteenth century, the concept of *kōnenki* was created to convey the European notion of the "climacterium."[57] Climacterium was originally used to describe the dangers associated with many critical transitions throughout the life cycle, regardless of age or gender. By the early twentieth century in Europe, however, it referred only to the female life cycle and indicated a span of several years during which, among other changes, menstruation ceased. At the same time, the concept of "menopause" was formulated in the gynecological literature to indicate the specific event of the end of menstruation.[58] Japanese doctors, more than one hundred of whom went to Germany to study medicine at the turn of the century, found a need to invent rather cumbersome technical words in Japanese to gloss these alien concepts.[59] However, by the 1930s these technical words had been dropped in favor of the by now well-established "ordinary" word of *kōnenki*, which continues to this day, in both medical and popular literature, to signify a gradual transition in female midlife lasting anywhere from ten to twenty years. There is still no widely used term in contemporary Japanese to express in everyday language the event of the end of menstruation, although there is, of course, a technical term (*heikei*), much as menopause was a technical term in English until as recently as forty years ago and little used in daily parlance. Nor is there a specific word in Japanese to convey the experience of a hot flash.

Although the end of menstruation did not seem medically significant to turn-of-the-century Japanese physicians, the newly discovered autonomic nervous system was of great interest. This idea, when it was first clearly articulated in Germany in 1898, caused a stir in medical circles everywhere. In Japan it "fitted" the holistically oriented physiological approach characteristic of Sino-Japanese medicine. Later, in the 1930s when a close association was postulated between the endocrine system and the autonomic nervous system, Japanese physicians comfortably adopted this idea and postulated a connection between *kōnenki* and disturbances in the autonomic nervous system, an association that the majority of Japanese physicians and women still accept today.[60]

Stiff shoulders, headaches, ringing in the ears, tingling sensations, dizziness, and so on are the symptoms that form the core of *kōnenki* discourse. These symptoms are the product of an unstable autonomic system, set in motion by declining estrogen levels. This account is contingent upon "local" biology in which neither hot flashes nor sweats, usually assumed in the West to be the characteristic symptoms of menopause, are very evident. This difference can perhaps be accounted for in part by diet.[61]

As Japanese physicians keep abreast of the medical literature published in the West, one might expect that, in a country actively dedicated to preventive medicine, there would be considerable pressure to prescribe long-term hormone replacement therapy to middle-aged women as a prophylactic against heart disease and osteoporosis, as is now done in North America. Here again, local biology plays a part, because mortality from coronary heart disease for Japanese women is about one-quarter that among American women and their rate of osteoporosis is half as frequent (although it is estimated that Japanese women become osteoporotic twice as often as do Japanese men.)[62] These figures, combined with a mortality rate from breast cancer that is about one-quarter that of North America, have given Japanese gynecologists little incentive to enter into the international debate over the risks and benefits of hormone replacement therapy. Most Japanese physicians are, in any case, deeply concerned about its potentially dangerous side effects. Herbal medicine (*kanpō*) is the treatment of choice in Japan, together with the encouragement of good dietary practices and exercise habits.[63] Epidemiologically speaking, therefore, *kōnenki* is not big news in Japan, although this situation is starting to change a little as some gynecologists more actively promote comprehensive health care for middle-aged women.

The end of menstruation has not been a particularly potent signifier to either doctors or women in Japan, in part because the Japanese concept of reproduction implies much more than a clearly demarcated biological process: it represents replication and continuity of the household above all, and this social continuity usually transcends concerns about the biology of individual women. *Kōnenki* is still regarded as a natural part of the aging process, and until recently it was assumed that, except in a minute number of pathological cases, women would simply "ride over" (*norikoeru*) any physical distress that might occur at this stage in life. I well recall one Japanese gynecologist asking me, with more than a touch of jingoism, "Why do Western women make such a fuss about menopause?" Over the past twenty years the stereotype of a leisured life leading to a distressful *kōnenki* has emerged, so that certain of the *shōwa hitoketa* are assumed to have lost the necessary willpower to deal successfully with this stage of the life cycle. They have, in effect, become too individualized and Westernized.

CONCLUSIONS

Life-cycle transitions are usually represented as social and cultural transformations that take place upon a universal biological base. My findings from Japan indicate that we should conceptualize both culture and biology as contingent and part of an ongoing dialectical exchange throughout the life course. Local biologies profoundly influence but do not, of course, determine the construction of a discourse about aging. What confounds the issue is that scientific discourse about menopause assumes the existence of a universal body, but this assumption is not always confirmed by professional knowledge and subjectivity in local settings.

The moralistic rhetoric associated with *kōnenki* is obviously unacceptable, as is the assumption that most middle-aged women in Japan live a leisured life. If, however, the concept of *kōnenki* is entirely abandoned because of its negative associations, to be replaced by the pathological approach commonly taken to menopause in North America, then little will have been gained. There is much to be learned from a deconstruction of the dominant ideologies about middle-aged women on both sides of the Pacific ocean.

NOTES

1. Nancy Matsumoto, "Women Who Don't Need Men," *PHP Intersect* (October 1988): 42–43.
2. Karōshi bengo dan zenkoku renraku kaigihen, *Karōshi* (Death from overwork) (Tokyo: Mado-sha, 1990).

3. "Kōreisha Kenshō Seitei o Teian," *Asahi Shinbun* (A proposal to establish a charter for the aged), September 8, 1990.

4. Michel Foucault, *Discipline and Punish: The Birth of the Prison* (New York: Vintage, 1979); David Armstrong, *Political Anatomy of the Body: Medical Knowledge in Britain in the Twentieth Century* (Cambridge: Cambridge University Press, 1983); Ian Hacking, *The Taming of Chance* (Cambridge: Cambridge University Press, 1990).

5. Elliot Freidson, *The Profession of Medicine* (New York: Dodd, Mead and Co., 1970). Irving K. Zola, "Medicine as an Institution of Social Control," *Sociological Review*, no. 20 (1978): 487–504.

6. Ian Hall Thorneycroft, "The Role of Estrogen Replacement Therapy in the Prevention of Osteoporosis," *American Journal of Obstetrics and Gynecology*, no. 160 (1989): 1306–1310; Gail Sheehy, *The Silent Passage: Menopause* (New York: Random House, 1992).

7. Margaret Lock and Deborah A. Gordon, eds., *Biomedicine Examined* (Dordrecht, Netherlands: Kluwer Academic Publishers, 1988); Peter W. G. Wright and Andrew Treacher, eds., *The Problem of Medical Knowledge: Examining the Social Construction of Medicine* (Edinburgh: University of Edinburgh Press, 1982).

8. Ludmilla Jordanova, *Sexual Visions: Images of Gender in Science and Medicine between the Eighteenth and Twentieth Centuries* (Madison: University of Wisconsin Press, 1989); Margaret Lock, "Models and Practice in Medicine: Menopause as Syndrome or Life Transition?" in *Physicians of Western Medicine*, eds. R. A. Hahn and A. D. Gaines (Dordrecht: D. Reidel Co., 1985), 115–139; and *Encounters with Aging: Mythologies of Menopause in Japan and North America* (Berkeley: University of California Press, 1993); Emily Martin, *The Woman in the Body: A Cultural Analysis of Reproduction* (Boston: Beacon Press, 1987).

9. Linda Birke, *Women, Feminism, and Biology: The Feminist Challenge* (Brighton, Sussex: Wheatsheaf Books Ltd., 1986); Judith Farquhar, "Objects, Processes, and Female Infertility in Chinese Medicine," *Medical Anthropology Quarterly*, 5 (1991): 370–399; Marian Lowe and Ruth Hubbard, eds., *Woman's Nature: Rationalizations of Inequality*, The Athene Series (New York: Pergamon Press, 1986).

10. Margaret Lock, *Encounters with Aging: Mythologies of Menopause in Japan and North America* (Berkeley: University of California Press, 1993).

11. Margaret Lock, "New Japanese Mythologies: Faltering Discipline and the Ailing Housewife in Japan," *American Ethnologist* 15 (1988): 43–61.

12. Lock, *Encounters with Aging.*

13. National Women's Health Network, *Taking Hormones and Women's Health* (Washington, D.C.: National Women's Health Network, 1989).

14. Patricia Leiland Kaufert and Penny Gilbert, "Women, Menopause, and Medicalization," *Culture, Medicine, and Psychiatry*, 10 (1986): 7–21.

15. Lock, *Encounters with Aging.*

16. Sasaki Shizuko, "Kōnenki o do ikiru" (How to live with Kōnenki), *Onna no Karada to Iryō* (Tokyo: Nihon Fujin Kai, 1988), 6:2–4; Igarashii Masao, "Kōnenki to rōka genshō" (Menopause and old age symptomatology) *Nichibo Ihō* (1987): 1–2.

17. Sharon Nolte and Sally Ann Hastings, "The Meiji State's Policy toward Women, 1890–1910," in *Recreating Japanese Women, 1600–1945,* ed. Gail Lee Bernstein (Berkeley: University of California Press, 1991), 151–174.

18. Mitsuda Kyōko, "Kindaiteki Boseikan no Juyō to Kenkei: Kyōiku Suru Hahaoya Kara Ryōsai Kenbo e" (The importance and transformation of the con-

dition of modern motherhood: From education mother to good wife and wise mother), in *Bosei o tou* (What is motherhood?), ed. H. Wakita (Kyoto: Jinbunshoin, 1985), 100–129.

19. Mochida Takeshi, "Focus on the Family" Editorial Comment, *Japan Echo* 3 (1980): 75–76.

20. Ōkurasho Insatsu Kyoku, *Katei no kiban no jūjitsu* (Enrichment of the Japanese family base), Ohira sōri no seisaku kenkyūkai hōkokusho (Reports of the Policy Research Bureau of the Ohira cabinet), no. 3 (Tokyo: Ōkurasho Insatsu Kyoku, 1980).

21. David Plath, *Long Engagements* (Stanford: Stanford University Press, 1980).

22. Kōseishō jinkō mondai kenkyūsho, *1989 jinko no doko—Nihon to sekai* (Where are the 1989 population trends going? Japan and the world) (Tokyo: Kōsei Tōkei Kyōkai, 1989).

23. Ogawa Naohiro, "Population Aging and Medical Demand: The Case of Japan," in *Economic and Social Implications of Population Aging. Proceedings of the International Symposium on Population Structure and Development, Tokyo,* (New York: United Nations, 1988), 254–275. "Toppu wa 112 sai," *Mainichi Shinbun,* November 9, 1990; Higuchi Keiko, "Women at Home," *Japan Echo* 12 (1985): 51–57. Hosoya Tsugiko, "Rōjin kango no tsuma no sutoresu" (The stress of wives nursing their old folks), in *Gendai no Espuri* (Tokyo: Shibundo, 1987), 151–162.

24. Keizai kikaku chō, *Nisen nen no Nihon* (Japan in the year 2000), Keizai shingi kaichō kitenbō unkai hokoku, (Tokyo, 1982).

25. Ōkurasho Insatu Kyoku, *Katei no kiban no jūjitsu.*

26. Kōseishō Hakusho, *Arata na Kōreishazō to Katsuryoku aru Chōju Fukushi Shakai o Mezashite* (Toward a new image of the aged and a vigorous long-lived society with good welfare) (Tokyo: Kōseisho, 1989).

27. Fujin Hakusho, *Kōrei sha fukushi* (Social welfare in the aged society), ed. Nihon Fujin Dantai-Rengōkai (Tokyo: Horupu Shuppan, 1989).

28. Hosoya, "Rōjin kango no tsuma no sutoresu." See also Higuchi, "Women at Home."

29. "Rōjin Kaigo Josei in Zusshiri" (Nursing the elderly is a burden on women), *Tōkyō Shinbun,* September 13, 1990.

30. Serizawa Motoko, "Aspects of an Aging Society," *Review of Japanese Culture and Society* 3 (1989): 37–46.

31. "Rōjin Kaigo Josei ni Zusshiri." *Tōkyō Shinbun.*

32. Keizai Kikaku chō, *Nisen nen no Nihon.*

33. Ōkurasho Insatsu Kyoku, *Katei no kiban no jūjitsu.*

34. See Mochida, "Focus on the Family." See also Eto Jun, "The Breakdown of Motherhood is Wrecking our Children," *Japan Echo* 6 (1979): 102–109.

35. William Kelly, "Rationalization and Nostalgia: Cultural Dynamics of New Middle-Class Japan," *American Ethnologist* 13 (1986): 603–618.

36. Kyūtoku Shigemori, *Bogenbyō* (Tokyo: Sanmaku Shuppan, 1979); Murakami Yasusuke, Kumon Shunpei, and Sato Seizaburō, *Bunmei to Shite no ie shakai* (Household society as civilization) (Tokyo: Chūō Kōron Sha, 1979).

37. Kōjino Imazu, Hamaguchi Esyun, and Sakuta Keiichi, "Shakai Kankyō no Henyō to Kodomo no Hattatsu to Kyōiku" (Strategic points in the social environment and the development of children), in *Kodomo no Hattatsu to Kyōiku* 1 (Child development and education, vol. 1) (Tokyo: Iwanami Shoten, 1979),

42–94; Monbushō, *Tōkōkyohi mondai o chūshin ni: chūgakko, kōtōgakko ron* (A discussion of junior and senior high schools: Focus on school refusal) (Tokyo: 1983).

38. Margaret Lock, "A Nation at Risk: Interpretations of School Refusal in Japan," in *Biomedicine Examined*, 391–414. Margaret Lock, "Flawed Jewels and National Dis/Order: Narratives on Adolescent Dissent in Japan," Festschrift for George DeVos, *Journal of Psychohistory* 18 (1991): 507–531.

39. Karōshi bengo dan zenkoku renraku kaigihen, *Karōshi*.

40. See Eto, "The Breakdown of Motherhood." See also Kyūtoku, *Bogenbyō*.

41. Higuchi, "Women at Home."

42. Mary Saso, *Women in the Japanese Workplace* (London: Hilary Shipman, 1990). Mary C. Brinton, *Women and the Economic Miracle: Gender and Work in Postwar Japan* (Berkeley: University of California Press, 1993).

43. Carol Gluck, "The Meaning of Ideology in Modern Japan," in *Rethinking Japan*, eds. A. Boscaro, F. Gatti, and M. Raveri (Folkestone: Japan Library Ltd., 1990), 283–297.

44. Pierre Bourdieu, *Outline of a Theory of Practice* (Cambridge: Cambridge University Press, 1977); Michel De Certeau, *The Practice of Everyday Life* (Berkeley: University of California Press, 1984).

45. H. D. Harootunian, "Visible Discourses/Invisible Ideologies," in *Postmodernism and Japan*, eds. M. Miyoshi and H. D. Harootunian (Durham: Duke University Press, 1989), 63–92.

46. Funding for primary research reported in this paper was provided by the Social Sciences and Humanities Research Council of Canada. Interviews lasting between one-and-a-half and two hours were conducted in their homes with 105 women. Approximately one-third were Kobe housewives, one-third were factory workers in south Kyoto, and one-third lived and were occupied in farming villages in southern Nagano, a fishing village in Shikoku, and a forestry village in Shiga. Names appearing in the text are fictitious. Interviews with physicians reported above were conducted in 1984 and 1986.

47. Hakuhodo Institute of Life and Living, *Japanese Women in Turmoil: Changing Lifestyles in Japan* (Tokyo: Hakuhodo Institute of Life and Living, 1984).

48. James Scott, *Domination and the Arts of Resistance: Hidden Transcripts* (New Haven: Yale University Press, 1990).

49. Robert Smith, *Ancestor Worship in Contemporary Japan* (Stanford: Stanford University Press, 1974).

50. Takie Lebra, *Japanese Women: Constraint and Fulfillment* (Honolulu: University of Hawaii Press, 1984).

51. David Plath, *Long Engagements*.

52. Lock, *Encounters with Aging*.

53. Margaret Lock, "Ambiguities of Aging: Japanese Experience and Perceptions of Menopause," in *Culture, Medicine, and Psychiatry* 10 (1986): 23–46.

54. In a 1984 survey that I conducted with over 1,300 women aged forty-five to fifty-five inclusively, three occupational groups were included: farming women, factory workers, and full-time homemakers. The middle-class urban sample was selected from the register of names and addresses available at many city halls in Japan. The register used is classified according to residential areas. Two areas regarded as representative of middle income families were selected and every

woman (525) between ages forty-five and fifty-five was noted and mailed a questionnaire. This was followed up by a reminder postcard and then a second mailing of the questionnaire to those who had not responded. After the first mailing 191 usable questionnaires were returned, after the postcard 68 more, and after the second questionnaire another 75 were returned giving a total of 324 usable responses. The usual response rate to Japanese mail questionnaires is between ten and fifteen percent.

The factory workers were selected by first making contact with the director of the Kyoto Industrial Health Association who facilitated the distribution of 405 questionnaires to fifteen factory managers, who then passed out all of the questionnaires to women of the appropriate age. Replies were sent back by mail directly to the researchers. A second group of 145 women working in small silk weaving factories were contacted by personal distribution of the questionnaire to factory managers after receiving the support of the local union in the form of a letter of introduction. I obtained 377 usable responses from this sample.

The final sample of 650 farm workers was selected through the support of the public health department of a large country hospital. The questionnaires were distributed by traveling public health workers to the women's organizations of forty-five villages. Responses were mailed directly back to the researchers and yielded 434 usable responses. A second, smaller sample of 176 usable responses was obtained through the cooperation of the local head of the department of public health, who introduced the researchers directly to the local women's organizations.

This survey was designed to be comparable with one conducted in Massachusetts using 8,000 women and another in Manitoba with 2,500 women aged forty-five to fifty-five inclusively. Lock, *Encounters with Aging.*

55. Lock, *Encounters with Aging;* Lock, "Ambiguities of Aging."

56. Margaret Lock, Patricia Leiland Kaufert, and Penny Gilbert, "Cultural Construction of the Menopausal Syndrome: The Japanese Case," *Maturitas* 10 (1988): 317–332.

57. Nishimura Hideo, *Josei to Kanpō* (Osaka: Sōgensha, 1981).

58. Yasui Hiromichi and Hirauma Naokichi, "Kanpo dekangaeru kōnenki shogai to wa donna mono deshoka," *Fujin Gaho* (September 1991): 370–379.

59. Yamada Kazuo, "Kōnenki no Rinshōmen," (Clinical aspects of menopause) *Rinshōigaku* 9 (1927): 1095–1102.

60. Donald Sheehan, "Discovery of the Autonomic Nervous System," *AMA Archives of Neurology and Psychiatry* 35 (1936): 1081–1115. Lock, *Encounters with Aging.*

61. Lock, *Encounters with Aging;* Herman Adlercreutz, Esa Hämäläinen, Sherwood Gorbach, and Barry Goldin, "Dietary phyto-oestrogens and the menopause in Japan," *The Lancet* 339 (1992): 1233.

62. WHO, *World Health Statistics Annual* (Geneva: World Health Organization, 1991). Philip D. Ross, Hiromichi Norimatsu, James W. Davis, Katsuhiko Yano, Richard D. Wasnick, Saeko Fukiwara, Yutaka Hosoda, and L. Joseph Melton, "A Comparison of Hip Fracture Incidence among Native Japanese, Japanese Americans, and American Caucasians," *American Journal of Epidemiology* 133 (1991): 801–809.

63. Margaret Lock, *Encounters with Aging.*

FOUR

Social Relations as Capital

The Story of Yuriko

Robert J. Marra

INTRODUCTION

It is a typical weekday morning. Grandpa has not yet returned for break-fast from his morning gateball game. His son is still at the fishmarket, auc-tioning the morning catch. His daughter-in-law is scrambling to retrieve her two sons from their early morning cram school lessons and drive them to high school on time. Grandma has been hard at work in the kitchen.

The nature of Grandma's work in the kitchen, however, does not con-form to stereotypical expectations. She has not been making breakfasts and packing lunches; that is her daughter-in-law's job. Rather, she has been entertaining a parade of neighborhood women who began arriving shortly after daybreak. Some came for idle banter; most came for advice and assistance in solving a variety of personal and financial problems.

I lived with Grandma and her family for more than a year. At first I was puzzled by her daily barrage of visitors. Grandma did not seem so special to me; in fact she seemed a little bit crazy. Why were all of these women asking her for advice?

As I grew to know her and her family better, the reason for the "parade of state" became clear. Grandma, whom I will call Yuriko, had taken both her natal and marriage families from financial deprivation to wealth and high status in the village. She had done so through hard domestic work and thrifty management of the family's financial assets. The morning en-tourage came to draw on this experience to solve their own problems.

What follows are a brief description of the social environment that frames Yuriko's life, an overview of her life from the prewar era to 1992, and an analysis of what her life and values have meant for her family and how those values articulate with the more modern values of the 1990s. Though not particularly different from the lives of other Japanese country women of her generation, Yuriko's life represents a set of values that most Americans unacquainted with Japan find surprising. Contrary to stereo-typical American expectations, she and the other women of her village have little if any desire to become more Western in their ways. Nor do they conceive of gender equality along Western lines; for them, Western equality is much too complicated and bothersome. Rather, they prefer their separate and unequal worlds. In both the private world of the home and the public world of the village during daylight hours, woman is boss.

THE SOCIAL ENVIRONMENT

Figure 5 is a sketch of the neighborhoods in the village where Yuriko was born and still lives today. The village is narrow and shaped like the Greek letter omega (Ω). In 1974, a road was built along the harbor. Until then, the village had only one central road running its entire length, with a row of houses on either side. The houses on the harbor side were wedged between the harbor and the road; those on the hill side were wedged between the central road and the adjoining mountains. One way the villagers characterize themselves is by who lives on the harbor side of the central road and who lives on the hill side. Before the harbor shore road was built, this distinction was extremely important because hill-side fishermen had to secure rights of passage through harbor-side homes to access their fishing boats. Now, however, with the advent of the harbor shore road, the demolition and conversion of several older houses into alleys, and the building of modern houses with central hallways at the same level as the living quarters, this distinction has become more symbolic than functional.[1]

By far the most important social distinction in the village is neighborhood designation. People from the same neighborhood value their relationships with their neighbors above all other relationships outside their natal and marriage families. This distinction is important enough that I have illustrated the neighborhood boundaries on Figure 5. The reasons for this are economic, social, and political. Fishermen from the same neighborhood have fished together in groups for more than one hundred years. Since nearly the same families have been occupying the same houses for centuries, generations of neighbors have worked together. This economic relationship eclipses the kinship relationship except in times of family anniversaries and other special family events, which I discuss later in this chapter.

Socially, neighbors represent the neighborhood to the larger village community. Sports events are organized by neighborhood. The women's association is organized by neighborhood and collects accident insurance funds from all households, prepares meals for social or religious events, and so on.

Politically, the neighborhood is the smallest cohesive segment of the village that operates as a political body. Possible ordinances or legislation are presented to the neighborhood as a group, the male members of which

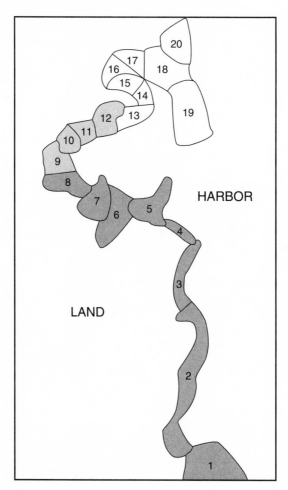

Fig. 5. Yuriko's village, subdivided by neighborhood. The shading indicates the three main wards of the village. Adapted from *The History of Fishing in Katsumoto-cho*, Fukoka: Totsuban Insatu, 1985.

then debate the matter. The consensus is presented to the village neighborhood association by a designated male representative, who then tries to influence other representatives to vote along the lines that this neighborhood deemed appropriate.

Politically speaking, these neighborhoods can be divided into three large groups coinciding perfectly with their historical ward boundaries. Neighborhoods one through eight on Figure 5 constitute the eastern ward of the village and can be seen as socially and politically distinct from the other two wards for a variety of reasons. One important reason is that these fishermen tended in the past to focus on net fishing, whereas the other wards engaged primarily in yellowtail handline fishing. The women of the eastern ward were historically much more active in supporting their husbands' fishing endeavors; they were responsible for netmending, an activity unnecessary in the other wards. With the demise of net fishing in the village, many of the women in the eastern ward became fishmongers, retailers who purchase fish sold at the fishing cooperative in the morning and resell it at the farmers' market. (Located in this ward, the fishing cooperative is the main source of fishermen's income.)

Neighborhoods nine through twelve are the central ward of the village, recognized as the hub of daily economic exchange within the community. In this ward both sides of the central road are lined with small shops and produce stalls that provide almost any household necessity. The number of households in this ward whose primary income derives from fishing is decidedly lower than in the other wards. Yuriko was born in this part of the village, and her natal family home is still headed by her older brother.

More important than the stores in this ward is the morning farmers' market. The fishermen's wives come here to buy their daily necessities, such as fish purchased by the fishmongers at the cooperative and brought for resale here. Every morning before dawn the women of the farming households on the hills overlooking the village rise to pick their vegetables, collect their eggs, and bring them down to their storefront stalls in town. There they sell to the fishermen's wives just as they have been doing since Tokugawa times. Lively exchanges and bartering over prices typify the morning farmers' market, a scene of seeming pandemonium that dwindles into silence as the noon hour approaches.

If one were to leave the central shopping area and chat with a housewife on her way home to the western neighborhoods (numbered thirteen through twenty in Figure 5), one would notice an immediate change in the central road. Stores abruptly cease, and the hills that shroud the other two wards steepen into a cliff, confining homes to a narrow strip of land between cliff and harbor. All eight neighborhoods in the western ward consist primarily of fishing households; Yuriko's marriage household is one of the exceptions in not garnering any income from fishing.

In addition to neighborhood divisions and the side of the village one lives on, social distinctions are based on kinship. Kinship lines are unequivocally bilateral; however, the length of the lineage that people speak of as being related is remarkably short. Second cousins are not considered relatives, even though the blood relationship is known.

Household composition has not changed since Tokugawa times, although the size of households has greatly decreased. In the ideal pattern, grandparents share their home with their married, eldest son, his wife, and his two children. Upon retiring, the grandparents move to the retirement part of the house, where they lead lives largely separate from their son's family. The difficulty is for the younger siblings, especially the males, who must leave the home and establish new households of their own. Housing space is at a premium in the village; only one newly created neighborhood has space available for housing construction. Many sons find new homes by being adopted into a family that lacks a male heir, marrying the family's eldest daughter.

Stem and branch family relationships are clearly known and accepted. (A stem family is one to which a number of households, called branch families, trace their ancestral roots.) However, because most families are fishing households and have a revolving, low supply of capital, the relationship between stem and branch families does not resemble the extended, economic family relationship found in agrarian northern Japan.[2] In this village, the stem and branch relationship comes to the fore only during the year's major annual festivals and, for specific families such as Yuriko's marriage family, at the time of weddings or the anniversary of the passing of a revered elder.

YURIKO'S LIFE

Yuriko was born in 1924, the eldest daughter of eight children, with three older brothers. Her father was a fisherman in the middle ward of the village in the era before fishing cooperatives came to southwestern Japan. The wholesaler to whom he sold his catch supplied him with all of his fishing equipment. Because of the monopoly he held on the fishermen's livelihoods, the wholesaler offered low prices for the catch and charged exorbitant prices for equipment, leaving his fishermen in a constant state of indebtedness. This circumstance weighed heavily on Yuriko's natal family, for they had many mouths to feed.

Shortly after Yuriko's youngest sibling was born, her mother became ill and remained so for many years. As the eldest daughter, Yuriko was responsible for taking care of her family. At that time, there was no running water, only brackish water from the village wells. Very few homes in the village had electricity, and hers was not among them. Firewood had to be collected for cooking.

Perhaps I will never know how Yuriko felt about her hard lot at a young age, but one fact is undeniable: she worked from morning until night seven days a week. She spent hours lugging water from the wells, washing clothes, collecting firewood, and cooking. Add shopping, cleaning, preparing baths, and caring for others' needs, and it is easy to project that fourteen-hour days of constant labor were her norm.

To her surprise, her family survived. Without much money, Yuriko succeeded in feeding and taking care of them. It was then that she first learned the lesson of being a good neighbor and saw how her personal image in the neighborhood could affect her family's survival. She also began to develop her reputation as a good provider and someone who would make a good wife.

Yuriko was born into a fishing household in the middle ward of the village. With its market and relatively few fishing families, Yuriko's reliance on her neighbors, and theirs on her, followed the law of supply and demand. She needed supplies of various sorts, and although her neighbors had them to sell, she had no money to purchase them. The neighbors, on the other hand, needed food, and Yuriko had fish from her father's catch that could be set aside to feed her neighbors rather than sold through the wholesaler. A barter system developed that fostered her image as a good family provider and a good neighbor.

But just when her family circumstances became manageable, World War II changed everything. All five of her brothers went to war, and only two would return. Without sons to help with the fishing, her father's catch decreased markedly, lowering the family income, increasing the family's debt to the wholesaler, and taking away from Yuriko the one resource that had enabled her to care for her family's needs. With the onset of gas rationing, her father's fishing activities were curtailed completely, and his boat was sequestered for military transport purposes.

During the war years Yuriko became the main provider of food as well as the main caregiver in the family. Added to her list of responsibilities were foraging in the forest for food, collecting shellfish along the beach, and participating in various war-preparedness activities with the neighborhood young women's association. As in the prewar years, her work helped the family survive extremely difficult times. According to Yuriko, the war years taught her the value of good relations with one's neighbors. Even though she had nothing to offer in return except a limited supply of time and labor, her neighbors continued to supply her family as though nothing in their relationship had changed. Although Yuriko was able to feed her family through her own ingenuity, she might not have been able to acquire her family's clothing and household supplies without her neighbors' help.

I asked Yuriko why her extended family did not come to her assistance. Her answer reflected both the times and the law of supply and demand. Supplies and food were precious commodities. All of Yuriko's male family members were fishermen; all had been put out of work by the war, and most had been drafted. Their resource base was the same as hers.

By 1946 her oldest brother had returned from combat, built a Japanese-style, single-oar boat, and resumed fishing with his father. (The other surviving brother moved to Nagoya.) Shortly thereafter her brother married, and it became his wife's responsibility to care for the family. Around this time Yuriko's father decided that she too should get married. He arranged for her betrothal to a man in one of the village's western neighborhoods. She married and moved into her new home, the bride of the eldest son of a fisherman who had retired early due to various health problems.

The circumstances of Yuriko's marriage family were perhaps as difficult as those of her natal family. Her father-in-law was out of work, so there was no money. Her husband had eight younger brothers and sisters, the youngest of whom had been born just six months before Yoriko's first child; thus Yoriko had small children to care for before she even started having two of her own.

However, there were two important differences between this home and her natal home. In the short term, the most important difference was that it had its own well. This meant no more lugging water through town. It also meant that she had a valuable resource to share with her neighbors. By sharing, she further enhanced her image as a good neighbor and family provider.

The long-term difference is that she married into a stem family. This gave her a ready-made network of branch family connections extending beyond the neighborhood and even into the farming households in the overlying hills. From her perspective and that of her father, she had improved her lot in life by marrying into a family that would allow her to use two sets of connections, kin and neighborhood, to improve the family welfare. The barter system and law of supply and demand that had served her well in her natal family quickly came into play for her marriage family. In the early years the commodities she could provide her neighbors and family members were water and work; in return she received a portion of the first crop or first catches of the season.

As her natal family had done, Yuriko and her marriage family survived those early years. Shortly after she married, several leading fishermen in the village took advantage of the Occupation's 1949 legislation reorganizing Japan's fishing industry and created the village's first postwar fishing cooperative. Yuriko's husband became one of the cooperative's first (and youngest) employees, in charge of unloading fishing boats, recording catches, and preparing the town catch for shipment and sale in Fukuoka. Her husband's small income brought money into her home after nearly ten years of largely doing without it.

But before Yuriko's husband could be paid, the fishermen who organized the cooperative and became its leaders had to devise a plan for raising initial capital to run the cooperative. They turned to their traditional support groups, the neighborhoods. Each neighborhood was organized into two subgroups, a young men's association and a young women's association. The men's responsibility was to sell as much of their old equipment as possible to outside parties. The women's responsibility was two-pronged: they were to volunteer at the cooperative to help land and record their husband's catches. Then they were to be given the transaction receipts from their husband's catches and put part of it aside as savings. Through the efforts of these neighborhood groups, the village economy recovered in just a few years and has been doing well ever since.

Because Yuriko's husband was a paid cooperative employee rather than a fisherman, she became the leader of her neighborhood women's association and one of the leaders of the association villagewide. Rather than simply volunteer at the cooperative for a brief time as the others did, she assisted her husband for many hours every day, thereby making it acceptable in the villagers' eyes for her husband's salary to be drawn from their catches and earning her considerable personal respect from the other women in the village. She worked in this way for almost four years, by which time the cooperative was doing well enough that it could take on additional paid help and she could return primarily to her family duties. Yuriko considers those four years to be the low point in her life for two reasons. First, she was forced to spend considerable time away from her small children (her mother-in-law looked after them), then handle family responsibilities for long hours at night. Second, she never cared much for eating fish; she says that working with live, slimy, smelly fish on slippery docks was totally repugnant. Since that time, she has not eaten raw fish.

Years now passed. Yuriko's younger child and her mother-in-law's children grew up and gradually married and moved out. Because she had gone so long without money, Yuriko was able to make do with very little. With more money from her husband's income and fewer mouths to feed, she began saving. By 1982 her parents-in-law had died, and her husband, her son, and her daughter-in-law were working, bringing three incomes into a household of six (grandparents, parents, and two children). Under those circumstances they had more than enough income to demolish their old house and build a brand new one, as modern as any and larger than most city homes in Japan. The new house symbolized Yuriko's image and her contributions to the welfare of her family.

DISCUSSION

Because her daughter-in-law was working full-time, responsibility fell to Yuriko to care for her two small grandsons and get them off to school every day. Her willingness to do so and thus permit her daughter-in-law to be employed full-time further enhanced Yuriko's reputation in the village, and in fact was the reason she started her "kitchen consulting business." Other women her age began seeking her advice on relations between mothers-in-law and daughters-in-law, questions of daughter-in-law employment, and childcare concerns. After that, questions broadened to financial, marital, and other affairs until she became recognized as a village sage. Some mornings she could not stand to have visitors, whereupon she would either not answer when someone came calling, or if I were there, she would tell them she was busy cooking for me and ask them to come back later.

Yuriko turned sixty in 1984, the year I was living there. By all accounts she had "made it": she had shepherded two families through difficult times, and both were doing well. Throughout her life she had worked hard, had given freely of her time and herself to others, and had held all relevant women's associations leadership positions along the way. In doing so, she had established a positive personal image that began in her natal neighborhood in one ward, was extended through her marital neighborhood to the second ward, and went villagewide through her work at the fishing cooperative. She now had leisure for the first time in her life, although some of it was being taken away by neighbors and friends seeking advice. Despite this "problem," she was looking forward to spending her golden years in the relaxed company of friends and family.

As noted previously, I do not consider Yuriko's life to be remarkable or extraordinary in any way relative to other Japanese country women of her generation, beyond the fact that she worked exceptionally hard through trying times and circumstances. Her life typifies the Japanese work ethic of hard work that yields deserved rewards. For social scientists, though, her life and her personal reputation have implications that shed light on what rural Japanese women see as their role in life and the mechanisms they can use to garner capital for themselves and their families.

The recorded history of the fishing industry in Yuriko's village goes back to the early 1700s, and it is clear from that history that the enterprise of fishing has been a male domain throughout. Various taboos against women either entering the sea or working on fishing boats are well recorded and still strictly adhered to by the older generation of villagers, though people in their forties and younger are somewhat less bound by these traditions.

Women in the village (and in many parts of Japan) grow up in a centuries-old tradition of a dual social structure. One aspect of this structure is public in a Japanese sense: women's public status relative to their husbands is deferential. The other is public and private in a Japanese sense, consisting of two parts: compared to their deferential public status relative to their husbands, women have a private status within their households where they are in charge, managing family and financial affairs. Women of this village also have their own ranked hierarchy of public social relationships that revolve around personal reputation, including such factors as age, personality, image, family's perceived prosperity, and how a family's circumstances have improved or declined under a woman's supervision.

For the village women of Yuriko's generation, reputation is the most important form of capital they can accrue. Reputation encompasses all five factors in the preceding list but concentrates heavily on the improvement of one's family's perceived prosperity. Yuriko is among the more successful examples from this village: not only are both her natal and marriage families better off now than when she began to take responsibility for them, but within her marriage family she has accommodated a new form of female enterprise that was not available to her during her younger years—work for pay.

During Yuriko's youth, there were no paying jobs for women in the village. Successful homemaking was a woman's only means of improving her reputation. Over the last twenty years, however, the fishing cooperative has hired a number of female employees, the majority of whom perform functions similar to those of "office ladies" in Tokyo corporations. At the morning farmers' market, a number of small shops have opened up and are managed by younger women of the village's central ward, making these women both the public and private heads of their households.

Yuriko's daughter-in-law was fortunate enough to be hired by the fishing cooperative upon graduation from high school, approximately twenty years ago. Now she has become the chief accountant for the morning fishermen's market, the economic mainstay of the village. While rising to this position, the daughter-in-law had two sons, now teenagers, who were largely raised by Yuriko so that their mother could work full-time and provide a third income to the family. At a time when most other women her age were turning household responsibility over to their daughters-in-law, Yuriko permitted her daughter-in-law the freedom to pursue a career. Yuriko's rewards for doing so include a beautiful, new home and an added reputation for being liberal and farsighted. People refer to Yuriko as *kanshin na mono*, or admirable—a designation that irks her daughter-in-law no end and leads to testy interactions between the two women.

Yuriko's motivation for permitting her daughter-in-law to work was surely the financial betterment of the family. However, in permitting her to work, Yuriko has enabled her daughter-in-law to receive the *kanshin na mono* designation when Yuriko passes away, since that permission allowed her daughter-in-law to advance into one of the few and most prestigious full-time positions available to women in the village. Most other positions for women in the village are part-time, and mothers either bring their small children along or work only during the school day. Yuriko and her daughter-in-law may be at the forefront of a new system that permits women with small children to work full-time while their able-bodied elders provide child care. Many people in the village say that the trend appears to be in this direction, although the main limiting factor is job availability. It will be interesting to see how this scenario develops over the next ten to twenty years.

That the villagers are talking about future trends in female employment brings out two points that are important to consider in any discussion of Japanese women. First, as has been noted elsewhere,[3] contrary to Western stereotypes about rural Japanese women the women of this village are relatively content with their rural lifestyles and show very little inclination to "escape" to the big cities of Japan. In the 1970s and early 1980s village demographic patterns did show an egress of younger men and women to the big cities. By the mid-1980s, though, many of them had returned with stories of higher incomes but also higher stress levels and a lack of free time. Their experiences seem to have influenced the younger generation, since demographics show the majority either remaining in the village or leaving for a few years after high school graduation and returning to stay by their early twenties. This trend has certainly reassured the elders of the village who, when I was conducting my fieldwork, were worried that their home was becoming a village of senior citizens.

The reasons for this change in demographics are numerous. For the fishermen, the economy is good, and over time they can count on a reasonable income. Fishermen work hard, and, when the weather is good, may go for weeks on end with almost no sleep to bring in the largest possible catch. It is a matter of pride and independence; they make as good a living as any average salaryman and do it for their own businesses. To them it is inconceivable that salarymen would want to put in long hours and suffer *karōshi* (death from overwork) for someone else's benefit.

The women are now enjoying a more relaxed, modern lifestyle than they believe could be available anywhere else. Neighborhood friendships and kinship ties ensure a ready support base that they would lack in urban Japan. Modern rural homes are typically larger and have more conveniences than city homes. Younger women now have part-time employment opportunities, with the possibility of full-time employment in the future. The food is as fresh and the air as clean as it gets; why would anyone want to live anywhere else?

The lifestyles of the women of this village, then, contradict a prevalent Western notion that Japanese women want to become more like Western women. By and large the village women are content with the separate but overlapping worlds of men and women. Time and time again I talked with them about my life with my wife and two daughters. My wife works full-time and is the primary earner for our family. We share responsibilities for household duties. The women of the village thought it embarrassing that my wife's income should be greater than mine but commendable that I could do household chores. They did not trust their own husbands either to get things done in the house or to do them properly.

Compared to Yuriko's early life, the younger women of the village have relatively easy lives. Like their Meiji era forebears who assimilated useful components of Western society that would aid Japan in its industrial development, these women have assimilated more than just the modern conveniences of their homes. They have assimilated aspects of modern Western womanhood that mesh well with their way of living, leaving behind those parts that would complicate their lives and village social structure. They like their women's and men's worlds, separate and unequal; they view the division as positive rather than negative.

A fisherman's wife has considerable autonomy in the home. In the late afternoon or early evening, the fisherman eats and then leaves to fish all night, returning at dawn. Again he eats, bathes, and then sleeps during the day. He gives his wife his catch receipt in the morning, and she has complete, unobstructed license to handle the daily household affairs in any manner she chooses.

From the wife's perspective, then, separate and unequal worlds mean freedom: freedom to pursue the relative advancement of her household as she deems appropriate; freedom from worrying about the fishing economy (except where new equipment purchases are concerned, in which she has substantial say); and most recently, freedom to pursue part-time work and garner additional funds for the family. It was Yuriko's effective use of these freedoms that gained for her the social capital—her personal reputation—that she enjoys today. It is her continued use of them in the 1990s that will ensure the continuity of her family's high social status into the twenty-first century.

NOTES

Research for this chapter was made possible by Andrew Mellon Predoctoral Fellowships (1983 and 1984), the Japan Iron and Steel Federation Endowment Fund of the University of Pittsburgh (1983), and business travel for the Japan–U.S. Friendship Commission and the National Association of Japan-America Societies, Inc.

1. In Japanese society it is customary to remove your shoes upon entering someone's home. However, in traditional homes, central hallways were at ground level and made of compacted dirt. It was expected, therefore, that people would keep their shoes on in the hallway until they stepped up into a raised room on either side (usually floored with tatami mats). In the Japanese way of thinking, the central hallway of a traditional home was actually an "outside" tunnel on the inside of the home. Someone could enter the home and pass all the way through without actually entering a room. Fishermen on the hill side of town, who needed access to their boats that were parked at the back of the houses on the harbor side of the road, simply walked through the house and exited out the back on their way to work.

In modern Japanese houses, the central hallway is elevated to the same level as the rooms in the home. The flooring is made of the same material as found in

the rooms; therefore one has to take off shoes in order to enter. This changed the custom, and now no one goes through anyone else's modern home to get to the boats. Instead one goes around, going down alleys or through vacant lots where homes once stood.

2. Keith Brown, "The Content of *Dozoku* Relationships in Japan," *Ethnology* 7 (1968), 113–38. Keith Brown, "*Dozoku* and the Ideology of Descent in Rural Japan," *American Anthropologist* 68 (1966): 1129–48.

3. Sumiko Iwao, *The Japanese Woman: Traditional Image and Changing Reality* (New York: The Free Press, 1993).

FIVE

The Traditional Arts as Leisure Activities for Contemporary Japanese Women

Barbara Lynne Rowland Mori

Traditional arts such as flower arrangement (*ikebana*) and the tea ceremony (*chadō*) are increasingly popular in Japan and have practitioners abroad as well.[1] Given the rapid rate of change in many aspects of Japanese society, especially the areas of accepted activities for women, the popularity of the traditional arts raises questions as to why women follow them, what opportunities and satisfaction they provide for women, and whether they have changed to meet the needs of women. This essay will explore the role of leisure activities, particularly those that are identified as traditionally Japanese, in the lives of contemporary women.

The traditional arts such as *chadō* are popular ways for women to spend their leisure time because these arts affirm traditional views of women as nurturing and supporting others in society. At the same time, they allow women to pursue personal goals of self-expression, artistry, the development of managerial skills. These personal goals might be defined as selfish and opposed to community norms of sacrifice and self-abnegation for women, but pursuit of them through traditional arts is deemed acceptable. The study and practice of traditional arts enables women to do what society expects of them as well as exhibit their personal skills and pursue friendships and activities that otherwise might place them in conflict with their roles in society. Many of the women interviewed expressed a sense that this participation let them "have their cake and eat it, too," following prescribed roles for women, yet escaping from the home and the demands of the roles of wife and mother. Participation in *chadō* allows for both acceptable public activity related to the art and private personal activity in the area of cultural learning.

The public perceives *chadō* as preparing women to take on the roles of wife and mother by providing training in deportment, food preparation, etiquette, and social understanding. This perception has enabled it to acquire followers, primarily through the promotional efforts of the Sen family.[2] *Chadō* is also perceived as an acceptable activity for older women. It thus has found a place for itself in the two peak times in women's lives when they are most likely to be involved in activities outside the home. The first period is between the ages of eighteen and twenty-six, just after completing their education and before marriage. During this time, the family places relatively few demands on the young women, who work full- or part-time or take lessons outside the home in traditional arts, cooking, or Western arts. The second period begins when the women's children have completed their education and left home, allowing women more free time. These two periods of women's involvement have proved important to the financial survival of the *chadō* schools.

Although initially a practice for upper-class women and later the wives of wealthy middle-class men, *chadō* has spread outside class boundaries because of its acceptance as a means of socializing young women and as a pastime and source of financial support for older women. It is part of the curriculum of many schools at various levels (junior and senior high and junior college) and is often provided by businesses as a perquisite for female staff. It can be practiced for very modest sums of money, since the cost of the basic equipment is minimal.[3] Although the affluence of Japan and the increase in leisure time for many women (particularly urban wives and widows of salarymen) has made this activity more accessible, *chadō* has retained an elite association. Its class and elite associations are an attractive feature of its practice for many women.

LEISURE

Noting the universality of leisure activities, sociologists have identified these activities as important for establishing culture, socializing the individual, and constituting the "arena where the intimate bonds are established and maintained."[4] "Leisure activities serve as an expression of social solidarity and norms to reaffirm the larger social order through display of artifacts that give physical shape to collective representation of myths."[5] Participation in particular leisure activities arises out of an individual's "taste," which is defined as a "preference exercised in response to normative pressures."[6]

Leisure activities such as *chadō* are important in the life of a society. Like the formal education system, leisure activities are a form of learning that prepares individuals for their societal roles. However, where formal education is restricted to certain age groupings, classes, and periods,[7] informal education through leisure activities may continue throughout an individual's life. Practice sessions (*keiko*) of *chadō* under the instruction of one teacher may include individuals of different social and economic backgrounds and different ages, ranging from young children of seven or eight to older men and women in their sixties, but are more likely to be groupings of individuals of similar age and background, at a similar level in their *chadō* studies, who associate with one another outside of practice.[8]

Urasenke is the school that has been most active in encouraging women to study *chadō* practice. Since it is also the largest school of *chadō* in Japan, chosen by an estimated seventy percent of all people who study *chadō*, I selected it for my research.[9] Students and teachers were interviewed either in their homes or where they study and teach.[10] My research was based on the concepts of grounded theory and symbolic interactionist analysis.[11] Grounded theory emphasizes the development of understanding of events from the observed context, and symbolic interactionist analysis focuses on the ways in which individuals create meaning to order their behavior in context. Therefore, this chapter emphasizes the manner in which *chadō* teaches a particular way to view the world and various kinds of patterned behavior, and focuses on the way women who teach and study *chadō* use it to structure their worldview as well as the meaning they give to their actions and choices. It is essential to represent the *chadō* world as its practitioners see it and to assess it in terms of the context of Japanese society.[12]

This approach to *chadō* differs from much existing scholarship on the topic in that it focuses on the people involved in the art rather than on its history, philosophy, or artistic development. This study does not emphasize the men who created the art or those who control it, but instead investigates the experiences of those who practice it, teach it, and study it, the majority of whom are women. I am therefore mainly concerned with the interests of women in the practice of *chadō* and the way it fits into and helps define their lives.

Most of my informants are women who do not question the values of the society in which they live. They accept their society's hierarchical order and the idea that there is a proper place for everyone and everything. These women seek to fulfill as best they can the roles assigned to them in Japanese society, while finding personal enjoyment and meaning within those roles. It is important that information about these women's lives be available to others who seek to understand the source of support for existing traditions and the reasons behind that support.

CHADŌ AND INCREASED LEISURE TIME

In Japan since the 1960s women, and especially urban homemakers, have increasingly been interested in a variety of leisure activities, particularly the traditional arts of flower arrangement (*ikebana*) and *chadō*. The reasons for this development include growing affluence, nostalgia for things Japanese, and an increase in free time for such pursuits. Changes in family composition and size, the nature and amount of household duties, and the definition of the role of housewife have encouraged women to look to the traditional arts, among other activities, as areas for personal growth and enjoyment. The urban homemaker lives in a small apartment and purchases rather than makes or grows most of the food and items she uses. Chores are eased by the use of machines, and her job has shifted to that of competent manager and wise consumer.[13] The family is also more likely to be a nuclear family with two children and no in-laws to care for, at least for a number of years. Thus, there are periods of time in her life when she will have fun and leisure without heavy housework or dependent duties. However, the definition of good wife and mother still requires some sense of sacrifice or devotion to duty, and this affects the type of activities she will choose to fill her leisure time.[14] As one thirty-five-year-old *chadō* student and mother of two boys in high school reported,

> When my household is going well, I seem to concentrate well. If I have some worries on my mind, I can't do well. I never used to go to [*chadō*] practice at a particular time because I had to make sure that my children went to school and my husband to work. After they left, I would clean the house and then go to practice. But I would try to be home before the children got home. My priority is as a housewife, and so I have to do housework before I can do anything else.

Another woman who has studied *chadō* for twenty years said, "Even when I was in Kyoto, I had to do housework first. Then with my free time, I could practice tea."

The traditional arts have a special appeal for middle-class women in that these arts advertise themselves as providing self-improvement and educational opportunities that enhance a woman's abilities as wife, mother, and hostess. Women are encouraged to take up traditional arts in order to learn Japanese cultural practices to pass on to their daughters. As one *chadō* student who is also studying Noh drama said,

> They talk about *wabi* and *sabi* [Japanese aesthetic concepts] and Japanese traditions. Japanese know generally about that from their grandparents. This changes from generation to generation, but it is difficult to know what to pass on. Tradition is something that is being made. The key idea for each time should be taught. We seem to be going round and round. What is Japanese culture and tradition? It is hard to put into words.

Another student remarked, "I did flower arrangement and crocheting. The reason I chose *ocha* (tea ceremony) was that there is no limit in exploring *ocha*." "The fact is there is no end to studying *chadō*. *Chadō* is not only serving tea, but also the collection of all kinds of Japanese art," observed another.

Of the students I interviewed, most reported that they were studying *chadō* in order to learn Japanese culture and tradition. The practice of *chadō* requires knowledge in many areas besides *temae* (the various ways of preparing and serving tea.) The student learns gardening and tea-house architecture which affects the kinds of *temae* done, the placement of utensils in the room, and the choice of utensils and items for the alcove (*tokonoma*) appropriate to various holidays and seasons. Students also learn the history behind certain celebrations and the appropriate symbols, artifacts, and lore of certain holidays. Therefore, besides learning what is appropriate for *chadō* on such occasions, students also learn how to celebrate them in their own homes. They thus improve their knowledge of the arts, home decoration, and food preparation and service. The students see this training as enabling them to maintain a sense of Japanese identity. Because so many Western things and ways of behaving have entered their lives, some students fear they may lose any sense of being distinctively Japanese. Said a Tokyo woman, "One reason [I began studying] is I was married to a man who was raised with *chadō*. The more I studied, the more I realized that I was Japanese. When I look around and see people without any knowledge of *chadō*, I wonder whether they have any nationality or not. So I think I am very lucky to have had a chance to get into *chadō*."

An important aspect of studying tea that attracts students is the opportunity to learn formal etiquette, which they feel will help them to be better wives and hostesses.[15] Etiquette is seen as more than just a list of rules for learning how to greet a guest or how to bow correctly. Etiquette enables human relations to progress smoothly and embodies a set of values that guide human interaction. The ways people interact with one another are an expression of social values of respect (*kei*), balance (*wa*), and sincerity (*makoto*.)

When asked what she felt was important to teach her students, a *chadō* teacher replied. "I want the students to learn about everyday manners and also the establishment of Japan, information that is gradually being lost. I want them to make these ideas an important part of their daily lives."

Another teacher, when asked why she thought her students came to study, responded, "First of all, interest in history and the beauty of *chadō*. People studying Japanese culture and art acquire an interest in *chadō*." When asked about how she felt people viewed her as a *chadō* teacher, another answered, "They say my manners are good and that I have an elegant occupation."

Manners reflect character. Teachers report that they learn much about their students from the way in which they interact with others. *Temae* performance allows the teachers to see into the students' souls and characters. One teacher said that by observing the *temae* of her students she could tell how far along they were in their spiritual development.

The Urasenke school of *chadō* directs its appeal to those spiritual interests and includes a meditative, semireligious component.[16] It stresses in particular the relationship between *chadō* and Zen Buddhism. Meditation is often part of the lesson (before beginning, students may sit *seiza*—a formal posture with legs tucked underneath as one meditates), and calligraphy by Zen masters grace the *tokonoma* (*Cha zen ichimi,* "the taste of tea and Zen are the same," is a common phrase). Stories of Zen teachers are recounted to illustrate the concepts such as respect (*kei*). One student expressed appreciation of this spiritual aspect, saying "I really like *chadō.* I don't think about evil when I am around *chadō.*"

Chadō also exerts a personal appeal by providing opportunities to meet and form friendships with cultured people (teachers and fellow students) while pursuing activities that are socially sanctioned as erudite. "I feel happy when I meet many various kinds of people and we are able to understand each other without words," said one student. "Most of my students who have studied for a very long time continue because their friends are still doing it. They want to do it together," commented one teacher. *Chadō* creates opportunities to enhance and display personal creative abilities and social status as well as find like-minded friends.

Although its rituals may seem esoteric, the world of *chadō* is not a static, encapsulated world remote from the lives of real people. The attraction of *chadō* is not that it is a museum piece, but that it is contemporary. Its practice is relevant to the lives of its teachers and students. The women who study and teach *chadō* are not longing for a mystical past; they are rarely interested in the philosophical and semihistorical stories of the practice of *chadō* by past masters. The women are more interested in how *chadō* relates to their own lives and interests. Conversation in the tea room concerns the present: what they are doing, the meaning of symbolic objects, or the way to execute a particular movement or to place flowers. They talk about the future: what they will do together to prepare for an upcoming event, to take a lecture on tea utensils, or to celebrate someone's birthday. They discuss the lives of individuals they know. Therefore, *chadō* changes as the interests of men and women who practice it change. Urasenke has come to offer classes in cooking and lectures on the symbols of the New Year and Japanese literature. The school offers tours not only of tea houses and public presentations of tea, but also of famous sights all over Japan and of Hawaii. The interpretations of the meaning and value of *chadō* by its current teachers and students are an important part of the change that keeps the art form current and popular.

REINFORCEMENT OF ROLES:
PROFESSIONAL WOMEN AND WOMEN'S STATUS

Japanese society privileges social roles and their obligations over personal goals and interests. Women are expected to fulfill the social roles of wife and mother before pursuing personal interests, and when they do, those personal interests must enhance skills needed in those social roles or stem from commitment to those roles. Women who engage in activities of a public nature emphasize that they are doing so as "ordinary women" and as "mothers and housewives." Yet they are able to use these roles as a shield for their personal choices to allow them to move into areas that have been restricted to men.

Most of the women interviewed did not question the social view that women's lives belong primarily to the family or in the private rather than public sphere. They asserted that the family comes first; things that take time from the family must be rationalized as either not really taking time from the family, as necessary to fulfilling family-oriented tasks, or as enhancing the public reputation of the family. Their outside activities must be manageable around family needs, improve their housekeeping skills, or enhance status and provide contacts to further family goals, such as securing better marriage prospects for children.[17]

Professionals in *chadō* are women who, with approval of family and teachers, have given up the roles of wife and mother in order to make a total commitment to their art and teaching. Women who combine a teaching career with mothering subordinate *chadō* to family demands. Because doing both is difficult, few women attempt it. "When my children were born and were growing up, I did not study or teach *chadō* until my youngest child went to junior high. During that time, I did housework only." This teacher's statement illustrates how difficult it is for women to steadily pursue teaching careers. Some can take up professional work in *chadō* only after completion of duties as wife or mother, after children are grown and out of the house or the husband has died. Married women who work professionally while raising children are usually those for whom *chadō* is part of a larger family concern with the art. They are the wives of tea masters or artisans or other professionals connected with the culture of *chadō*.

In addition to the occupation of teacher, *chadō* also offers employment to women in other capacities directly and indirectly related to the various schools. Women are hired by Urasenke in positions as maids, clerks, utensil dealers, tour guides, and classroom lecturers. Women in these roles are expected to know something about *chadō* practice as well as the job for which they are specifically employed, and many women who work in the various office and retail jobs study privately.

Like professionals, amateurs who study *chadō* find their training is usually not an unbroken continuum. A young woman may begin to study *chadō* because her mother insists that she do so as "bride training." She may pursue this in a desultory fashion for one to three years either while attending high school or junior college or upon completion of formal education until marriage. Sometimes she will come to enjoy it and continue, only to drop out when she marries and her time is taken up with running a household and raising children. "I was studying *chadō* from my elementary school days, but I started being really serious after my children started going to school," reported a student who was moving toward acquiring her teaching credential.

When the children are all in school, a woman may be busy with the PTA, taking the children to private lessons, helping them with homework, and so on. But she will have more leisure time than before. She may become aware that as part of her role as mother, she should pass on a sense of Japanese cultural identity, yet be unsure what constitutes Japanese culture. She may feel a need for advice about social occasions that require her attention to detail and order. Since more women live apart from extended families in the cities, advice on cultural identity, gift giving, and proper attire for social events such as weddings or funerals is often sought from the tea teacher. The student may return to *chadō* as a way of learning these things and as a familiar activity.

While I was interviewing a teacher at her home where she taught, a woman came in and joined the lesson. She presented her record book (where each preparation she had done was recorded) to the teacher and was told to serve as a guest for the next student doing a preparation. The teacher said, "You look familiar but I don't remember your name. When were you here last?" The woman replied with her name and said it had been twelve years since her last lesson, but now that her children were all in school she was free to take up where she had left off, if the teacher agreed.

A woman's friends' opinions will affect her decision to return to *chadō*, as will her husband's attitude and willingness to pay for lessons. It is difficult for a husband to refuse either to pay or to allow household money to be used for activities that promote his wife's education and identification as a cultured person. This is particularly so if the wives of other respected men are engaged in similar activities and she explains it as important for teaching the children proper manners and values. He even has less cause to disapprove if she uses her own funds.[18]

Others come to take up *chadō* as an activity in widowhood. "I have a friend whose husband passed away. Her daughters persuaded her to study *chadō*. They said that by doing *ocha*, she will be well mannered and lead a good life that is calm and composed. They want their mother to lead a happy life like mine," said an elderly student. A Tokyo teacher said, "After my husband's death, I could choose either to remarry or to remain single. I chose to live on my own. I started tea seriously then, which is very different from the practice I used to have before my marriage. I could not go through a day now without tea."

Because women tend to outlive their husbands and to live longer than in the past, they are becoming a significant segment of the population. Widows form a growing group of students in *chadō*. One woman whose husband was retired and who was studying with friends who were all widowed said that her friends jokingly encouraged her to become a widow quickly so that she could join them on their trips to visit famous tea huts and Buddhist temples.

Chadō has been successful in attracting women to its practice because it has stressed its ability to teach skills useful in fulfilling the role of housewife and is thus seen as an established arena for "bride training." It also stresses knowledge of Japanese cultural practice and is thus able to teach women practical skills and values to pass on to their children. Time spent pursuing *chadō* is seen as enabling women to perform domestic roles, not seduce them away from home and family. It is also seen as an acceptable pastime for an older woman, something to keep her busy and involved in her own life and not meddling in the lives of her children. One woman said, "I have two sons, and thus I will have two daughters-in-law. One of the reasons I began to study *chadō* was so that I would not be a bother to my daughters-in-law."

Though a concern for family and her role in it is the most important factor affecting a woman's *chadō* participation, her status is also an important motivator. A woman's status (in her own eyes and those of her friends) can be seen as a reflection of three criteria: husband's work and family (social class); fulfillment of the social roles of wife, mother (assessed by children's accomplishments), daughter-in-law, and homemaker; and public involvement in the community (activities outside the home). The first two are based partly on her ability to manage others. *Chadō*, with its emphasis on creating and maintaining a particular ceremony that requires the manipulation of symbols, spaces, and people, helps teach such management skills. *Chadō* teachers are very clear that they are teaching people how to manage their lives and the lives of those with whom they interact to produce a pleasurable encounter and to create and maintain social occasions in which things are accomplished harmoniously and effortlessly, or at least appear so.

The third criterion of a woman's status is what she herself does. The women who were interviewed emphasized that they were interested in *chadō* because it offered them a positive and flattering view of themselves. When asked how others saw them in light of their practice of *chadō*, most responded that others saw them favorably because of their involvement in the art. In the eyes of their friends and neighbors, *chadō* was identified with depth of character, spirituality, grace, beauty, accomplishment, creativity, erudition, and culture. *Chadō* gave them more in status in the eyes of their friends than, say, playing tennis or other sports.

CREATIVITY AND PERSONAL DEVELOPMENT

Creativity is associated in the Western mind predominantly with individual egotistic expression and originality. The product of this process is attributed to one individual who sometimes receives social approval and reward for this achievement and is expected to subordinate all other roles and interest to this endeavor. However, this is only one aspect of the creative process. Artistic endeavor may also serve to reinforce social values and practices, and this aspect is more acknowledged in *chadō*.

Japanese women who study *chadō* do not seek to be lone isolated artists working in private studios who periodically emerge to present objects for critical review and acclaim.[19] Instead, they have chosen an interactive art, where creativity is expressed in a group context and through exchange with others. There are occasions on which *chadō* is presented to an audience of observers and in this way is similar to other presentation arts, but this is not the heart of *chadō*.

Although one can use tea ritual (*temae*) to make a bowl of tea for oneself, the ritual is not intended for solitary practice. *Temae* incorporates action by the host and guest, in which the guest is not merely a passive consumer of what is prepared but has an active role to play in the unfolding and significance of the ritual. The host rarely makes tea for herself alone.

According to Grand Masters Sen Sōshitsu and Tanaka Sen-O, the art of *chadō* is the experience of a combination of elements—movement, utensils, space, personality, and occasion—that is meant to be shared.[20] When it is accomplished, nothing remains except the memory of the experience, the sharedness of feelings. Its value and meaning cannot be recorded, preserved, or analyzed, and they cannot be separated from the involvement of the participants. The individual's talents and abilities are blended with others.

Most of the time spent doing *chadō* is in lessons, often but not always, or even mainly, with a goal of actual performance. A person may study for years before ever performing in a public or semipublic setting. The intimacy between teacher and students and among students is one of the attractions of *chadō*, and most of the enjoyment comes from attending the lessons.

As a new teacher said, "It is sort of like a salon. They talk about their problems and other things, and catch up with the latest news about themselves for the past week. People who are about the same age discuss their problems and try to solve them together. Others who work come to relieve their stress at my place."

An older Tokyo student said, "I come here not only because of tea, but also because there is much social interaction with people who are studying with me, and because of the personality of the teacher. All those factors have inspired me to continue tea for fourteen years without taking a day off from practice sessions."

The product of *chadō* is not the tea you drink, the bowl you drink it from, or the room you drink it in, but the people who drink and make tea.

"The tea master strove to be something more than the artist . . . art it-self."[21] Art is not a product but a process. A dance, poem, *temae*, or paint-ing is not the object of the doing but a by-product and means to achieving personal perfection.

According to one teacher, "In order to have a balanced life one must be in harmony with her real or actual life through her religious culture and spirit. Before doing anything beautiful, one must be linked to her real life. Then Japanese culture will be born. This is all part of *wa, kei sei, jaku*, which is to have a well-balanced life."[22]

"At first I started studying *chadō* for the sake of a good marriage, but now I do this for my mental training. My mother often tells me these days that I am calmer than before," reported one student when asked about her purpose in studying *chadō*.

As Kato notes, the art was developed by tea masters of the past who de-voted themselves to art as a total commitment and who developed a phi-losophy around its practice.[23] "The concept of perfection, however, was different. The dynamic nature of their philosophy laid more stress upon the process through which perfection was sought than upon perfection itself."[24]

Students practice *chadō* as a means of becoming better people. "Tea is for the purpose of teaching harmony and respect among persons. They take lessons to become splendid people," observed one teacher. All the teachers interviewed responded that the purpose of teaching *chadō* was not primarily to teach the art form, the rituals, its history, or Japanese culture, but to teach people etiquette, how to become better people, and how to in-teract smoothly and pleasurably with each other.

As seen from responses to a UNESCO survey as well as in the inter-views, this sense of personal development is combined with enjoyment.[25] The women study *chadō* because it is fun, as the following responses show: "It looked like fun and I thought I would enjoy it. There was a *chadō* club when I went to *jogakkō* (high school equivalent through 1945). When I went to the club and saw everybody doing it, I wanted to learn also" (a woman who later became a *chadō* teacher). "I liked the atmosphere. Since I tend to be scattered around my daily life, I love the tranquillity and calm feeling rising inside of me during *temae*" (a teacher). "My family says that I look the happiest when I practice tea. As for myself, it is an enjoyment and also a hardship. It is a part of my life and I cannot think of a life without prac-tice" (a widow). "I became interested in the beautiful movements and I wanted to do it myself" (a young woman).

MALE-FEMALE RELATIONS AND PERCEPTIONS OF STATUS

Chadō reflects the rest of Japanese society, as Smith illustrates, in that it is male dominated.[26] For most of its history it was an exclusively male art form.[27] In the *iemoto* system, the top positions, some of which are inherited, are reserved for men.

The *iemoto* system is a network of relationships among teachers and students. The head of the school is a hereditary position at the top. The head is surrounded by teachers who were students and disciples of his father and over time adds his own male students to this group. In Urasenke, these male students are referred to as *gyotei* and are responsible for carrying out the wishes of the head of the school. They also teach students of their own, who in turn are considered students of the head. Some of the *gyotei* inherit their positions from their fathers and some are given the rank by the head of the school on the basis of services they offer. Some *gyotei* are appointed after being apprenticed in the Urasenke program. They are house boys who serve in the grand master's home and thus come to learn *chadō* from him directly. These positions are usually only available to men. However, an exception to this rule was Hamamoto Sojun Sensei, a woman *gyotei*, who gained this rank because she was appointed as teacher to the present grand master when he was a young child. He honored her as his teacher and adviser until her death a few years ago.

For most of its five-hundred-year history, *chadō* has been an activity for men. Women were not allowed to teach, perform publicly, or receive certification (permission to study and perform tea ritual) until after 1894. Given the relatively short period of time in which their participation has been accepted, it is interesting to note that the art in modern times is predominantly identified with women.

Since 1894, when women were first allowed to become teachers and perform in public, they have come to constitute eighty percent of the membership.[28] As the Urasenke school has moved to take advantage of the interest of women, it has created new organizational structures and activities. This has provided professional training and leadership positions for women. Men's dominance of leadership positions is predicated upon the idea that women are not able to devote one hundred percent of their time and talent to *chadō* because their energies and loyalties belong first to family obligations. This idea is being challenged by a number of women (usually unmarried or widowed) who have demonstrated a commitment and ability similar to those of men. Often these positions are in newly developing areas such as teaching abroad and in new organizations such as the group formed to teach *chadō* in English. Male students interviewed indicated no reluctance to study under female teachers or any difficulties in accepting direction from female students in superior positions.[29]

In other social and work situations in Japan, the act of preparing and serving tea to another is an expression of deference and dependence and viewed as a symbolic act expressing the asymmetry between the sexes. Within *chadō* itself, it does not have the same connotation. The host and guest roles are held by either men or women, and considerations of rank do not usually determine who takes these roles, especially during the lesson. *Chadō* in the tea room does not present many situations in which women as status inferiors are required to celebrate men's status superiority through the performance of tea ritual.

The dichotomy between public and private spheres of activity is an important factor in assessing the activities of women. The public arena has often been reserved for men. Access to this arena has become a goal for women and a measure of women's success and acceptance in wider society. However, the expanding sphere of women's activity and acceptance in the public arena sometimes leaves the impression that men and their activities are the standard by which women's activities and worth are measured—that there is greater value in succeeding in the public rather than the private arena. This view is not necessarily shared by women interviewed in this study, who identify as drawbacks of public recognition its numerous duties, obligations, and tendency to leave individuals open to criticism. When the product of the art is the self rather than an object from which one can psychologically distance oneself, the scrutiny of the public may be unwelcome. Many women indicated that they prefer to be privately known among friends and acquaintances as artistic and cultured rather than have any great public renown. They prefer to limit their public activity to the local community or the world of the practitioners of *chadō* rather than enter the public world of media and institutions. Those women who were professionals and who as members of the Sen family had a widely recognized public identity were not unwilling to have influence and power to use what they had, but they did desire to be less under scrutiny and free from criticism of their actions.

CONCLUSION

Chadō, an interactive art that develops skills in nurturing and supporting others, developing the self, and creating a tranquil environment, is a popular way for women to spend leisure time because it offers avenues for creativity and enjoyment. Women augment and support their roles as wives and mothers while they socialize with other women in a beautiful setting away from some of the demands of these roles. They attain social recognition for their talents and taste in a limited and comfortable sphere. Traditional arts enable these women to fulfill social demands while engaging in an activity they find personally rewarding. *Chadō* does not appeal to all women but it has an appeal to many who support the school financially through the fees they pay for lessons and the purchases they make of utensils and kimono. To understand the lives of women in Japan, it is necessary to see how choices such as studying *chadō* in their leisure come not only from their understanding of their place in society and the requirements of their roles as wives and mothers, but also from their desire for personal identification as talented women. As women redefine their lives and situation in society, *chadō* may receive less of their support.

NOTES

1. I use the term *chadō* to refer to the tea ceremony as an art form as practiced by the Urasenke school of tea. There are many Japanese words that translate to "tea ceremony" in English. *Sadō* is the common generic word used to refer to the practice of making tea. The term *chadō* is used to distinguish it as an art form and subject of study. Currently Urasenke is using the term *Chanoyū* (literally, hot water for tea) to refer to the tea ceremony, but the term *chadō* was predominantly used while I was doing my research. The ceremony is also sometimes simply referred to as *ocha* (tea) by practitioners. The "Golden Age" of *chadō* as defined by Rand Castile in *The Way of Tea* (Tokyo: Charles Tuttle, 1976) and others, is identified as the sixteenth century when *chadō* had its origins in the practice of Sen Rikyu and others. However, today enrollment in schools of tea is greater than at any time since World War II. Urasenke, which keeps its membership records in a computer file, claims two million adherents in Japan and abroad. However, it is not possible to verify these figures because Urasenke, like other schools, does not open its records to outsiders. There are approximately forty-five branches and numerous study groups (affiliations that are recognized and often receive support from Urasenke headquarters) outside Japan. Most are located in the United States and Europe; there are also groups in Russia, China, Korea, Thailand, and South America.

2. *Chadō* and other traditional Japanese arts are practiced by different schools that are the hereditary province of a particular family. The Urasenke school of tea is the province of the Sen family, and the position of grand master is inherited through the male lineage in that family. The women of the Sen family are important in the popularity of *chadō* and the position that *chadō* has acquired as a socializer of women. Yumyosai's (1852–1917) wife, Yukako Shinseiin (1850–1916), was instrumental in promoting *chadō* as part of women's training by having it included in the curriculum of the newly established girls' schools; Sen Sōshitsu, ed., *Chanōyu: The Urasenke Tradition*. trans. Alfred Birnbaum (New York: Weatherhill, 1989), 49. Sen Kayoko (d. 1980), mother of the present grand master, Sen Sōshitsu XV Hounsai, was also instrumental in promoting *chadō* in Japan and abroad, particularly in Hawaii, and in designing tea sweets, utensils, and ritual. Sen Tomoko, wife of the current grand master, is also active in promoting *chadō* as principal of the Urasenke Senmon Gakkō (Urasenke training school); she presents *chadō* throughout Japan and has created a new tea sweet. Shiotsuki Yaeko, older sister of the present grand master, has her own teaching locations in Tokyo and has published, at last count, thirty books on Japanese etiquette and various other topics; she travels, giving lectures on *chadō* and etiquette.

3. The initial outlay for lessons is small. To begin studying, all a student needs is *kaishi* (paper on which to place sweets), *sensu* (a small folding fan), and *fukusa* (a

small square of cloth, usually silk for wiping utensils), which are sold as a set with a small carrying case. The cost of lessons depends on the status of the teacher and the frequency of lessons and is about ¥3,000–5,000 per month (roughly $30–$50 in 1995). As the student progresses, she will be encouraged to attend more frequently and to purchase new wiping cloths yearly (they wear out). She will not be expected or encouraged to acquire tea utensils unless she wishes to teach. She will be allowed to come to practice in Western clothes, but will be encouraged to wear kimono, especially if she plans to participate in any public presentations, because the movements will be affected by the wearing of kimono. Because kimono must be worn for public presentations, women should be comfortable doing *temae* (tea ritual presentations) in kimono.

4. Neil H. Cheek, Jr. and W. R. Burch, Jr. *The Social Organization of Leisure in Human Society* (New York: Harper and Row, 1976), 91.

5. *Ibid.*, 156.

6. *Ibid.*, 130.

7. For most women who go beyond high school, the intervals are 6 (elementary school), 3 (junior high school), 3 (high school), and 2, reflecting junior college rather than university.

8. While I was doing research in Japan for my dissertation, my son (then aged eleven to thirteen) also took lessons with two of my teachers from the Urasenke Senmon Gakkō. At first he studied with a group that included a foreign graduate of Midori Kai (a program teaching *chadō* to non-Japanese at the Urasenke headquarters), an English teacher at the school, a seller of tea utensils, and myself. Later he studied with a group that met in the evening and included an office employee of Urasenke (who was the daughter of the owner of a small store), two women who were wives of salarymen in their late forties and early fifties, a retired college teacher in his sixties, and two girls of farming background who were current students at the Senmon Gakkō.

9. A. L. Sadler, *Cha-No-Yu: The Japanese Tea Ceremony.* (Tokyo: Charles Tuttle and Rand Castile, 1962); Castile, *The Way of Tea.* I used three main research methods: participant observation (personal experiences as a student attending Urasenke Senmon Gakkō in Kyoto from 1983–1985), in-depth interviews with thirty teachers and fifty-five students in several sites in Kyoto, Tokyo, and Yokohama, and observations of teaching and other situations relevant to the topic, such as attending gatherings for tea (*chakai*) and public presentations of tea at temples and shrines (*Okencha* and *Okucha*) by Grand Master Hounsai. All teachers and students interviewed were observed in the lesson setting at least once, and many were observed as often as five times a week. The teachers ranged in age from thirty-three to eighty-two. The students included those training to be professionals and those who considered themselves amateurs and ranged in age from sixteen to sixty-five. The opportunity to interview and observe the teaching of *chadō* in these various settings has not formerly been open to researchers. *Chadō* is a private activity. The support of the grand master and the Sen family was instrumental in gaining access and completing the interviews. Without their support, it would not have been possible.

10. Settings for observation and interviewing were chosen on the following criteria: distance from the Sen family's direct observation and control, size of area

(large city, rural), intensity of study (professional training or amateur; daily, weekly, or sporadic lessons), and type of study situation (institute, junior college, temple, private home). See Barbara Lynne Rowland Mori, "The Tea Ceremony: A Transformed Japanese Ritual," *Gender & Society* 5, no. 1 (March 1991): 86–97; and "Chadō: A Symbolic Interactionist Analysis of Transmission, Adaptation, and Change." (Ph.D. dissertation, University of Hawaii, 1988).

11. Herbert Blumer, *Symbolic Interactionism* (Princeton, New Jersey: Prentice Hall, 1969). Joel Charon, *Symbolic Interactionism: An Integration* (Englewood Cliffs, New Jersey: Prentice Hall, 1985). Barney G. Glaser and Anselm Strauss, *The Discovery of Grounded Theory* (Chicago: Aldine Publishing, 1967); and *Theoretical Sensitivity: Advantage in Methodology of Grounded Theory* (Mill Valley, California: Sociology Press, 1978). Erving Goffman, *The Presentation of Self in Everyday Life* (New York: Doubleday, 1959); *Encounters: Two Studies in the Sociology of Interaction* (New York: Bobbs Merrill, 1961); *Behavior in Public Places: Notes on the Social Organization of Gatherings* (New York: Free Press, 1963); and *Frame Analysis: an Essay on the Organization of Experience* (Boston: Harvard University Press, 1974). John Hewitt, *Self and Society: A Symbolic Interactionist Social Psychology*, 3rd ed. (Boston: Allyn Bacon, 1984). John Lofland, *Doing Social Life: The Qualitative Study of Human Interaction in Natural Settings* (New York: Wiley, 1976). Bernard N. Meltzer, John W. Petras, and Larry T. Reynolds, *Symbolic Interactionism: Genesis, Varieties, and Criticism* (Boston: Routledge and Kegan Paul, 1975). Howard Schwartz and Jerry Jacobs, *Qualitative Sociology: A Method to the Madness* (New York: Free Press, 1979). Sheldon Stryker, *Symbolic Interactionism; A Social Structural Version* (Menlo Park, California: Benjamin/Cummings, 1980).

12. One of the concerns I had as a researcher was the ability of an outsider to accurately represent the lives and experiences of the women, particularly because Japanese is not my native language. To deal with language concerns, I had my interview transcripts and translations reviewed by native speakers. In almost every setting, I discovered my subjects had their own way of testing my knowledge of *chadō* and its practice before granting interviews or allowing further observation of the group. In almost all instances, my affiliation with the Sen family was verified and I was asked to make tea. As I had no difficulty in getting interviews and often teachers and students who were interviewed introduced me to others, I gathered that I passed their tests. In my reports, I have made every attempt to portray the women with integrity.

13. Learning to do *temae* and perform public tea gatherings requires a great deal of coordination among people and things. *Chadō* is seen as an opportunity to learn important managerial skills. Teachers mention to their students that learning to do a *chaji* (a four-and-a-half-hour meeting for tea, which includes several preparations of tea and food) requires all the managerial skills of a general in charge of any army. They note that Oda Nobunaga (1534–1582) and Toyotomi Hideyoshi (1536–1598), ambitious warlords of humble background, required their generals to learn it for this reason.

14. Lebra's interview subjects' comments on their perception of their mothers show that a mother's self-sacrifice was an important criterion for being seen as "good." Those mothers who indulged themselves or who did not have a difficult time were not described as "good." Takie Lebra, *Japanese Women: Constraint and Fulfillment* (Honolulu: University of Hawaii Press, 1984).

15. For a discussion on the role of etiquette in the creation of civilization, see Norbert Elias, *The History of Manners*, vol. 2 of *The Civilizing Process*, trans. Edmund Jephcott (New York: Pantheon Books, 1978).

16. For a discussion of the religious connotations of *chadō* practice, see Jennifer Anderson, *An Introduction to the Tea Ceremony* (New York: State University of New York Press, 1991) and Dorinne Kondo, "Symbolic Analysis of the 'Way of Tea,' " *Man*, n.s. 20, no. 2 (1985): 287–306.

17. Men who were interviewed most frequently cited improvement of job opportunities as their main reason for studying *chadō*. Young women often said they studied in order to improve their marriage prospects. Older women said *chadō* provided contacts through the teacher and fellow students to potential mates for their children.

18. Many women have access to their own money from savings before marriage, money given to them by their mothers, or from their own part-time employment.

19. The women who practice *chadō* often engage in making artifacts such as tea bowls, tea scoops, sewing bags for utensils, *kobukusa* (small squares of brocade on which hot objects or utensils are placed), *fukusa* (wiping cloths), and calligraphic scrolls, but this is all very secondary to the learning of *temae*.

20. Sen, *Chanoyu*. Sen-O Tanaka, *The Tea Ceremony*. (Tokyo: Kodansha International, 1983).

21. Kakuzo Okakura, *The Book of Tea*. (New York: Dover Publications, 1964), 61.

22. *Wa, kei sei, jaku* refers to the precepts of harmony, respect, purity, and tranquillity taught by Sen Rikyu, a founder of the Sen schools of *chadō*.

23. Shūichi Kato, "Notes on Tea Ceremony" in *Form, Style, Tradition: Reflections on Japanese Art and Society*, trans. John Bestor (Tokyo: Kodansha International, 1975).

24. Okakura, *The Book of Tea*, 40.

25. UNESCO, Asian Cultural Centre. *The Traditional Forms of Culture in Japan* (Tokyo: Taito Printing, 1975).

26. Robert J. Smith, "Gender Inequality in Contemporary Japan," *The Journal of Japanese Studies* 13, no. 1 (Winter 1987): 1–25.

27. Sadler, *Cha-No-Yu*.

28. Castile, *The Way of Tea*.

29. This does not mean there are no objections to the increasing presence of women in the art. Older men in the Urasenke headquarters are uncomfortable with women in positions of importance. Though many recognize women's skills in the art, they often feel that women—who are expected to be softer and politer—are not good at the in-fighting within the system to gain advantages for their constituencies. Some men are uncomfortable with the role of tea in "bride training," which they feel devalues the art form. They also feel that attention to the interests of women detracts from *chadō* as a discipline. However, *chadō* currently has more difficulty attracting men than women. Some believe this is because the profession has been devalued by the presence of women, but interviews with male students who did not continue indicates that it is the length of apprenticeship and the boring aspects of being held in minimal jobs with little content for years that causes men to drop out. In 1982, the grand master selected eight men

for special admission to the Urasenke Senmon Gakkō, with tuition and living costs (dorm fees) covered if they would enter the *mizuya* program (apprenticeship) after graduation. Only one of the eight did, and that person has recently dropped out. The reasons he gave for not continuing had to do with the menial tasks assigned (he was often made to water the street in front of the house or to wait for delivery of packages), lack of study provided (he hoped to be spending time learning new *temae* or improving the ones he already knew, but he was given no opportunity to do this), and indifferent treatment by older teachers. He made no mention of women's involvement or devaluing of the art as a reason for ceasing his apprenticeship. The feudalistic, Byzantine nature of the system seems to be more of a discouragement to men than is the presence of women, given the competing opportunities for employment in other better-paying occupations.

SIX

Producing Mothers

Anne Allison

In early July 1987, my son had just completed his first three months at a Japanese nursery school (*yōchien*). When I picked him up the day before summer vacation, his teacher instructed me on how to monitor David's behavior during the break: keep practicing skills he was learning at school, keep up friendships with children who attended the same school, and keep up the basic routines and schedules at home that are maintained in school. Saitō-*sensei*, the teacher, also mentioned that David was being given a calendar that we might use to chart his summer activities.

The calendar was cute, as such items are for Japanese children: brightly colored with anthromorphized animals brushing their teeth, putting on pajamas, and cleaning up toys. Accompanying it were stickers displaying different kinds of weather (cloudy, rainy, sunny) and different activities (playing, swimming, biking, tidying up), so that the events of specific days could be recorded. David and I marked some of his days in this fashion, but we regarded the calendar as more an optional amusement than an everyday routine and did not fill it in consistently.

Six weeks later, on the first day back from summer vacation, Saitō-*sensei* asked me for the calendar. Confused when I told her it was still at home, she asked if I hadn't completed it as had been expected by using the stickers and adding descriptions to mark what David had done each day during the vacation. We discovered, in talking, that I had missed the first few minutes of a mothers' meeting in which these instructions had been explicitly given. I had therefore misread the calendar's meaning, interpreting it as a gift rather than an assignment: its intended purpose was to monitor David's activities while away from school and provide the teacher with a record. I offered an apology for my negligence and Saitō accepted it, but she was implicitly chastising, pointing out that her job would be made more difficult now. Knowing what children did in their hiatus from school helped her to assess the problems they might encounter upon returning.

Even more serious than this missing information was the implication that the schedule and daily regimen of my child over vacation had been lax. If David had spent his break in too a loose a fashion, Saitō suggested, he would have problems reintegrating into nursery-school life. Mothers are expected to monitor the lives of students away from school in a manner that is monitored itself by the school authorities through methods such as these calendars. If and when a child slips, the responsibility lies with the mother.

School, as this incident helped elucidate, is a totalizing (pre)occupation in Japan: an endeavor that is not delimited to the school building or school day but, rather, infiltrates and shapes every aspect of the child's life. And mother, as my relations with a Japanese nursery school for fifteen months demonstrated almost daily, is the expected implementer of this extension of school practices into the child's home and playtime.

"KYŌIKU MAMA": THE EVERYDAY INSTILLER OF EVERYDAY EDUCATION

In this paper I examine the relationship between two institutions, school and motherhood in Japan, to see how this intersection is shaped by school ideology and practices and how it is experienced by mothers. Broadly I am interested in the syndrome of the *kyōiku mama* (education mother): the type of mother so committed to furthering the education of her child that she does everything from sharpening pencils, making midnight snacks, and pouring tea for a studying child to consulting with teachers, investigating the range of schools, tutors, and *juku* (cram schools) available, and even attending class herself in subjects where her child is deficient. *Kyōiku mama* is a term both of respect and reprobation: it conveys respect for mothers who are successful in seeing children through the competitive Japanese school system and reprobation for the pressure they consequently exert on children whose days, nights, and energies are consumed by study. *Mamagon* or "mother godzilla" is another term encoding only the second half of the *kyōiku mama* relation, condemning mothers who relentlessly police their children's study habits.

Here my focus is not on the entirety of the *kyōiku mama* phenomenon, a phenomenon that has arisen since World War II in the era of economic rebuilding, national mobilization of the school system, and urban demographics that have encouraged close mother-child relations in which women supervise the education of their children, often single-handedly in the absence of hardworking husbands. My aim rather is to look at one phase of the *kyōiku mama* life cycle: a mother's role when her child enters nursery school. I investigate the interrelationships between school and mother in producing the behavior of "education motherhood" and pursue two questions: How does the school manage, shape, and monitor a woman's behavior in her role as mother, and how do women experience the expectations placed on them by the school system and the educational demands of Japan's super-competitively schooled society?

I have chosen the nursery school as the site for these investigations despite the arguments made by such scholars of Japanese education as Lois Peak. Peak minimizes the importance of the mother's role in the socialization of children to school, asserting that "Japanese believe that the home and the school are so dissimilar that it is difficult for the family to teach the behavior the child will need in the classroom.[1] In Peak's view, the school provides the atmosphere for *shūdan seikatsu* (group life), which is the key structure to such institutions as the Japanese workplace. She argues that *shūdan seikatsu* could never be replicated at home because children are central to family life and mothers indulge them as spoiled dependents. Being spoiled causes the children to engage in *amae*, a behavior inimical to that expected of students. Home, and specifically the child-mother relationship, is therefore not only inconsistent with the interpersonal dynamics of school, but also must be actively transcended and displaced in the school environment.

Emphasizing that nursery school is oriented far less to academics in Japan and far more towards the adoption of group dynamics that will be the foundation of all future educational and social endeavors for the child, Peak further discounts the role of mother. Her implicit assumption is that the energies of *kyōiku mama*–hood are activated primarily at the time of entrance exams taken by less than one percent of nursery school children entering elementary school and by only about six percent of children entering junior high school. Since the vast majority of Japanese youth do not sit for entrance exams before the age of fifteen, Peak claims that these earlier exams are far less important in the educational lives of Japanese children than is often assumed. Accordingly, she asserts that mothers play a significantly lesser role in socializing children to school life than the institution of the school itself.

Norma Field has argued a different position in a recent paper on the infiltration of school life into the sphere of what should, or once did, constitute play for children in Japan.[2] Presenting statistics on the high rates of stress-induced diseases in elementary school children and noting that half of all fourth through sixth graders attend cram school that lasts often until nine o'clock at night, Field depicts the rigors of a study regime that begins long before the age of fifteen and the children's first entrance exams. Field emphasizes the habituation of test taking that even young children are subjected to as preparation for the major tests they will take upon entrance to high school and college.[3] Every skill and subject they are taught involves barrages of tests, exercises that instill in the child an "atomized, mechanistic mode" of acquiring knowledge through cramming (Field 1992, 22). The effect, writes Field, is to inscribe a purpose and regimen into every activity; even play is organized to mold the child into a good student.

In contrast to Peak, Field believes that it is the anticipation of entrance exams that determines how Japanese children are treated, instructed, and managed at even the early stages of their educational careers. Field argues that children are expected to perform as early as "age zero" (she cites the popular books of Iibuka Masaru who urges mothers to educate children even in utero), an expectation that seeps into all domains of a child's life (Field 1992, 9). Concluding that childhood has disappeared in contemporary Japan, Field notes the absence of any activity, relationship, or domain that offers a reprieve to the child from the pressures to perform. Performance thus becomes interminable. The realm of mother and home become not an antidote to school, as Peak suggests for every stage except that of taking entrance exams, but rather the very mechanism for extending study management into realms outside school.

Making performance continuous and insinuating it into the child's daily life is an effect of Japan's *gakureki shakai* (academic pedigree society). The careers of adults (even women who assume roles as mothers) depend almost entirely on the colleges they attend, which depend upon the passing of entrance exams before college and high school, which depends in turn on the schools they attend as children.

No matter how one assesses the *gakureki shakai*—as the foundation of Japan's economic prowess built up from the ashes of wartime defeat or the great price extracted from Japanese citizens for living in an economically secure but competitive society—few dispute its dominance in that society or the consequences for those who are unwilling or unable to meet its demands.[4] Children learn at an early age the connection between their success as students and their future success as adults in the networks of work and social status. My argument here is that mothers play a pivotal role in both embedding into the child the continuous study and performance patterns of a *gakureki shakai* and offer the child a measure of emotional security and intimacy with which to survive these demands.

My position takes something from the arguments made by both Lois Peak and Norma Field: from Peak, the notion that mothers and home give children a special attention that schools can and will not, and from Field, the notion that daily study routines that exceed the dimension of school and entrance exams mobilize children into the regime of a *gakureki shakai*. The position of mothers vis-à-vis the educational imperatives aimed at their children is, in my view, therefore contradictory; mothers impose a behavioral regimen onto the child consistent with that of school but outside its parameters, yet they also cushion the child from this regimentation with nurturance and comfort. Mothers are not unaware of these contradictions and often describe the anxiety and resentment they feel at being compelled (by the school, society's demands, and husbands or mothers-in-law) to push their children into habits of study and performance that they then try to make easier with treats, indulgences, and creative pleasures. One effect of this double-edged mothering, for both mother and child, is to make desirable that which is obligatory: to encase the tasks of learning and performing in acts of love and play so pleasant that they disguise and thereby instill the tasks at hand.

THE DISCIPLINE OF SUMMER VACATION

Diverse media strategically advise mothers how to cultivate desirable behaviors in children. Newspaper columns, special television programs, books, mothers' magazines, articles in children's magazines and comics, and handouts from school with directives or hints for mothers all convey messages that display a high degree of ideological consistency. One of the most basic premises of all this mother-focused discourse, no matter what the age or level of the child, is that mothers need to direct the child's energies in ways that will make learning at school easier and more productive.

An article entitled "Summer Discipline Strategies for Hurrying a Child's Independence" appeared in a popular mothers' magazine in August 1987.[5] This "independence" (*jiritsu*) is not the ability or inclination to chart one's own course and act without the help of others, but rather the ability to internalize certain habits of self-maintenance that are expected of students. My reading of this article coincided with the end of summer vacation and the reprimand I received from David's teacher for failing to complete his summer calendar. Interested, I found the discussion consistent with the emphasis Saitō-*sensei* had placed on maintaining the "flow" of school life during vacation to avoid disrupting a "rhythm" of patterns and routines needed while school is in session (Kitsumura 1987, 26). Curious that this very consistency with school was encoded in the word "independence," I began to understand that the meaning of this concept is heavily shaped by the demands and constraints of Japan's schooled society and addresses those behaviors needed in order to survive and succeed in it. In short, "independence," so often advocated in discussions about raising and training children in Japan, means the development of patterns, skills, and attitudes that enable the child to adopt and perform successfully the labors of school (and later, work).

Significantly, the word "discipline" (*shitsuke*) in the article refers not only to children but also to their mothers. A mother is supposed to instill discipline in her child by exhibiting it herself. Significant as well is the fact that the prime authority in "Summer Discipline Strategies" is a nursery school teacher, precisely the figure who monitors the child's relationship to school and mediates this relationship with the mother on an everyday basis when school is in session. The tone of this teacher's voice in the text is as subtly reprimanding as was Saitō-*sensei*'s when speaking to me of the calendar. The first point that Ariga-*sensei* makes is that "the independence of life rhythms begins by gaining strength in breakfast" (Kitsumura 1987, 26). Acknowledging that it is easy to slip into a more relaxed pattern over vacation, Ariga-*sensei* emphatically warns against this tendency.

> There are many cases of children losing the rhythm of nursery school life over summer vacation. The children will ask if they can stay up later because it is vacation, and the mothers will permit a new bedtime. But doesn't this cut a new pattern? If children stay up late they'll also sleep in later. . . . Pretty soon a chain has set in and the life rhythm has been broken. And if this continues for forty days, once September comes these children will be drowsy all morning long. (Kitsumura 1987, 26)

Her solution is for mothers to establish "fun" routines in the morning. Mother and child should participate together in morning exercises transmitted on a local radio station and share a hearty breakfast, over which they can linger and communicate as they rarely have time to do on a school morning.

Ariga-*sensei* warns against laxness. Recognizing that mothers welcome summer vacation partially because they do not have to make the elaborate lunches (*obentō*) that their children take to school, she says, "This feeling of liberation has a connection to being neglectful and careless" (Kitsumura 1987, 29). Criticizing mothers who make big dinners but scant breakfasts or who combine breakfast with lunch, she asserts that breakfast is "the source of children's energy, and if a mother neglects this she is taking something from her child's energy level" (Kitsumura 1987, 29). "Give breakfast meaning by communicating with your child," Ariga urges, and then outlines an entire list of techniques for routinizing the vacation days of both mother and child. In her advice, the two most important guidelines are scheduling activities in an orderly fashion over the break and maintaining a consistency between these summer routines and those of school. Accordingly she urges mothers to maintain friendships that their children have established at school by arranging playdates with these friends. Ariga acknowledges that mothers may be seeking a "liberation" from such activities, which can take place almost daily during the school year and consume vast amounts of the mothers' energy and time. "But a woman must think of what's good for her child rather than what's relaxing for her," she says. Children take pleasure in their friendships with others. Further, these interpersonal ties are what constitute the *"ningenkankei"* or human relationships of any social group in Japan, including the *shūdan seikatsu* first introduced at nursery school. Consequently, playdates during vacation are of critical importance for the children and a critical responsibility of the mothers.

Other behaviors that she addresses as desirable for establishing a child's "independence" include learning to pick up one's toys after play, wash hands after being outside, gargle, make friends, keep clean, and eat nutritious food. For each of these desired goals, the teacher offers strategies for their inculcation such as getting a child who has poor eating habits to help out in selecting and preparing the ingredients for healthy meals. The suggestions are often ingenious and elaborate, such as the "trick" Ariga used herself with a son who liked trucks but hated washing his hands. She made a path out of masking tape from the door of their house to the bathroom so he could continue to drive his trucks from outside to the sink, where the chore of handwashing became coupled to, and transformed by, a play that he liked. Ariga points out that this technique worked far better than simply ordering the child to clean his hands.

In the same vein, she encourages mothers to do whatever is necessary to make a particular chore or routine pleasurable and fun for the child. If gargling is to be started the next day, for example, she suggests that mothers go out and buy a cute new cup with which to begin and associate the process. Such a technique is preferable to merely ordering a child because the former, by making a routine "feel good," is more effective. Mothers should underscore this "feel good" quality by articulating it in words to the child: "When you wash your hands, it feels good, doesn't it?" (Kitsumura 1987, 34). Finally, Ariga-*sensei* speaks of transforming one's house so that it mimics important features of the classroom. The rationale is that spatial and physical consistency will facilitate the habituation of certain routines for the child. "There is a way to make the habits followed at nursery school continue into the home. In short, let's make the conditions the same in the bathroom [for example] as at school. Put towels at the same height. This makes a big difference. Children who see this will follow the same habits as at school" (Kitsumura 1987, 34).

By the end of this article, I was exhausted by merely imagining the various strategies recommended by Ariga-*sensei*. I wondered to what degree such suggestions were taken seriously by Japanese mothers. How fully might they be implemented on a daily basis, and how much were they formed by expectations on the part of nursery school officials?

As I had already discovered, nursery schools (as somewhat distinct from day-care centers) expect a very committed and extensive involvement from mothers to assist children to adopt and adapt to the routines of nursery-school life.[6] Nursery-school policy implicitly assigns to mothers the role explicitly articulated by Ariga: mothers must make habitual and desirable such routines as eating one's lunch, cooperating with others, following a teacher's rules, and keeping clean. The purpose is to make the integration into school easier for children. The place, space, authority, and practices of school life are given a prior and superordinate position. Mothers are to make this goal realizable and assimilatable for children. In doing so, they act as culturally constructed mothers and self-sacrificing managers of home, family, and children.[7] In other words, an ideology of motherhood is linked to and adopted by an ideology of education and productive performance instituted through a school system. I now turn to the subject of how a nursery school issues both recommended strategies and compulsory directives that presuppose as well as construct this mother-school link.

PRODUCTIVE MERGENCES:
MOTHER'S LOVE AND SCHOOL'S DISCIPLINE

In April 1987, my family moved to a middle-class neighborhood thirty minutes from downtown Tokyo. I would be conducting a postdoctoral research project in this setting on the interrelationships between domesticity and motherhood, examining how women assigned to the domestic sphere manage and are managed by this role. My main interest was not the gendered division of labor per se: the fact that work as a career is still constructed as primarily a male role and domesticity is still constructed as primarily a female role, even as women enter the ranks of the labor force in ever-increasing numbers and a new antidiscrimination law forbids the hiring and promotion of workers on the basis of gender.[8] Rather, given that the domestic sphere has continued to be feminized in this stage of industrialization and late capitalism in Japan, I was interested in how this domestic feminization is both shaped by institutional relations and managed and experienced by a class of women positioned most clearly within domesticity—married mothers who are not working outside the home.

Putting my son in a local nursery school proved fortuitous for my research. I made contacts that developed into interviewee groups, and equally important, I became involved myself in the institutional environment of a nursery school.[9] From this position I could observe and participate in the routines of motherhood centrally organized and directed by the school. I learned how crucially determined and organized mothers' lives are by the school system their children enter and also how creative and tireless most mothers are in carrying out this school-ordered labor in the home. Here I draw on the data and experience I acquired in the context of "Yamaguchi Yōchien" as mother-anthropologist in 1987 to 1988 to discuss what I perceive to be a dialectical relationship between home (mother) and school.[10]

I intend to be neither totalistic nor exhaustive in my presentation. Yamaguchi Yōchien is a private school in a middle-class neighborhood that caters to families with stay-at-home mothers. The mother-school-child dynamics would be realized differently in day-care centers, which cater more to mothers who work outside the home. Although my remarks are specific to this school and environment, the ideological behaviors and expectations for mothers are duplicated in principle, if not exactly in the same forms, elsewhere in Japan.

Before being accepted into Yamaguchi Yōchien, every child must undergo an interview at the school along with the child's parents.[11] On the day of our appointed interview, the principal (*enchōsensei*) greeted us, spoke briefly about the school, and then called David's teacher (Saitō-*sensei*) into the room. Almost immediately Saitō-*sensei* turned to me, rather than my husband, and pointed to the booklet entitled "Guidebook to Entering School" ("Nyūen no Shiori"), which was at the top of a huge pile of introductory materials. Skipping the first page ("Goals to aim for before entering school," a list of skills and behaviors a child should have mastered before entering school), Saitō turned to page two and the heading "Things to Prepare at Home."[12] Included here were four categories: things used in transit from home to school, such as shoes, boots, overcoats, and raincoats; meal-related items, such as a cup, napkin, chopsticks, *bentō*-box (*bentō* are lunches contained in the box), and *bentō*-bag (the bag in which to put the *bentō*-box); classroom-oriented items, such as a hand towel, a bag to carry back and forth from school, a bag for inside shoes, a bag for gym clothes, and a smock to wear inside school; and dusters. During the time we spent talking Saitō focused on two subjects: the things I needed to make for David before he started school and the places on his belongings where I needed to attach his name labels (listed on page six under the heading "Method of Attaching Badges"). Saitō-*sensei* was animated as she spoke—friendly, welcoming, and engaged. The matters of which she spoke, however, were almost exclusively ones of regimentation: how the child's clothing and belongings must conform to school standards and how (implicitly) this conformity must be carried out by and through the mother.

At home I reopened the pages in the guidebook that Saitō-*sensei* had so insistently pointed out and realized the enormity of the tasks at hand. Not only were there a number of specific items to purchase, make, or affix labels to, but many of these were specified further in terms of dimensions or materials. For the hand towel (*otefuki*), we were advised to use towel material but make it in the size of a handkerchief, thirty centimeters from tip to tip, with a hoop at one end for hanging. We needed to make four hand towels, two for everyday use and two for reserve. I wound up buying two towels and remaking them into the school *otefuki* because I could find no such item with the required details in the shops. Later other mothers said that some of the nursery-school paraphernalia is indeed available for purchase, but that a "good" mother will still make as much as she can on her own.

Another item, the *tesage*—according to the guidebook, the bag used to "carry all those things that the school-dispensed satchel [*kaban*] cannot"[13]—proved to be the most complicated object and an arduous task for me, since I lacked a sewing machine and other mothers to advise me on how closely to heed the specifications in the guidebook. The bag was to be thirty centimeters high, forty centimeters long, five centimeters in depth (so that it can stand upright), have a handle, and be made out of a thick piece of cloth. Mothers were advised to "please make an easy-to-use thing with your own hands." Similarly the bag for gym clothes (*taisōgibukuro*) was to be thirty centimeters long, twenty-five centimeters wide, and have a drawstring that pulls to one side. The bag for indoor shoes (*uebakibukuro*) was requested without specific dimensions, as were the meal items and the two dusters (used to clean the room—an activity that all children are expected to participate in). Smocks, as I learned fortunately in time, could be purchased at the school; for those making them by hand, the design and positioning and number of pockets were designated.[14] Labels needed to be attached to or written on all these items. What should be written (class and name in some cases, just name in others), where precisely it should be affixed (lower left corner on bags, lower right corner on any piece of clothing, and in the middle on the towels and indoor shoes), and what size it should be (eight by four-and-a-half centimeters for gym clothes) were clearly spelled out.

As is apparent to the reader, a mother's involvement at this preliminary stage of "readying" the child for school is already extensive and heavily prescribed. Why precisely the involvement and preparation are so elaborate and why the elaboration comes in the form of specifying precise dimensions can be explained in part by the school's desire to homogenize the children by making their dress and belongings uniform and in part by the school's desire to impose order, any order, on the children as their entry into a new disciplinary regime. That this initial regimentation takes place in the arena of the personal—things worn on bodies and things that accompany bodies from home to school—signals an ordering of the child at a level that is not only everyday and ordinary but also individual. As Foucault has written, social order is inscribed on a person's body;[15] so too is the new order of the educational regime written into the very things that come into closest bodily contact with the child: shoes, gym clothes, shoulder bags. These accoutrements, as much as the school routine, render a wholescale and continuous transformation of the child into student. As Aida Yuji has written about the Japanese worker: "Certainly, looked at from the outsider's perspective, work doesn't remain within the finely demarcated hours of worktime. When actual worktime is over, people [in the West] become private persons. But in Japan work is not compressed into the eight hours of actual worktime as it is in America. For the whole 24 hours a day a worker cannot forget that he is a worker."[16]

The ideology of identity merging with work that Aida articulates for the adult Japanese male is similar and thus continuous to that of a child's identity being merged with school.[17] This mergence begins with nursery school and is operationalized by the mother.[18] She labors "with her own hands" to supplement and encourage a school order in the domain of the home that the child is leaving for the first time. It is not surprising then that transitional objects figure highly in the retinue of "things to prepare at home," objects that bring home into school as much as they bring school into home. It is also not surprising that these transitional objects are transportational: the plethora of bags that contain those essentials of nursery school life that move continuously between home and school. The *tesage* (large school bag), for example, is not only the most complicated and major sewing project for the mother, but it is also a container that must be filled and emptied daily. Every afternoon she must look inside the *tesage* and the *kaban* (school-issued yellow bag) for memos and dirty clothes that she must launder overnight. Every morning she must refill the bags with essentials for the day's schooling. And at the week's end on Saturday, she must launder smocks and handtowels and wash and scrub the indoor shoes (*uebaki*).[19]

Each day the mother must perform two other domestic jobs. The first is sending the child off in a clean and ironed uniform, which usually means ironing the jacket and pants or skirt of the uniform and laundering as well as ironing a white shirt.[20] The second is making the *obentō*, which are highly elaborate meals of five to six small courses that mothers spend as much as forty-five minutes preparing on the four lunch days of the week.[21] These *obentō*, like the child's uniform and equipment, are tended to at home but under the supervision of the school.

The school supervises the *obentō* in three ways. First, explicit rules and recommendations are made in speeches by the principal, talks with the teacher, and handouts and memos that are sent home from school. Such recommendations include that certain easy-to-eat foods be favored in the beginning, harder-to-eat foods be added gradually, no sweets or drinks ever be allowed, only chopsticks and *furoshiki* be used by third-year students,[22] heatable aluminum *bentō*-boxes be used during winter months, foods the child dislikes be added to eliminate "food fussiness," and *obentō* be nutritiously balanced. Second, *obentō* must be eaten in their entirety and in a timely fashion by the child. When children cannot perform this task, they are given assistance, encouragement, or reprimands by the teacher, and their mothers are consulted, as I was for almost the entire first two months of David's attendance at Yamaguchi Yōchien, to make an *obentō* that their children can consume.[23] Third, lunch is a ritualistic event with different stages: washing hands, singing the lunch song, giving thanks to Buddha and one's parents, pouring tea (done by the two "class helpers" for the day), laying out the *obentō*, eating, putting the *obentō* away, throwing away trash, and cleaning hands. This ritual blends personal discipline and collective life (*shūdan seikatsu*) so that everyone is expected not only to eat correctly but also to eat correctly as a member of a group.

The mother's role is to make an *obentō* that the child can easily, willingly, and happily eat. The mothers I knew (including myself, much to my own distraction and bemusement at times) would consequently expend great energy and time crafting an artistically appealing as well as nutritiously balanced meal for the child. The result is something like: a box with its three sections filled with two pieces of different kinds of tempura; a fruit salad of three strawberries, two grapes, and one banana cut into the shape of a caterpillar; and a smooth bed of rice embroidered by a thin line of seaweed finely crushed. There might be a small flag of Norway stuck into the rice, an aluminum muffin cup with two small hamburgers stuck together to make a bear, and two small containers, one with sauce for the tempura and one with ketchup. The *bentō*-box would be put into a *bentō*-bag; the utensils would be put into a utensil holder; a cup would be put into a cup bag; and a clean handkerchief would be added every day. All of this would then be put into either the *kaban* or the *tesage* and taken out by the child at school, who, it is hoped, would eat with gusto and contentment. When this doesn't happen, the teacher reports back to the mother to offer hints or warnings. In David's case, Saitō-*sensei* came to our house for an invited dinner with four *obentō* cookbooks—one for each season—with the suggestion that I study these for the help I obviously needed.

Schools expect mothers to interface home and school in other ways as well. At Yamaguchi Yōchien, mothers were expected to attend mothers' meetings about every six weeks, meet with the principal about three times a year, participate in the daily "farewell ritual" when children, teachers, and parents all line up to say good-bye to each other, and be involved in the school's three big annual events.[24] We were asked to instill and monitor proper behavior at home, make our children sociable by arranging frequent playdates with other Yamaguchi Yōchien children, and maintain certain schedules, routines, and activities consistent with those at school and conducive to developing specific skills.

Prior to summer vacation, Yamaguchi Yōchien's version of "Summer Discipline Strategies" was issued both verbally by the teacher and in two written directives. One directive, entitled "Promises for Summer Vacation," used child-oriented language accompanied by pictures. The other, entitled "The Way to Spend [*sugoshikata*] Summer Vacation," was directed to the mothers. The child's guideline, printed on heavy paper and obviously intended to be hung on a wall, listed a series of "let's" suggestions: "Let's get up early [there is a picture of a clock that reads 7:00]. Let's go to bed early [the clock reads 8:00]. Let's not forget our greetings. Let's brush our teeth after eating. Let's not overeat or overdrink cold things. Let's take a nap. Let's return home at 5:00. Let's pick up. Let's wear a hat in the sun. Let's not run out in front of cars. Let's play outside."[25] The handout to mothers listed sixteen specific behaviors to ensure that children upheld, including keeping an early bedtime, restricting snacks between meals, participating in radio exercises, brushing teeth after eating, obeying traffic rules, picking up one's belongings, and continuing to practice joining hands before and after meals. The phrase used under the subheading for behaviors concerned with health was: "Let's live according to correct rules" (*kisoku tadashii seisakatsu o shimasho*). "Correctness" was clearly an ideal that the school did not want to leave to chance or individual interpretation.

WOMENS' EXPERIENCES AS EDUCATION MOTHERS

To my Western sensibilities, Yamaguchi Yōchien was engaging in overkill; too much of our lives was being advised or supervised by the school system. Or, to put this differently, how "correctly" my son was adjusting and conforming to the nursery-school regimen had become too dominant a concern in both my life and my relationship with David. As the hypothetical Westerner referred to by Aida in the quote above, I come from a social order where the boundaries between school, work, and home are more clearly demarcated and where domestic activities such as preparing a child's lunch and arranging playdates are considered personal and outside the school's authority. How, I wondered, do Japanese mothers experience the expectations, demands, and regulations placed on them by the school system in Japan? To what degree do they heed those demands, and how do they conceptualize the various relations and implications involved?

The data I use here are preliminary. I have selected responses from only a few of the thirty-five women I interviewed intensively and extensively over fifteen months; the full interviews will form the basis of a much longer manuscript on Japanese mothers. These interviews and the discussions I had with mothers in an endless and endlessly changing playdate network of children who visited each other's houses almost every afternoon after school revealed that few of the Japanese women I encountered expressed any overt criticism of the various directives put out by Yamaguchi Yōchien. Some would welcome a non-lunch day because of the respite this gave them from *obentō*, and some would complain occasionally of the constant laundering and scrubbing of their child's white shirts and white indoor shoes. Most of the women spoke of their daily schedules as "full," "busy," and "active" and mentioned having little free time to do anything unrelated to child or home. They said their bedtimes usually coincided with those of their children (typically 9:00) because women were too exhausted to stay up any later.[26] However, all this activity, incurred in part by the demanding routines of a child's nursery-school life, was rarely bemoaned or thought to be too heavy or excessive a price to pay for having a child attend nursery school. These women thought that they should be involved in their children's education, that this was their responsibility and not that of their husbands, and that the school had the authority to dictate and monitor quite specific behaviors for both them and their children.[27]

Most of the women with whom I spoke felt that, by staying at home, they gave their children a decided advantage in two ways. Their presence and support at home made going to school easier and happier for the children and made the nursery-school experience as valuable as possible in furthering the children's academic careers. These women viewed nursery school as a first step toward later learning, even if nursery school is not significantly academic itself. And because nursery school is important for the child's educational development, a mother's love, support, and energies in the school domain were deemed important. In these discussions, women revealed what I have called earlier a contradiction in the role of the so-called education mother: that a mother must both ensure that a child conforms to educational rigors and routines and also offer a cushion or prop with which to survive them. No woman articulated her position as contradictory or dialectical. A few did, however, specify particular events, practices, or behaviors at Yamaguchi Yōchien that concerned them and caused them to question how they, as mothers, should respond appropriately.

Noguchi, for example, told me that her son was experiencing stress over the upcoming Sports Day. A skill that he would have to perform on the day and that was being practiced daily at school was difficult for him, and his deficiency had been pointed out by the teacher. As a result, the child was now asking to stay home from school, which Noguchi had allowed one day, but did not want to permit routinely. She finally gave him the option of dropping out of school; since he was still four and only at the first-year level, she figured he could reenter the next year. But the child chose not to drop out because he did not want to stop seeing his school friends. Given that the boy would be remaining at school, Noguchi saw no solution to his problem over Sports Day except for him to endure it. Consulting with the teacher was unthinkable to Noguchi, for she feared that the teacher would regard her comments as criticism and act even less charitably toward the child.

Other mothers mentioned similar reactions to specific policies or specific teachers at Yamaguchi Yōchien. One day at Noguchi's house, four other mothers with children in David's class were gathered, and all except one expressed similar concerns about the upcoming Sports Day and the role Saitō-*sensei* was playing in it. Two other children were experiencing stress like Noguchi's child. The mothers' interpretation was that Saitō-*sensei* was working all the children too hard and was being particularly hard on those children who were not mastering the required skills quickly enough. Some of these children were being criticized in front of the other children, which is harsh punishment in a school system where the peer group is so central. Noguchi recounted another story about Saitō-*sensei*, who had been the teacher of her first son, now aged ten. He too had been deficient in a Sports Day activity; in the weeks of training leading up to the event, he had been routinely criticized both in front of the other children and the mother. On the day itself, Noguchi tried to greet Saitō and, hearing again of her son's failings, bowed deeply, along with her husband, for all the grief they had caused the teacher. Angry about Saitō's continued criticism, the Noguchis felt that they nevertheless could take no action because any complaint to the principal would be reported back to Saitō and be likely to make her more, rather than less, harsh on the boy. As for their son, the event deeply scarred him and, convinced that he lacked any aptitude whatsoever, he refused to participate in any group sports or physical education in school for years.[28]

Other mothers mentioned other behaviors, policies, or attitudes on the part of teachers that concerned them. Several were troubled by the schoolwide tendency to let children work out their own problems even if this meant that certain children were getting bullied by others. A handful of mothers complained about Saitō's tendency to play favorites. Three mothers in particular said that she was too harsh on their children: too critical and demanding and not as overtly nice and friendly as she was to other children. However, none of the mothers citing specific problems with Yamaguchi Yōchien indicated that they would take the matter up with either the teacher or principal. Their preference was to endure the situation by giving their children extra love at home or, in one case, considering transferring the child to a different school at the end of the school year. The common attitude was that encountering problems, hurdles, or difficulties at school is, to some degree, expected and, to some degree, must be regarded as a kind of challenge for the children. Hence, although these women were troubled by certain aspects of the school situation and concerned about their children's wellbeing, none were willing to either confront the school authorities or let their children stay home from school. The bottom line seemed to be not whether their children were always having a good or easy time at school, but whether school was adequately preparing them for later life (specifically, later school life). And on this score the mothers seemed in general agreement that Yamaguchi Yōchien was a good school.

On the issue of school authority, no mother explicitly complained of the school being too intrusive or assertive in its monitoring of a mother's role in her child's education. Occasionally, however, a woman would give an example of how she had been criticized for some failing. One woman who worked in her mother-in-law's rice store was reprimanded for not spending enough time with her child, a criticism that was given in the context of reporting the child's problems in picking up a certain skill (jumping rope).[29] Other women were urged to exert greater efforts in getting their children to perform some behavior. Often women simply reported their conversations with teachers—conversations that could occur almost daily after picking children up at school. The women expressed concern that their children weren't mastering some skill, seemingly agreeing with the teachers' assessments both of the children's progress and the mothers' duty to help a child develop school-related skills such as jumping rope, eating lunch, washing hands, gargling, paying attention, and chinning on the uneven bars. Sometimes mothers appeared tense and nervous about continuing negative reports from teachers. Many mothers worried about the parent-teacher conferences (held approximately one month prior to the end of school) and about the home visitation, a visit the teacher makes to the home of each student in part to assess the home environment.

A number of my friends received rather negative reports of their children during the parent-teacher conferences. One mother was told that her daughter was effectively incompetent in every task, skill, and behavior expected of children her age. An example given was that she failed to draw triangles the "correct" way. When this woman (Tanaka) pointed out that Sachiko drew triangles at home all the time, she was told that her drawing order was incorrect. Privately my friend laughed, telling me that she found the teacher's worldview too rigid and her assessment of the girl ridiculous. Yet she did not tell the teacher this, nor did another friend whose son received a similarly bleak report that the mother also, in private, did not accept. In the case of Tanaka, she was concerned enough about the disjuncture between her pedagogical values and those of the teacher and school that she considered placing Sachiko in a university "feeder" school for first grade. This "escalator" system ensures that children, after completing the initial entrance exam to get in, will be passed until they graduate from high school. Tanaka hoped that pedagogy in such an atmosphere would be less rigid and a student's progress less rigidly assessed.

Some women expressed grave reservations about the educational system and its competitive effect in contemporary Japan. Iide said that she didn't think Japanese mothers had a choice: "Even if we have worries, we need to make our children study." She admitted that her husband's view was different, that he didn't care if their children attended university or not as long as they were happy and managed to make a living for themselves. But Iide disagreed with him: "We have no choice [*shigatta ga nai*]. All mothers in Japan need to 'hang in there' [*ganbaru*] and make their children do the same."

Another woman (Mori) in the same interview group expressed a different position.

> Even if we get our children to study hard, well, that's the image of us Japanese, right? A home where men are absent because they are working and mothers and children only concentrate on studying. . . . My worry is that we are just producing kids who fit into the mold. In school it is stressed that there is one right way to do things. So we and the school keep enforcing this idea, the one-pattern idea. Plus we have to keep teaching our children to follow authority and be subordinate to their superiors. They must learn how to agree with what others say and do: to go around saying *"hai hai"* [yes, yes] all the time.

Mori stated that she would not send her children to cram school in the future and merely wants education to be a process that enables her children to live healthy, self-reliant lives. "In this society, since one can't go very far without education, I hope they do okay in school. [But] I just want them to be average and able to face anything because they are boys. Even if they don't make it into a company, they can become bakers. As long as they work hard [*ganbaru*] and have a good nature."

The other three women in Mori's group were sympathetic to her position, and many other women I spoke with were similarly worried, distraught, or anxious about the school system and the challenges in their children's future. Most, however, expressed resignation in the face of a system that they were sure would determine their children's future whether they liked it or not. Given this situation, most also spoke of how they tried to make the chores of learning and adjusting to school regimen as pleasurable and endurable as possible. In this context, they referred to "skinship" (a westernized word): the importance of spending as much time with children as possible, which was linked to an understanding that school is an ordeal for a child. A mother's love and labors were thus connected to the difficulties a child faces in entering and attending school. The love is a type of compensation as well as incentive for the labor. I came to see that school is not expected to be, nor criticized for not being, a particularly happy time for children. School is about working hard, learning to adjust, and traversing a system of hurdles that is often unkind but inevitable. Thus the highly elaborate *obentō;* the beautiful *tesage;* the constant efforts to arrange and host playdates; and the endless devices used to get children to gargle, wash hands, greet others, learn to count, recognize characters, take turns, brush teeth, and practice skills being taught at school—all these are ways of both expressing maternal love and assisting a child to fulfill school's performative demands.

Although some women, as I have noted, could articulate conscious concerns and doubts about the school system, few women questioned the role they were expected to play in encouraging their children to perform. Only one woman clearly expressed personal doubts about the energies she expended that effectively entrapped her children within the performative circuit. She knew she was acting right as a mother, she said, but these motherly acts of sitting next to her older boy as he studied and making sure her younger son learned how to adjust to nursery school only pulled these boys deeper into a school system she was not as sure was so right. This woman, a model of the type of peppy and resourceful mother who completes every domestic chore with elaboration and turns every learning task into a game or adventure, had fallen, she confessed, into the throes of a deep depression.

CONCLUSION

My aim in this chapter has been to challenge the generalizing of the "education mother" syndrome and to question how real mothers, in the context of a Buddhist nursery school in a middle-class Tokyo neighborhood in the late 1980s, are expected and compelled to assist their children in adapting to school. Unlike those scholars who argue that the educational role played by mothers comes at a later stage in their children's schooling, I show that the institution of a school itself demands a much earlier involvement that expects mothers to carry an educational agenda into the very patterns and routines of daily life. It is at this level of daily life that children are situated into a performance structure and ethos that complements and thereby extends performativity learned at school. The mother, who must incorporate this continuous education into the vacations, playtime, and home is often burdened with feelings of anxiety and doubt. The role of *kyōiku mama*, by this assessment, is thus neither simple nor generated solely or even primarily by mothers themselves. Rather it is a relationship between mothers, children, and a school system that has been situated within the political and economic relations of Japan's postindustrial labor market. As Norma Field suggests, children are being programmed at ever earlier ages to assume a posture of productivity that will continue into later life. Mothers, I would suggest, are being programmed into and by the same model.

NOTES

1. Lois Peak, *Learning to Go to School in Japan: The Transition from Home to Preschool Life* (Berkeley: University of California Press, 1991), 6.

2. Norma Field, "Child Labor in Prosperity: The Implications of the Japanese Schooling Crisis" (paper presented at the Children at Risk conference in Bergen, Norway, May 1992).

3. Compulsory education stops at ninth grade, so all students take entrance exams upon entering high school.

4. For a critique of this principle, particularly with respect to the damage it does to children, see Horio Teruhisa, *Educational Thought and Ideology in Modern Japan: State Authority and Intellectual Freedom,* trans. Steven Platzer (Tokyo: University of Tokyo Press, 1988).

5. Kitsumura Ki, *"Yōji no Jiritsu o Hayameru Natsu no Shitsuke Sakusen"* (Summer discipline strategies for hurrying a child's independence) *NHK Okaasan no Kenkyūshitsu* 11 (August 1987). NHK is also the national (government sponsored) television station.

6. Boocock and Tobin describe some of the differences, both real and perceived, between nursery schools and day-care centers (*hoikuen*). Because entrance into the latter is determined by local municipal offices on the basis of a mother's work outside the home (Boocock states that the determination is made on the basis of need, but our family's "need" was denied in 1987 because I did not have a job that took me to an office for more than thirty-seven hours a week), day-care centers do not presume or demand a mother's involvement in her child's education as do nursery schools. This may be one of the major differences between the two, though Boocock argues that the differences of pedgagogy, care, and student organization are far greater than is commonly imagined. Sarane Spence Boocock, "Controlled Diversity: An Overview of the Japanese Preschool System" *The Journal of Japanese Studies* 15, no. 1 (winter 1989): 41-66; Joseph J. Tobin, "Komatsudani: A Japanese Preschool" *Preschool in Three Cultures: Japan, China, and the United States,* eds. Joseph J. Tobin, David Y. H. Wu, Dana H. Davidson (New Haven: Yale University Press, 1989), 12-71.

7. On the role of mothers demanded in preschool education, see also Fujita Mariko, " 'It's All Mother's Fault': Childcare and Socialization of Working Mothers in Japan," *The Journal of Japanese Studies* 15, no. 1, (winter 1989): 67-91. For other scholarship on Japanese preschools, see Tobin (1989) "Komatsudani"; Joy Hendry, *Becoming Japanese: The World of the Preschool Child* (Honolulu: University of Hawaii Press, 1986); and the entire winter 1989 (vol. 15, no. 1) issue of the *Journal of Japanese Studies* on "Social Control and Early Socialization." Thomas Rohlen's article "Order in Japanese Society: Attachment, Authority, and Routine" is particularly useful, and his analysis of the emphasis on routines within the classroom dovetails with the emphasis placed on a mother's monitoring of daily routines that I discuss here.

8. According to 1988 statistics reported in the *Asahi Shinbum,* sixteen million Japanese women work, one-third of them in part-time jobs. In service industries such as trade and insurance, more than half the workers are women. But only one percent of management positions are held by women, and only one percent of all women working hold managerial positions. A 1987 government white paper reported that women still manage the bulk of all housework in families where both adults have jobs outside the home (February 3, 1988: 12).

9. Because interviewing one-on-one seemed to make people uneasy, I arranged groups of three to six women who would convene, usually at my house, for sessions that lasted as long as four hours. Most of these groups met more than once, and one group met for twelve sessions.

10. "Yamaguchi Yōchien" is a pseudonymous name. *Yōchien* means "nursery school."

11. The interview usually takes place months before the new school year, which begins in April. David had been accepted in absentia because a friend, whose child had been the only other foreigner to attend Yamaguchi Yochien, wrote a letter presenting our case. The interview for us was then pro forma and constituted an introductory meeting.

12. There were ten "goals to aim for before entering school." These included seven skills the child should be able to accomplish on her own without a mother's help: getting up on time, going to bed on time, eating by oneself, going to the toilet, washing oneself, putting on shoes and clothes on by oneself, and separating from one's mother. There were three additional goals: develop a positive attitude about going to school and get rid of resistances such as "I don't want to go," abandon babytalk, and learn the route to school by going the same route everyday.

13. At our school, the *kaban* were yellow shoulder bags with the school's insignia printed on the front. Children could put into these *kaban* their *bentō* bags and other small items, including memos and directives sent from class.

14. At Yamaguchi Yōchien children wore uniforms to school and changed into smocks upon entering the classroom.

15. Michel Foucault, *The History of Sexuality, Volume 1: An Introduction,* trans. Robert Hurley (New York: Vintage Books, 1980).

16. Aida Yūji, *Nihonjin no Ishiki Kōzō* (The structure of Japanese consciousness). (Tokyo: Kodansha Gendaishinsho, 1972), 67.

17. Unlike Aida, I regard mergences such as worker and man and student and child to be compelled by concrete institutions such as corporate and educational practices. According to Aida, these behaviors emerge automatically in Japanese culture rather than as the effect of socialization.

18. I am speaking here of the child's mergence with school and student, but actually the mergence of a man with his work is also enabled by the domestic work that women perform as wives and mothers. Men can stay late at work only because they have wives who are tending to the home. Children and men who participate in these responsibilities assume, by definition, a different relationship to their place of work.

19. School runs six days a week in Japan. At Yamaguchi Yōchien class ran until 1:30 every day except for Monday and Saturday, which were short days (no-lunch days) ending at 11:30.

20. Uniforms are bought through the school in two sets: one for spring and summer and another for fall and winter. The winter uniform consists of a jacket and short pants or skirt; the summer one includes pants or a skirt with suspenders. Long-sleeved shirts are worn in the winter and short-sleeved in the summer. Hats change as well: felt ones for the winter and straw hats for the summer. Uniforms are changed on a designated day for both seasons unless the weather is extremely unseasonable.

21. The "o" preceeding *obentō* is the honorific. Lunch boxes were referred to as both *"obentō"* and *"bentō"* in the school setting.

22. *Furoshiki* is a traditional cloth used to wrap things. First- and second-year students may use *bentō* bags within which to place their *bentō*-boxes, but the third-year students must use the *furoshiki*, which, like chopsticks (versus forks), are considered both more difficult to use and more traditionally Japanese. For further discussion of this ideology see Anne Allison, "Japanese Mothers and *Obentōs:* The Lunchbox as Ideological State Apparatus," *Anthropological Quarterly* 64 (October 1991): 41-66.

23. I have written about this in detail and the entire process and ideology surrounding school *obentō* elsewhere. See ibid.

24. The three big annual events are the Dance Festival (*bon odori*), held in the summer, Sports Day (*undōkai*), held in the fall, and Winter Assembly (*seikatsu happyōkai*). Each entails rigorous training and preparation on the part of the children for approximately six weeks before the event.

25. There is almost an unwritten understanding that children should return home at 5:00 from playdates or playing outside their homes, which is the time that women often set out to do their shopping for dinner. In the neighborhood where we lived, a school chime went off at 5:00 and could be heard for blocks around. Friends in other neighborhoods reported the same phenomenon.

26. Many said, however, that they would get up later when their husband arrived home, usually to make him something to eat.

27. There was actually much discussion about gender roles in our group interviews. About one-third of the women mentioned a desire that their husbands participate more fully in child raising and—the flip side of this desire—that they could be liberated more often from the home and its duties. About the same percentage of women said they wished to work when their children became older. Almost all the others stated that they would pursue some activity—charity, hobby, further education—at some later point. Still, no one expressed a longing to exchange her own life as mother for her husband's life as worker.

28. A teacher in the third grade eventually got Noguchi's son to participate again by refusing to believe the boy's statement that he was totally inept.

29. The implication was that the mother should be practicing with her child at home, a suggestion that was also made to me when David had similar trouble with jumping rope.

SEVEN

Nurturing and Femininity

The Ideal of Caregiving in Postwar Japan

Susan Orpett Long

This chapter explores the Japanese cultural ideal of female nurturing. Historically created, the ideal has influenced several generations of Japanese women, serving as a standard by which they measure their behaviors, or by which they measure their rejection of "tradition." This ideal has also influenced several generations of Western views of Japan, creating a smokescreen through which we frequently misinterpret Japanese women's lives. While nurturant behavior may be an ideal, accepting the ideal as reality misses the elements of women's choices, the very real stress that accompanies nurturing, and the relationship between nurturing and power in Japanese society.

American descriptions of Japanese women since World War II have frequently focused on the importance of women's domestic roles as mothers, wives, and caregivers of the elderly. From the 1950s stereotypes of the subservient Japanese wife to the 1970s image of the perfect homemaker to the 1980s caricature of the "education mama," Japanese women have been presented in the West as nurturers. Attempting to demonstrate that change is occurring in Japanese society, the media report on single "office ladies" who prefer international travel to marriage, on housewives who take up golf, and on the rise of the career woman. But even these depictions rely on the stereotype of the "happy homemaker" with whom these "new women" are contrasted. The rejection of the ideal seems only to reinforce its importance.

We might ask why the ideal and its rejection continue to make "news" in the United States. Kuzume argues that these images may reflect more about American society than provide an accurate view of Japanese lives.[1] Is it because we are engaged in our own cultural debate about how the role of women relates to our concern for nurturance? Are idealized Japanese women held up to us as role models, and the aberrations presented as comic relief to our own cultural dilemmas? Or are they presented as objects from which we measure cultural distance?

Characterizing a group of people is always a problematic enterprise. In cross-cultural descriptions, some differences are overemphasized, whereas others are underemphasized. Foreign journalists and ethnographers may initially be overwhelmed by the differences from their own society, and in attempting to capture and explain these differences to others, they make implicit comparisons with what is familiar to them.[2] Yet that which is "familiar" may not be an accurate portrayal of their own society, but only of their limited experience of it. For example, an American career woman working in Japan may be struck with what she sees as a lesser commitment to career among Japanese women. These Japanese women may place their jobs lower on their list of priorities than her colleagues in the United States would. This implicit comparison is to a group of highly educated American professional women, yet a broader look at American society might suggest that women working at discount stores and on production lines make choices similar to those of their Japanese counterparts. Thus, the American career woman discovers difference in Japan, but the difference is not based solely on culture, since the "Japanese" attitude or behavior of which she had been unaware (or chose not to acknowledge) is also found among members of her own society. Frequently, it seems, the identification of difference involves value judgment, leading some to conclude that Japanese women are just a decade or so behind women in the U.S. and that they will eventually catch up to the seemingly higher status of women in the West.

If cross-cultural comparison overemphasizes differences between societies, it underemphasizes the existence of variation within a society. The lives of some women in Japan may approximate our models of them as exemplary nurturers. Others actively reject a nurturer's life style, and still others may wish to live in accordance with this cultural ideal but find themselves in circumstances that do not accommodate their dreams. The working class women described by Kondo and the wealthy women described by Lebra and Hamabata may hold similar views of femininity in the abstract, but in the reality of their day-to-day lives, the ideals take on different meanings.[3] To better understand the relationship between femininity and nurturance, we must look not only at the ideal, but at the variation in behavior and interpretation found in the reality of contemporary Japanese women's lives.[4]

To analyze the relation between nurturing and femininity in Japan, I begin by distinguishing between cultural ideals and lived experience. The ideal identifies mature women with feminine nurturing. In actual women's lives, people make choices regarding the extent to which that role will be carried out. Nurturing others is stressful as well as potentially fulfilling. The ideal may represent a form of oppression that keeps women from having a larger voice in society, or it may represent a realm of meaningful activity that allows them freedom from capitalist exploitation. Japanese women have many different perspectives on the relationship between nurturing and women's roles.

The identification of nurturing with femininity is neither biologically based nor an indelible aspect of Japanese culture. As with gender roles in all societies, that identification is a cultural ideal that is a product of the experiences of particular historical periods and particular social classes. This ideal influences the lives of contemporary Japanese women, not in a deterministic way, but as a tool of interpretation and evaluation of their own lives and of the lives of others. This chapter explores the influence of the cultural ideal of nurturance as it affects the lives of Japanese women in the 1980s and 1990s.

NURTURING IN JAPAN IN HISTORICAL PERSPECTIVE

"Nurture" refers to the process of raising or promoting the development of another. The English term suggests the meanings of feeding, fostering, training, and nursing. The Japanese term for "nurture" is *yōiku.* This is a word made up of two Chinese characters: *yō,* meaning to bring up or cultivate, and *iku,* to raise or bring up. As in English, it connotes feeding, fostering, and nursing. In both the United States and Japan, this term has become associated primarily with women's roles. Feminist literature on gender differences has argued whether this association is biologically based or socially constructed. Our own cultural mythology in the United States is that such gender differences are "natural," and some feminist writers have taken stands that seem to support this belief.[5] Others argue that nurturing roles are psychodynamically or socially constructed—that is, that men are naturally just as good at nurturing, but that they are discouraged from utilizing or expressing these abilities by differential socialization.[6]

The idea of nurturance is incorporated into the definition of the caregiver role. Many of the English-language studies of postwar Japan stressed that the primary role of adult women was to care for their families. In the "new middle class," the nuclear family predominated.[7] With husband as salaryman putting in long hours at the office, the wife spent most of her time in a separate sphere, concerned with managing the household, raising children, and supporting her children's academic and her husband's business careers. She did so not only by taking care of their physical needs, but through such activities as attending PTA meetings and shopping for the requisite seasonal gifts to her husband's superiors. These duties, together with rigorous standards of home cleanliness and management, turned her into a "professional housewife."[8]

In the 1990s, as life spans have lengthened, women today are increasingly likely to be caring for a frail parent or parent-in-law. And in recent years a much larger proportion of Japanese housewives have joined the paid labor force. But there is little evidence that their role of family nurturer has been lessened, shared, or voluntarily restricted.

Historical and early ethnographic studies suggest, however, that the association between women and nurturing may not have been so close in the past: from the Tokugawa period (1600–1868) through World War II, older children, mothers-in-law, and even fathers frequently had major roles in childcare, while the primary duty of the middle-aged woman was to assist in the household's productive labor, whether in growing food, producing goods in cottage industry, or engaging in commerce.[9] Elder care was limited in scope, given the fifty-year life expectancies in that era.[10] Rather than viewing the role of nurturer as a natural women's role, researchers in recent years have pointed out that in the Meiji period (1868–1912), there was purposeful government policy to create an image of Victorian genteel women while continuing to utilize female productive labor, a policy intended to improve Japan's image abroad and maintain social control during rapid industrialization and social change at home.[11]

One of the ways in which government leaders created this association between women and nurturance was by establishing in the Civil Code a particular type of family system, known as the *ie*. The *ie* was a multigenerational household that ideally continued beyond the lifetime of any individual member. All living members were legally under the authority of the male head of household. The household head thus had responsibility for arranging marriages for the household's members and for preparing them for adult economic roles. The structural and economic need for both an adult male and an adult female in each generation meant that women were trained to assume duties of household management, particularly in wealthier families.[12] A woman's reproductive role was assumed; training in her productive responsibilities continued under her mother-in-law's direction if she married into an established household. Succession often occurred at the death of the household head, but the retirement of the older generation was not uncommon, with the new head couple responsible for the welfare of the retired generation as well as that of their own children and other live-in relatives or employees. The model for the *ie* system was that of the Confucian-inspired samurai family of the Tokugawa period. Nonetheless, that model has continued to influence people's vision of the ideal well into the postwar period.[13]

The Allied Occupation eliminated the legal basis for the *ie* and established a new family ideology that included equal rights for women, equal inheritance by all children, and free choice of spouse and career. Over the postwar period, behavior and attitudes have gradually changed.[14] Since the latter part of the 1960s, the majority of marriages have not been arranged. The total fertility rate has decreased to an average of only 1.5 children, and among households containing members sixty-five years or older, the proportion of three-generation households fell from fifty-four percent in 1975 to thirty-seven percent in 1992.[15] Although very high in comparison to other industrialized countries, the rate of marriage for women has declined from a 1971 high of 10.5 per 1000 population to less than 6 in recent years. The divorce rate rose gradually from a 1963 low of .73 per 1000 population until the mid-1980s, when it briefly stabilized at about 1.3 and then began to rise again in the 1990s.[16]

These legal and demographic changes, however, have not eliminated some continuities with earlier family models of marriage, child rearing, residing with elderly parents, and dividing labor by gender. The Japanese public explored American child-rearing practices through the mass media, and some people undoubtedly tried them. However these have now been largely rejected as inappropriate for Japan. Infants are fed on demand, and children continue to sleep with parents or grandparents and are indulged by family members based on the folk wisdom that children "before seven [are] among the gods." In public opinion surveys, the majority of adults responded that their ideal family would be a three-generation family and that when parents were widowed or ill it was best that they be cared for by their children (or daughters-in-law).[17] Fifty-seven percent of those over sixty-five live with a son or daughter, the highest rate of coresidence in the industrialized world.[18]

Regardless of the type of courtship—"love" or arranged—many young people in the postwar period expect some degree of romance. However, decisions about marriage continue to be influenced by parents and to focus on the candidate's background, educational achievements, and potential to fulfill the gender-bound roles of breadwinner (for men) and mother and household manager (for women). Once children are born, most couples experience a greater separation of their daily activities, with the wife often retiring from paid employment at least until the children are in middle school.

The cultural ideal of nurturance is not sufficient to explain the continuity with the past. Women's focus on the nurturing role is reinforced by continued discrimination in the business world, despite constitutional and legal guarantees of equal opportunity and nondiscrimination. Companies may assert that discrimination against women workers is not technically based on gender but rather on seniority; because women retire more often than men to raise children or change jobs, they are likely to have less experience than men their age. Yet the companies' expectation that women will bear children and stop working to raise them, at least for a number of years, has led to the hiring of women in lower-track positions where pay, benefits, and responsibility are less than those of their male counterparts with similar educational backgrounds.[19] This must enter into the economic calculations of a family when deciding whether the wife should continue working or retire, and it reinforces the belief that marital roles are complementary. The wife may be more valuable to the family through support of her husband's and children's careers and through her provision of care for chronically ill elderly parents or in-laws. The cultural ideal of women's nurturing does not ensure that a woman will assume that role, but indirectly may make that her most rational choice.

THE NATURE OF NURTURE IN JAPAN

As an American woman, I have been struck in my observations by three aspects of Japanese nurturing. These are the emphasis on physical comfort, the avoidance of conflict in providing care, and the totality of the caregiving experience. I do not claim that all caregiving behavior in Japan is characterized by these features, but the words and actions of caregivers I have interviewed, surveyed, and observed suggest that these are important elements in understanding the nature of caregiving as a cultural ideal.

Caudill and his colleagues conducted studies of Japanese and American mother-child interaction in the 1960s. They found that the Japanese mothers responded to their infants' cries physically (picking up, feeding, coddling, and so on), whereas the American mothers were more likely to respond verbally to their infants' cries.[20] Dr. Phyllis Braudy Harris, a gerontologist, and I observed in Japanese nursing homes in 1990 that physical care (cleanliness, grooming, and so on) is excellent, but in most of the institutions we visited, there appeared to be less emphasis on the kind of mental stimulation that would be found in an American home providing similar quality physical care. In Japanese husband-wife relationships as well, American researchers have commented on the extent of physical care of husbands. Wives often assist husbands with putting on or taking off their overcoats, pay close attention to their physical welfare, and serve meals to them when they come home late or tea and snacks to them on weekends.[21]

The importance of "being there" as evidence of providing physical comfort was pointed out in a home nurse's comment to a woman caring for her sixty-five-year-old husband, who had black lung disease and required oxygen twenty-four hours a day. The patient and the visiting nurse were reviewing his most recent outpatient visit to the hospital. Despite the man's complaints, the physician had insisted that blood and X-ray examination revealed that he was doing well. "So," the man reported to the home nurse, "if the doctor says I'm doing well, how can *I* [assert myself and] say something is wrong?" Rather than respond to the patient, the nurse turned to his wife and said, "You should go with him to the doctor next time." When the husband protested that suggestion, the nurse continued to the wife, "You understand the [oxygen] machine well, but you haven't been to the hospital with him for a while, so you're not up on his current condition." Although the wife was providing excellent care for her husband at home, the nurse was gently criticizing the wife for not "being there."

Conflict avoidance emerges as a major cultural theme in studies of Japanese communication styles and social interaction.[22] Although conflict is frequently present, to express personal feelings such as anger or frustration is viewed as disruptive of human relationships.[23] To nurture is to shoulder the other's burdens, relieve stress, and create a calm environment. Anger and confrontation are thus antithetical to good caregiving. Anthropologist Steven Smith, who has studied alcohol use and abuse in Japan, tells the story of a woman who, in order to keep her alcoholic husband from embarrassing the family by going out to the liquor store in his pajamas, continued for years to go out to buy his sake whenever he so demanded.[24] Margaret Lock writes of a mother whose son had "school refusal syndrome." The son remained in the attic of their home, refusing to come downstairs. His mother continued to carry food up to him for two years.[25]

A woman I met when she was in her late thirties told us of her experience caring for her grandmother for six months. The grandmother was ninety-four years old, severely demented, and had a broken hip. The woman's husband did not help, and her daughter was studying for her high school entrance exam. "All of my energy was gone!" she told us. She then added that her grandmother wandered at night. "If I took her outside, she would eventually calm down and be able to go to sleep. I always took her out while my husband slept. He is a hard worker, with many responsibilities at his job." This woman saw her role as family caregiver, meeting the needs of her daughter for quiet study time, her husband for rest at home, and her mother-in-law for supervision. Performing her role maintained the peace of the household. Despite her own exhaustion, this woman would not confront any of them with her own problems or consider asking them to compromise their needs to help her.

The third aspect of the Japanese cultural ideal of nurturance is the expectation that caregiving is a totalizing experience. Nurturing children, husband, and elderly parents has been considered a woman's major role. Other obligations and desires should not be allowed to interfere with caregiving obligations. Because working women are expected to be home to prepare dinner and bath before husbands return, many work "part-time" (usually meaning four or five full days per week) for significantly less pay and no benefits. Women physicians I interviewed in the late 1970s frequently selected their specialties and practice styles to maximize the flexibility of their daily schedules; it was more important to meet family obligations than to compete for more prestigious and economically rewarding positions.[26] Anne Imamura notes that even women who do not work pursue leisure activities only when their housework and caregiving obligations are fulfilled, but that such free time is very limited.[27] Women who become involved in activities outside the home often justify their involvement as an extension of their role as parent, whether by becoming an officer in the school PTA, joining a consumer or citizens' movement, or taking a job to pay for tutoring for a child.

Caudill's study pointed out that the physical nature of comfort provided for infants was related to the fact that the Japanese mothers usually remained in the same room as their infant, rather than leaving them (even in sleep) in a crib in another room.[28] Several Japanese friends have commented to me that playpens used by many American families seem to them like prisons that contain babies and limit their contact with other family members. Although more common in recent years, babysitters were rarely used in the past, so that a stay-at-home mother stayed at home most of the time, taking the baby with her when she needed to go out. The perceived necessity of the mother's full-time attention to caregiving activities reflects something about the cultural ideal, even if individual women choose to work full-time, to hire babysitters, or to use playpens.

Caretaking of the frail elderly is similarly thought to require nearly full-time attention, not only when a parent or parent-in-law is demented and must be watched for reasons of safety, but also when a physically ill person demands continual attention. Again, elder sitters are rarely used. One woman interviewed was caring for an 83-year-old mother-in-law who was wheelchair-bound because of a broken femur, but was mentally alert. Since their marriage the woman and her husband have lived together with her mother-in-law in a small, suburban apartment. The husband is a truck driver. The caregiver complained of chronic back pain, and of her mother-in-law's physical and mental dependence on her:

> She's dependent on me, so she doesn't want me to leave the house. I only slip out for 15 minutes every few days to shop for groceries. She wants no visitors. My daughter comes, but only once or twice a year. So I have no help. My husband is no help at all with his mother.
>
> Since 1986 when she broke her leg, I have had a week's break twice when we put her in an institution for a "short stay." Once was for my daughter's wedding. The other time was for my brother-in-law's funeral.

The cultural ideal of providing care thus requires the full and undivided attention of the caregiver. In telling an interviewer that she goes for days without leaving her home, the woman quoted above is not only attempting to elicit sympathy but also conveying to us the quality of the care she provides for her mother-in-law as judged by Japanese cultural standards. Ideal nurturing thus seems to mean providing for another's physical comfort, avoiding the open expression of conflict, and the near complete attention of the caregiver to meeting the needs and desires of the recipient of her care.

CAREGIVING AND IDEAL WOMANHOOD

The ideal of the selfless woman is one who provides ideal care. Selflessness is consistent with an ideal of harmonious social relationships based on empathy and dependence and with Buddhist notions of the merging of self with the unity of the universe.[29] The ideal of the selfless woman was promoted by the government in pre-World War II and wartime Japan as being both feminine and patriotic. The anticipation of the needs of others is glorified in the cultural notions of *amaeru* and *amayakasu;* passive demands for dependency (*amaeru*) are matched by parental (or other superior) care and indulgence (*amayakasu*).[30]

The notions of dependency and selfless womanhood combine in two feature films about elder care made in the 1980s. *Yakusoku* (*A Promise*) and *Hanaichimonme* (titled as *Gray Sunset* in English) both deal with families faced with the increasing senility of an elderly relative. Although the style and content of the two films differ, both present family members as emerging more mature, more whole as a result of the caregiving experience. In both films, the adult sons of the demented old people play active roles in decision making, but it is the daughters-in-law who provide most of the physical care. At one point in *Hanaichimonme,* the demented old man reaches out to nurse at his daughter-in-law's breast, a symbolic request for nurturance. The film utilizes such images to relate the daughter-in-law's own healing through caring for her father-in-law to the nurturant symbol of the bodhisattva.[31] The films seem to hold out the promise of mature (i.e., ideally nurturant) womanhood: the satisfaction of fulfilling an important, socially recognized role; the reintegration of the nuclear family; increased intimacy with spouse, children, and siblings; the pleasure of interpersonal relations; and the gratification that comes from serving others. Painter (this volume) describes a TV drama with a similar message. A woman tries to decide whether to marry a man whose elderly parent she would have to care for. In choosing to marry him, she gains the satisfactions of the heroines in *Yakusoku* and *Hanaichimonme.*

According to the message of these films and TV shows, proper nurturing reaps success and fulfillment. On the other hand, social critics have used film and print media to point out the dangers of less than ideal nurturing. Educators, sociologists, and social critics blame mothers for overindulging their children.[32] They claim that contemporary mothers attempt to compensate for lack of paternal involvement with their children by providing too much maternal attention. The film *Kazoku Gēmu* (Family game) portrays a father who is totally out of touch with his family, a mother who pushes her children to pursue the Japanese dream of university entrance and white-collar employment, and two sons who in their own ways rebel against their parents, the dream, and the norms of society. The term "family" has no meaning, and their lives are parody.

None of these media attempt an accurate, descriptive portrayal of the caregiving experience. Their images of women are similar to the stereotypes the American public holds of Japanese women, but these are the works of Japanese writers and producers intended for Japanese audiences. Female nurturance is assumed. The significance of caregiving is debated at a level of abstraction once removed from the reality of the lives of Japanese women. The interpersonal problems and the aging of the population that characterize postindustrial Japan are simultaneously resolved in the ideal of the selfless woman.

THE EFFECTS OF THE CULTURAL IDEAL

This section examines data from several recent survey and interview research projects in which I have been involved, a Japanese survey on husband-wife relationships, and interviews and a questionnaire study on caring for frail elderly relatives. Women's responses to questions about caregiving and relationships in these studies show that the nurturing ideal does influence the way they live and reflect upon their lives. But the other effect of the cultural ideal is that it has masked, at least for the American public, other aspects of women's lives: the degree of choice in decisions about caregiving, the amount of stress in caregiving roles, and the relationship between social power and caregiving.

Husband-wife Relationships and Childrearing

In late 1988 and early 1989, the Hyogo Institute for the Study of Family Issues conducted a survey of husband-wife relationships in Japan and the U.S.[33] In Japan, over 1300 families with first or eighth graders in the Kobe public schools completed the survey. Their responses indicate that although there is substantial agreement about women's roles in family life, several factors seem to influence the way in which the ideal is played out in daily housework, childrearing, and paid employment. Nearly eighty-five percent of the respondents agreed with the statement that "Men should be out working; women should be in the home." A similar proportion of respondents believed that a father should actively participate in raising his children. This suggests support of an ideal in which women are caretakers of the home and family, but also indicates that men should nurture and discipline as well.

However, as in the U.S., there is a gap between that ideal and actual lives. Regardless of their work status, both women and men reported that the wife does nearly all of the housework and child rearing, although there were some differences based on the wife's employment status.[34] Husbands of women who work part-time almost never participate in child rearing. Husbands of women who are self-employed on work full-time are only slightly more likely to participate. Yet a larger proportion of these women reported that certain tasks are primarily done by others—extended family members or hired help. But even then, wives continue to do most of the housework, have the major responsibility for child rearing and seem to remain the family nurturer.[35]

The somewhat greater degree of paternal involvement reported in self-employed families may be because home and business are often in a single or nearby location, or perhaps because the self-employed husband has greater investment in his children in that he expects one of them someday to take over the family business. Thus self-employed families may be able to come closer to the ideal of paternal involvement with their children.

Despite the ideal, long work hours, and other workplace expectations often keep other [i.e. not self-employed] men away from home past the time young children are in bed. The realities of daily life may keep them from realizing that ideal despite their continued belief in it. This then might reinforce the commitment to women remaining in the home while the husband goes out to work.

This study not only verifies our ideas about *who* does housework and child care. It also sheds light on how and why female nurturing occurs. The majority of parents who completed the survey believe that mothers should be at home, otherwise they cannot physically care for their children. The continuity of role complementarity in which women should "be there" is indicated by the sharp division of tasks between husband and wife and by the small amount of joint decisionmaking reported by the respondents.[36]

I have claimed that Japanese caregiving is characterized by avoidance of open conflict. The survey data are consistent with this ideal. Almost ninety percent of respondents reported arguing with their spouses less than once a month, and nearly sixty percent less than once or twice per year.[37] The totality of the caregiving experience—another distinctive feature of Japanese caregiving—is also clear in this survey. Housework and child care are expected to be the primary, even all-encompassing occupations of a married woman. Our respondents indicate their acceptance of this view in both their attitudes and their reported behavior.

Why do women continue to accept this role even when they are working outside the home? To fully answer this question is beyond the scope of this survey, but the data suggest that many women would agree with a woman physician's response to a question about the compromises she was making in her career: "Isn't raising children to become good people also important work in society?" In the survey results, activities most clearly thought to be the wife's job were attending school meetings and parent-teacher conferences (ninety-five percent of the respondents) and taking care of children when they are sick (ninety percent).

The data show the dangers of accepting the ideal as the full picture. This study suggests that *not* achieving the cultural ideal may be either a matter of choice (as among the full-time workers who elect to work and to hire some outside help) or of compromise with the realities of their situations. Because the educational status of husbands and wives were closely correlated, it seems likely that the low proportion of full-time housewives among junior high school graduates may be related to the family's financial need for the wife's income. The lack of involvement of fathers in child rearing may be a result of the demands of the workplace, which in turn are based on the assumption that women are at home to care for the home and children. Mothers who have chosen to work full-time continue to view themselves as fulfilling the ideal of nurturing despite their greater absence from the home, or at least present themselves that way to outsiders who arrive with questionnaires. When there is less choice, working women may view their work outside the home as an extension of their caregiving role because their income is needed for meeting their children's physical and educational needs. The ideal may remain similar, but its interpretation varies with the family's circumstances.

Elder Care

Recent studies of elder care also illustrate the nature of caregiving and the effects of the cultural ideal on those who nurture.

Opinion surveys of Japanese adults of all ages indicate a continued preference for family caregiving of the impaired elderly and a sense of responsibility to provide such care.[38] Campbell and Brody found that older women were more in favor of using formal services, perhaps projecting their own fears of becoming a burden on the family, and that the younger generations took a more positive stance on family responsibility.[39] In fact, family caregiving remains a legal requirement. All children are expected to share in the responsibility for caring for elderly parents.[40] It also remains the norm. Less than two percent of those sixty-five and over are in nursing homes, and ninety percent of the physically or mentally impaired elderly receive family care.[41]

As in the United States, women in Japan are most likely to be the primary caregivers of impaired elderly relatives.[42] Elderly women are less likely to receive caregiving from their spouses than from other female relatives not only because they often outlive their husbands, but also because gender roles throughout the life course encourage nurturant behavior of women more so than of men. In an exploratory study of seventy-five caregivers in Shiga prefecture, eighty-six percent of the caregivers were women.[43] These caregivers receive help from husbands (primarily for heavy work such as airing bedding, bathing the elderly family members, and taking them to the doctor), children, siblings, and others, but frequently this assistance is provided only when the primary caretakers must go out or are involved in the time-consuming task of feeding the elderly. But as one woman commented, "My husband [age 52] does not try to help [his mother] at all. He believes that women are supposed to take care of patients."

A significant part of this caretaking emphasizes physical comfort. In an open question asking about the type of assistance the caregiver provides, feeding, washing, bathing, dressing, shaving, and toileting were most often mentioned. Many of these elderly people were bedridden. Japanese society seems willing to accept a high proportion of "bedriddenness" compared to other industrialized countries. Perhaps this is because it is easier to provide care for a bedridden person than for a mobile patient, especially one who suffers from dementia. Buddhist-based cultural notions of fate and death along with the lack of distinction in Shinto between physical and mental states of being may have contributed to a lack of emphasis on aggressive rehabilitation. It is also more difficult for people who are weak to get up from futon bedding on the floor than from raised beds. A greater acceptance of dependency in the caregiver–care receiver relationship may also make being bedridden more acceptable than it would be in a society that stresses independence.[44] In recent years, however, rehabilitative services are becoming more common. Many hospitals now have physical and occupational therapists, jobs that barely existed twenty years ago. But the warehousing of elderly, bedridden patients in *rojin byoin* (hospitals for the elderly) continues.

Even in such places, and even more so in homes and in day care programs, bathing is a comfort rich in symbolic meaning as well importance to hygiene.[45] Despite the difficulty of getting into a tub, all but the severely impaired were helped to bathe in the large, specially adapted tub found in all of the facilities we visited. For those at home, there are day care services that some people use solely for the reason that mobile *ofuro* (bath) units make home visits. Physical comfort, if not mobility, remains an important goal.

Confrontation of elders or the direct expression of emotion is avoided because it is socially disruptive. Those who upset an ill elderly person by showing anger create greater tension in the household. In particular, a daughter-in-law who stands to inherit property is seen as acting inappropriately and ungratefully if she complains about her role. Yet there is no doubt that caregivers experience tremendous stress. In a 1987 survey in Tokyo, more than three-quarters of caregivers indicated that they felt mental exhaustion, and in a 1985 survey in Yokohama, over half said that they were depressed.[46] If these complaints cannot be verbally expressed, dissatisfaction may be indicated somatically. Physical illness is culturally acceptable and even expected.[47]

The all-encompassing nature of the nurturing role is also found in elder care. The Shiga survey and our interviews that supplemented it showed how extensive caregivers' complaints are about lack of time to themselves, as in the story of the woman who felt she could only leave home for fifteen minutes every few days for groceries.[48] Another woman caring for her own mother wrote at the end of her questionnaire, "I feel tremendous stress because it's so difficult to maintain a life of my own." Moreover the burdens of caregiving, especially the perceived necessity of the caregiver's physical presence, create conflicts with other caregiving roles. In the Shiga study, a number of respondents noted that their greatest problems were their inability to attend PTA meetings at their child's school or go to parent-teacher conferences for fear of leaving the elderly parent alone. Others noted that the caregiver role also conflicted with personal needs for sleep and relaxation. Nearly forty percent of the respondents had been forced to either stop working or cut back on their hours in order to provide care for the elderly relative, possibly adding to the family's financial strain.

This group of respondents was selected because they were providing home care, so in a sense they represent those already fulfilling the cultural expectation of self-sacrificing nurturance. Although there is variation in such factors as who provides the care, who assists, and the seriousness of the elder's disabilities, the points raised earlier about the effects of the cultural ideal—how women must choose or be forced to compromise the culturally ideal role—show little variation in this particular sample. However, several discussions have captured the social difficulty of making alternative choices. A young woman studying in the United States read a draft of the report of our Shiga study. She wrote back to us:

> As a member of the generation whose parents will soon be over sixty-five years old, as a daughter whose mother had been taking care of her mother-in-law for twenty years, and as an educated, working, married woman, I have always been worried about how I would be able to take care of my parents and parents-in-law without quitting the job and making [a] mess [of my] "face" in the traditional Japanese society. For women who have new and rational ideas, it is obvious that they would be torn between the traditional social norm and the new values. . . . [The government] took it for granted that women are resources of unpaid caregiving services. . . . The important thing is, I believe, that no matter who assumes the caregiving role, the person can freely choose his or her own way of parent care without considering the social stigma.

Another woman we met in Japan came to similar conclusions about the need for greater choice in the caregiving role through her experience in caring for her mother with Alzheimer's disease. By joining a support group for family members caring for relatives with dementia, she learned how to care for her mother, but also, she says,

> I gradually realized the size of this social problem, that it was not only *my* problem, but a women's issue. Now young woman have a choice to stay home and raise their children or to put them in day care. But with elder care, we have no choice. It destroys our own life and the life of the family. I decided to protect myself while caring for my mother, but it was exhausting, and I wanted to give up. Now [that she is in the nursing home] I feel free, but also guilty. . . . It is a bitter, heavy feeling. . . . I think a lot about my own old age. I have two daughters, one working and one in college. I want to raise my kids to not have these feelings. I tell them to put me in a nursing home if I become crazy. I don't want to be a burden.

Her story indicates that choosing alternatives to the nurturing role has social and emotional consequences. She has provided in the past, and will again provide, care for an elderly relative, but her interpretation of that role shows that she does not share fully in the cultural ideal. Her story also points to another effect of the ideal: the stress created for those who do fulfill that role. There may be joys and satisfactions as suggested by the films *Yakusoku* and *Hanaichimonme*—a few people who completed our questionnaire mentioned these rewards. But the great majority of the respondents feel the burdens most heavily. While the granddaughters of Campbell and Brody's study voiced willingness to care for their parents when they become frail, the cry of the Shiga respondents seems far more poignant. A forty-six-year-old woman told of the criticism she always feels, that her caretaking is never good enough. "My husband's brothers don't help her directly, but tell me, 'A TV program said to do this. Why don't you do it like that?' and so on. I often feel badly that they seem to think that her problems are my fault."

One sixty-seven-year-old man who, together with his wife, was caring for both of his parents wrote, "My son and his wife think that they will take care of us, but I've been caring for my father for ten years, and it's too much! When I am old, I don't want my children to have to care for me."

Nurturing is not simply a matter of filling a cultural role. In Japan, the ideal of caregiving promises satisfaction and personal fulfillment, but the reality also creates a sense of burden and guilt. If we are to understand the meaning of nurturance in a particular society, we need to focus on the individuals who make personal choices, balancing satisfactions and burdens in the context of their own lives.

NURTURING AND GOVERNMENT POLICY

Just as industrialism and the government aided in the creation of the "good wife, wise mother" and "professional housewife" roles for women (which have served the government well), the economic and political systems continue to shape women's roles. Rosenberger's chapter in this volume brings out the tension between the media and state expectations of women. In recent years, Japan has experienced a labor shortage, especially of unskilled workers. Many companies prefer not to hire foreign guest workers and thus turn to a historical source of additional labor: women. Unlike the factory women of the late Tokugawa and prewar eras, young unmarried women no longer constitute the majority of the female labor force because a declining birth rate and young women's demands for higher education have led to decreased numbers and availability of workers in their teens and early twenties. Rather, it is older, married women who are available to work, but these women are more likely to have conflicts between work and family roles, caring for children or for elderly parents.

Some have argued that the best way to ease the pressure on the labor market is to encourage higher birth rates. After many years of anticipation that birth control pills would be made more widely available (that is, not only for treatment of gynecological problems), in 1992 the government postponed that move indefinitely. However, policies that would encourage women to stay home and raise larger families are in direct contradiction to the immediate need for women's labor.

Another factor in favor of creating policies to encourage women to take on the nurturing role more fully is the staggering sum it would cost the government to build enough facilities to care for the elderly. According to demographic predictions, by 2025 nearly one-fourth of the Japanese population will be sixty-five or older, with the largest proportional increases in the over-seventy age bracket—the age group most likely to suffer from chronic diseases. Even if building enough nursing homes were feasible, it seems unlikely that they could be fully staffed by Japanese women willing to accept the low pay, low status, and heavy labor that professionalized bodily care of strangers demands. So it is in the government's interest that women provide unpaid care to their own family members, despite the burdens that this imposes on the women. On the other hand, the personal nurturance provided in the home might be more satisfying to both the elderly person and the caregiver than institutionalized care, particularly if conflict could be expressed more openly and if nurturing need not require such total interpersonal and physical commitment. Increased services to caregivers as well as to the elderly and greater availability of support groups would help to ease the burdens of nurturing.

Nonetheless, as some women themselves note, providing appropriate care is not an individual problem but a social and political one. Those who create family policy and labor policy may themselves be unaware of the implications of their assumptions about nurturing and women's roles. The cultural ideal may hinder their ability to recognize the choices and burdens that affect actual families. The greater involvement in policymaking of those who have made hard choices and carried the burdens may make a difference. Given the low representation of women in the highest ranks of business and government in Japan, it seems that grass-roots citizens' movements, local government, and women's groups, together with media support, have the greatest potential to improve the social power of nurturers to make meaningful choices about their roles.[49]

CONCLUSION

Laws and gossip, living arrangements, self-evaluations, and film portrayals all contribute to an ethnographer's understanding of a cultural ideal. These sources all show that the Japanese concept of nurturing is closely identified with the notion of ideal womanhood. It involves physical proximity, the maintenance of social harmony, and undivided attention to the needs of the other.

Such a cultural ideal is "real" in the sense that it influences the behavior and attitudes of people in their daily lives. We see how evaluations based on the ideal of nurturing add to caregiver stress in the cases of the home nurse's comment to the former coal miner's wife and the criticism from the brother-in-law who thought he had seen on a TV show a better way to care for his mother. The cultural ideal influences women like the daughter-in-law who had had only two weeks off from caring for her mother-in-law in four years, and those only to meet other family obligations. It leads survey respondents to report infrequent arguments with husbands and a sense of primary responsibility for child rearing despite a belief in the value of paternal nurturance. The ideal influences how women present themselves to outsiders curious about their lives, because they want to portray themselves in a positive light according to their values and cultural expectations.

If we are to understand these women's lives, we need to move beyond the ideal. The ideal may be rejected, as by those dual-career families who hire outside help and the Japanese woman living in the U.S. who saw herself as having "new and rational ideas." It may be accepted, as by the woman who supervised her grandmother's confused night wandering or the many women who agreed with the statement that a woman should be at home. Or the ideal may be compromised. Junior high school graduates who work part-time may agree with the ideal of staying at home while children are small but justify their work outside the home as lack of choice or as an extension of the nurturant role. The woman who felt both freedom and guilt at placing her mother in a nursing home clearly rejects the ideal at one level, but at the same time, she was preparing to start caring for her mother-in-law.

Such ideals must be seen in context. They are not accidental or coincidental, nor are they biologically determined. They are intimately linked with the division of labor and capitalist society's needs for production and reproduction. As those needs compete, the ideal may become less clear, and the strains on individual women can be expected to increase. For some, the role of nurturer may remain attractive, particularly when women face continued discrimination in the labor market and the deaths of middle-aged salarymen are attributed to overwork. But as Japanese women become more vocal about the strains of their role as nurturers, they will undoubtedly challenge not only that role, but also the system that has created and supported the identification of nurturance with femininity.

NOTES

I would like to acknowledge the contributions of colleagues Noriko Iwai and Phyllis Braudy Harris, with whom I worked on the two studies that provided data for this chapter. Phyllis Braudy Harris, Robert Marra, Anne Imamura, and Noriko Iwai have provided helpful comments on earlier drafts of this chapter.

1. Yoshi Kuzume, "Images of Japanese Women in U.S. Writings and Scholarly Works, 1860–1990," *U.S.-Japan Women's Journal,* English Supplement No. 1 (August 1991): 6–50.

2. See, for example, Deborah Fallows, "Japanese Women," *National Geographic* 177 (April 1990): 52–83.

3. Dorinne K. Kondo, *Crafting Selves: Power, Gender, and Discourses of Identity in a Japanese Workplace* (Chicago: University of Chicago Press, 1990). See also the chapters by Roberts and Creighton in this volume about women working on production lines and in discount stores. Takie Sugiyama Lebra, *Above the Clouds: Status Culture of the Modern Japanese Nobility* (Berkeley: University of California Press, 1992). Matthews Masayuki Hamabata, *Crested Kimono: Power and Love in the Japanese Business Family* (Ithaca: Cornell University Press, 1990).

4. See Sumiko Iwao, *The Japanese Woman: Traditional Image and Changing Reality* (New York: The Free Press, 1993) and Margaret Lock, *Encounters with Aging: Mythologies of Menopause in Japan and North America* (Berkeley: University of California Press, 1993).

5. For example, see Alice Rossi, "Gender and Parenthood," *American Sociological Review* 106 (1984): 1–31.

6. For example, see Nancy Chodorow, *The Reproduction of Mothering* (Berkeley: University of California Press, 1978). See summary in Susan A. Basow, *Gender Stereotypes and Roles,* 3rd ed. (Pacific Grove, California: Brooks/Cole Publishing Company, 1992), 63–64 and 235–236.

7. Ezra F. Vogel, *Japan's New Middle Class,* 2nd ed. (Berkeley: University of California Press, 1971).

8. Suzanne H. Vogel, "Professional Housewife: The Career of Urban Middle Class Japanese Women," *Japan Interpreter* 12 (1978): 16–43.

9. See Kathleen S. Uno, "Good Wives and Wise Mothers in Early Twentieth Century Japan" (paper presented at panel on Women in Prewar Japan, Pacific Coast Branch of the American Historical Association and the Western Association of Women Historians joint meeting, San Francisco, 1988); and "Women and Changes in the Household Division of Labor," in *Recreating Japanese Women, 1600–1945*, ed. Gail Lee Bernstein (Berkeley: University of California Press, 1991), 17–41. Robert J. Smith and Ella Lury Wiswell, *The Women of Suye Mura* (Chicago: University of Chicago Press, 1982).

10. Life expectancy at birth in 1949 was 53 years. In 1993 it was 76.3 for men and 82.5 for women.

11. Uno, "Good Wives." Sharon H. Nolte and Sally Ann Hastings, "The Meiji State's Policy Toward Women, 1890–1910," in Bernstein, *Recreating Japanese Women*, 151–174. Yoshiko Miyake, "Doubling Expectations: Motherhood and Women's Factory Work under State Management in Japan in the 1930s and 1940s," in Bernstein, *Recreating Japanese Women*, 267–295. Margit Nagy, "Middle Class Working Women during the Interwar Years," in Bernstein, *Recreating Japanese Women*, 199–216. See also Sharon Sievers, *Flowers in Salt: The Beginnings of Feminist Consciousness in Modern Japan* (Stanford: Stanford University Press, 1983).

12. Jane M. Bachnik, "Recruitment Strategies for Household Succession: Rethinking Japanese Household Organization," *Man* 18 (1983): 160–182.

13. See Smith and Wiswell, *Women of Suye Mura*.

14. Susan O. Long, *Family Change and the Life Course in Japan*. (Ithaca: Cornell University East Asia Papers, No. 44, 1987).

15. Kōseishō, "Kokumin Seikatsu Kiso Chōsa" *Kōsei no Shihyō* 39, no. 12 (1992).

16. The divorce rate in 1993 was 1.52 per 1,000.

17. Long, *Family Change.*

18. Kōseishō, "Kokumin Seikatsu Kiso Chōsa." *Kōsei no Shihyō* 40, no. 11 (1993).

19. According to Japan's Equal Opportunity Employment Law, women must now have access to career-track positions. However, enforcement of this law is weak, and many women continue to prefer the flexibility of noncareer-track jobs.

20. William Caudill and Helen Weinstein, "Maternal Care and Infant Behavior in Japan and America," *Psychiatry* 32 (1969): 12–43.

21. William Caudill, "The Cultural and Interpersonal Context of Everyday Health and Illness in Japan and America," in *Asian Medical Systems: A Comparative Study*, ed. Charles Leslie (Berkeley: University of California Press, 1976), 159–183. Sonya Salamon, " 'Male Chauvinism' as a Manifestation of Love in Marriage," in *Adult Episodes in Japan,* ed. David W. Plath (Leiden: Brill, 1975). Suzanne Vogel, "Professional Housewife."

22. Harumi Befu, *Japan: An Anthropological Introduction* (San Francisco: Chandler, 1971). Takie Sugiyama Lebra and William P. Lebra. *Japanese Culture and Behavior,* rev. ed. (Honolulu: University of Hawaii Press, 1986). S. Ramsey, "To Hear One and Understand Ten: Nonverbal Behavior in Japan," in *Inter-cultural Communication,* 4th ed., eds. L. A. Samovar and R. E. Porter (Belmont, Calif.: Wadsworth Publishing Co., 1985). Edwin O. Reischauer, *The Japanese Today: Continuity and Change* (Cambridge, MA: Belknap Press of Harvard University Press, 1988). Robert J. Smith, *Japanese Society: Tradition, Self, and the Social Order* (Cambridge: Cambridge University Press, 1983).

23. See Ellis S. Krauss, Thomas P. Rohlen, and Patricia G. Steinhoff, eds. *Conflict in Japan* (Honolulu: University of Hawaii Press, 1984).

24. Stephen R. Smith, "For the Sake of Sake: Negotiating a Drinking Role in Japan" (paper presented at the Annual Meeting of the American Anthropological Association, Chicago, November 22, 1987).

25. Margaret M. Lock, "A Nation at Risk: Interpretations of School Refusal in Japan," in *Biomedicine Examined*, eds. Margaret Lock and Deborah A. Gordon (Dordrecht, Netherlands: Kluwer Academic Press, 1988) 377–414.

26. Susan O. Long, "Roles, Careers, and Femininity in Biomedicine: Women Physicians and Nurses in Japan," *Social Science and Medicine* 22 (1986): 81–90.

27. Anne E. Imamura, *Urban Japanese Housewives: At Home and in the Community* (Honolulu: University of Hawaii Press, 1987).

28. Caudill and Weinstein, "Maternal Care."

29. See Brian Moeran, "Individual, Group, and Seishin: Japan's Internal Cultural Debate," *Man* 19 (1984): 252–266.

30. Takeo Doi, *The Anatomy of Dependence* (Tokyo: Kodansha, 1973).

31. William Deal, "Japan as an Aging Society" (paper presented at the conference on Dementia: Moral Values and Policy Choices in an Aging Society, University Hospitals of Cleveland Alzheimers Center, April 27, 1990).

32. For examples in English, see Hayao Kawai, "Violence in the Home: Conflict between Two Principles—Maternal and Paternal," *Japan Quarterly* 28 (1981): 370–378. Fumie Kumagai, "Filial Violence: A Peculiar Parent-Child Relationship in the Japanese Family Today," *Journal of Comparative Family Studies* 12, special issue (1981): 337–350.

33. Iwai Noriko, *Amerika no Fufuzo to no Hikaku: Kenkyū Hōkokusho* (A comparison with the image of husbands and wives in the United States: A research report) (Kobe: Hyogoken Katei Mondai Kenkyūjo, 1990). Susan O. Long and Iwai Noriko, "Personal Patriarchies: Women's Employment and Marital Relations in Japan" (paper presented at the annual meeting of the American Anthropological Association, New Orleans, December 2, 1990).

34. Of the women who responded to the survey, half of the high school and vocational school graduates were full-time homemakers. More college and especially junior college graduates were likely to be at home at this stage of life, but only thirty percent of junior high school graduates were full-time homemakers. The great majority of women in all employment categories consider that housework is primarily their responsibility.

35. In general, husbands participate regularly in only a few activities, such as talking with the children or playing games or sports with them.

36. Samuel Coleman, *Family Planning in Japanese Society: Traditional Birth Control in a Modern Urban Culture* (Princeton: Princeton University Press, 1983). Walter Edwards, *Modern Japan Through Its Weddings: Gender, Person, and Society in Ritual Portrayal* (Stanford: Stanford University Press, 1989).

37. Fewer than eighty percent of American wives reported arguing with their husbands less than once or twice a month, and only twenty-eight percent less than once or twice a year.

38. Linda G. Martin, "The Graying of Japan," *Population Bulletin* 44 (1989): 1–41. Marvin B. Sussman and James C. Romeis. "Willingness to Assist One's El-

derly Parents: Responses from the United States and Japan," *Human Organization* 41 (1982): 256–259. Ruth Campbell and E. M. Brody, "Women's Changing Roles and Help to the Elderly: Attitudes of Women in the United States and Japan," *The Gerontologist* 25 (1985): 584–592.

39. Campbell and Brody, "Women's Changing Roles."

40. *Kodansha Encyclopedia of Japan* 6:99a.

41. Ruth Campbell, "Nursing Homes and Long-term Care in Japan," *Pacific Affairs* 57 (1983): 78–89.

42. In a survey of bedridden elderly, the Japanese National Council of Social Welfare found that sixty-one percent of elderly bedridden men were being cared for by their wives, but only eleven percent of bedridden women received care from their husbands. Half of bedridden women received care from a daughter-in-law and another twenty-eight percent from their own child. See Campbell and Brody, "Women's Changing Lives," and D. Maeda, "Family Care in Japan," *The Gerontologist* 23 (1983): 579–583.

43. Phyllis Braudy Harris and Susan O. Long, "Daughter-in-Law's Burden: An Exploratory Study of Caregiving in Japan," *Journal of Cross-Cultural Gerontology* 8 (1993): 97–118.

44. Compare Christie W. Kiefer, "The Elderly in Modern Japan: Elite, Victims, or Plural Players?" in *The Cultural Context of Aging*, ed. J. Sokolovsky (New York: Bergin and Garvey Publishers, 1990), 212–220.

45. Emiko Ohnuki-Tierney, *Illness and Culture in Contemporary Japan: An Anthropological View* (Cambridge: Cambridge University Press, 1984). See also, Scott Clark, *Japan, A View from the Bath* (Honolulu: University of Hawaii Press, 1994).

46. D. Maeda, K. Teshima, H. Sugisawa, and Y. S. Asakura, "Aging and Health in Japan," *Journal of Cross-Cultural Gerontology* 4 (1989): 143–162. Okamoto Takako, "Zaitaku Chihōsei Rōjin no Kaigosha no Nayami" (Problems of caregivers of demented elderly in the home), *Rōnen Shakai Kagaku* (Social gerontology) 10 (1988): 75–90.

47. Ohnuki-Tierney, op. cit. Margaret M. Lock, "Protests of a Good Wife and Wise Mother: The Medicalization of Distress in Japan," in *Health, Illness, and Medical Care in Japan*, eds. Edward Norbeck and Margaret Lock (Honolulu: University of Hawaii Press, 1987), 130–137. In the study by Maeda and his colleagues, seventy-eight percent of the caregivers expressed anxiety about their own health, and seventy-seven percent expressed anxiety about care in the future. Maeda, *et al.*, "Aging and Health." Okamoto found that after "no time for self," the most frequently checked complaints were physical exhaustion, lack of sleep, and uncertainty about the future. Okamoto, "Zaitaku Chihōsei Rōjin no Kaigosha no Nayami."

48. Harris and Long, "Daughter-in-law's Burden."

49. Susan O. Long and Phyllis Braudy Harris, "Festival for a Cause: Culture and Participant Mobilization in a Japanese Social Welfare Movement" *Sociological Focus* 26 (1993), 47–63.

EIGHT

Mother or Mama

The Political Economy of Bar Hostesses in Sapporo

John Mock

SKETCHES OF HANAYAMA HOSTESSES

Machiko

Machiko was twenty-three in 1976. She had moved to Sapporo five years before from a small city in eastern Hokkaido. The third daughter of a shopkeeper, she had a commercial high school degree and intended to work for a company. After arriving in Sapporo, she learned that the salary was less than half of what she could earn working with a cousin in a small bar in Susukino.

She took a job at the bar, which was quiet, with a solid, loyal patronage of businessmen. She worked as a hostess, bartender, and waitress, as did her cousin and one other woman. She wrote to her mother every week and talked on the telephone occasionally. She planned to get married in the not too distant future but hoped to keep working until she had her first child. She resided alone in the neighborhood of Hanayama.

Sachiko

Sachiko was from a very small town in the southern part of the Ishikari plain, not far from Sapporo. She had a very difficult childhood with a father who drank heavily. As the oldest daughter, she apparently bore more than her share of the problems. She stopped going to junior high school some time in her second year, and she says that no one, neither her family nor the school, ever made any serious effort to persuade her to go back. She was twenty-six in 1976 and had been living in Sapporo for about ten years. She worked in a large cabaret and had had a number of jobs there and at other clubs, including standing nude in a cage that circulated the ceiling. At the time of this study, she was working as a hostess and making a substantial income. She also had several male friends who gave her expensive presents and paid her rent. It was not clear that any of the men knew of any of the others. She had several bank accounts and a number of other investments, including somewhat suspect deals, the details of which were never clear to me.

She had no contact at all with her family and, when pressed, talked about them in cold, hostile terms. She came to Sapporo specifically to be a bar hostess and said that she had sexual contact with all of her bosses. She also said that one of the reasons that no one made any attempt to get her to return to school was that one of the teachers was interested in her. She never specified exactly what that meant, but she laughed when I asked if she had been a virgin when she came to Sapporo.

Yoko

Yoko was thirty-two in 1976 and one of the oldest working hostesses in Hanayama. She was probably my best informant. She was a successful hostess: while not particularly pretty, she had a quick wit and the ability to make almost anyone laugh. During the sixteen years she lived in Sapporo, she saved scrupulously and, by 1976, had substantial savings that she invested widely. She also had a high weekly income from the small nightclub where she worked as a hostess. In fact, of all the hostesses interviewed in the neighborhood, her income was the highest.

Yoko was the oldest daughter of a farm family in northeastern Hokkaido. She came to Sapporo in order to avoid becoming a farmer's wife. After graduating from junior high school, she worked for a small manufacturer in Sapporo for four years while living with an aunt and uncle. She quit that job and went to work as a hostess when she was twenty years old. She said that she had engaged in prostitution in the early years but had not thought it worthwhile. In 1976, she had a male friend who paid her rent and gave her substantial presents and to whom she maintained loyalty. By 1981, her benefactor had disappeared, she had moved into a much nicer apartment in another part of Sapporo, and her income was even higher. By 1991, she was running her own establishment, had her fingers in a number of other ventures as well as managing her own very substantial investment portfolio, and had a younger male friend whom she introduced rather proudly in English as her "boyfriend."

Her relations with her family were strained by distance but on the whole quite good. She maintained regular contact with her parents and with the uncle and aunt with whom she had lived when she first came to Sapporo. By 1991, she was a wealthy woman who spent her time managing her own bar and her wide array of investments and studying things "she had never had time for," like English and calligraphy.

THE *MIZU SHŌBAI*

Japanese who work in entertainment industries—the *mizu shōbai*, the water trades—make up a distinctive occupational category. The history of entertainers and entertainment is as old as Japan itself (Plath 1964). The term *mizu shōbai* comes from the Edo period when entertainment either occurred on boats or in the walled or otherwise guarded "gay quarters" of various cities (Shoji 1967; DeBecker 1971). There is even a substantial artistic tradition based on the "Floating World" of *ukiyoe* prints, and any number of literary works and literary references. All of these continue as an ongoing counterculture in premodern and modern Japan (Hane 1982).

Bar hostesses (*hosutesu-san*) constitute a large and important segment of the *mizu shōbai*, which developed out of and adapted to Japanese industrialization (Bornoff 1991). The hostess occupation is notable because it is one of the few in which Japanese women can gain economic and social independence, even though many hostesses lack extensive education.

I examine the characteristics found among hostesses in the Sapporo neighborhood of Hanayama to look at the patterns of individual and social interaction and functions, to examine the changes that have occurred during the past sixteen years, and to see if these young women became bar hostesses because of the glamour of the "big city," as Laura Jackson (Jackson 1976) asserts, or because there were few other viable economic options.[1]

CHARACTERISTICS OF THE HANAYAMA HOSTESSES

In the Sapporo neighborhood of Hanayama, approximately a kilometer from the "gay quarters" of Susukino, the hostesses were young women mostly in their early twenties with little formal education, who had an occupation that made unusual demands on their time, a high degree of social and economic independence at the price—or benefit—of social isolation, a distinctive set of social and ethical values, and a set of behavioral and taste markers including dress, speech patterns, and domestic arrangements.

In 1976, almost all of the hostesses came from the small towns, small cities, and rural areas of Hokkaido, although there were a few from Sapporo and other parts of Japan. Almost all of them said that they had come to Sapporo for employment and to get away from the places where they grew up. All of them felt that Sapporo was a far better place to live than their home towns. Many of them had difficult childhoods and migrated to Sapporo to put distance between themselves and their families. By 1991, the situation had changed somewhat; the neighborhood included foreign hostesses—primarily from the Philippines, Thailand, and Korea—and a high proportion of hostesses from other parts of Japan. As Sapporo has grown from a regional to a national city, its entertainment industry has grown, providing more hostess jobs.

Education

The average level of formal education for a Hanayama hostess in 1976 was middle school—just under nine years—a very low level for young Japanese.[2] The Hanayama hostesses in 1976 had a low average educational level because none of them had more than a high school education (only a few of the thirty-eight had graduated from high school), and several had been expelled during junior high school. One even asserted that she had been pushed out of the sixth grade.[3] This meant that many were ineligible for virtually all other reasonably well paying occupations.

By 1991, the hostesses' average level of education had risen strikingly to eleven-and-a-half years. However, educational requirements had also risen. In a society where approximately 92 percent of the population graduates from high school, any average below twelve years is decidedly subnormal.[4] In Japan, where formal education and the ability to pass examinations are among the most important considerations for economic upward mobility, the hostesses' low levels of formal education considerably limited their social and economic opportunities. The hostesses see themselves correctly as having little potential for economic or social mobility through normal channels. Poorly educated Japanese women have little chance of making a living wage, although opportunities appear to be increasing, at least in good economic times, because of the shortage of labor in Japan (Okamura 1973; Roberts 1994).

The hostess occupation differs from most other occupations in Japan in a variety of ways. It emphasizes affective, social skills and has an unusual environment and working hours. The job of the hostess is to make the (male) customer feel relaxed and happy, thereby encouraging him to consume food and drink, patronize the establishment regularly, and advertise that establishment to other potential customers. The usual means of effecting this task is through flirtation, flattery, laughter, and "mothering."

Hostesses can be divided into two categories: large-establishment hostesses and small-establishment hostesses. Hostesses working in large establishments usually deal with groups of men, often on company expense accounts. The hostesses will skillfully interact with each other and with the customers at the table to promote a party atmosphere. This interaction pattern is complex, and it takes some time to acquire the necessary skills and sensitivities. One Hanayama hostess described an interaction this way:

> Now that is easy. We [she and the other hostesses] found out right away who they [the group of three male customers] were. Machiko's customer was a little shy and formal, so I teased him a bit about being ceremonious. After he had a little to drink, he relaxed. When he relaxed, so did everyone else. Machiko would have done the same thing if mine had needed it. We've been working for quite a while and you learn these things. It is much easier

if there are several of us, we can help each other. . . . I suppose that it takes some time to become sensitive, but that is our job. If we do it well, we make money and it is more comfortable.

This hostess said it had taken three or four years before she felt reasonably comfortable and competent in her job. She thought that her income had increased proportionally with her skills during this period.

Hostesses in large establishments such as cabarets and nightclubs are usually paid both a commission on customer consumption and a high percentage of a hefty service charge levied on the customer per hour per hostess. Hostesses in smaller establishments are usually paid a flat wage roughly commensurate with their value to the establishment. This difference in the basis of income means that in the smaller establishments, the hostesses have little pressure to be aggressive, though they still have economic incentives to perform their duties well.

In the small bars (often seating only a dozen or so patrons) the atmosphere is relaxed. Unlike the large establishments, often great, barn-like structures filled with people, blasting music, and a floor show, the small bars tend to be dark and quiet, although equally smoke-filled. The hostesses here often double as bartenders or waitresses. In the small bars, the hostesses talk to the customers, often at greater length than in the cabarets and certainly to greater depth—or will leave the customers alone. Since the hostesses do not rotate, the possibility for something other than superficial communication exists. The atmosphere of the small bar is usually one of quiet comfort. Each small bar attempts to build up and maintain a cadre of steady customers, some of whom may come in several nights a week.[5]

In the past decade, an important change in the small bars has occurred with the development of the *karaoke*, "empty orchestra," machine, which enables customers and hostesses to sing to professional backup music. In these bars, the hostess is expected either to sing well or to be funny or attractive in the attempt. Older hostesses might specialize in traditional folk ballads, the *enka* or *minyō*, and younger hostesses may be able to sing along with English popular tunes.

Economic Position

The economic position of the hostesses varies according to where they are employed. The cabaret and nightclub hostesses average a higher income than do those in the small bars, but there is also a wider range of income among the large-establishment hostesses. Because the small-bar hostesses inevitably establish fairly close personal ties with their employers, the cabaret and nightclub hostesses' job security is considerably more problematic. Among the Hanayama hostesses in the middle 1970s, the cabaret and nightclub hostesses averaged less than two years of tenure in a job; the small-bar hostesses averaged over four years. More recent discussion suggests that the differences in tenure may be increasing because the large-establishment hostesses are more occupationally mobile and the tenure of the small-bar hostesses is staying relatively constant.[6]

Small-bar hostesses tend to receive a relatively steady income. Cabaret and nightclub hostesses' wages vary widely from month to month. The cabaret hostesses' incomes in 1976 varied from as much as ¥400,000 a week to as little as ¥60,000 ($1,300 and $200 at 1976 rates). As a group, the hostesses averaged between ¥100,000 and ¥150,000 ($300 and $450) per week or $15,000 to $22,500 a year in 1976 dollars. The most successful cabaret hostess (identified as "Yoko" in the opening sketch) was making ¥400,000 a week in 1976. By 1981 she had increased her income to almost ¥600,000 a week, an income that she still received as a small-bar owner in 1991 (in June 1991, ¥600,000 was more than $4,500). Moreover, in 1991, she also had significant income from investments. In 1991, she said that she thought she would make about ¥35,000,000 (about $270,000). Further, it is unlikely that all of her income would be declared and taxed.

Although Yoko's income from 1976 to 1991 appears to be far above average, the economic position of the hostesses is strong. Almost all of the hostesses make high wages, certainly much higher than they could make in other types of employment, given their educational levels. Even if they had better educational credentials, as women they would be restricted to low-paying and insecure employment. Teaching and the civil service are exceptions to this rule but are only available to women with high levels of education. These professions are secure, often with lifetime tenure and high status. However, they share with hostessing an occupational immobility. Women tend not to be promoted to high positions in schools and the civil service, just as there are few positions to which hostesses can be promoted. Female teachers can become principals; there are high-ranking female civil servants; and hostesses can become *mama-san* (bar managers). However, women have, on the whole, much shorter career ladders than men do.

Hostesses are unusual in their degree of economic and social independence. Twenty years ago, Linda Perry stated flatly: "A woman in Japan is, in effect, denied the possibility of being independent economically or socially at any comfortable level" (1975:33). Though hostesses seem to be an exception to Perry's assertion, opportunities for women have not expanded significantly in Japan during the past two decades.

Expressions of Social and Economic Independence

Hostesses express their economic and social independence in a number of visible ways including patterns of dress and domestic arrangements. The hostesses are less restrained in their dress than other Japanese women of the same age. One reason for their relative flamboyance is that attractiveness and sexiness are highly marketable items in their profession. Another reason is that the hostesses perceive themselves as modern and independent of family constraints that might censor their choices.

Another means by which the hostesses express their independence is through their domestic arrangements. Most of the hostesses interviewed in 1976 had their own apartments, yet no other apartments in the neighborhood were rented by single women. Further, the hostesses' apartments were far less "domestic"—that is, dominated by everyday furniture and artifacts—than were the other neighborhood apartments. The hostesses' apartment walls were adorned with modern Western-style prints and other artifacts clearly European in influence. Such items were rare in nonentertainer apartments. Most of the hostesses' apartments had Western-style beds, which are almost never found in nonentertainer apartments. All of these features served to distinguish the hostesses from nonentertainers and express their independence, both social and economic.

Other Distinguishing Features

Gender and age also distinguished the hostesses from the other residents of Hanayama. All of the hostesses were women between the ages of eighteen and thirty-five. There were relatively few nonhostess women of similar age living in the neighborhood.

The hostesses' working hours differed from their neighbors'; since they worked in the evenings and slept until about noon, the hostesses were active in Hanayama in the afternoons. Virtually everyone else in Hanayama who was employed outside the neighborhood was absent during this period, leaving only shopkeepers, landladies, the unemployed, and children. The hostesses' working hours thus isolated them from most of their neighbors. The landladies, several of whom had been hostesses or *mama-san* in the past, comprised the only nonentertainer group in the neighborhood with whom the hostesses had noticeable social ties. Even the shopkeepers in the neighborhood had relatively little contact with the hostesses.

NEIGHBORHOOD GEOGRAPHY

The physical geography of the hostesses' residences reinforced the hostesses' isolation. The hostesses all lived in the relatively new apartment buildings that started to replace single family dwellings in the neighborhood in 1965. The apartments were small and inexpensive in 1975. By 1990, many of the newly constructed apartment buildings were large and expensive. The sheer size of the new apartment buildings allowed the entertainers to hide in the crowd and therefore be even more socially independent and unconstrained. Most of the other apartment residents were young, short-term residents of the neighborhood. With the exception of the landladies, the hostesses were surrounded by other people who were somewhat marginal to the social life of the neighborhood. Thus, the hostesses were both temporally and physically isolated in the neighborhood. Moreover, between 1975 and 1991, almost all of the single-family housing and the few duplexes in Hanayama were replaced by large and small apartment buildings, which effectively removed the other white-collar residents from the neighborhood, quadrupled the number of entertainers, and demolished what social cohesion there had previously been (Bestor 1985 and 1989; Mock 1980).

SOCIAL NETWORKS

The hostesses' working hours and apartment life contributed to the differences between the social networks that the hostesses constructed and those built and maintained by nonentertainers in the neighborhood. In 1975, most of the other residents had built or were in the process of establishing extensive neighborhood social networks. The size of these networks correlated with the members' length of residence in Hanayama and type of housing. Apartment dwellers had less extensive social networks than those who lived in single family houses. The hostesses of the neighborhood had markedly limited networks, ranging from those who knew only their own landladies to a few who had twenty or more contacts. The hostess with the largest network had thirty-eight contacts within the neighborhood—mainly other hostesses, landladies, and shopkeepers. The hostesses' networks were by far the smallest of any permanent residents'.[7]

For the younger white-collar housewives, including those who had just moved into Hanayama, the average number of contacts was more than one hundred. The other social groups in the neighborhood had even larger numbers of contacts. These networks were consciously built up and maintained with a complex interaction of gift exchange, information exchange, political activity in the neighborhood association and its block associations, and general social activity. *Idobatakaigi*, "conferences by the well," have continued to occur long after water has been piped into every home.

There are a variety of reasons for the difference between hostess and nonhostess social networks. In addition to the temporal and physical isolation created by the hostesses' unusual working hours and housing, the major reason is that the hostesses are not as interested as the others in building and maintaining strong residentially-based social networks.[8] They are disinterested in residential networks because they do not share the generally accepted Hanayama value that social networks are inherently worthwhile and should be developed under nearly all conditions. Though the hostesses may have been excluded from the other residents' networks, no one ever expressed that idea in the interviews. On the other hand, the hostess attitude is expressed quite well in the following comment:

> Why should I want to do that? One of the main reasons that I wanted to come to Sapporo was to avoid that sort of thing. In [the small Hokkaido city she was born in], everyone knows everyone else, and that is all they talk about. What this person and what that person did. I do not want that, I came here to live a modern[9] life, not like an Edo village.

Another hostess voiced a more temperate but similar response about residentially-based social networks:

> That is what old people do. I suppose it is very Japanese—I do it too, for business. I have contacts and friends, but not here. I do not think it is bad, it just takes a lot of time and effort, and there is no need for that sort of thing anymore. I would rather do other things. The only people I know here are Mrs. Sasaki [the landlady] and Mrs. Itoo [the neighboring landlady and a great friend of Mrs. Sasaki]. I do not even know the name of the hostess in the next apartment. I see the people I work with every day; I do not want to live with them. That is why I came here. . . . Yes, I think that I am typical of the people who work in [the entertainment district of] Susukino; a lot of them are like me.

The hostesses saw the construction and maintenance of strong, residentially based social relationships as being old-fashioned, "feudal," not worth the time and effort, and a constraint on their personal freedom. Most of them came to Sapporo not only to find what they considered to be interesting and high-paying jobs, but also to escape what they saw as the cloying culture of smaller cities, towns, and hamlets. Many of the hostesses suggested that the older residents were "too polite" and "too constrained by custom and ceremony."

In contrast, a younger white-collar woman expressed positive attitudes toward strong networks. Her attitude is fairly representative of attitudes found elsewhere in urban Japan (see Imamura 1978): "No, I don't think things are really different. You still need to know people to get ahead. I spend almost all day here, and I would feel very strange if I did not know the other people or at least some of them. It bothers me that I don't know quite a few people [almost all hostesses]. It makes it easier if you know people, doesn't it?" A young, male, National Railways (JNR) employee expressed similar sentiments:

> Right now, in my career, the important thing is to [get to know many people]. . . . No, not just at work, here in the neighborhood too. Not just because there are several older JNR employees here, although that is a very important factor. . . . Well, it's that I don't know who will be im-

portant in the future. Maybe the neighborhood association head will be the one to introduce me to someone who will be very important, maybe not. But if I know as many people as I can, then my chances are better, aren't they?

The difference between the hostesses' attitudes and those of the white-collar housewife and the JNR employee relates in part to their different positions in Japanese society. A housewife, even of the most transient type, expects to stay in Hanayama for at least several years. Because she is likely to have young children, she values the social support of older women and peers in the neighborhood and local groups such as the PTA (Higuchi 1975). JNR employees and other young white-collar employees consider the development of an extensive network—a "broad face" in Japanese usage—one of the most important ways of getting ahead. Like the young housewife, white-collar employees expect to stay in the neighborhood for at least several years, perhaps for the entirety of their careers. Thus both assume at least a minimum of stability.

The opposite is true of hostesses. Not only are they themselves very mo-bile—at least partly by choice—but so are those individuals whose worlds intersect with theirs, the other entertainers and their patrons. The average residence of hostesses in Hanayama was less than one year in 1975 and seems to have increased only marginally since then. This short tenure in the neighborhood appears to have been caused in part by the hostesses' desire to avoid entanglements or involvements within Hanayama. In con-trast, the average tenure for other residents of roughly the same age was almost three years.

Hostesses saw the neighborhood men as dangerous; if they got to know the men, the likelihood of unwanted attention, with all the related prob-lems and complications, would increase. Several of the hostesses said that they had been raped at least once (either in their home towns or in the place they lived in Sapporo—not necessarily in Hanayama) and under-standably did not want to repeat the experience.

The Hanayama hostesses reported that they paid various people, said to be *yakuza*, for protection in their jobs and in their outside lives. The *yakuza* are said to have arrangements with the local police that give the *yakuza* responsibility for the entertainment districts and, by extension, the entertainers. They appear to perform these social control functions quite effectively. As a general rule, there is little harassing of hostesses and almost none of the physical danger in the entertainment districts that one associates with similar districts in other parts of the world, including the United States. What physical danger does exist for the hostesses appears to be mainly in the residential neighborhoods.

It would be inefficient at best for a hostess to devote time and energy to develop and maintain a residentially based social network. The hostesses are not in the neighborhood long enough to reap the benefits, nor can they mix residential and occupational networks to benefit their careers. They are to some degree shunned by the other women of the neighborhood, and they themselves want to avoid involvement with any of the men.

Although hostesses form what Mayer (1969) calls a quasi-group, in the neighborhood of Hanayama they form a distinctive social set. The Hanayama hostesses are young women with low degrees of formal education, a profession that makes unusual demands on their time, and a distinctive set of social and ethical values. They are significantly differentiated from the mainstream population by their resistance to assimilation into the ongoing patterns of neighborhood social relationships and their ability to establish and maintain economic and social independence. Although the realities of Japanese society channel the hostesses into their occupation, the occupation—with its concomitant possibilities of economic and social independence—makes them anomalies. It is difficult for Japanese not of the *mizu shōbai* subculture to deal socially with the hostesses outside the professional milieu. Thus the social patterns of a residential neighborhood, which depend to a large extent on intragroup interaction, appear often to be interrupted and even destroyed by such a nonintegrating group (see Mock 1980).

PROSTITUTION

If prostitution is loosely defined as the explicit exchange of sexual activity for pay or some other economic benefit, then there were three types of prostitution among the Hanayama hostesses.[10] The first involved a straight business deal: so much money for so much time or for specific activities. The second type involved the exchange of nonspecified but mutually understood activities for partial or total economic support; that is, the woman's friend or lover might pay the rent and provide her with expensive gifts such as clothing. The understanding suggested exclusivity; the woman was not supposed to have other lovers or was supposed to be very discrete about having other lovers. This type is closer to the English word "mistress" than "prostitute." The third type involved receiving expensive gifts from various lovers in an understood, nonspecified exchange for sexual services.

Possibly as many as half of the hostesses in Hanayama acquired a significant percentage of their total income through direct pay or gifts—including things like rent—related to sexual activity of the second and third type. Although the hostesses, as a set, were viewed by most Japanese as having loose morals, most of the Hanayama hostesses were not engaged in prostitution of the first type. However, at least two other women, not of the *mizu shōbai* but rather otherwise "normal" housewives were engaged in prostitution. Obviously, the percentage of hostesses engaging in prostitution is higher than that of the nonhostess population, but prostitution is not exclusive to hostesses, nor are all—or even most—of the hostesses prostitutes. In fact, the small, inexpensive apartments in Hanayama may have attracted a higher percentage of prostitutes than more wealthy residential areas.

Prostitution added to the distance that separated the hostesses from the rest of the residents of the neighborhood but was not, in and of itself, a major factor in their isolation. In fact, discussion of the various hostesses and their activities—sexual, sartorial, and otherwise—constituted much of the daily conversation for almost every adult in the neighborhood. Each new outfit sported by a hostess seemed to constitute a local news flash.

SOCIAL FUNCTIONS

The hostess quasi-group performs at least three social functions. It facilitates male social transactions, offers both sexual and pseudosexual entertainment, and provides wives for marginal males. The first two functions are the more important. Hostesses, and to a lesser degree other female entertainers, provide the essential lubricant that enables Japanese male social transactions to occur.[11] The characteristics that a polite housewife is supposed to manifest tend to be the opposite of those needed to succeed as a hostess. Most housewives are extremely shy—which is considered proper, especially when they are young—and are seen as their husbands' private property. *Okusan*, the most common form of address for housewives, means a person from the innermost (*oku*) area of the house or compound. On those rare occasions when a visitor is invited into a home for dinner, the wife acts as mute cook and serving maid. Hostesses make their living by promoting a convivial atmosphere, and are young, attractive women who are seen as accessible to all men, not as the property of one man.

An astonishing amount of business in Japan is conducted in public coffeehouses, cabarets, bars, "snacks," and restaurants.[12] In the bars and snacks after regular company hours, social bonds are formed that establish the much publicized "group identification" in Japanese companies. Hostesses, particularly in the smaller bars, facilitate these relationships. Even in the cabarets and nightclubs, it is the hostesses who create the conditions that allow Japanese men to get to know each other in a "safe" environment.

So important is this first function that nearly all but the cheapest drinking establishments employ hostesses or hostess-bartenders. Even liquor stores that have a counter or a tiny partition for drinking on the premises often have a female shopkeeper who performs the hostess role.

In the bars and snacks, hostesses perform a second function. They provide the bulk of the entertainment, in place of the showgirls of the cabarets and nightclubs. To a certain extent all of these women are public and available for conversation, jokes, teasing, and looking at—if nothing else.

Their third function—marrying marginal males—derives from the Japanese custom of carefully investigating the background of a potential spouse. Hostesses are immediately disqualified from "good" marriages because of their occupation: as women who have been publicly available, they cannot return to being private. Hence they marry males of equally marginal backgrounds—if they choose to marry at all. Their substantial economic independence gives them perhaps more options to marriage than other Japanese women. In any case, marginal marriages are not necessarily impoverished; in fact, they can be very wealthy, although not socially acceptable.

CONCLUSION

The hostess occupation reflects Japanese consumerism. One of the great attractions to the profession is the hostesses' appearance of being able to purchase all of the items that one has been repeatedly told are essential for happiness. This attraction is especially powerful for the young, poorly educated migrants from rural areas and small towns. That businessmen are the major consumers of the hostesses' services suggests a closer than casual relationship.

It would seem that the driving force in the migration of the Hanayama hostesses from their natal towns into the big city of Sapporo was and is economic, although there are social and political motivations as well. None of these young women had options that were economically competitive with the occupation of hostess. Nearly all of them said that they became hostesses because of the money; no one talked about the glamour of living in the big city, although some expressed a wish to live a modern lifestyle. Many were running away from their families and the social environment in which they had grown up—various tales of sexual molestation and harassment were fairly common. One might suspect that, as young women, they did not fit readily into the mold prepared for them by the mainstream society.

If the women's choices are based on economics, so too are the external pressures on them. By discriminating strongly and effectively against women both in education and employment, Japanese society channels women with minimal education into the entertainment fields. These women have a choice, of course, but it is not an even one: they may choose marriage, which can mean poverty and certainly economic and social dependence and lack of freedom, or they may choose the water trades, which offer substantial economic gain and economic and social independence. Although marriage may not mean poverty and being a hostess guarantees neither economic gain nor independence, the two choices do tend to correlate with these effects. Thus, there is a stream of young women who become professional sex objects or, at best, a sort of modern version of the ancient Greek *hetaera*—bright, attractive, competent women who are denied full citizenship but fulfill a crucial role in society. The role of the hostess reflects both the exploitation of women who become hostesses and the exploitation of women who follow the mainstream path of marriage to middle-class respectability and the various restrictions that this path entails (Vogel 1963). By taking the alternate path, the hostesses gain considerably in terms of social and economic independence, but pay a substantial price for that independence.

NOTES

I thank Lorisa Mock for the several rereadings and editings of this chapter that made it as readable as it is. I am responsible for any errors or misstatements.

1. This chapter is based on more than a year of participant-observation in 1975 to 1976 and a series of short visits in 1981, 1990, and 1991. The primary source of information was long interviews with about a fifth of the total adult population of the neighborhood in 1975 and 1976. Subsequently, only spot checks and casual interviewing were done. In the original study, approximately 20 percent of the adult population of the neighborhood, including thirty-eight hostesses and eight landladies, were interviewed, most more than once. Much of the material discussed in this chapter came from multiple sources and could be cross-checked. The research was done almost exclusively in the neighborhood where the hostesses lived, not where they worked.

2. The average was 8.8 years in 1975 to 1976. Completion of middle school takes 9 years, the legal minimum required education. In the much smaller sample taken in 1990 and 1991, the average increased to approximately 11.5 years. In *The Japanese School: Lessons for Industrial America* (New York: Praeger, 1986), Benjamin Duke cites the Ministry of Education Statistical Handbook, asserting that ninety-four percent of all Japanese go to high school and ninety-eight percent of those graduate (Duke 60). This would mean that approximately ninety-two percent of all young Japanese have higher levels of formal education than the average hostess, at least in this Sapporo neighborhood.

3. Most of the hostesses left at the end of middle school, the legal minimum. Those who left earlier did so because they actively disliked school and were perceived as delinquent. Only two said they were "officially" expelled; the others said they stopped going and, after a greater or lesser amount of pressure to return, were just ignored by the school system. One hostess said that her middle school officially graduated her even though she did not attend the final two years.

Hostesses reported engaging in behaviors that ranged from sexual activity to delinquency, petty theft, and the like. The hostess who said she left school during the sixth grade, the final year of elementary school, asserted that she had been seduced by a teacher and stopped going to school to avoid him. All of the hostesses, even those who finished high school, seemed to have become sexually active quite early, and all expressed a strong sense of rebellion, although the targets of that rebellion were broadly dispersed.

4. In Japan, as in the United States, the percentage of students graduating from high school can be a very misleading figure because it suggests a level of education, not just years of formal education attended. In both countries, it is possible to attend and graduate from high school with a poor education.

5. See especially Spradley and Mann's treatment of the distinction between staff, regular customers, and casual customers. James P. Spradley and Brenda Mann, *The Cocktail Waitress: Women's Work in a Man's World* (New York: Wiley, 1975), 76–81.

6. Given the sample size, no statistical significance can be suggested. The original work in the mid-1970s included extended interviews with thirty-eight hostesses. Only ten have been checked since then, seven in 1981 and five in 1991 (with two of the 1981 group reinterviewed in 1991).

7. The only exception in the period under consideration was a small cluster of blue-collar workers who lived in company housing in one corner of the neighborhood until 1981, when the housing was demolished. These residents also had extremely small networks within the neighborhood.

8. Other entertainers who live in Hanayama are equally disinterested in such networks. When I use the phrase "nonentertainer," I am purposely ignoring a small group of nonhostess entertainers—bartenders, musicians, bounders, and other people who work in the various occupations in the entertainment district.

9. A "modern life" in this sense appears to mean personal freedom from family and other social obligations. Although part of this image clearly constitutes an attempt to remove oneself from the restrictions placed on Japanese women, it also, at least in part, reflects perceived American values and behavior patterns, primarily derived from films and television.

10. This definition attempts to exclude people such as housewives or anyone who benefits incidentally from sexual arrangements such as marriage. One of the problems in discussing prostitution is that the English word is so heavily value-laden. Much of this cultural load derives from the Judeo-Christian concept of sin, which is not widely held in Japan.

11. A quaint but pertinent historical note: it is said that when Japan was "opened" by the European powers led by the United States, one of the first responses on the part of the Japanese who had to deal with the barbarians was to have geisha—courtesans skilled in music, dance, and conversation—function as social buffers. As a result, geisha gained a great deal of respectability.

12. Extremely common in Japan, a "snack" is an establishment where food is served with the drinks.

NINE

Marriage, Motherhood, and Career Management in a Japanese "Counter Culture"

Millie R. Creighton

In this essay, I apply the phrase "counter culture," used by Susan Benson in describing American department stores, to the work culture of women in the Japanese department store industry.[1] Although work is an important arena of inquiry in all industrial or postindustrial societies, the desire to work, choice of occupation, and the value placed on work are linked to the social world in which people situate themselves and to their understanding of "other options, other constraints, other obligations".[2] Japanese women's work and career aspirations cannot be assessed independently from parental investment in education, the constraints imposed by Japan's permanent-employment system, the persisting social value given to the long-exalted role for women of *ryōsai kenbo* (good wife, wise mother), and women's own perceptions of the prestige and problems they reap from paid employment or homemaking work.[3]

In the mid-1980s the Japanese government passed a series of initiatives to expand female employment and career opportunities. Foremost among these was the 1985 passage of Japan's Equal Employment Opportunity Law (*danjo kōyō kikai kintōhō*, herein referred to as EEOL), which went into effect in April 1986. When the EEOL was passed, the government also established a special committee, entitled "Planning and Promotion of Policies for Women," and created the Institute for Advancement of Women in Employment as a cooperative endeavor between industry and the Ministry of Labor (MOL). I suggest these changes reflect a desire to participate in international life, rather than an internal shift in Japanese social values regarding women's roles. Had Japan not made such changes by the end of the United Nation's Decade for Women (1975–1985), Japan would not have been allowed to ratify the U.N. Resolution on Elimination of All Forms of Discrimination against Women.

Studying legal changes alone would present a very incomplete understanding of Japanese women's work goals and experiences, particularly when those changes seem not to have stemmed from internal shifts in social values or employment structures, but from a desire to appease international pressures. Rather than reduce work experiences to a few variables, Miller suggests that "a more comprehensive approach to understanding how work opportunities are distributed in modern society is to begin by looking at concrete work situations and worker interpretations of them."[4] This chapter attempts to provide such a look by presenting an ethnographic account of female employment in a particular Japanese work culture: department stores. Most of the field research on which this is based was conducted from 1985 to 1987, the period when the EEOL was passed and implemented. I examine the feelings, values, and goals of women department store employees I interacted with and interviewed. I assess their interpretations of their work experiences and of how the EEOL may, or may not, affect their working lives and the parameters of their own "counter culture."

Japanese department stores comprise a work culture that, like other work cultures, involves "the transmission of knowledge, attitudes and codes of behavior."[5] Structured around the pivotal interface of store employees and customers across the sales counter, it is a counter culture in several ways. Often the interests of the predominately female employees run counter to the interests of (a largely male) management. Social roles of women as domestic household consumers merge with employment roles as sellers, allowing women as retailers and as shoppers to view themselves across the counters, in alternate role possibilities.

This counter culture is not equivalent to countercultures that urge revolutionary or antiestablishment modes of life. Nonetheless, Japanese department stores both typify women's working conditions in Japan prior to the passage of the EEOL and serve as counter examples. In order to explicate this dual nature of department store counter culture, I must discuss general conditions affecting Japanese working women and the nature of the EEOL.

DEPARTMENT STORES, WOMEN'S EMPLOYMENT, AND THE EEOL

Women have been active in the Japanese labor force in fairly high numbers throughout most of this century.[6] Whereas women's employment was once concentrated in agricultural and later in manufacturing work, it has overwhelmingly shifted to the service sector. Within this sector, female employees have tended to concentrate in banks, securities firms, department stores, and other companies involved in retail and distribution.

Although the percentage of women in the Japanese labor force has been comparable to that of women in other industrialized countries, Japanese women have faced greater obstacles because of societal values that require concentrated maternal involvement in child care and because of the seniority-based structure of the permanent employment system. In *The Japanese Company*, Clark asserts, "It is admittedly true that no industrial society gives women genuine parity with men in economic affairs, but Japanese women are more rigidly discriminated against than their Western counterparts."[7] Given the Japanese employment system, where promotions and pay increases are made on the basis of years of service and training provided by one's company, the main problem for women has not been a discrepancy in wages.[8] Women were often hired primarily as *shokuba no hana* (office flowers). They were given only routine jobs and seldom allowed to enter the career track. Companies preferred to hire their "office flowers" from among new junior college and high school graduates, and a majority of companies refused to hire women who were four-year university graduates. The rationale given for this discriminatory practice was that women would (and should) quit at marriage to concentrate on family duties. Since junior college and high school graduates tended to be two to four years younger than university graduates, companies claimed they would receive the benefit of these additional years of employment before the expected marriage age. A possible rationale not mentioned was that these women's lower educational level justified their lower salaries and career prospects relative to their male work colleagues.

Single women employees between the ages of twenty-four and twenty-seven were considered "aging" and would likely experience the pressure of *kata-tataki* (a tap on the shoulder) through suggestions that they retire. Even if they managed to obtain jobs, "aging" four-year university graduates were not welcome to stay because, by working "too many years, they accumulated seniority and a commensurately higher annual salary, becoming with time costly labor."[9]

Older women returned to the work force in large numbers, usually after their youngest child had entered school, but as returnees they did not have the status of regular, full-time staff members. They were designated temporary or part-time labor. This reserve of cheap female labor suited the demands of the nation's permanent-employment system; the women could be hired or laid off in accordance with current economic conditions, allowing companies to retain all male employees in the "permanent employment" track even in a stagnant economy.[10]

The average age of female workers is rising because of demographic changes. The average life expectancy for Japanese women has risen to over eighty years, while the average number of children per woman has dropped to less than two.[11] Most women thus have "almost forty-five good years left to them after [becoming] relatively free from childcare responsibilities in their mid-thirties."[12] Many women fill these years by returning to work in simple, low-paying jobs, at a wage disadvantage because the

Japanese seniority-based permanent employment system grants higher pay rates for consecutive years of employment with the same company.

Against this background of women's limited career prospects, Japan's EEOL was passed. It bans sexual discrimination in recruitment and training; calls for equal treatment in welfare benefits, retirement, and dismissal for employees in the same level of employment; and urges employers to establish childcare leave for women and reemploy women at their former job statuses after an absence to bear or raise children.

The EEOL has been criticized for many reasons. Although the law prevents the previously standard practice of differentiating between a male work track and a female work track, the law as interpreted by the Ministry of Labor does allow companies to differentiate between a career track and a noncareer track. Companies are not required to treat all female and male employees equally, but only those employees in the same track. Companies are not expected to grant responsible work and promotion to noncareer-track employees (who are mostly women); they are only required to allow qualified women the possibility of admission to the career track formerly reserved for men. This interpretation underscores the significance of the word "opportunity" in the law's title. The law does not seek extensive changes in work organization to grant equal employment for men and women. Its aim is instead to provide a limited number of qualified women the opportunity for equal employment with men.

Although the law requires that women be admitted to the career track, government interpretations of the law point out that it does not require that men be allowed equal access to the noncareer track or to traditionally female jobs. The rationale for this discrepancy is that the law was meant to enhance career prospects for women, not change career patterns of men, nor threaten the jobs of women not interested in career advancement. Employees in the noncareer track are predominately women, and these women continue to be assigned low-ranking menial jobs such as filing, copying, greeting customers, and pouring tea. Companies still stipulate working requirements for noncareer-track women that are not stipulated for career-track employees. Many companies, for example, still require women in the noncareer track to live with their parents.

This interpretation of the law allows many companies to post advertisements for female employees and maintain working conditions that appear discriminatory by Western standards. When equal employment laws were implemented in the States, "help wanted, male" or "help wanted, female" had to be dropped from most job advertisements. In contrast, after the passage of the EEOL in Japan, companies could continue to specify a desire for female filing clerks and female employees in other low-ranking jobs traditionally viewed as women's work, even though advertisements were not supposed to specify males for higher-ranking or career positions.

Perhaps the most fundamental criticism of the new law is that it only asks that employers make efforts to treat women equally; it carries no penalties against violators. However, this is also true of similar laws in other countries. For example, many of the laws guaranteeing equal employment for men and women in Canada also carry no penalties for violators. Without penalties, the effectiveness of the Japanese EEOL will be largely dependent upon companies' ability and willingness to recognize and revise discriminatory practices. Two months after the law went into effect, a survey was conducted to determine firms' preparedness to comply with the new law. An overwhelming majority of the firms (79.9 percent) said the law would have no impact on their operations since they already "treated men and women employees equally," despite the fact that only 1.2 percent of the firms had women in positions above the rank of division manager.[13] Recent analyses suggest that little has changed in this regard. In his post–EEOL discussion of Japanese-style employment, Whittaker writes, "There is still great resistance to having female functional managers; estimates range from 2.5% of all managers down, depending on the definition, with little change over the past decade."[14]

Although department stores exhibit many of the same constraints on women's employment, relative to other types of companies in Japan they have emerged as a stronghold for working women in general and for career-minded women in particular. Moreover, this trend was recognized before the passage of the EEOL. An article published in 1982 notes that "women have not made much progress in improving their status in Japanese industry," but points out that "the department store industry has been a noteworthy exception, in taking the initiative in appointing women to management posts and opening the way to participation in administration."[15] As in most large corporations in Japan, department store management tends to be male-dominated. What makes department stores a special case, a "woman-oriented industry," are two circumstances: the overwhelming majority of department store employees are women (estimates run between sixty and eighty percent depending on the store and its location); and eighty percent of their customers are women. To cater to their overwhelmingly female clientele, department stores have been willing to promote women to high-ranking positions. A researcher for the Japan Department Store Association (*Nihon Hyakkaten Kyōkai*) indicated to me in an interview that this willingness stemmed from the realization that "it is better to have women [in management] to know how to sell to other women."

In light of this background, I explore the possible impact of the EEOL on women's working lives and investigate how women in the Japanese department store industry experience, interpret, and express their work culture. I will be particularly concerned with the extent to which the women see marriage and motherhood as compatible with career aspirations and the extent to which the managerial women role models motivate incoming women toward a career-orientation.

A WOMEN'S WORK CULTURE

Ishihara Ichiko, who rose to the pinnacle corporate position of executive director at Takashimaya department store, is well known in Japan as the first woman to be appointed to an executive post in the department store industry. Famous for her adopted slogan, "Think like a man, act like a lady, and work like a dog,"[16] Ishihara forged her way to the top of the industry by working extensive overtime hours, while reporting that she left by 5:00 P.M. so the company would not have to pay her overtime, and using her female perspective in matters such as kitchenware sales, which she boosted by introducing American cookware and food storage containers.

Conservative Japanese employment structures that separate male and female work tasks have actually helped women advance in department stores. Early in my research, an analyst for the Japan Department Store Association explained to me that "there are lots more female employees" than in other types of companies and that "management feels the supervisors of females should be females." He asserted that large numbers of female workers require greater emphasis on women's work morale. He believed that the presence of female managers helps to maintain morale because it "gives the underling female the feeling that she has some hope to rise up." A woman in a high-ranking advisory post at one department store also noted that female managers can avert a morale problem: "It is not a good thing to have men and women start together and capable women see that men are always promoted above them. . . . It doesn't matter when the ability of the men is obviously high or better than the female employees, but when it is not, there must be some sort of morale problem."

Interviews with female staff indicated that they perceived department stores as less male-dominated than other companies because of these factors. An employee of one store's pharmaceutical department said she chose to work at a department store because "department stores are a concentrated place of female employment. Still now in Japan most workplaces are dominated by men. Since there are so many women around, I thought that a department store was, at least, not as likely to be dominated by men as other companies." A woman who has worked both on the sales floor and in her store's planning offices said that "women want to work at department stores because they feel they have more to say than at some other companies. Department stores are part of the retailing system, and in a way the retailing system is part of the women's world."

Department stores have long set precedent in female employment. Mitsukoshi employed the first female sales clerks in Japan in 1895.[17] Though the majority of other companies refused to hire graduates of four-year universities, department stores were willing to make use of their talents.[18] Limited employment options elsewhere motivated many university graduates to seek department store jobs. One such woman who sold jewelry at Mitsukoshi cited limited options as the reason for her choice. "The primary reason was the job recruiting situation for girls who had finished four years of college. I was looking for a job in 1980, and the job choice was very limited for female university graduates then. If you were finishing a junior college it was different; there were many more job choices." The remarks of a woman on Seibu department store's art museum staff, whom I interviewed while she was temporarily posted in the United States, reveal that hiring prejudices against four-year university graduates remained strong even after the passage of the EEOL. "In the States everyone is so interested in getting an M.A. or Ph.D.—even women! I am so surprised at this. . . . In Japan if I say I have a four-year degree it is hard to get a job; people think it is too much for a woman to have a four-year degree. . . . No one wants you.

Although the majority of female employees quit within five to seven years, department stores are unlikely to exert pressures to coerce women to resign. A female public relations employee at Mitsukoshi contended that long before the EEOL, women could continue working once they married, even if they were pregnant—something many other companies would not allow. Since the store had an obligation to show concern for them, they were often removed from the sales floor during early pregnancy. "The beginning of pregnancy," this employee said, "is the most dangerous period, so women shouldn't stand so much but do other things. Typically they handle the register or do work in the back." Once past the initial months of pregnancy, women would return to the sales floor but be shifted to "appropriate areas" where their presence would not jar customers. She continued, "We do have some pregnant women working on the sales floor. Usually this is in maternity or baby goods. We don't expect them to leave from these areas even if they are very pregnant."

Department stores were leaders in introducing the programs and policies for women urged by the Ministry of Labor and the EEOL. At Seibu, the establishment of a system called the "Ladies' Board" allowed the proposals of female employees to be "relayed directly to the store managers as well as the entire management structure."[19] At the same time, Seibu introduced a strict merit system that based pay raises on ability without regard to gender.

Childcare leave systems were already well developed at many department stores long before the EEOL. A public relations employee outlined

Mitsukoshi's program, which allowed nine weeks of paid maternity leave and up to one year of nonpaid leave. "When a baby is born, an employee can take nine weeks off with pay. The employee decides whether this is before or after the baby is born. . . . After childbirth . . . employees can take up to one year off, but they won't be paid for this period. Afterward they can return to work with the same pay and rank as before."

Isetan adopted its leave program in 1971. In 1985 it was officially chosen by the Ministry of Labor as the "model childcare leave system."[20] It allows pregnant employees to take eight weeks off with pay before and after the birth of a child. A woman can also take up to a maximum of three years of unpaid leave and return to the same job. In keeping with strong societal values of intense maternal involvement, the Secretary to the President at Isetan points out that "this three-year period is to take care of the child." Afterward, the woman "is accepted back to the same level as that at which she left." She emphasized that in Japan, "There are so many companies where they would never accept former employees back. Once they leave, it's the end!" Women who choose to return to work after their sixteen weeks of paid leave are over may come to work one hour later than the normal starting time for up to one year after the baby's birth.

Department stores have also been pioneers in adopting policies of rehiring women who have left to raise children. In 1970, Odakyū department store initiated a program of reinstatement and status transference for its female employees. Under this program a woman could change her employment status from full-time to part-time and back to accommodate the demands of marriage or motherhood. If she resigned from the company, she was entitled to priority reinstatement within five years.[21]

Both Seibu and Tōbu department stores inaugurated license programs of reinstatement. Under these programs, women are issued a license allowing them to return to the company at their former status up to a maximum of ten years after their departure. (Seibu later extended this period.) Not all female employees are given this license; the right to return depends upon previous job performance. At the time of retirement the employee must apply for the license; the stores retain the right to decide whether to grant it. A public relations employee for Seibu claimed that approximately six hundred women had taken licenses under the program by 1986 and about thirty had already returned to work. Since the employees could have up to ten years off, she explained that the company still did not know what percentage of these women would actually return. An employee at Tōbu also noted that his stores' program, three years old in 1986, was too new to allow any conclusions. "Theoretically, a woman could quit for ten years and reenter. But the program itself hasn't existed anywhere near ten years yet, so I can't say for certain if there will be cases like this or not."

To further accommodate its working mothers, Seibu department store maintains its own in-store day-care facilities.[22] Women are allowed to take time off during the day to attend to small children. Seibu's associated supermarket chain, Seiyu Stores, adopted what it called a "baby care time system" for employees with children under two. Under this system, employees could take two hours off each day to care for their children by either coming to work late or leaving early. What was most novel about this system was that the daily childcare leave privilege was extended to both mothers and fathers. A spokesperson for the company reportedly boasted that the system embodied "the spirit of the Equal Employment Opportunity Law."[23] However, in 1986 such a system was too innovative for the Ministry of Labor. After the passage of the EEOL, the ministry surveyed other countries' childcare systems, including those that involved fathers, and reported to the press that "Japanese society is not ready to have the Ministry of Labor promote such leaves for men workers, especially because of men's inexperience concerning such matters."[24] This response reveals that the EEOL's passage was not intended to erode existing distinctions in male and female gender roles, nor differential involvement in parenting and child care.

Leave programs that included fathers were finally given recognition in 1991 with the passage of the *Ikuji kyūgyōhō*, the Young Childcare Leave Law. The law, which went into effect in 1992, addresses the reluctance to accept men as full partners in childcare, stipulating that parents of either sex must be allowed to take an extended leave after the birth of a child. When this law was passed, journalist and social commentator Kashima Takashi tried to assess the possible impact. He found a computer software company that had for ten years allowed fathers to take a year off after a child's birth. In questioning the company, he discovered that none had ever taken advantage of this option. Kashima concluded that the new childcare leave law may sound like a "rebel law," but that, law or no law, men could not really take such leave. As he states, "One reason is that both men and women find it difficult to break away from the notion that child rearing is part of the women's realm. A second reason is that it takes a lot of courage for men to take a long break for child rearing when evaluation within the company is still very much based on how long one stays in the office."[25] Thus, even the passage of a childcare leave law that includes fathers does not indicate that gender role distinctions have vanished or that men and women will easily take advantage of their newly defined legal rights.

Even before passage of the EEOL, female employees had a greater chance of obtaining managerial positions at department stores; their opinions and suggestions were more likely to be taken seriously by senior management. However, discrimination did and does exist. The Secretary to the President at Isetan said, "Management needs to use the strength of female ability. Even though there are greater chances for promotions in department stores, we are still much, much behind compared to American retailers." A female employee at another store stated, "I can't really say that discrimination doesn't exist. . . . Men rise in the ranks before women." One woman described the training program for first-level management that she underwent at age forty in her twenty-second year of employment: "There were eight women in the group. I knew most of them by face. The rest were twenty-two men, and so it was a bit different, of course. On the whole, these men were much younger than me because this training was for the initial management level, which most men try to get to by about thirty." A high-ranking female employee of one department store explained that management was divided into four levels. Drawing an analogy with college ranks, she likened the first two levels to the underclass and the two higher levels to the upperclass. She noted that many women have entered the first two managerial levels to work in the underclass, but no women have yet crossed the divide between levels two and three to graduate to upperclass status.[26]

In addition to the problems of obtaining the higher management positions, many employees complained about the paucity of women buyers. Although the overwhelming majority of department store customers are women, their buyers seldom are. One employee revealed her frustrations about this, saying, "Look at this store. This year [1986] in April it will have its first female buyer. The first! Can you believe it? It'll be in women's underwear. . . . At department stores eighty percent of the customers are women, but the buyers are all old men."

Some department stores maintain a paternalistic stance toward female employees. One major store unofficially requires all women who are not four-year university graduates to live with their parents during their early years of employment.[27] A female employee commented on this policy, saying, "In the old days perhaps the company president and executives thought that when girls lived with their families they behaved better." The company presents this policy as consistent with Japanese cultural expectations. According to one company spokesperson, "I think the company wants to have someone who can watch the new girls' life, especially when they join the company. . . . Parents also expect this and desire it. Parents feel that the company should take some responsibility for their young daughters. . . . I think all of this is something that must be very peculiar to Japanese society. The company wishes to have its employees' parents watch and control their children. And parents want the company to control and thus be responsible for their children." In an analysis of office ladies and female factory workers employed by Brother, Lo shows how the acceptance and expectation of such corporate paternalism resulted in lifestyle restrictions, such as an evening curfew, that regulated women even in their nonworking hours.[28]

The work routine for female department store employees can be tiring and boring. The Secretary to the President at Isetan says, "For those who don't understand the exciting aspects of retailing—well, just selling things is boring for them. Sometimes there are girls who quit within three days." Some positions are particularly tiring, including those such as "elevator girl," often sought after by many new employees as the most glamorous job. According to a spokesperson for Mitsukoshi, "The elevator girls get a lot more break time. . . . They have an extremely tiring job. They have to stand all the time and use their voice continually. It gets boring too. They are primarily there to give a good, sparkling impression to the customers. They can't express much of a happy smiling condition if we keep them at the elevators for more than forty-five minutes each time."

Unlike many women who are "office flowers," female department store employees are not usually expected to subordinate themselves to male colleagues. However, department store clerks must adopt a subordinate, subservient attitude toward their customers. This requirement stems from Japanese expectations of status inequality. Anthropologist Nakane Chie has characterized Japan as a "vertical society" that emphasizes rank differences among individuals and groups.[29] In Japan, customers are "outsiders" and guests of the store and thus rank higher than sales clerks. Clerks must exhibit the subservient behavior consistent with their inferior status. Because they must display appropriate status behavior and satisfy customers' demands for high service, women may find department store training especially demanding. A male employee of a manufacturing firm who trains new recruits discusses different corporate policies toward bowing: "It is said that department store instructors use a gauge marked in degrees. We don't use such a gauge. . . . We need not have such an exact bow. The bow is in the mind; if they have a respectful mind, the bow will be okay." In contrast, many female department store clerks mentioned the severity of the training: "We had to practice standing and bowing over and over. We had to practice against a wall with our back and butt against it. We had to stand as straight as that wall, and when we bowed our butt had to remain against it while only our backs moved."

Stores often regulate female dress and mannerisms more strictly than male dress because customers have more exacting standards for female clerks. According to one personnel director, if female clerks wear too much makeup or jewelry, do not dress according to expectations, or behave in ways considered inappropriate for women, Japanese customers will complain.[30] Therefore, many regulations govern personal appearance for women. Gravely serious, he stated the rules: "Women cannot have long hair. It should be shoulder length or shorter. If they have long hair, they can't bow right. [They] cannot use eye shadow that glitters—the kind that is currently very popular. They can only wear one ring at a time. They can only wear skin-color stockings. No patterns, bright colors, or pink lace nylons are allowed. [*As he mentioned the last item, he glared at my own choice of legwear for the interview.*] Their shoes must be dark blue or black, and the heel height must be under five centimeters."

The female employees at many stores are required to wear uniforms, whereas men are not. As the personnel director explained, at his store, women's uniforms indicate differences in female employment status or different job positions. "The general clerks all wear the same uniform. The uniform of female managers is different from the others. Elevator operators and information clerks have a separate uniform." Male employees at this store are required to wear name plates, but not a designated uniform.

The popular Japanese phrase "a man's face is his resume, a woman's face is her price tag" suggests that a woman's main assets are her youth and beauty. The phrase sums up the traditional position of women in the job market.[31] As is the case for "office flowers," women employees at department stores are sometimes primarily window dressing. According to the personnel director, "When we interview prospective female employees, we are looking for someone friendly and neat who is quick in motion. The smile is very important. We want those persons able to give a very good first impression."

Certain jobs (information clerks, elevator operators, greeters at doors or escalators) are focal points of customer interaction. These women dispense store information, but their primary purpose is to offer a decorative hospitality to the customers.[32] Women are commonly chosen for these positions by virtue of their general good looks, beatific smiles, and elegant bows. According to another personnel director, "This is a special group among the clerks. . . . Girls are selected for these positions from among the junior college and high school graduates. . . . The trainers look them over closely and make selections. . . . Most important is choosing tall girls with pretty bows."

The EEOL urges companies to provide training for women and to allow them access to the male-dominated career track, but it does not require that these opportunities be extended to all women employees. Companies have turned to multitracking, assigning women to either the career track or the noncareer track. The situation at department stores is similar, although the division between these two tracks is not so clearly drawn. Advanced training, promotion possibilities, and pay raises are likely for four-year college graduates, somewhat less likely for graduates of two-year colleges, and extremely rare for high school graduates.[33] This situation creates frustration and anger in many employees; it can also deter women with less education from taking an interest in their work. One employee, a high school graduate who was initially committed to her work, decided to quit when she realized that she would never be accorded the same treatment as university or even junior college graduates. "I thought I had tried to study other department stores and to try to improve myself on the job for three years. In the maternity area there is a fashion show every three months, and I worked very hard on these even on my days off. I worked very diligently at my job and gave it my best efforts, but when I found out that after three years the junior college students were entering at the same pay as me, I knew none of my efforts were really appreciated at all by the company."

Some high school and junior college graduates expressed concern that the new law would further limit their prospects. In many cases, university graduates were sympathetic to them, as is evident in one woman's comment that "the first year we were all at the same level, the same as high school or junior college graduates. But I've been here only one and a half years and I'm already at the same level as a high school or junior college graduate who's been here five or even ten years. Even if they work here a long time, they'll never rise at all. But the companies like to hire them. . . . They are the cheapest and they don't stay long." Another university graduate who entered her company in the same year concurs. "The company says that it spent more money on college graduates and that we bring in more money. But it's not true. We all do the same things, so naturally the high school grads don't like it. I'm sure they resent it."

As defined by the law, equal opportunity does not mean that men and women will necessarily perform the same tasks, even when they have been hired for the same track. One woman explained that her store has formalized this sexual division even for men and women on the career track. "During the first year, men have first-year 'men's work,' women have first-year 'women's work.' Women's work consists of things like throwing out the garbage, washing the rags, carrying bags. Lots of people hate it. During the first year they make you do the things everyone hates, but these things are different for men and women. So if we entered on equal terms with men during the first year, we get the same pay, but even if we are working in the same sales area, the work is very different."

The differential job descriptions indicate that tasks are assigned according to a traditional gender asymmetry where women are assigned tasks associated with domestic duties. These differential tasks are another clue that passage of the EEOL did not indicate a desire to overturn existing gender role distinctions.

Although not required to do so by the EEOL, Isetan department store began an experiment in 1986 that allowed selected female university graduates in the career track to perform the same work tasks as men. A woman involved in the experiment noted that she felt a responsibility to succeed for the sake of future female employees. "I am currently involved in an experiment within the company. Since my second year, I have been doing the same work as men. Normally, I would not be allowed to do second-year men's work. . . . The results have not been decided yet. If I am considered a failure, no one will be able to argue for men's and women's work being the same for a long while."

"JUST LIKE A JAPANESE GIRL"

This section deals with women employees' perceptions of themselves and each other and with their motivations to work. How well have women been socialized to fit into the career track given Japan's lifetime employment system? What are women's career aspirations? How are these goals related to marriage and motherhood?

Most Japanese women have been raised to consider the domestic realm their foremost responsibility, marriage and motherhood their primary goals. These attitudes, which have not changed radically in Japanese society for decades, are firmly held by women as well as by men.[34] In a study of working women with children in day care, Fujita discovered that the social evaluation of such women was based on how well they performed their domestic and childcare duties, not on their work positions or performance.[35] Socialization instills the belief that remaining unmarried will render life fearfully unfulfilling. One day during my research, I was talking with a group of women employees near an extensive display of Girls' Day dolls annually set up by the store during the weeks preceding Girls' Day on March third. Several of the women recalled their childhood delight with the tiers of elegant dolls annually displayed in their own households. But they also recalled their mothers' admonitions that the dolls had to come down immediately after Girls' Day. If not, they were always told, people would believe they were slovenly in their household habits, which could bring on the greatest threat for a girl's future: difficulty finding a husband and the horror of facing life as an unmarried woman.

A little later in life, the women were faced with repeated reminders of the urgency to marry. These often took the form of joking analogies, but the message was serious. One such analogy relates women to Christmas cakes.[36] It is the custom in Japan to purchase a Christmas cake for consumption on December 24 or 25. These cakes begin to flood the market from mid-December on, but most sales are made only on those two days. Social wisdom in Japan playfully suggests that women are like Christmas cakes. Before they reach age twenty, no one really wants them. The interest in them and the demand for them continues to rise until age twenty-four or twenty-five, at which time they command the greatest interest and can be sold at the best price. But they should not wait too long, because once they hit twenty-six, no one wants them anymore, and if they cannot be unloaded before the New Year (or married at latest by around age thirty), they will never find a buyer. Brinton uses the Christmas cake analogy to point out the extent to which Japanese women conform to social expectations and marry on schedule.[37] I emphasize that the joke not only reflects conformity to the age-appropriate timing of marriage, but also prompts such conformity. Young women may laugh at the joke, but they are nevertheless reminded that if they do not get serious about securing a marriage partner by their mid-twenties, they may be doomed to spinsterhood. Lo's account of factory workers shows that by the age of twenty-six many of these women began to think of themselves as spinsters with little hope of marriage or a better life than factory employment.[38] The recent rise in the acceptable marriage age has many Japanese saying that Christmas cakes have become New Year's cookies. However, the expectation to marry by a certain age, and the fears associated with not doing so, still appear to be strong, even if the age itself has risen.

In addition to fears about remaining single, women in management must counter questions about their capabilities. These questions are often raised most strongly by other women. Some express the belief that socialization has left women weak in managerial abilities. A section head for Keiō department store said, "If we're talking about women's products alone, women have an absolutely accurate eye for product selection. . . . However, women are slow when it comes to decisiveness in negotiating large-scale contracts, so that area is better suited to men."[39] Women are often conceptualized as too emotional for management. A shop master for Seibu stated, "Women have a tendency to be overly sensitive to detail when it comes to management. In comparison, I feel that men are very talented in managing women."[40] A woman who spent ten years in the interiors department at Seibu, then worked as a part-timer at Isetan, believed that women in the workplace create more problems than men. She said that "squabbling" occurs "more in department stores than elsewhere because there are a lot of women working together. That kind of squabbling doesn't happen with the men, but it's always present among women. . . . Women are just a lot more troublesome."

Patterns of coworker relationships among female staff members contrasted with those of male workers. In his bank study, Rohlen noted that *senpai-kōhai* (senior-junior) relationships were clearly demarcated along sex lines. The expectation that *senpai* and *kōhai* are individuals of the same sex is a severe disadvantage for women because patronage is a significant factor for career advancement in the Japanese employment system.[41] In department stores, male employees had firm notions of *senpai-kōhai* relationships, whereas female employees had weak or even no notions of such relationships. A ten-year female veteran of the industry stated, "Lots of us were good friends. Usually you made friends at the same sales floor or department. Of course someone there might be your *senpai*, but after a while everyone gets mixed up and you can't really tell a person has worked at the store longer unless they are considerably older. Men . . . are more aware of status differences and who their *senpai* are."

In addition, identification with the group of employees with whom one entered the company—a trait often attributed to Japan's employment system—was strong among men but weak among women. Female personnel consistently noted that loyalty to and identification with one's entrance group diminished with time, whereas identification increased with those in one's area, regardless of age or year of entry. One woman claimed, "I think your close friends don't necessarily have anything to do with the year that you entered the company. It has more to do with the people you work with. You tend to become close to the people in the same sales area." After twenty-two years of employment, one female manager revealed that, in contrast to men, her identification with her entrance cohorts (only about five of whom remained) was limited to an ability to recognize them. She stated, "Among the men, it seems that they keep rather close association with the men who joined the company with them throughout their entire career. But this is not true for women. For some years after joining the company they will remain close . . . but eventually this fades away. Naturally I can still recognize anyone who joined in the same year if I see them at the store."

For decades the majority of women have been denied corporate rewards, but companies often indulged women with irresponsible work attitudes.[42] An American woman, employed as an adviser to foreign customers, expressed astonishment at some of her Japanese colleagues' work habits. She said, "The women are sweet and wonderful, but so extremely childish. Even if they tell you they are career women, I can't believe they think of themselves as that, or else they have no concept of what it means. They have no sense of commitment, no responsibility, make no attempt, and don't even entertain notions of anything."

Many women do desire responsible positions, but the rigors of Japan's career employment system and its "disregard-the-clock-come-early-stay-late" attitude make them wonder if a career is worth dedicating their lives to.[43] Realizing this, the American woman added, "The system is so harsh that maybe women just give up, or else they never try to begin with." Many Japanese women felt that the work ethic permeating Japan's lifetime employment system was too demanding for all employees. One said, "Japanese people go overboard when it comes to work. They think it is only natural to work long hours every day and still take home extra work for their days off. All the men do it, all of them, and they do it all the time. In that sense they really don't ever have vacations."

One woman expressed the opinion that men are able to cope with the situation for two reasons: first, because they have no choice, and second, because they know exactly what to expect in the future. Men understand what the promotion system means for them and exactly how or when they will rise in it. Even if they do not like the system, they can at least plan for it. As of yet, women do not feel assured that the career track makes them any similar promises of security. As one employee commented, "When starting out, men also get the most boring, difficult work, but they *know* they will rise in the future. They can bear through the early years because they have this assurance. Women don't think it's ever going to happen, so why should they put up with washing the rags all the time?"

Even if women are willing to make sacrifices, they are often unwilling to assert desires for managerial positions out of fear they will appear selfish, something the Japanese employment system discourages for both sexes.[44] One employee said, "Comparing a specialist to a generalist, I want to be a specialist. I never think in terms of managerial ranks or raising my position. I don't want to appear selfish to the company by saying that I want to be higher or a manager. But I want to use my ability." Despite wanting to be considered a specialist, this licensed dietician refused to describe herself as one because "in Japan it sounds too strong for a woman to say 'I'm a specialist.' "

Many women expressed a great deal of ambivalence. They wanted to continue working, preferably in challenging jobs, but they also wanted to become wives and mothers and were not certain that they could cope with both roles. Some preferred the option of changing companies at some point in their lives. Given the Japanese emphasis on maintaining relationships within a particular group, they thought returning to the same company after a long absence would be difficult, even if allowed by the new reinstatement programs. A clerk at Isetan said, "I want to keep working. I can't stand the idea of being stagnant just because I get married, but I don't necessarily think I will keep working at Isetan." A Tōbu employee agreed. "I want to keep working always, but whether at a department store or not I don't know. Young childhood is a very important period. I don't think it's possible to naturally integrate work with this . . . so maybe I'll quit at childbirth and look for another job later. I think it would be difficult to just quit a company and then go back to the same place. It would be better to start again somewhere else."

Many women were eager to pursue their careers but feared that success in the job market would interfere with success in the marriage market.[45] Japanese women must cope with fixed societal concepts of *kekkon-tekireiki*, the years considered suitable for marriage. Long past the upper limits of *kekkon-tekireiki*, (usually given as from twenty-four to twenty-seven, now possibly extended to thirty), a middle-aged manager who has worked at

Matsuzakaya for over thirty years expressed a twinge of regret over never marrying. "I used to think I would quit when I got married, but I never got married, so here I am. Sometimes I regretted not being married and wished that I would get married. But then again, I thought that working was more interesting." This sparky, attractive woman was self-confident and proud of her department store career. She derived particular satisfaction from being made a buyer. She once said, "When I became a buyer, that was the biggest thing in my life. There are very few women buyers in Japan; nearly all the buyers are men. . . . I think that this is the best thing that happened to me here. I felt like the company was recognizing my abilities when it made me a buyer." Although satisfied with her life and proud of her accomplishments, she still occasionally cracks jokes about her single status. In reference to the axiom that one can buy anything at a department store, she said, "I buy everything at Matsuzakaya. But I can't buy a boyfriend here; it'd be good if I could."

The women of managerial or supervisory status with whom I interacted in two years of research were all at least twenty-seven years old, and most were well over thirty. All had passed the age of *kekkon-tekireiki*, and all were unmarried. Some of these women had aspired to a career position from the beginning; others became seriously interested in retailing after working in the industry for several years. None of the women had consciously decided to remain single. Upon graduating, all thought they would marry someday. Almost none of these women described marriage and motherhood as something they had rejected or even "lost out on." Rather, husbands and children had simply not materialized in the course of events. A thirty-five-year-old who had recently returned from a stint as manager at one of Mitsukoshi's European stores laughed when she recalled her decision to go to a junior college rather than attend a four-year college so that she could work for a couple of years and quit when she married. She said, "When I started here, I had no idea I'd work fifteen years. I wanted to work for a little while, then quit when I got married. Here I am." Another woman, a forty-year-old manager, admitted that when she was younger she felt disappointed she had not married, but by the time she was in her mid-thirties she had accepted the possibility she would never marry and was satisfied with her career.

One woman in her mid-forties had aspired to a career position since early in her employment. With a directness not applauded by Japanese values, she had fought for raises and argued for promotion whenever she believed gender bias was postponing her advancement. She had always wanted responsible work and had always wanted to marry. The marriage just never happened. At some point, she had dealt with the possibility that she would never have a family, and, having done so, she was, at forty-seven involved in work that she found exciting and productive. She mentioned that her greatest difficulty had come from external pressure to marry, but this had also vanished at some point. Her family and other well-wishers had begged her to quit her job and pleaded with her to get married. This pressure on her was most extreme between age twenty-five (at that time already a late age for a woman to marry) and age thirty (the absolute, last hope, end of *kekkon-tekireiki*). Once she passed thirty, however, everyone seemed to give up. She was allowed to pursue her own lifestyle and career unfettered by family objections. She recalled that as a young woman she was terrified of reaching the end of *kekkon-tekireiki*, but that when it finally arrived, she ironically experienced it as a welcome release offering a new freedom from family and societal pressures.

For over a year I worked closely with one female manager who still had not resolved the conflict between her career and a desire for a family. I met her when she was thirty-five years old. At our first meeting, although we had not been discussing the issue of marriage at all, she suddenly and adamantly asserted that she had no interest in marrying. Her assertion was so strong that I suspected it was an attempt to deny her true feelings. I reproved myself for my thoughts and decided they were probably based on similar interactions with members of my own culture and did not apply to this Japanese woman. Working with her for a year, it was clear that she took great interest in her role as a public relations director for a large department store.

Shortly before my son was born, I went to visit her for the last time, taking along a female Japanese friend. This was not a formal interview; the discussion quickly turned into an intimate conversation among three women. It was early December, already a time when people discuss year-end plans and new year hopes. In the midst of the conversation, my department store friend suddenly blurted out that she was getting married in the coming year. Somewhat surprised, I foolishly congratulated her. She then confessed that for some time she had been terribly worried that she would never marry or have children. She explained that she had not set a wedding date, nor did she even have a partner in mind. However, at thirty-six she felt that if she were ever to marry and have children, she would have to get started immediately. She was, therefore, steadfastly determined to marry before the end of 1986.

Despite her current career successes, a woman still within the range of *kekkon-tekireiki* expressed the fear that she was getting "too old" for marriage. She joined Seibu after majoring in journalism. Having spent her two days of vacation each week taking classes in curatorship from "morning until night," she was rewarded with a longed-for transfer to Seibu's art museum staff. In 1986 she was one of the few employees, and the only woman, chosen from all Seibu stores to go abroad for specialized training in her field. She felt that "it was a very big thing for me to be chosen."

Although she was excited about her work, she had reached the age of twenty-five, and her mother's warnings that she would have difficulty finding a husband were always on her mind. She discussed the forces that seemed to be driving her to choose between a career and a family, stating, "My age is not so easy because people try to get married and quit the job. . . . I think my age is a turning point. I still don't know. I want to do my career, but I want to get married, have a family, have a child—just like a Japanese girl. Now I want to work for the museum here and live in America, but I can't avoid my age or concerns for my future either. My mother always says to me, 'It's too late, it's too late!' " This employee went on to express her dreams of organizing a traveling exhibition. Hearing her boast about her company's innovative art museum policies, it was difficult to imagine that she could easily give up her professional goals. "If," she said of the art staff, "we want to take a challenge, we must take a risk. We like challenge."

Many young women saw the challenge of entering the career track as a risk—not the risk that they would fail at their jobs, but that they would never marry. It strikes me as highly relevant that of all the women I randomly met and interviewed in managerial positions during two years of active research, not one had ever been married.[46]

Other research reinforced my growing suspicion that women in managerial positions tended to be single. A 1982 article on women in the distribution system focused on interviews with four female department store managers. Of the four, three had never been married and one was divorced. The women who had never been married made statements resembling those given by my interviewees. One said, "I originally began the study of interior decoration because I wanted to have an attractive home. However, I became so absorbed in arranging the interiors of other peoples' homes that to this day I haven't created a home of my own."[47] Another commented, "I also believed until a certain age that it was normal to get married, but after this age passed, I became determined to continue working for the rest of my life. . . . If there were a man understanding of these aspirations, I'd consider marriage, but so far I haven't met such a person."[48] The divorcée claimed that her marriage ended because she was unable to cope with both homemaking and her job. She also stated that nearly all female managers at her store (Shibuya Seibu) were single. "The work of a shop master calls for such extremely hard labor, both physically and mentally, that in the Shibuya branch, there are only two women shop masters who have children; the rest are all single women, middle-aged and older."[49] I was told about many other women in management positions. Even among these cases, the only married woman had an American husband, not a Japanese.

I do not mean to suggest that there were no married women with high-ranking career posts in department stores. As indicated, the executive director of Takashimaya was married (now widowed) and the mother of two. However, she represents a special case: as the daughter of a diplomat, she was actually raised outside Japan and the Japanese social context. Given her high status, younger junior clerks were unlikely to interact with her or perceive her as a role model.

I was interested in how junior-ranking women employees viewed their senior-ranking counterparts in managerial positions, women with whom they did interact. In explaining why department stores were more willing to promote women to management than other companies, department store senior personnel often claimed that it inspires younger women. The presence of women managers is supposed to provide living proof that women will be promoted and give junior women something toward which to aspire. Based on extensive interaction with these young women, it seemed to me that what struck them most clearly about their seniors was not that they had become managers, but that they had not become wives and mothers. The middle-aged, unmarried women I knew as managers had for the most part come to terms with their singlehood and the fact that they had never had children. Having faced these issues, they appeared quite happy and involved in life. Deriving great satisfaction from past career accomplishments, they had further goals and little self-pity. However, when I asked younger women about their shop masters and supervisors, rather than applauding their accomplishments, the first response tended to be "*kawaisō ne!*" ("It's pitiful, isn't it!"). I knew the pity was for the senior women's single status.

Occasionally there are voices in Japan that question whether marriage should be the route sought by all women. These voices are exemplified by the book, *Kekkon shinai kamoshiranai shōkōgun* (The "maybe I won't marry" syndrome).[50] Yet as Brinton shows, the vast majority of Japanese still get married during the culturally designated appropriate ages.[51] In a society of near-universal marriage, where failure to marry by a certain age evokes pity at best and social rebuke at worst—the so-designated middle-aged (over thirty) managers, proudly presented by the company as models of what young women may aspire to be, seemed instead to be perceived by these young women as stale, unconsumed Christmas cakes or Girls' Day dolls that had been left on the shelf. Like these other fearful reminders of the horrifying possibility of spinsterhood, their unmarried seniors served for many younger women as a living reminder of mothers' admonishments. If you are not ladylike, if you do not behave in a wifely or motherly manner, you will never get married. If you aspire too high, if you fight too hard for raises or promotions, if at twenty-five you fail to realize it will soon be too late, you will never get married.

IMPLICATIONS FOR CHANGE

This account of Japanese women's work experiences in the department store counter culture is not intended to suggest that Japanese society is unchanging. Rather, it raises doubts that legal changes such as the introduction of the EEOL can have any major impact on female employment roles without a corresponding shift in social values. Japan's permanent-employment system is structured around a gender dichotomy in which wives are totally dedicated to their families, thereby allowing men to be totally dedicted to the firm. Brinton points out that in order for Japanese women to realize greater career opportunities, there must be a concomitant change "in husbands' expectations that wives bear almost full responsibility for housework and child care."[52] The statements of women working in the department store industry clearly also call for a concomitant change in employment expectations for men so that overtime work decreases to a level consistent with other industrialized countries.[53] Such a shift would allow men to take greater responsibilities in family matters and make the career path for men an option more women perceive as viable for themselves.

Shifting role definitions have already created increased career opportunities for women in some arenas. If we look across the counter, we see that interpretations of women's consumer role, long a domestic responsibility of women in Japan, have changed. Women once were responsible for the family budget and made purchases, but they did not control the family budget or purchasing decisions.[54] The fact that women now control the budget and make purchasing decisions according to their own tastes has prompted increasing career opportunities for women.

In the 1980s, Japanese manufacturers, marketing specialists, and distribution experts woke up to the fact that most of their potential customers were women who controlled the family budget. Companies that dealt in real estate, securities, automobiles, computers, or anything else formerly considered "for men only" began struggling to appeal to women. Although marriage and motherhood remain the primary roles for women, the "good wife and wise mother" is no longer expected to limit herself to inconsequential tasks and small purchases. Her control of the family budget, once the province of men, has been acknowledged by the world of finance. Securities brokers have devised new strategies to appeal to homemakers. Four new money-management magazines designed for homemakers appeared in 1986. Department stores began offering classes for women in economics and stocks.

Just as department stores value the understanding and knowledge of women managers to sell to other women, many companies have begun to value women in career positions to increase sales or corporate appeal among homemakers. Investment brokerages, automobile manufacturers, real estate companies, and so on have become increasingly receptive to promoting women. Japan's largest advertising firm, Dentsū, opened an affiliated company called Dentsū Eye, run almost entirely by women, because businesses were demanding advertising that appealed to female buyers.

Since consumer-oriented industries need to court female customers, including working women, they have begun to institute services to make work demands more compatible with domestic expectations. Department stores, for example, remain open later to accommodate working women. Many stores have devoted great effort to "home shopping," which allows customers to order by phone the items they see advertised on television.

The Tokyū department store in Jiyūgaoka decided that full-time working women would appreciate some help completing their household tasks. The store developed a special service in conjunction with the Tokyū commuter train line. Working women could leave their grocery shopping lists at the train station on their way to work, and the store would have the groceries waiting to be picked up when the women were returning home. This service was particularly well received because of the Japanese emphasis on fresh foods, and the corresponding expectation that wives shop daily.

Expectations of consumer activity may serve to impede women's career options or goals, especially if women feel required to expend time and effort keeping abreast of the latest trends. However, a growing awareness of women as the nation's primary consumers has opened up different avenues of employment and enhanced career possibilities. New consumer services directed at working women may make work and family roles more compatible. As the secretary-general of the Japan Consumer Association declared, the growing realization that eighty percent of the country's consumer market is female, and not the recently passed Equal Employment Opportunity Law, results in new career opportunities for women.[55]

CONCLUSIONS

Discussing marginality in Japan, James Valentine states, "The most obvious case of marginality at work is the professional woman, or at least a woman in a 'man's occupation.' "[56] In a seeming contradiction, he contends that professional women are not as marginal as adult men who have reached a certain age without marrying or fathering children. In order to understand this apparent contradiction, I suggest that the marginality of professional women involves more than a simple failure to assume one's "proper place" and gender role.[57] It involves a "confusion of categories."[58] Unmarried women who devote themselves to careers are problematic and hence marginalized to a certain extent. However, they are less marginal than unmarried men because they have accomplished a role switch, crossing from one social category (wife and mother) to another (career person), essentially becoming "sociologically male" in the process. A more problematic situation arises when, rather than switching roles, a woman expects to straddle both roles by combining career and family expectations. This situation is the most problematic because it creates a greater overlapping of categories, a more severe confusion of social definitions.

It seems clear that although the EEOL allows career-oriented women into male-dominated professions and managerial ranks, it was never intended to disrupt existing social concepts of a gender role "balance" or the expectation that each sex fulfill different roles. Strong resistance to eliminating differential gender roles is indicated by the Ministry of Labor's initial reluctance to support childcare and leave programs aimed at both mothers and fathers and the continued acceptability of advertising "for women only" for traditionally female jobs.

A perceived conflict between career and domestic roles makes it difficult for many women to develop or assert their career goals. Despite claims by some social analysts that women no longer see wife and mother and career roles as incompatible, young women employees in my department store study still saw high-ranking female superiors—their potential role models—as women who have succeeded in their chosen careers only at the cost of marriage and motherhood. For most of the younger women, giving up marriage and parenting was too high a price for career fulfillment. The presence of large numbers of unmarried managerial women served not to inspire these young women to further their career goals, but to confirm their belief that success in the job market conflicts with success in the marriage market.

Despite increased career opportunities, the socialization of women still emphasizes their roles in the domestic sphere. The tradition of separate spheres—men in the public work world and women in the domestic realm—finds expression in patterns of female work relationships that differ from the industrial norm in studies of male employees. Among women department store employees, the diminished role of *senpai-kōhai* relationships and the lack of identification with their entrance cohort group lead to the hypothesis that the more diffuse, generalized roles typical of the domestic realm may be carried over into female work relationships.[59]

The persistence of gender socialization suggests that any real change in attitudes toward female employment must be social and not just legal. A law such as the EEOL, based on foreign concepts and adopted to appease external opinion, cannot be truly effective without a corresponding change in underlying Japanese social values regarding gender roles and the relationship between work and domestic life. The department store employees clearly suggested that policies supported by the EEOL (such as temporary retirement and reinstatement programs) did not correspond with Japanese values emphasizing the devout maintenance of ongoing personal relationships with all members of one's work group. Most of the women were not inspired to model themselves after a female executive role model like Ishihara if it meant making a lifetime effort to "Think like a man, act like a lady, and work like a dog." They suggested the need to restore a balance between work and domestic roles for both sexes by decreasing the workaholic emphasis on excessive overtime commitments for those with careers, whether male or female.

Against this backdrop, it is relevant to note that the dominance of women as consumers in contemporary Japan has expanded career options for women. Women have long been expected to be responsible for the household budget as part of their domestic duties. In modern Japan it is now assumed that women are also in control of family finances, employing their own personal tastes and judgment in making most of the nation's consumer decisions. Decades before the EEOL, women had better chances of rising to managerial ranks in department stores than in other companies because department stores found that such women's judgment and perspective helped sell products to their primarily female customers. As other industries that formerly catered to men awaken to the fact that women make most of the purchasing and now many of the financial decisions, it seems likely that career opportunities for women will increase within these industries. The rationale is both economic—utilizing female talent to sell or appeal to women—and consistent with a new interpretation of long-standing cultural values that define consumer decisions as an important aspect of women's social and domestic responsibilities.

NOTES

The research presented in this chapter was largely conducted under a Fulbright-Hayes (Department of Education) grant. Earlier versions were presented at a roundtable convened during the 1989 Association for Asian Studies meetings in Washington, D.C., at the 1989 annual meetings of the Western Conference of the Association for Asian Studies held in Long Beach, California, at the 1990 Japan Studies Association of Canada conference held in Vancouver, B.C., and at the 1991 annual meetings of Asian Studies on the Pacific Coast held in Bellingham, Washington. Earlier versions or parts of this chapter are presented in different frameworks in the Women in International Development (WID) working paper series distributed by Michigan State University and in *Canadian Perspectives on Modern Japan*.

I thank Bev Lee, Takie Lebra, Ueno Chizuko, and Dawn Currie for their comments on earlier versions of this chapter. I also thank Stacy Pigg (along with Bogart) who lent me her apartment to use as a sanctuary while I was working on this version, thereby helping me to juggle my own mother and career roles.

1. Susan Porter Benson, *Counter Cultures: Saleswomen, Managers, and Customers in American Department Stores, 1890–1940* (Urbana: University of Illinois Press, 1986).

2. Sandra Wallman, "Introduction," in *Social Anthropology of Work*, ed. Sandra Wallman (New York: Academic Press, 1979), 8.

3. Mary C. Brinton, "The Socio-Institutional Bases of Gender Stratification: Japan as an Illustrative Case," *American Journal of Sociology* 94, no. 2 (1988): 300–334. D. H. Whittaker, "The End of Japanese-Style Employment?" *Work, Employment, and Society* 4, no. 3 (1990): 321–347.

4. Gale Miller, *It's a Living: Work in Modern Society* (New York: St. Martin's Press, 1981), 296.

5. Herbert Applebaum, "Theoretical Introduction," in *Work in Market and Industrial Societies*, ed. Herbert Applebaum (Albany: State University of New York Press, 1984), 3.

6. For example, based on figures provided by Shinotsuka Eiko in *Nihon no toshi rōdō*, 1982, Brinton argues that the percentage of women in the labor force has not changed remarkably between 1920 when 38.2 percent of the labor force was female, and 1980 when the figure was 37.9 percent. Mary C. Brinton, "Women and the Economic Miracle: The Maintenance of Gender Differences in Education and Employment in Contemporary Japan" (Ph.D. dissertation, University of Washington, 1986), 22. Such an interpretation counters the popular misconception that Japanese women are now entering the labor force in larger numbers, with evidence that Japanese women have long made up a significant proportion of that labor force.

7. Rodney Clark, *The Japanese Company* (New Haven: Yale University Press, 1979), 234.

8. Women's wages were fifty-three percent of men's in 1985. Ueno Chizuko, "The Position of Women Reconsidered," *Current Anthropology* 28, no. 4 (supplement) (1987): s75.

9. Dorothy Robins-Mowry, *The Hidden Sun: Women of Modern Japan* (Boulder: Westview Press, 1983), 173.

10. Thomas P. Rohlen, " 'Permanent Employment' Faces Recession, Slow Growth, and an Aging Work Force," *Journal of Japanese Studies* 5, no. 2 (1979): 235–272.

11. According to the 1990 Japanese Yearbook of Statistics, the current life expectancy for Japanese women is 81.77 years. Sōmucho Tōkei Kyoku, *Nihon no Tōkei: Heisei 2 nen* (Tokyo: Ōkurashō, 1990).

12. Sugahara Mariko and Takeuchi Hiroshi, "Japanese-Style Management and Women's Entry into the Job Market," *The Wheel Extended: A Toyota Quarterly Review* 12, no 4 (1982): 27–32.

13. "Sex Equality in Promotion Not Achieved Yet at Cos.," *Japan Times,* June 8, 1987.

14. Whittaker, "The End of Japanese-Style Employment?" 326.

15. Toyota, *The Wheel Extended*, 24.

16. Ibid., 25.

17. Although sources agree that Mitsukoshi was the first to hire female clerks, there is some discrepancy regarding the date at which this occurred. Sievers claims it was in 1901. Sharon Sievers, *Flowers in Salt: The Beginnings of Feminist Consciousness in Modern Japan* (Stanford: Stanford University Press, 1983), 86. The 1895 date was taken from a Mitsukoshi Press Release Publication of May 11, 1986, page 14.

18. In a 1981 Ministry of Labor survey, seventy-three percent of all companies said they would not hire women who were graduates of four-year institutions.

19. Kuroda Setsuko, Makiya Yoko, Mizuno Junko, and Maeoka Sakiko, "Women Creating a New Wave in Distribution: Part 1, Working Women Describe Their Experiences," *The Wheel Extended*, 18.

20. Issobe Mayo, "Ministry Promoting Childcare Leave Systems," *Japan Times*, May 5, 1986.

21. Kuroda *et al.*, "Women Creating a New Wave," 18.

22. This is significant because the limited hours of most available day-care centers neither permit women to do any overtime work nor allow for enough commuting time if they live far from the city center (as families with children often do). On the other hand, Ueno Chizuko has pointed out to me that some social commentators in Japan are skeptical of such in-company day-care centers and concerned that these will result in children becoming "hostages"; mothers could be forced to work long hours because they will have no excuse for leaving at the end of the normal working day.

23. "Seiyu's 'Baby Care Time' Starts for Parent Workers," *Japan Times*, July 3, 1986.

24. Issobe, "Ministry Promoting Childcare Leave Systems."

25. Kashima Takashi, "Chiisaku umareta ikuji kyūgyōhō," *Sekai* 7 (July 1991): 20.

26. This interview was conducted on February 14, 1986.

27. A woman who had worked at the store for over twenty years and had never married pointed out that the company did, at some point, allow single women to live on their own.

28. Jeannie Lo, *Office Ladies / Factory Women: Life and Work at a Japanese Company* (Armonk, New York: M. E. Sharpe, 1990).

29. Nakane Chie, *Japanese Society* (Los Angeles: University of California Press, 1970).

30. During 1985 I was employed as a guide and translator at the American Pavilion at Expo '85, which was held in Japan. My experiences agree with this description; there were Japanese visitors to the fair who would complain to the pavilion management if they felt female guides wore too much makeup, looked sloppy, or behaved in what they considered an unladylike manner. Although there were daily customer complaints about women on the staff not being tidy enough, there were never similar complaints about men. Some of the men teased about this, saying that this reflected the relative merits of male and female grooming on our work teams, but the women, unanimously agreeing that we were at least as tidy as the men, felt it reflected higher customer expectations of women employees.

31. Sugahara and Takeuchi, "Japanese-Style Management," 32.

32. They will also be asked questions that have nothing to do with the store and are hence required to have broad knowledge.

33. This was the claim of a Japan Department Store Association researcher. It should be noted, however, that many of the women born before 1950 who hold high-ranking or managerial posts are high school or junior college graduates because a four-year university education for women was much rarer at that time.

34. A government survey conducted in 1986 revealed that eighty percent of women and seventy percent of men believed that men and women "are not equal" (Issobe Mayo, "Ministry Explains New Employment Law," *Japan Times,* April 7, 1986) and that sixty-three percent of men and forty-nine percent of women agreed with the traditional division of labor where men work and women keep house (Issobe, "Ministry Promoting Childcare Leave Systems").

35. Fujita Mariko, " 'It's All Mother's Fault': Childcare and Socialization of Working Mothers in Japan," *Journal of Japanese Studies* 15, no. 1 (1989): 67–91.

36. See, for example, Millie R. Creighton, "Contemporary Japanese Women: Employment and Consumer Roles," in *Canadian Perspectives on Modern Japan,* eds. T. G. McGee, Kate Elliot, and Bev Lee (Vancouver: University of British Columbia Institute of Asian Research, 1990): 56–88; and Mary C. Brinton, "Christmas Cakes and Wedding Cakes: The Social Organization of Japanese Women's Life Course," in *Japanese Social Organization,* ed. Takie Sugiyama Lebra (Honolulu: University of Hawaii Press, 1992): 79–107.

37. Ibid.

38. Lo, *Office Ladies / Factory Women.*

39. Quoted in Kuroda *et al.,* "Women Creating a New Wave in Distribution," 20.

40. Ibid. The discussion preceding this comment seemed to imply that women have personality characteristics undesirable for the workplace and that their capacity for detail is not desirable in management. The quoted comment is a response to the statement that "this trait is best utilized when it is developed positively, with women concentrating on the finest details, instead of working in a negative, fussy way."

41. Thomas P. Rohlen, *For Harmony and Strength: Japanese White-Collar Organization in Anthropological Perspective* (Los Angeles: University of California Press, 1974), 123.

42. Illustrating this point, Clark writes, "Women . . . were spared the rigors of competition. . . . Women were able to regard authority lightly. . . . Girls frequently came late for work when it suited them, or disappeared into the office kitchen when their sections were particularly busy" (*The Japanese Company,* 208).

43. Robins-Mowry, *The Hidden Sun,* 178.

44. For example, Lebra asserts that *wagamama* (selfishness) is an inacceptable motive in Japanese society and hence, "Even though a woman may be enjoying her career as the best way of fulfilling her personal wishes, this must not be confused with an approval of *wagamama.*" Takie Sugiyama Lebra, *Japanese Women: Constraint and Fulfillment* (Honolulu: University of Hawaii Press, 1984), 297.

45. Both Lebra and Robins-Mowry suggest that success in the career market might indeed detract from success in the marriage market. See Lebra, *Japanese Women,* 312; and Robins-Mowry, *The Hidden Sun,* 133.

46. During this entire time, I only met one woman ranking higher than sales clerk who was married, and she was not a manager or supervisor. In fact, she was also not a member of the regular employment system; she had not gone through the company's career track. Although she had a high-ranking position with a great deal of authority (Secretary to the President), it had been created for her, and she had been employed after her children were grown.

47. Quoted in Kuroda *et al.*, "Women Creating a New Wave in Distribution," 23.

48. Ibid.

49. Ibid.

50. Tanimura Shiho, *Kekkon shinai kamoshiranai shōkōgun* (Tokyo: Shufu no tomosha, 1990).

51. Brinton, "Christmas Cakes and Wedding Cakes," 79–107.

52. Ibid., 102.

53. Japanese workers do work many more annual labor hours than most of their Western counterparts. Recent indications suggest that the number of overtime hours for Japanese workers is decreasing, but there are deceptive aspects of such accounting. It is common for career-minded employees to report little or no overtime even though they are working many overtime hours, as Ishihara claimed she did to forge her way to the top of the department store industry. Since the mid-1980s, some companies have been limiting the number of overtime hours that even permanent employees are allowed to work. In one such case, the company passed a regulation that no one would be allowed to work any more than a certain number of overtime hours per week. The announcement for the new regulation, however, pointed out that the company could not deny employees the right to spend their off-work hours involved in pursuits of their own choice at their workplaces. The obvious interpretation was that employees were supposed to put in as much overtime as before but report less.

54. Managing the household budget has long been expected of wives in Japanese society and is frequently mentioned in popular literature as far back as the Tokugawa period. For example, a story by the well-known writer Saikaku described one wife's initial virtues and dedication to her marital role by stating, "She made all entries in her housewife's cash book with the utmost care." Ihara Saikaku, *The Life of an Amorous Woman and Other Writings*, trans. and ed. Ivan Morris (New York: New Directions, 1963), 83.

55. Suvendrini Suguro, "Japanese Women Tighten Control of Purse Strings," *Japan Times*, June 12, 1986.

56. James Valentine, "On the Borderlines: The Significance of Marginality in Japanese Society," in *Unwrapping Japan: Society and Culture in Anthropological Perspective*, eds. Eyal Ben-Ari, Brian Moeran, and James Valentine (Honolulu: University of Hawaii Press, 1990), 43.

57. See Ruth Benedict, *The Chrysanthemum and the Sword* (New York: Meridian, 1946).

58. Mary Douglas, *Purity and Danger* (London: Routledge & Kegan, 1966).

59. Describing the domestic realm of Japanese women, Takie Lebra claims that "the women's domestic role is characteristically diffuse, unpunctuated, multiple, or generalized" (*Japanese Women*, 301).

TEN

Careers and Commitment
Azumi's Blue-Collar Women

Glenda S. Roberts

But now, [lowers voice] women have begun to change greatly. They no longer maintain the household. They dislike raising children. That is what it has come to. . . . Today, who is going to maintain the household? I think that Japan has already started on the road to ruin, since so few people are alert to this. Unless women awaken, and take hold of themselves, more and more good women will be made fools of by these new social trends.

The quotation above is excerpted from a speech given in 1984 to the assembled employees of the shipping center of the Azumi Corporation (not its real name), a large-scale manufacturer of lingerie and leisure wear located in the Kansai region of Japan. I spent one year there in 1983 to 1984 learning about the lives of blue-collar women workers.

What are the social trends so scorned by Azumi's president? The most egregious is that of the increasing participation of married women in the workforce. Much to his dismay, more and more Azumi women were staying on after marriage for ever longer terms of service. In doing so they were challenging cultural norms that see women's contributions to the household budget as supplementary and women's main role as housewives and mothers. Why did married women so persistently remain on the job? What obstacles did they face in working continuously through childbearing and rearing? What do their experiences tell us about blue-collar women and lifetime employment?

AZUMI: THE CONTEXT

Azumi was different from many manufacturers in that most of its women were regular, not *pāto*, employees.[1] Most other manufacturers experienced an economic decline after the oil shock of 1973 to 1974, leading them to "rationalize" their workforces through such practices as lessening the number of recruits taken each year, encouraging early retirement, and hiring *pāto* workers, largely homemakers whose household budgets were feeling the pinch (Fuse 1979; Shinotsuka 1983). In contrast, Azumi grew steadily in the 1970s, and it was not until the early 1980s that it began to notice a downturn. At this point Azumi started its own rationalization drive, greatly reducing the scale of the "main office" factory (which had been its first), ceasing to hire new blue-collar workers, and shifting workers to jobs at another location. It had already established subsidiaries in rural areas of Japan and in other parts of Asia where labor and overhead were much lower than in the urban setting where I worked.

In 1983 when I entered Azumi I found, to my surprise, that my immediate work group consisted mostly of married women with long years of service to the company. Some of them had started after junior high school or high school and stayed through marriage and pregnancies. Others entered after their children began school, but entered as regular employees because the company was expanding. Whatever the case, the women felt lucky to have jobs as regulars when most women of their age could only find jobs as *pāto*. They shared the desire to keep their jobs. One of my coworkers described our work group as the "survivors," those who had stuck it out through years of being under the thumb of a tough boss, standing firm regardless of their husbands' disapproval of their working or the company's hints that perhaps they were getting too old for the work. Thus, my sample, mostly married blue-collar women working as regular employees for a major corporation, is not the norm. From them, though, I learned the reasons why lifetime employment as a full-fledged regular employee is difficult for a blue-collar woman worker.

Nationwide, Azumi had roughly four thousand employees, nearly 75 percent of them women. When I began the study, 49.9 percent of Azumi's female workforce consisted of saleswomen. Office workers were next at 34 percent, with factory workers following at 13.5 percent. Designers were the fewest at 2.5 percent. Azumi had increased its female workforce by about 33 percent from 1974 through 1985. The percentages of women employed in the various job categories, however, fluctuated a great deal in accordance with company policies to streamline operations, increase the sales force, and shift the bulk of the manufacturing work to rural and overseas subsidiaries.[2]

The percentage of married women in the nonagricultural workforce has increased steadily in the decade preceding this study, from 51.3 percent of the female workforce in 1975 to 58.8 percent in 1985. If we include those who are divorced or widowed, the figures are 62.1 percent and 68.2 percent respectively (Rōdōsho Fujinkyoku 1987, 16). Azumi has shown a similar trend, going from 16.3 percent in 1974 to 18.6 percent in 1984. In Azumi these figures are skewed downward by the large proportion of saleswomen. If we exclude them from the calculations, the percentage of married women went up from 25.4 percent in 1974 to 39 percent in 1984.

At the main office factory, 48 percent of the women were married. By comparison, 81 percent of Azumi's male employees were married.

As of March 1, 1984, there were 18 men and 224 women in the main office factory. Of the women, 49 percent were married. The average age of the women was 29.65; of the men, 39.06. All the women were regular employees, except for eight *pāto*. The average length of service of female regular employees was 10.11 years; of male regular employees, 11.16.[3]

The inspection and packaging section (I&P), where I worked as a packager, consisted of eighteen women and one man. Ten of the women were married, one widowed, and seven unmarried. Of the married and widowed women, all but one had children. Two of the women were *pāto*. The *kakarichō* (subsection chief) oversaw the operations of the entire section. The subsection chief was a woman, Murakami-*san*, unusual in this company. The I&P had no section chief; Murakami-*san* reported directly to the factory manager. Workers in the section packaged, labeled, and inspected garments. Four of us were assigned to packaging and labeling, one (the man) to shipping, eleven to inspecting, one to office work, and two to facilitating the work flow. Those two held the lowest supervisory rank, that of *shisutaa* (from the English word "sister"). Management assigned the term *shisutaa* to these work facilitators in the 1960s when there were many young recruits who needed a little extra "sisterly" supervision and advice. Each *shisutaa* had many charges at once and was enjoined to keep them in line. Unlike informal senior-junior relationships in which, as Rohlen (1974) describes, seniors foster a young male employee's path upward, *shisutaa* did not have the ability to affect the promotion of their female charges, nor to negotiate or bargain with the *hanchō* (supervisors of groups of about thirty employees) or any higher supervisor on behalf of their charges.

The pace of the day was brisk and the work atmosphere stern, in part because of our *kakarichō*. She did not allow us to chat, chew gum, hum, or whistle on the grounds that such conduct would impede our concentration. Breaks ended at the bell, and people would begin to get back to their stations before it rang. Indeed, sometimes employees worked through portions of their breaks. There was no loitering in the halls or restrooms. Some people would linger to chat in the cafeteria after lunch, but most would bring their snacks upstairs to the break areas of each section and converse there. For most of my year at Azumi, I worked mornings.[4] I soon discovered that if I wanted to become at all familiar with my coworkers, I would have to arrive early for the prework snack that some chose to eat together and stay until the 12:40 P.M. bell rang to signal the impending end of the lunch break.

At 5:10 the dismissal bell rang, but only the *pāto* were free to leave. The regular employees remained for an extra ten minutes to clean the shop.

That done, we formed a circle and were dismissed. If no overtime was required, most workers then rushed downstairs to the locker room to change into street attire and hurry to catch the train or ride their bicycles home.

In April 1984 the company decided to dissolve the factory's inspection and packaging section and transfer most of its workers to the shipping center, to do similar jobs. This change afforded me the opportunity to experience a different setting: the new I&P division was over three times the size of the old factory's section. It was headed by a male *kachō*, one male *kakarichō*, two female *hanchō*, and four *shisutaa*.

EMPLOYMENT AND *RYŌSAI KENBO*

Most of my coworkers' husbands were regular employees in local factories or small businesses, or else they worked for Azumi. Until the mid-1970s, most urban women married to salaried employees did not have jobs outside the home, though they may have taken in piecework. Had my coworkers planned to work after marriage? If not, what made them change their minds? Had they forsaken the traditional role of *ryōsai kenbo* (good wife, wise mother) as Azumi's president so feared, or was this new pattern another interpretation of that role?

A woman who tries to "have it all"—a family and a career of her own—is definitely beyond the bounds of the *ryōsai kenbo* role. Instead, women are encouraged to work until marriage, quit to raise a family, and reenter the labor force, if at all, after the children are grown. The resulting pattern of employment, shown in figure 6, is known as the "M-curve"; it shows the rate of employment declining between the ages of twenty-four and thirty-four (NIEVR 1988).

Until the first peak is reached in the mid-twenties at 65.2 percent, women's participation in the paid employment sector is considered normal and is encouraged socially as well as economically. During this period, women's desire to work is most congruent with ideological assumptions about women's role. The downward trend begins in the age range twenty-five to twenty-nine with a 22 percent drop and reaches its lowest point at the ages thirty to thirty-four, dropping 9 percent more. This represents the period of greatest conflict between women's continued employment and their roles as wives and mothers. Role contradictions notwithstanding, 33.8 percent of women are employees during this period of the life cycle, in the "trough" of the M. Granted, some of them are single women, widows, or divorcées for whom the continuation of work poses less of a cultural dilemma. However, many of these female employees are married and have young children. My research focuses on this age group, the one that faces the most severe role contradictions. What the M-curve fails to show is how many in the trough and at the second peak are work-

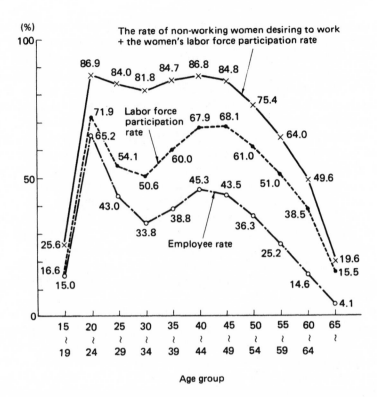

Fig. 6. The rate of nonworking women desiring to work and the women's labor force participation rate. The labor force participation rate and the employee rate are based on the 1985 "Labor Force Survey" by the Statistics Bureau of the Management and Coordination Agency. The rate of nonworking women desiring to work is based on the 1982 "Employment Status Survey" by the Statistics Bureau of the Management and Coordination Agency. The employee rate consists only of workers employed by companies. The labor force participation rate also includes the self-employed and family workers. National Institute of Employment and Vocational Research, *Women Workers in Japan,* 1988, 26.

ing as full-time, regular employees. Many may be temporary workers, dispatch workers, or *pāto.*

Although the professional housewife model for women is still very much in evidence today, changes in the economy and society are modifying women's response to it. A 1985 report published by the Women's Bureau of the Ministry of Labor notes that salary increases have not kept pace with rises in the price of housing and education. These factors lead women to seek employment outside the home even after they have families. With the current restructuring of the workplace, they have the op-

portunity to do so. Reluctant to add to their tenured workforce, employers created *pāto* jobs in large numbers. As a result, women are working as
employees outside the family in record numbers. In 1975 female employees in the nonagricultural workforce made up 59.8 percent of all female
workers. By 1985 they made up 68.2 percent. Takenaka (1989) notes that
the gains come mostly from married, middle-aged women reentering the
workforce. This has made the second peak of the M-curve higher.

Furthermore, in the 1980s, women's average length of service in their
companies climbed steadily as more women postponed quitting their jobs.
Age at marriage and at first birth increased. The number of births per
woman had fallen to 1.53 by 1992 (Tsuya and Mason 1992). These trends
combine to make the M-curve's trough increasingly shallow. Also, the
span of years between early retirement at marriage and reentry after
childrearing is decreasing. The notion that a woman's primary responsibility is to her home remains strong, however, and employment policies
and practices, although gradually changing, are largely premised upon a
male career model.[5] Hence the trough in the M-curve, although filling in,
is still apparent (see figure 7).

Most of my coworkers at Azumi were either in the trough of the M or at
the second peak, trying not to slip down the slope until they had reached retirement age. By virtue of being regular employees despite also being wives
and mothers, they were bucking the system. Married Azumi women who
were staying on the line from age fifteen, as well as those who were mid-
career entrants, had chosen a controversial career trajectory. Why?

Most took a job for economic reasons, to help pay for housing or for educational or other child-related expenses.[6] My coworkers agreed that married women work to maintain a certain living standard. Even though they
strive to maintain that standard, some feel it is too high, and that people
have given in to greed and extravagance. But all felt that their husbands'
salaries had not kept pace with the increase in the cost of living or with the
higher standard of consumption. The commentary of Shimizu-*san*, a thirty-
two-year-old mother of two who had worked at Azumi since age fourteen,
is illustrative: "Even if it's only a little, it helps out with the household
finances. The standard of living has risen greatly. A house didn't have a refrigerator ten years ago. . . . Now there's one in every house, and a car for
every two people, one per household. It's because we have these things and
the living standard has risen that more and more people are working."

Nishitani-*san*, a married woman with two children and one on the way,
focuses on the consequences of rising educational standards:

> It's funny to call it luxury, but one wants spending money. People want
> videos and things. And we've come to spend money on kids that we didn't
> used to spend. Luxuries like home tutors, cram schools. Before it used to be
> okay just to send your child to the regular school program, but that's not

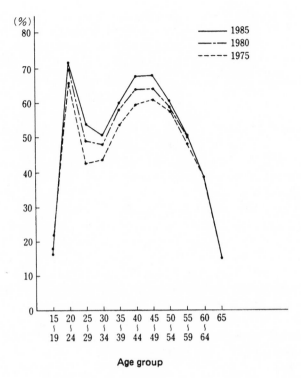

Fig. 7. Women's participation in the labor force by age group. Takenaka, 1989, 289.

good enough anymore. So if you want to give your child the same as the next, it costs money. Because luxury has become commonplace in our lives, we can't get by on just our husband's salaries, so we have to work. That's how my family is. We could get by on Father's [my husband's] salary alone, but we want more than that. We want to do this and that for the kids. Give them nice clothes and toys. At this point nice toys are enough, but once they get to elementary school, we want to give them supplemental education, and that takes money.

Nishitani-*san* plans to quit the company as soon as her oldest child enters elementary school because she does not have access to after-school day care. But she says that then she will look for a job as a *pāto*.

Kamida-*hanchō*, a married thirty-seven-year-old mother of two who has been with Azumi since junior high, emphasizes the practical—it is a waste of resources to have a woman at home when she could be out working, especially in view of the cramped quarters typical of modern housing. Moreover, the market for in-home piecework (*naishoku*) has shrunk, so if a woman wants to earn income, she almost has to go out:

Well, household finances are probably a part of it, but it's a waste for women to just sit at home. For instance, nowadays when you talk about houses, it's a *danchi* [apartment complex]. There's hardly any women's work like washing and cleaning left to do. In the old days, it took a day to do the garden. Even *naishoku* isn't as available as it used to be. There aren't many kinds of *naishoku*. Since there are lots of people with spare time, they decide to work, even if only a little.

Kamida-*hanchō* does not seem to be of the opinion of most homemakers in Imamura's 1987 study: that a homemaker's main job is the education and care of her children. Instead she emphasizes the lack of productive work for a homemaker who lives in an apartment complex. To Kamida-*hanchō*, this is a waste of her talents.

Another coworker noted that, because a homemaker has to operate within her husband's salary, there are those with extra and those with nothing to spare, and she pitied the latter. Although I have no hard data, my impression is that most of my coworkers would have had difficulty managing the budget on their husbands' income alone. If they stayed at home, they would not be emulating the upper-middle class homemakers of TV dramas who wear designer clothing, hire private tutors for their children, drive luxury cars, attend culture classes, meet at upscale cafes for lunch, and the like. Instead, they would be stuck in the house, in perhaps morally uplifting but depressing penury.

According to Nishitani-*san*, who at thirty-two had sixteen years of regular service at Azumi: "I envy them. [*Laughs*] But for me, I'm more suited to being outside. Three meals plus a nap sounds appealing, but I couldn't stand just doing housework. I want to have my own interests, and there are many things I want to study. I think it would be a lonely existence."

People often say that homemakers have an easy life because their husbands support them. Perhaps this slightly derogatory image of professional housewives indicates a decline in the social assessment of their value. One rarely hears of *ryōsai kenbo* these days, but *san shoku hirune tsuki* (three meals and a nap) is on the tip of many tongues, male and female.

WOMEN'S ASPIRATIONS FOR PROMOTION

Women did not aspire to promotion, perhaps because they knew that their chances for rising very high in the ranks of the company were slim and realized the difficulties of combining a challenging job with household responsibilities. Although I asked if they considered opportunities for promotion in their evaluation of a job's worth, almost everyone said that she did not think of such things.[7] Fujii-*san* said: "I don't think of such things. Maybe it's funny for me to say that as long as I can work it's okay, but I don't have any desire to climb." In any case, one could not take a test for promotion without the recommendation of one's superior. Whereas some superiors are glad to recognize a woman's potential and invite her to take the test, most are not.[8]

As indicated in the speech by Azumi's president, which extolled the virtues of the professional housewife and warned of the dangers of other gender roles for Japanese women, Azumi was built on the premise that eager young women would enter the company, work for several years, perhaps gain the rank of *shisutaa* or even instructor or *hanchō*, then marry and retire to realize their true destinies as wives and mothers. Azumi did not want highfliers; such could not be accommodated in a promotion system with such a low ceiling for women. Moreover, the jobs to which female production workers were assigned were so physically taxing that it was unlikely that many would stay on for a career. Those two who made the grade to *kakarichō*, Murakami-*san* and Tahara-*san*, were anomalies: the former remained single, the latter divorced.

The promotion system was orderly as far as it went, but when young women at the first peak of the M began pushing the limits, there was no place for them. Their wages rose, but the company did not invest in extensive training for them, or plan for them to become all-around experts in operations and management, as they did for male employees. When the company, desperate for workers, hired middle-aged married women as regular employees, it added stress to a system already in trouble. It challenged the cultural assumptions upon which Azumi had based its personnel practices and upset the company's hierarchical power relations. It was ironic that the president of the same company that hired these women was lecturing to them that married women belong in the home, but the gender role that suited an earlier era was definitely out of sync with the economy of the 1980s, and the managers had not foreseen, nor did most of them approve of, the changes that were taking place. Contradictions abounded. My coworkers had their own doubts about the choices they were making to be married employees. Work on the shop floor was all the more challenging for such women because it contradicted a gender role to which they themselves subscribed, at least to some extent. Those who did feel justified in stretching women's role to include work after marriage often did not feel that women should strive for promotion beyond the lower levels. Women sometimes even held other women back from achieving.

CAREERS: FOUR CAMEOS

Perhaps the best way to understand the commitment involved in working as a regular employee at a large company such as Azumi is to examine the personal accounts of women who have had relatively long careers.

Through their stories we can see what it takes to manage within a system geared toward men. Here are the careers of four of Azumi's survivors.

Usui-hanchō

Usui-*hanchō* works at the factory, supervising its dealings with the subcontractor. She entered Azumi in 1968, straight from junior high school. She decided on this company because she liked to make things and was in a sewing club at school. She came to the factory on an observation trip and liked it because it was so clean and pretty. Although two of her friends joined the company at the same time, they ended up quitting after two or three years because they lacked enough interest in the work to do well. Usui feels that she has been able to continue so long because she was extremely interested in sewing.

She sewed on the sewing production line for her first eight years. At some point she was made *shisutaa*, although she did not say when. When she transferred to the I&P section at age twenty-three or twenty-four, she became *hanchō*. This was also the time when she married. When asked if before marriage she had planned to remain at work after marriage, she replied, "No. [*Laughs*] I yearned for retirement at marriage. But just when I got married was when I really got into being a *hanchō*—the work began to appeal to me. Before that I thought I'd definitely quit if I got married. But since I started really enjoying the work, I thought I'd quit when I got pregnant instead. But even when I got pregnant, I felt after all that this work really suits me, so I couldn't quit."

Marriage, the responsibilities of being *hanchō* of a new division, and pregnancy all came quickly. Usui-*san* had her first child at age twenty-six and her second at twenty-eight. She continued to work as hard as ever, doing overtime and refusing to take the two years of childcare leave time:[9]

USUI: I have a rather strong sense of responsibility. Even right after having my children, I did overtime. Also, I didn't take childcare time for either child. Together it would have been four years, but I never took one day.

GLENDA: Because you were *hanchō*?

USUI: When you're a *hanchō*, you can't take it. They didn't ask me not to take it, but I knew how terrible it would be being *hanchō*, having the responsibility—to take an hour off. When I was pregnant, too, I did overtime quite a bit.

GLENDA: Weren't you tired?

USUI: Yes, but there was nothing to be done about it. When I was *hanchō* I didn't feel any particular problem with doing overtime, but since coming to production, I've been dissatisfied with the overtime that we have to do as a result of late samples or late materials, because during normal hours we have idle hands. If you make the delivery date clear, and materials arrive on schedule, then overtime is unnecessary. But if materials aren't together, or you have that sort of trouble, then you end up having to do overtime almost every day. I was pretty much able to do overtime because I had the understanding of my mother-in-law, who would look after the kids for me, and my husband, who could pick them up for me. But some people can't do that, and even so, I sometimes had to make them do it. So overtime on account of late materials was a big headache.

Usui-*san* made these sacrifices for a post that provided her with ¥3,000 per month in recompense for her extra duties. In 1983, at the exchange rate of 240 yen to the U.S. dollar, this was about $12.00. One would think that the job must have been especially enjoyable. Yet listening to her account of the first few years of being a *hanchō* under Murakami-*kakarichō*, it is difficult to conclude so:

At first it was okay, but the worst time lasted for two years, and within that, one year especially was bad. The problem was that when I became *hanchō* I was put in charge of a kind of work with which I was unfamiliar, and the people underneath me knew more about it than I did. They asked me question after question. So I lost my ability to think, in such a position. I felt I couldn't do it myself. So for half a year I kept telling Murakami that I'd like to quit the job [but stay at Azumi].[10] But there was the problem of what I'd do if not that, and moreover, there was no one to take my place, so Murakami told me that, given these circumstances, I should think over what was to be done. I'd be mortified to quit defeated, so I gritted my teeth, tried hard, and got on the right track. I became able to answer the questions they asked me and handle problems that came up.

Just when I was thinking that at this rate I wouldn't be quitting while down, Murakami asked me if I still wanted to change jobs. She said that if I had quit before when I wanted to quit, the bitterness would have perhaps remained, but now that I myself was satisfied with my job, and since personal relations also had returned to normal, it wouldn't be as if I were quitting in such a bad position, and the bitterness wouldn't remain. So then she asked me if I'd like to change. [Moreover, at this point there were two employees whom Murakami-*kakarichō* had groomed to replace Usui.] For that worst one year, I was totally lost. At first people would forgive me even if I made mistakes, but I wasn't very good at handling the questions some would ask me. So I took responsibility for everything—and didn't have room to move. It wasn't good, but I tried very hard. When I left the group, the person who had subjected me to the most questions, Sakurai, said she understood now how unreasonable she had been in what she had said, now that she knew the job and had experienced it for herself. In the end she said she understood the humanity [*ningensei*] of the *hanchō* and she apologized, weeping. Everyone had said bad things about me, but in the end everyone apologized and said they'd been mistaken. I was very happy. At that point, for the first time I was glad I had taken on the job of *hanchō*. I'd suffered with it for a long time, but it was good that I had accomplished such a task.

It is common in Japanese companies for people to be transferred to divisions of the organization in which they have no expertise, on the principle of sink or swim. One executive was transferred from sales to the top position in the health and safety division. He had to learn the job from step one, having no prior knowledge of health or occupational safety matters. It is particularly difficult in the beginning when one's subordinates know more about the job than oneself, as in Usui-*san*'s case. She commented that the job was psychologically unnerving and that she lost weight because it was so challenging. She had felt that everyone treated her as an enemy at first. It took two years before she felt comfortable in the job and the people understood her well.

It is possible that all new supervisors experience a hazing similar to that of new employees until they show that they have mastered the job and are worthy of it. I noticed some unusual behavior when Murakami-*kakarichō* was replaced by Machida-*kakarichō* in January 1984. Several people complained that he knew nothing about inspection and was a poor decision maker and that the *shisutaa* and some of the other workers were behaving disrespectfully toward him, ordering him about and being lax in their work. It could be that they were simply having a field day after the severity of Murakami-*kakarichō*, but they may also have been testing him to see how far he could be pushed. In any case, Murakami-*kakarichō* would not let Usui-*san* step down from being *hanchō* until she had overcome these obstacles and could leave with her head held high. At Azumi, overcoming hardship and seeing a challenge through to the end are viewed as being good for the individual.

After leaving I&P, Usui-*san* faced a different challenge. She had been out of production work for six years, and now she had to readjust to it:

> Inspection has a severity about it. Since there were few people, it was easy to achieve discipline, and it was hard to take time off. If one piece came back from the shipping center, it was dealt with rather severely; it was not looked upon lightly. But when I went back to production, I felt the strain of the physical labor because you don't stop sewing on the machine—it's straight through from 8:30 to 5:00 [with breaks at lunch and 3:00]. At first it was hard to get used to, since the environment was so different, but I adjusted fairly quickly because I had done the same work five or six years earlier. Within one month I was keeping up with everyone in the sewing division. I had been used to using my head more as a *hanchō*, but now it was a question of dexterity. My hands couldn't keep up. Plus the sewing methods of years ago and those now are completely different, so it took a year of hard work to get used to it. Just when I felt it had really sunk in, I returned to the job of handling the outside orders. My present job is also difficult, but not because of physical labor. It's the nervous strain.

Although Usui-*san* said that she had not been in her present job long enough to be sure, she thought that she might start liking it as she grew accustomed to it. She was not sure if she would stay on until retirement, but she had just taken out a company housing loan that would take ten years to repay, so she wanted to stay at least that long. It is obvious that she was an enthusiastic and talented employee with a determination to keep working. It is also quite unlikely that she would have been able to continue her career at Azumi without the cooperation of her husband and mother-in-law.

Kamida-hanchō

Kamida-hanchō joined Azumi's shipping center at age fifteen and continued through marriage at age twenty and the birth of her two children. As in Usui-*san*'s case, her mother-in-law took care of the children while they were young. *Kamida-hanchō* is six years older than Usui-*san*, but their experiences within the company were similar. *Kamida-san*, however, has remained a *hanchō* and was even urged to take the test for promotion to *fukushunin*. She passed the test and was given an additional ¥10,000 per month besides her *hanchō* allowance. This meant that, with bonus, she received an extra ¥300,000 per year ($1,250 at 240 yen to the dollar). No others her age remain in the shipping center, except for two men.

Kamida-hanchō survived her early experiences of hazing with her sense of humor intact: she is a vivacious woman, full of self-confidence. Whereas Usui-*san* had misgivings about being *hanchō* and wanted to step down, Kamida-*san*'s confidence seems never to have faltered. Usui-*san* said that she had dreamed of being a homemaker at marriage, but Kamida-*san* insisted on working. When asked if she had planned to continue working after marriage, she replied, "Yes, because those were the conditions under which I had my *omiai* [arranged marriage]. 'I want to work after marriage. Is that all right?' That was up front in the conditions. Since they [the prospective groom and his family] said it didn't bother them, I said all right."

Kamida-*san* said that the hazing she underwent hardened her. It left her with a zeal for work and a passion for a lively and quick-paced workshop. Indeed, one of the difficulties she had in her job as *hanchō* was getting the women, particularly the young ones, to work with the same dispatch that she does. She commented:

> KAMIDA: People nowadays are dull [*tsumaranai*]. They're spoiled by the work, you could say. There's no liveliness, is there? Don't you feel everyone is lazy? Whether they're supposed to be in a rush or not, they do it at their own pace. It seems like there aren't any people like me anymore, who feel they have to make the deadline if someone says to hurry. In my day, if they said we were in a hurry, we had to make it on time. People nowadays don't have that feeling. My group goes at an ordinary pace, so I get fidgety. I get annoyed. At the selective inspection group they're pressed for time, so you don't have that. Everyone is frantic.

GLENDA: Do you think it's better to be frantic?

KAMIDA: You're really doing work that way. The reason you are coming to the company is to work, after all. And on the basis of that, you get paid, right? So if you don't keep them hopping, somehow. . . . You have to break them in, so you work frantically, and in exchange for that, when there's time you can catch your breath, and you can let things pass. During busy times you have them work hard for you, and in compensation, when you have time to spare, you let it pass even if they're chatting. It's no good to be lazing around day in day out. I've wondered what you have thought since you have come, observing that work style. Maybe you thought "Gee, are they all [lazy] like this?" Don't you think they're a bit sluggish?

GLENDA: Well, sometimes . . . but it's hard to strike a balance.

KAMIDA: Yes, it is, isn't it?

GLENDA: If you're too rushed every day, it's awful.

KAMIDA: But now, downstairs, the new work is terribly piled up. They're doing overtime, you know. Because they aren't putting out during the regular day, they have to do overtime. If that's the case, they have to work extra hard during the day. There are times when I can't understand that, since I was brought up in a different age.

I remember my surprise when Kamida-*san* expected me to agree with her that a frantic work pace is better than a steady, ordinary one. In fact, being accused of working at what is called "my pace" is tantamount to being labeled a selfish, disloyal worker (selfish because others are trying their utmost; disloyal because the company has deadlines and needs workers to put forth extra effort at times). To Kamida-*hanchō*, activity in itself was valuable—after all, that is the meaning of work, the reason one is paid. She saw it as a fair exchange. Workers owed it to the company to work hard during busy periods or else put in overtime. What she did not consider was that the shop was often shorthanded. Many workers complained that the company was unreasonable in expecting so few to do so much in a normal day, but to Kamida-*hanchō*, the problem lay in the workers' attitude, not the company's unrealistic demands. She did, however, allow the workers to relax their pace and chat a bit during slow periods. At the I&P, in contrast, the *kakarichō* never relaxed her vigilance.

When Kamida-*hanchō* was pregnant, regulations at the company were stricter. The union had not yet negotiated for the one-year extension of the one-hour-a-day childcare time. Moreover, the work environment made no exceptions for pregnant employees. Nevertheless, Kamida managed to survive the treatment, and, as a result, she now thinks that pregnant women are overindulged.

GLENDA: You've always been at Azumi, right? Even after marriage.

KAMIDA: Yes, and had two kids. I did take maternity leave, though.

GLENDA: You did? Was it easy?

KAMIDA: There wasn't anything like nowadays, where you can go home one hour early [at 4:10]. For my oldest, I worked straight to 5:00 P.M. I asked them if I could leave early but they said that since Grandma was at home, they wouldn't allow it, and they turned me down.[11] With my younger child, I could go home at 4:00 P.M. for just one year. People now get two years, right? It's changed a lot, the treatment. With my older child I didn't go home early, and there certainly wasn't any stuff like sitting down if you were pregnant. Even if we were really showing, we didn't sit, we moved around. I think that people nowadays are indulged.

GLENDA: Which way is better?

KAMIDA: Just because someone is pregnant is no reason to treat her respectfully, have her sit, and treat her with care. I think it's best for a pregnant woman to move around as much as she can. Nowadays, even the people who work with someone who's pregnant will bring her a chair and say "Please have a seat" and this and that. Even the people around her look upon her indulgently, don't they? If I say, "It didn't used to be that way," I'll just be told, "Well, times have changed," and that's that, isn't it. But I always did it that way—I came through having done it that way. Even when I was pregnant, I was a *shisutaa*. I stepped down once. I was a *shisutaa* until my son was born, and I stepped down when I was really big and I was to begin pregnancy leave. Within a year I was asked to be a *shisutaa* again. Then after a while they asked me to be a *hanchō*, and so I was. I was still young so I could work at a good clip. If it were now, I couldn't do it.

Such an attitude on the part of a *hanchō* does not betoken a receptive attitude toward implementing improvements in women's working conditions.

Because Kamida-*hanchō* said that her work was more important to her than the household, I wondered if she had a particularly cooperative husband. I asked her which she thought consumed her husband's attention more, home or job. She replied:

KAMIDA: My husband seems to do both well, but if it's one or the other, he seems to put more emphasis on work. He doesn't take time off. I guess that I, too, stress work more than home. Grandma always says, "It seems that work is more important to you than the household!" I think this isn't good of me. Somehow or other I always seem to end up giving priority to the company. I think I'd better change my mind about that, but . . . inasmuch as I'm working, it just won't do to change it.

GLENDA: You mean there is a conflict?

KAMIDA: Yes. I think I should change, but I can't. Maybe I'd feel differently if I were an ordinary [without rank] employee, but since I have responsibility, sometimes I have to sacrifice the home some.

Both Usui-*san* and Kamida-*san* felt responsible toward their work, but Usui stepped down from her *hanchō* position and devoted more time toward her household, whereas Kamida-*san* always gave her job priority, despite her mother-in-law's criticism and her own ambivalence. It seemed impossible to hold a position of responsibility within the company and still run a household; the demands were simply too great.

This finding is compatible with that of Takie Lebra (1981, 1984, and "Gender and Culture," 1992). In her research on career women, Lebra found that household support by natal kin—especially mothers—was often instrumental in enabling a daughter to build a successful career. Of the four women at Azumi under present discussion, two (Shimizu and Kamida) lived with mothers-in-law, and one (Usui) frequently depended on her mother-in-law and younger sister for child care and on her husband to manage household and childcare tasks. In cases such as these, where household incomes are much lower than those in entrepreneurial elite families, in-laws may be more willing to lend a hand in household responsibilities. Usui-*san* noted that her mother-in-law knew Usui-*san* was suited to work and that staying at Azumi was better than quitting to work elsewhere, since she would not enjoy the same salary or benefits. Thus Usui-*san* gained her mother-in-law's cooperation. Usui-*san*'s salary at Azumi was on a par with her husband's salary and the loss of it would have been a heavy blow to the family finances.

Usui-*san* was typical of Azumi women in gaining the cooperation of her family. Of thirty Azumi factory women with young children, nineteen depended on family members—be they in-laws or natal kin—for child care. Eight had husbands who could be relied on to pick up children from the day-care center.

Shimizu-san

Like other women with long careers, Shimizu-*san* said she gave 70 percent of her energy to the company and only 30 percent to her household. However, unlike the others, she decided to quit the company and give more time to the children's school activities when her second child entered first grade. Shimizu-*san* was thirty-one at the time of the interview.

Shimizu-*san* lived with her parents-in-law and had left the child rearing up to them. A very resourceful and bright woman, she entered the company after junior high school. Her family was not well off, and her mother had died when she was ten years old. She said that she hardly knew of a world beyond the district where she lived, let alone anything about Azumi located several miles away in another district. It was with some trepidation that she set off for the company on her first day, worrying that she would get the train transfers wrong and get lost. Nevertheless, she soon found her bearings. She became *shisutaa,* then *hanchō* at age twenty-one. She reached the position of sewing instructor by age twenty-four before returning to being a line employee at the birth of her first child in 1977. She stepped down because she wanted to take the extra hour off for childcare, which was impossible for an instructor to do:

> There's no way someone with the responsibility of subforeman can take one hour off per day and keep up with the job. Also, one's workers resent it. You don't have to take the childcare time, but I wanted to. Also, you wouldn't be able to ask as much from your workers [if you took it]. Usui-*san* was the *hanchō* of the I&P section, and she didn't step down when she had her first child—she refused to take the childcare time. Yet, after a while, Usui decided that the job of *hanchō* didn't suit her, so she went back to the sewing division. In my case [as instructor], I was subforeman for more than one hundred people, not just a *hanchō* for twenty or so. When everyone is working hard, you can't just take off early, saying *osaki desu* [I'm leaving ahead of you]. I figured I couldn't handle my home and job well if I kept the post but left early every day. I figured that you can always get other jobs, but you can't do so with your home life. So I decided I'd worked hard for eleven years, and now it was time to take it a little easy for the two years of childcare time, and then work hard again afterwards.

In the fall of 1978, Shimizu-*san*'s second child was born, whereupon she transferred to the inspection and packaging section to be in charge of quality control. At this time she, her husband, and her children moved from their apartment to the home of her in-laws. She noted that the only way she could continue working now that she had two children was if they moved in with her husband's parents. Once they moved in, she became responsible only for cleaning up after dinner, doing her own family's laundry every evening, and supervising her children's homework. Her mother-in-law handled the rest. This arrangement apparently brightened the life of her mother-in-law, who had become depressed after her son's marriage to Shimizu-*san* but improved greatly after the birth of her grandchildren.

In the spring of 1985, Shimizu-*san* retired from the company. Her second son was about to start elementary school, and she wanted to be able to attend school activities herself rather than send Grandma in her place. She said the children would feel much happier that way. Moreover, her husband might soon face a transfer to a distant location, and she wanted to be able to go with him. She did not, however, intend to become a full-time homemaker. She wanted to find a job as a *pāto,* which would allow her more flexibility to attend to her children. In preparation for that, she was going to use her nine months of unemployment insurance to pay for training as a professional bridal assistant so that she could find work in wedding halls to dress brides in their ceremonial kimono. Moreover, she planned to take classes in sign language, thinking that skill, too, might be useful someday. She would also go to driving school and obtain her license, increase her activities in her religious organization, and start a high school equivalency course. She remarked that it was important to stay as active as possible and that the future looked bright. An added motivation for such activities was to mimimize friction between herself and her mother-in-law. During the interview, which took place before she retired, she commented on this:

> Both my husband and father-in-law feel there's no need for two women to be at home, so they agree to my going out to work and leaving the household affairs to Grandma. They tell me to work hard and save. I think the reason brides and their mothers-in-law don't always get along is they have to see each other twenty-four hours a day. But if one isn't around during the day, the other who stays home can take it easy—stretch her legs—so in that sense, the way Grandma and I are doing it is better for both of us.

When Japan urbanized, women who in the past would have farmed their parents-in-laws' land found themselves without employment except for in-home piecework. The trend toward urbanization coincided with the rise of the image of the thrifty and industrious professional housewife who devotes herself to her family. Even now that outside work is available to married women, the rationale behind such work is that it contributes to the household. My informants at Azumi who coresided with their mothers-in-law justified their careers in terms of their economic contributions to their households, but they also noted an important side-benefit: their jobs kept them from the constant critical scrutiny of their mothers-in-law while allowing both mother-in-law and daughter-in-law a measure of autonomy, to the benefit of their interpersonal relationship.

Nakada-san

Nakada-*san*, who had fourteen years of service at age forty-two, was a widow with one teenage son. Her career contrasted sharply with those of the other three women. They had started as fresh recruits from junior high school; she entered the company in midstream. They were go-getters; she was a plodder. In her own words:

> NAKADA: The first place I ever worked was a sewing factory, but not Azumi. I made pajamas and negligées. It was a small company. I worked there for five years. Then, when I got engaged, I quit and stayed home doing nothing for a year, got married, and stayed at home until he died. Then I returned to my parents' house and started working at Azumi in 1970 [at age twenty-nine]. At first I was in the sewing division. You'd think I'm healthy just looking at me, but actually I'm not so strong, and I couldn't keep up. It was too tiring. So I changed to putting the finishing touches on stuff from subsidiaries and inspecting them.

GLENDA: Did you ask to be transferred?

NAKADA: Yes, I did. It was within the same section. At the sewing job I felt extremely rushed and couldn't keep up the pace—it was partly line-work. In less than a month I was ready to quit. The place I had worked at before wasn't so hard. It was all relatives and friends who worked well together and had a good time. Azumi is a big company and therefore hard, naturally. You enter a point in the line, and if you can't keep up with the flow, it piles up and stops at your station. So I worried a lot and told my mother I wanted to quit, but she said if I said such a thing, I could take my child and get out of the house. We had several quarrels over this, with her asking me to leave. Anyway, I changed to the other job, and then when the I&P section was set up downstairs, I entered as an inspector and spent about eleven years there.

In this case the company was willing to find work suitable to the em-ployee. Because Nakada-*san* was able to transfer to a different sort of job, she was able to remain in her mother's household. Her mother's attitude might sound harsh, but in accordance with Japanese society, her parents' obligations to support her ceased when she married into the Nakada household. Her mother was willing to take her and her child back, but could not afford to support them even if she had wanted to. Nakada-*san* commented that she returned to her own family rather than going to her husband's because she hoped that it might be easier to remarry. However, she never did fulfill this wish.

After several years in the sewing division, Nakada-*san* was transferred to inspecting in I&P, then transferred again in 1983 to the shipping center, where she readied cosmetics and leotards for distribution. I asked her why she moved to the shipping center.

Gradually, Murakami began saying it'd be a good idea. I had developed a dislike for inspection work. I didn't want to do that sort of work until I got old. And when defective goods were returned, I had to go to everybody and apologize and I had to stand a long time [on the job every day]. Moreover, Murakami would get angry at me, and once I made a mistake, I'd make an-other and another. It just so happened that the *kakarichō* at the shipping cen-ter asked if there was anyone the factory could spare to work at the shipping center, and Murakami recommended me. I thought any place would be fine if there was a job for me. I'm glad I made the move; I like it better at the shipping center.

Nakada-*san* was obviously not a star worker, but she had managed to stay on for fourteen years. Why was she not pressured to quit? Most work-ers who were slow at their jobs, made mistakes, or lacked enthusiasm were the first to be pressured into leaving. Perhaps Nakada was kept on because management was sympathetic to her household situation, or because Nakada herself never gave the company sufficient reason to try to force her out. In her own estimation, she was not a star employee, but she did do overtime even when she did not want to and was careful to keep her opinions to herself and not cause trouble. She was a quiet person, shy unless you talked to her alone, and certainly never offensive to anyone. Fortunately, she was able to settle into a section of the company that she found moderately enjoyable, but she still wished she could remarry and be rescued from having to earn a living. At the end of the interview she confided, half-jokingly:

> If the company heard my interview, they'd say they didn't need employees like me, and they'd ask me to quit! I'm only working because I have to. I'm not a go-getter. That's my temperament. I envy people who do things quickly with dispatch—like Shimizu-*san*, who makes clean-cut decisions. I just mumble, and you can't depend on me. Before, when I was at the factory, I wanted to quit as soon as my son graduated if I had to keep doing inspection. But now that I've changed jobs, I think I can work until retirement. If there were someone who said, "You needn't work, stay at home for me"—someone who would bring in lots of money for me, you know? [*Laughs*][12]

UPDATE

Eight years have passed since I initially interviewed these four women about their careers at Azumi. In a return visit in 1992, I reunited with them. All spoke warmly of their children, noting where they were in school and talking of their plans for them.

Usui-*hanchō* has remained at Azumi, as energetic as ever. She uses personal computers in her work now. She trained herself in the evenings, reading manuals and studying through correspondence courses. The company subsidized one-third of her expenses.

Kamida-*hanchō*, too, has remained at Azumi. She oversees inspection quality control now, and the company occasionally sends her to Tokyo for quality control seminars. She noted that much has changed at Azumi since the mid-1980s; two-thirds of the inspection and packaging workforce are now *arubaito* (young people working part-time). Turnover is high, which is a headache for production schedules. Her son has graduated from a private college and now works as a salesman. After finishing high school, her daughter entered a two-year technical school for childcare training and now works at a public day-care facility. The two children still live at home. Kamida-*san*'s mother-in-law, who had taken care of the children throughout their childhood, fell ill and needed care herself the last year of her life. Though Kamida-*san* feared that she would have to quit her job, the children, then in college, shared nursing duties; thus Kamida-

san was able to stay at Azumi. She noted that she would have quit had it been a choice between hospitalizing Grandma or caring for her herself at home, since she owed her so much for all of her support. She, her husband, and the children plan a trip to the U.S. in 1993—their first travel abroad. They had become tired of hearing about all of their friends' and acquaintances' trips abroad and decided to experience it for themselves.

Shimizu-*san* took on a variety of jobs in her home after leaving Azumi. She now sews lingerie at home for some big-name companies. She spoke with pride of her accomplishments over the last few years: she obtained her high school equivalency diploma through night school and steered her older son into a college-track high school (the younger will take exams next year). Although retired from Azumi, she still keeps in touch with her former coworkers.

Nakada-*san* remains at the shipping center and plans to stay there. Although she suffered a serious illness a few years ago, she has recovered. Her son has grown up and left home to live and work on his own. She told us he has talent in gymnastics and may try for the Olympics in the future.

CONCLUSION

What can we learn from these blue-collar survivors? First, their lifestyles and, to some extent, their values differ from those of the well-educated professional housewives of whom we often hear (Imamura 1987; Iwao 1993; Suzanne Vogel 1978). Indeed, they have much more in common with the confectionery *pāto* of Kondo's (1990) study or Haruko, the farming woman of Bernstein's (1983) work. The veterans of Azumi value their jobs highly, marshaling their considerable energies toward their careers as regular employees while simultaneously being wives and mothers. It is a rare person who can maintain this balancing act. In Japan the demands on a regular employee in a large firm are so great that they practically necessitate a full-time manager in the home, if there is to be a home. As Osawa Mari (1994) deftly illustrates, the counterpart of the *ryōsai kenbo* is, after all, the overworked salaryman. To be both requires a supportive family situation, willingness to go the extra mile for the company, and determination to put one's duty to the job above one's right to take childcare hours or sick leave, not to mention vacation days. Moreover, it takes courage and tenacity to insist on staying even when one's bosses or coworkers—or sometimes one's own family—would prefer that one leave.[13] As long as corporate culture is based on strictly separate gender models, I do not expect to find great numbers of Japanese women aspiring to lifetime employment in the mainstream. But we can learn much from those who do.

NOTES

1. I refer to Japan's part-time workers using the Japanese term, *pāto* (derived from the English), so as not to confuse their meaning with ours. *Pāto* work does not necessarily connote shorter hours; indeed, many manufacturing *pāto* work as many hours as regular employees. The difference lies in benefits, wages, and job security, which are vastly inferior to those of regular employees.

2. As do many lingerie companies in Japan, Azumi had its own sales force, trained to sell its product line exclusively in Azumi boutique sections of department stores as well as in separate Azumi shops. The sales clerks were Azumi employees, but their working hours conformed to those of the stores where they were employed.

3. This is long in comparison with nationwide statistics for average years of service for women, which was 6.5 years in 1984.

4. I started out working afternoons, arriving after lunch, but after a few weeks switched to mornings.

5. Examples of such practices are frequent job location transfers, expectations of after-hours socializing, heavy overtime schedules, long working hours in comparison with Europe and the U.S., scant vacation time, and so on. These practices necessitate a great deal of commitment to one's job and are based on the assumption that a man's spouse will take complete care of his household. The concept of full-time, career-oriented employee carries with it the expectation that this employee will be first and foremost a company man. Rarely can a married woman employee meet this expectation and still have a family left to go home to. Thus we have the paradox that although Japanese women have had certain employment rights guaranteed them in the post-World War II Labor Standards Law, a combination of cultural gender norms and expectations for career employees has kept them from coming anywhere near the male pattern of job tenure. The rights granted by law are pregnancy leave for fourteen weeks at 60 percent of one's pay and childcare time that allows a woman one-half hour of rest twice a day during work to care for her infant until the baby is two years old. Miyaji Mitsuko and Honda Junryo, *Onna no Rōdō Kijunhō* (Tokyo: Rōdō Junpōsha, 1986), 27.

6. If the woman were divorced or widowed, however, she worked for the basic necessities. The income of the mother alone is usually insufficient to provide for "extras" such as new appliances, a car, a house, or additional schooling for the children.

7. Part of women's reluctance to express a desire for promotion might also stem from reserve, as openly seeking promotion would be deemed as aggressive and hence negative behavior. Robert Cole, in *Japanese Blue Collar: The Changing Tradition* (Berkeley: University of California Press, 1971), notes that male factory workers were hesitant to admit that they desired promotion, but they did attribute such aspirations to their coworkers. The women I interviewed, however, did not attribute to other women a desire to climb, nor did they admit such a desire for themselves.

8. Since 1986 the company has asked several women under forty, including Fujii-*san,* to enter a training program for the next promotional level and to take

the test upon completion of the program. Fujii-*san* passed and has since learned the duties of her new post, which requires office and computer skills. In 1988 she was asked to test for the next higher credentialed level, *fukushuji*. She was thrilled to be included among those considered for promotion. She said about one-fourth of the people testing at this level were female employees. One factor encouraging the company to invest in Fujii-*san* is her family circumstances. Her husband is chronically ill, and the firm knows that Fujii-*san* intends to continue her job until retirement at age sixty.

9. Azumi's union made an arrangement with the company whereby the childcare time would be taken for one hour at the end of each day and could be taken for up to two years after birth.

10. She also remarked at another point that the fact that she was having difficulties balancing home and work duties contributed to her desire to step down from being *hanchō*.

11. This was in violation of the Labor Standards Law.

12. Nakada-*san* was not the only middle-aged employee who wished to find a partner. Taniguchi-*san* (age forty-eight) was still hoping, and so was Matsumura-*hanchō* (age thirty-six). Murakami-*kakarichō* (age forty) said that she had not had the luck to find a spouse, but should not be treated as different from other women because of it. To the Japanese, marriage is not only considered a natural step in the process of life, but it is also essential to being recognized as a mature adult (Lebra 1984:78). The next step is having children—how often my coworkers urged me to have a baby! Without one, I was excluded from the conversations on childcare, and in their eyes I had not yet fulfilled my duty to my mother—how happy she would be, they told me, if I had a baby!

13. For a detailed account of women's working lives at Azumi and their strategies to keep working, see Glenda S. Roberts, *Staying on the Line: Blue-Collar Women in Contemporary Japan* (Honolulu: University of Hawaii Press, 1994).

ELEVEN

Popular Reading

The Literary World of the Japanese Working Woman

Nobuko Awaya and David P. Phillips

For the foreigner intent on learning about Japanese culture, details of the lives of young Japanese women are often obscured by analyses that seek to define limitations on women in Japanese society. Though numerous studies focus on the two most typical women's roles, the office lady and the housewife, they overlook the growing number of women who delay marriage or decide to remain unmarried. The implicit assumption that there are few alternatives for Japanese women beyond marriage needs to be updated.[1] Both nonfiction and fictional literature from the 1980s and 1990s suggest that a quiet revolution is occurring in women's values. This literature points to the fact that some women are postponing their marriages in order to devote more time to advancing their careers, traveling abroad, or simply enjoying freedom prior to taking on the responsibilities of married life. Though the majority of jobs open to women are still not career-track positions, these jobs are no longer just a means to save money before marriage, but to help single women maintain financial independence while exploring their options.

One of the most cogent pieces of evidence that values are changing is the body of popular literature read by the working woman. Some Japanese women writers have been exploring topics that were previously unpopular. Female protagonists in novels are getting divorces, establishing single-family homes, and pursuing careers.[2] And many women actually entering marriage today have more demands and expectations of their marriage partners. Recent literature exposes a fact often hidden from mass media: many young Japanese women are forging new alternatives for their future. Part of their search for alternatives has led to the popularity of literature that has helped young women to redefine their roles. This literature provides a blueprint for change by focusing on issues of image and identity. Before investigating why women are attracted to the current popular women's literature and how such literature reflects the aspirations of this generation, it is useful to review the recent shifts in beliefs and attitudes that have helped to influence the current audience of young women readers.

In contemporary Japan, women's consciousness of the issues of women's liberation did not occur as a popular movement. Rather, women who were intent on pursuing careers came to realize that they were stymied by glass ceilings at the workplace that restricted them to secretarial and reception work or to other noncareer-track positions. They began to explore other avenues to fulfillment. In the 1980s, popular television programs and movies began to include numerous scenarios in which women were having affairs, pursuing success in double careers as homemakers and working women, or just striking out on their own. Though the media cannot provide an accurate measure of the extent to which values were shifting, its focus on new roles for women indicates the fascination with which viewers pondered the topics of marital infidelity and the foibles of the "career woman," as she is known in Japanese. Popular media has raised television and film viewers' consciousness of women's roles in society. It highlights the fact that more women were openly expressing their dissatisfaction with their role in the workplace and searching for alternative models. Instead of saving money solely for marriage, some office ladies started saving for foreign study programs, hoping to gain experience abroad that would provide new opportunities upon their return to Japan or else to meet and marry a foreigner.[3] Such goals suggest an attempt to bypass the social system and to search outside Japanese society for opportunities for personal growth. If the system proved so rigid that it would not allow women to alter their roles or protest against early marriage and childbearing, growing numbers of office ladies were willing to travel away from Japan.

Other office ladies have grown disillusioned with the life that awaits them after marriage. They are typically young, single women with high school diplomas or junior college degrees and full-time, noncareer jobs. Having already achieved substantial financial independence and freedom, including the opportunity to live alone, they are questioning the wisdom of exchanging their jobs for marriage.[4] They have seen their classmates marry and face a lifetime of duties as homemakers for working husbands, giving up their freedom, their jobs, and their financial independence. As a result, many single women have become more selective in their choice of spouse and in their career and life options.[5] Nonfiction books like Matsubara Junko's *Onna ga Ie o Kau Toki* (When women buy homes), which describe options available to single women, have become best-sellers by providing titillating new images of the glamour and success that await the single career-woman.[6] Following the trend to study the motivations and aspirations of the single woman, Tanimura Shiho wrote *Kekkon Shinai Ka Mo Shirenai Shōkōgun* (The "maybe I won't marry" syndrome) in 1991, analyzing the changing roles of single women in Japanese society. In the afterword to her book, Tanimura expresses her frustrations and her hope.

It is only fairly recently that I have begun to experience the same resignation as others who feel that they may not get married. . . . Yet, now that I
have written this book, I have begun to see this vague position of "maybe
not getting" in a positive way. I believe that this change in my outlook is due
to the interviews with each of the people I met. All of these women realized
that they might not get married, all had anxieties about such a future, all of
them were alone, and yet all of them had the spunk to keep on going.[7]

Tanimura demonstrates to her readers that there are alternatives to marriage and affirms the lives of women who explore these options.

Though new options have become available to Japanese women since
the early 1990s and more women are expressing dissatisfaction with their
roles in the workplace and the home, a large number are still leaving work
for marriage or childbearing.[8] In major metropolitan areas, however,
many women are keeping their jobs.[9] This phenomenon is relatively recent, as shown in national survey data that reveals significant shifts in attitudes concerning marriage and work.[10] When people of both sexes were
asked in 1989 if they agreed with the statement "Men should work, and
women should stay home," nearly fifty-two percent of the men and thirty-
seven percent of the women agreed with the statement.[11] In comparison,
in 1991 only thirty-five percent of the men and twenty-five percent of the
women agreed. Women's attitudes about marriage are also changing. In
1987 less than fifty percent of the women interviewed felt that they preferred marriage to staying single, and almost thirty-eight percent of them
would prefer to live alone if given the choice.[12]

In the past two decades, changes in women's values have affected their
attitudes toward work and their role in society. In addition to surveys and
demographic data, popular culture reveals that the expectations and aspirations of working women in Japan are changing.[13] This chapter provides
a glimpse of how women's popular literature has contributed to women's
changing aspirations. We examine the novels of Yoshimoto Banana and
Hayashi Mariko, two authors who are currently among Japan's most celebrated writers of women's literature. Their readers generally range in age
from teenagers to women in their early to late twenties and are mainly
students and working women. The authors' works point to a common
theme: the search for a better quality of life and reaffirming images of
identity.

YOSHIMOTO BANANA: BREAKING AWAY FROM THE MAINSTREAM

Yoshimoto Banana is one of the youngest successful women novelists.[14] By
1987, at the age of twenty-three, she had forged a new style that won her
many young women readers and a number of curious male readers as
well.[15] The women at the center of her novels overcome obstacles to per-

sonal happiness through a combination of luck, perseverance, integrity, and a devil-may-care attitude that defies social conventions. Such characters start from scratch in building their own identities. Likewise, Yoshimoto has built her own public identity from scratch. As her work has gained popularity, Yoshimoto has capitalized on her public persona as an author. Because she looms larger than life to her readers, many of them are just as fascinated with Yoshimoto the celebrity as they are with the lives of her fictional characters. The stories she tells are partly iconoclastic and partly resonant with traditional values. Because she draws from familiar ideas such as the importance of forming close relationships and at the same time includes subject matter that focuses on marginalized people, her characters seem both mainstream and eccentric. It is perhaps this blend of the familiar and the unusual that makes her literature so attractive to her reading audience and feeds speculation about her own beliefs. Such fence-sitting gives her literature a safely *risqué* quality by challenging without threatening.

Yoshimoto's fiction centers on young women's efforts to discover themselves. Most of her writing is in the romance novel genre (*renai shōsetsu*). Yoshimoto departs from the familiar territory of other romance novelists by avoiding verisimilitude or realistic depictions of the average woman's life. Her plots revolve around characters who live on the margin. Two of her most popular novels are *Kitchen* (1987) and *Tsugumi* (1989).[16] *Kitchen* relates the story of Sakurai Mikage, a college dropout who is left an orphan by the death of the grandmother she had lived with most of her life. Mikage is befriended by a man who was a college classmate. He lives with his father, a transvestite who poses as his mother. The plot of *Tsugumi* is equally implausible. It is about the teenage years of a young woman, Tsugumi, who was born with life-threatening and disabling congenital defects. Tsugumi is demanding, selfish, and quick to tell people exactly what she thinks of them. Such behavior is normally to be avoided in Japanese society, but Tsugumi flaunts her disregard for social niceties. Part of the attraction of such far-fetched plots for the reader is their avoidance of a realistic venue. The improbable circumstances that characters such as Mikage and Tsugumi are placed in have two purposes: they force the characters to hone their survival instincts, and they allow the reader to empathize from a safe distance.

Iconoclastic behavior holds a fascination for the reader who is unable and unwilling to be iconoclastic or antisocial, yet who is frustrated by the constraints of daily life. Yoshimoto inhabits her stories with marginalized people who have the luxury of being able to indulge in such behavior. The effect of marginalization on individuals is a continual theme in her novels. She uses marginality to emphasize the fearlessness and power of her characters. Once they have rejected worries about marriageability, the yardstick with which conventional society judges young women, they are able to pursue journeys of self-discovery. Free from social constraints, stripped of the expectations that burden the normal Japanese young woman, they appear to the reader as explorers, at once rebellious and appealing. The reader thus has the twofold pleasure of vicariously appreciating the experience of life on the edge and being reassured that she will never have to go through such experiences.

The grounds for ostracism in Japanese society are broad. It is difficult to understand the isolation of many of Yoshimoto's characters without an awareness of the importance marriage plays in their lives. In modern Japanese society, marriage and childbearing have been the key to social acceptance for most women. Feminism in Japan has its roots in discussions in the 1880s and 1890s over whether education for women should focus on preparing them for marriage.[17] The views of early feminists, who argued that education should do more, clashed with expectations of the era that women be good wives and wise mothers.[18] Yet we find in much popular woman's literature today that the institution of marriage is not questioned. Such challenges would be too radical for these works to be accepted by the mainstream audience of women readers. Romance and marriage remain important goals for many single women.

Contrary to convention, in *Kitchen* the character Mikage ignores her options for marriage. She is painfully aware that her ostracism by society is due, in large part, to her inability to fit the mold of the other young women around her who are pursuing marriage. She is also learning to deal with the pain of personal loss. Having lost her only close relatives, Mikage finds herself forced to develop new skills for survival. She passes through several stages of self-realization. Though at first she is "left here, all on my own, putting all my efforts into just trying to cope," as she starts to adjust to her new life she discovers that "although I want to cry I can't. I feel strangely elated."[19] Her pain and her awakening to life are tinged with an existential sadness. She thinks to herself, "There are times like this when the realization that I am who I am becomes very painful."[20] Pain and isolation, as well as her freedom from the roles and responsibilities of family, become the departure points for her journey of self-discovery.

The kitchens in this novel prove to be symbols of the security for which Mikage longs. They are oases. She says, "I think my favorite place in the world is the kitchen. It doesn't matter where it is, or what kind of kitchen it is. As long as it's a kitchen, I can cook there. I'm happy."[21] Mikage variously describes the kitchen as a place she would like to die in, a place to cook in, a place to grow attached to, and a place to share with others. But the safe feeling that kitchens seem to exude does not shield her from her problems. Instead, she contemplates the maturation that is occurring within her. "I have to grow up more and more, and go through many experiences, and fall down to the depths many times. I'll go through pain again and again . . . but I won't give up. I won't back off."[22] It seems fitting that Yoshimoto's depiction of her source of strength, the kitchen, is so insular and nurturing.

The creation of highly unusual characters such as Mikage helps to explain the popularity of Yoshimoto's work. Although Mikage is orphaned and young, she is amazingly independent and able to vocalize her feelings. The reading audience of *Kitchen* is composed mostly of young women in their late teens and early twenties. Their sense of isolation is not as great as that of Mikage, and they have their families to depend on. However, Mikage's situation mirrors on a smaller scale their own adolescent crises and attempts at self-exploration.[23] A number of Yoshimoto's themes reflect the deepest concerns of young Japanese women. Yoshimoto's favorite subjects are young women who experience the isolation that comes from not knowing the roles they are expected to fill.[24] Following graduation from high school or college and in the early years of employment, the young woman has to answer for herself some of the most difficult questions in her life: What type of future do I want? Can I pursue a career? Will I find a husband who will allow me to pursue a career? Do I want to raise children right away? Even for high school students, these questions loom in the immediate future.

These questions reflect the commonality of young people's struggles to reach maturity as they search for role models. Characters like Mikage who are able to question accepted values and examine alternatives are meant to stimulate the reader's own existential search. Yoshimoto depicts self-discovery as a series of experiences of pain and joy. The uniqueness of her approach is her ability to guide the reader toward accepting her marginalized characters as role models. She does not merely create characters that her readers can empathize with. Rather, in the process of identifying with Mikage's plight, readers can associate her range of emotions and problems with their own. They have the satisfaction of watching each step in her progression. Readers may even gain confidence in the ability to shape their own future and to experience the range of emotions that Mikage allows herself. Through her example, readers learn that it is all right to feel overwhelmed and that, no matter how isolated they may feel, they are not alone in coping with the struggles of day-to-day life.

Mikage's status as an orphan marginalizes her. She must undergo a number of hardships in order to regain her sense of belonging. She is without a family. She has no expectations for marriage. And, as a single, unemployed, female college dropout, she has few career opportunities. Yet Mikage does not let these sobering facts crush her spirit. In *Mangetsu*, the sequel to *Kitchen*, she decides with bravado to teach herself the art of cooking.[25] She is amazed when she is eventually taken on as an assistant for a famous teacher who runs a cooking school. At the same time, she recognizes that she stands apart from her students. She describes the rigid control that governs their lives. "They lead a life of happiness. No matter what they learn, they have been taught—probably by loving parents—not to extend themselves beyond the bounds of this happiness. But they don't know anything about real joy. As to which approach to life is better, it is not something that the individual can choose. Life is such that each person lives it as he or she must."[26] Coming face to face with students who are sheltered from real-life experiences, Mikage finds comfort in her life as an outsider.

Yoshimoto is speaking through her protagonist, suggesting to her readers that their lives, though secure, may lack the breadth and emotional richness of Mikage's existence. She is challenging the status quo, claiming that, by subverting the process of self-discovery, prescribed social roles preclude experimentation. She demonstrates that the rewards for wandering from the path of acceptable behavior are a heightened consciousness and a deeper range of emotions. Mikage experiences these emotions, although her awareness of isolation makes her fate seem bittersweet.

> One experiences happiness by avoiding as much as possible the realization that one is entirely alone in life. I think how nice such a life would be. I would wear an apron and laugh like a delicate flower. After a great deal of bewilderment, I would fall in love and get married. How wonderful! It is a story that is both exquisite and graceful. When I am really tired, or when I get a rash, I relieve the loneliness of the evening by calling all my friends. Even though their voices help, at such times I detest every aspect of my life, including my birth and my upbringing.[27]

Her self-hatred is directly related to her marginalized position in society. Yet, despite her envy of other women who can slip so easily into marriage and who are careful not to step outside the bounds of propriety, Mikage is not satisfied with such a mundane solution to her loneliness.

Mikage has met a fate that few young women in Japanese culture have shared. She is part of an isolated segment of society deemed socially unacceptable, and yet her marginalization also confers privilege. James Valentine observes, "The potential for some marginals in Japan to remain marginal to any group, thus lacking collective support for a strong alternative identity and world view, may encourage detachment from fixed perspectives on self or society, and give the individual a sense of cultural relativism that, despite social and material difficulties, constitutes a form of awareness which is prized in itself."[28] With her alternative identity, Mikage is in a position that is both enviable and unattainable. As an outsider, she can be bold and make risky choices. She feels comfortable dropping out of school, although she shies away from people who might criticize her for doing so. Commenting on a former boyfriend, Mikage remarks, "While looking at his face in profile, I thought that he was the type of person who would take control and force me into action, doing things like help me to find a new apartment and make sure I came to classes. I loved his healthy attitude, and I really looked up to him, but at the same time I was sick of myself, since I was unable to follow along with what he wanted. But that was in the past, when I was the way I used to be."[29] Recognizing this past self, Mikage realizes that she has become much more independent and freewilled. She no longer wants to be dependent on another person and learns to gauge her own strength by standing alone.

Though Mikage experiences great sorrow during her journey of self-exploration, this sorrow is combined with a fierce determination to forge ahead, even when she is not sure what she is searching for. She is different from many other young women who resign themselves to their fates and become passive and nonthreatening to the male world. Yoshimoto's depiction of Mikage is just one example of how she uses her characters as mouthpieces. She establishes new role models that help young readers cope with life. In a particularly desolate scene near the end of *Mangetsu*, Mikage says, "Standing alone in this exceedingly lonely garden that I had never been in, I felt that this time I really was all alone. People are not controlled by the power of external forces. In the depth of my heart I realized that defeat comes when one gives up inside."[30] Although she goes through periods of feeling ineffectual, Mikage has developed a mechanism for fighting her fears of helplessness: she recognizes that these anxieties are common to all people and can be resisted.

To understand Mikage's story, which ends with her finding happiness in the arms of the man she has fallen in love with, we must turn to Yoshimoto's motivation for writing *Mangetsu*, the sequel to *Kitchen* that tells of Mikage's miraculous transition from shiftless youth to career woman. Yoshimoto writes:

> The novel *Kitchen* was altogether too sad. The protagonist was a *maguro*[31] from beginning to end and just flopped around, without any real verve. The aftertaste of such a story was very strong. But I didn't dislike the story, so I decided to write the sequel, "Kitchen 2" [*Mangetsu*]. In the sequel, I was happy that I was finally able to write a work that would make people think, "So this is the way that people should be." And I became able to depict a character who, as a working woman, looked cheerfully around herself each day. Women are strong![32]

Uncomfortable with the lack of resolution in Mikage's life, Yoshimoto altered the story, developing a happy ending that neither shows Mikage as a traitor to feminist rights nor shows her to be dissatisfied with her existence. Mikage has come full circle, learning first how to survive as an outsider and then reintegrating with society through her career and relationship. Yet she has learned a great deal about herself in the process and discovered that she can relinquish her position of isolation without sacrificing her independence. Her story becomes a role model for young readers to follow.

In Japan, the personal story of others has always been a social tool for learning by example. The I-novel (*shishōsetsu*), a literary form that gained popularity in the 1910s, arose from the tradition of authors who wrote fictional or semifictional accounts that were based loosely on their personal lives. Consequently, the I-novel came to be accepted as a literary form that records the inner workings of the minds of some of Japan's most well-known authors. Although this style of writing has been declared passé by most contemporary authors, Yoshimoto and others have made use of it, imbuing their characters with elements of their own personality. Yoshimoto, however, refutes any attempt to include her fiction in the I-novel genre. She comments,

> When I am asked where the characters in novels come from, I answer that people make them up on their own, so they are probably taken from a part of the author's own personality. But they are definitely not meant to be direct representations of the author. I think that, in my case, one can make such a statement about the character Sakurai Mikage in my novel *Kitchen*. . . . I feel that I am not as optimistic a person as Mikage. Yet, though I was not writing an I-novel, using my imagination I primitively composed the story.[33]

Though she denies the I-novel appellation, her work is regarded as closely reflecting her philosophy and personality. She has achieved celebrity status, and her remarks are closely scrutinized to enlighten readers about her approach to life. Judging from interviews in literary journals, Yoshimoto is comfortable espousing her opinions on such varied subjects as religion, the aspirations of teenage girls, and the "correct" approach to life. Her boldness and her fame heighten the appeal of her fiction to her readers. Consequently, Yoshimoto's beliefs and values, as publicized in the mass media, become inextricably related to the public's interpretation of her work. She intentionally blurs the boundary between author and character.

> If I could develop the skill when I am writing a novel of using words to convey to paper everything in my life—everything about me during that period in my life, the good weather and the bad, my struggles and my joys, places I have been, my health, the pain I experience when I fall in love, light and darkness, films I have seen, books I have read, television I have watched, people I have met, times I have gotten angry or felt compassionate, all of these thousands of bits of data—this would mark the limits of my talent.[34]

Her public persona as a spokesperson overshadows her fictional characters and should be considered in any analysis of her writing.

Yoshimoto presents a different type of role model in the novel *Tsugumi* (1989).[35] The main character, a young woman of the same name, is marginalized as a result of a life-threatening congenital illness. The novel tells of an improbable romance between Tsugumi and a young man she meets. Using Tsugumi as an example, Yoshimoto demonstrates to her readers that pleasure and happiness are impossible without personal suffering and pain. Maria, who is Tsugumi's cousin and closest friend, observes her objectively. "Tsugumi said, 'If you want to gain something, you can't ever help losing something at the same time.' . . . Her words meant to me that Tsugumi must have something she has kept to herself. She must have lost something and gained something else. Tsugumi's notion of self is so firmly established, that I never thought there might be things she has gained or lost. I felt that my understanding of Tsugumi as a person had suddenly come into focus."[36] Maria remarks on two qualities that Tsugumi has that most young Japanese women do not possess. Tsugumi is a survivor, who feels that she has lived for so long because she has had to experience a great deal of pain and suffering. Also, in contrast to other young women, she knows exactly who she is and what she wants. In a conformist society where many young women are manipulated through life's stages, Tsugumi is a breath of fresh air. She is admired by her family and especially by Maria for her spunk and her will to live. However, her illness prevents her from having a normal life. Treated like a misfit, she learns to play the part, becoming tough and developing the mischievous side of her personality to prove that she still has control of her life. And in a most un-Japanese manner, she discards all social conventions, preferring to shock and titillate. Maria says, "She is ill-tempered and rude. She is vulgar, has a filthy mouth, is whining, self-centered, spoiled, and terribly stubborn. She will discover what a person hates to hear most, wait for the perfect timing, and at the appropriate time blurt out the words calculated to irritate the most. She is really like a devil."[37]

The characters of Tsugumi and Maria, just like the character of Mikage, have been created by Yoshimoto to demonstrate young people's struggles between conformity and rebellion. Whereas Mikage both conforms and rebels, Tsugumi and Maria act as "halves" of the same persona, with Tsugumi representing rebellion, and Maria following the safer path of conformity. Maria is, for the most part, content with her life. Tsugumi is seething with desires, demands, and a need for affection. Maria, who is uncertain about her own identity, admires Tsugumi's strength. Tsugumi, in turn, senses Maria's indecisiveness.

In a twist that places her firmly within the I-novel tradition, Yoshimoto reveals that she recognizes the "Tsugumi" within herself. She ends the afterword to the novel with a confession: "By the way, *I* am Tsugumi. That terrible personality—I can only think that it's me."[38] Instead of one image

in the form of the character Mikage, here Yoshimoto has created two images to represent the conflict the author shares with her readers. When
Yoshimoto states that she is Tsugumi, she does not intend to suggest that
Tsugumi's life is based on her own, but rather that she shares basic elements of her persona with Tsugumi.

Tsugumi's actions demonstrate the struggle required to achieve personal fulfillment. Such fulfillment is in direct contrast to more traditional
measures of success such as marriage or child rearing. Comparing their
own lives to those of Tsugumi, readers are reassured that their own struggle will not be as difficult. In the process of reading the novel, they empathize with Tsugumi's fate. However, they identify with the character
Maria, who is more familiar to the readers because she is much more like
them. Yoshimoto's final words turn this relationship of identification up-
side down. Readers who have assumed that Tsugumi was too wild and
nonconformist to represent the author's feelings are shocked that Yoshimoto identifies strongly with Tsugumi. The impish Tsugumi and the author become parts of the same rebellion, daring readers to take possession
of their lives.

Even though she upholds the value of traditional institutions such as
marriage and the family, at the same time Yoshimoto empowers her readers by demonstrating that women can challenge accepted values and
speak out without fear of ostracism. By gaining independence, characters
such as Mikage and Tsugumi learn that they can relate to men as equals.
Such strength, which is neither stereotypically masculine nor feminine,
comes through people's realizations that they do not need to be trapped in
gender roles. Yamada Emi, another novelist who writes for young women,
comments on the trends that have sparked the popularity of romance novels: "It has reached the point where the majority of readers like women
characters who are strong. I'm sure that the reason why there are so many
readers who find books boring unless men and women are treated equally
is that there has been a change in [the values of] this generation."[39]

Yet the strength of Yoshimoto's characters is not the only factor contributing to the popularity of her stories. Her readers are fascinated with
her own approach to life as expressed by those characters. Her characters
stand alone, fiercely determined, honest, sensitive, and willing to learn
from the world around them. Tsugumi battles her illness and against all
odds proves that she can lead a relatively normal life. Mikage fights to
map out her identity and learns in the process that women, as well as
men, can be aggressive and goal-oriented. Both are aware of their own
mortality, and this awareness pushes them to their limits in comprehend-
ing the mechanisms that shape their lives. As Mikage says, "No matter
what happens, I want to continue to be aware of the fact that some day I
am going to die. For if I can't keep conscious of this fact, it is not possible

to feel alive. Maybe feeling this way is what has made my life turn out the way it has."[40]

In contrast to the role models of traditional literature, these women face the fear of isolation and focus their will to live on their own development. They are like the unnamed woman in Yoshimoto's short story "Gekkō" (Moonlight), who adjusts to life by controlling the love that seems to oppress her. "It is painful to think about those things which one is attached to. I feel like I am about to be smothered by something like a painful prayer, something that is harder to bear than our tenacious attempts to cling to life. When I am able to make myself stop thinking about such things, I can finally rest at ease."[41] These thoughts reveal one of the most innovative aspects of Yoshimoto's writing: her ability to communicate the motivations of her characters to her audience in an intense, personal voice. She plays on the reader's desire for genuine emotions and creates stories of people who are able to verbalize their dilemmas succinctly.

Yoshimoto has composed a fictional world that contrasts with the dreary, everyday world of the office lady.[42] Her stories present women who have rejected the training in the arts and secretarial work that are the standard route to marriage and respectability.[43] These women have striven to develop the innate, unique aspects of their personality. It seems ironic, given Yoshimoto's low opinion of their occupation, that such a large proportion of the people who read Yoshimoto's novels are women who are or will become office ladies. Perhaps the popularity of her works can be considered their form of silent protest.

Yoshimoto the author and Yoshimoto the media sensation exist as inextricably linked entities. Many of her readers look to her for guidance through the characters she portrays. The loyalty of her readers is perhaps best explained by her ability to develop a fictional approach to describing and analyzing their most pressing problems. Yoshimoto's characters go through the painful steps of self-discovery, learning in the process about their identity, their ability to be independent, and how to feel comfortable in society without relinquishing their freedom. Although the characters who inhabit her novels may not actually help readers become "closer" to their idol, the literature allows them to become more familiar with the persona that the author has projected. Discussing her career as a writer, she comments, "People who know their own weaknesses and strengths are beautiful. I want to become that kind of person. I have lost the outlook I had as a child, in which anything seems possible. Yet all the things I have done every day of my life remain in my hands, my heart, and my head."[44] Her writing has popularized the image of the woman who, free of family obligations, aims to forge a new identity. Just as some women are redefining their lives and career goals, Yoshimoto and her characters are learning to dispose of the gender-laden baggage of social expectations. These characters demonstrate that it is possible to change one's life, not merely through the attainment of material success, but through a better understanding of oneself.

HAYASHI MARIKO: CELEBRITY AND SOCIAL COMMENTATOR

Japanese women essayists are constantly aware of the male critic and create images of women with men's ideals in mind. They tend to write about beautiful women who are poetic, graceful, and well-dressed. But the work of Hayashi Mariko exposes this type of literature as a sham.[45] Focusing on the oppression of women by men's standards of beauty, appearance, and passivity, her writing shatters preconceived images and reflects her anger that women's literature promulgates conformity to such standards. Her first novel, *Runrun o Katte Ouchi ni Kaerō* (Let's buy a scooter and return home), released in 1982, was a powerful work that condemned the cult of the beautiful woman. She writes the following in her preface.[46]

> I truly wonder if there is any reality to a work that reads like the following: "She woke up in her bed, with white sheets wrapped around her. Getting up, she drank some milk, and went to see a man at the café." So what if the woman gets dumped by the man! No matter what develops in the scenario, it is always trying to be fashionable . . .
>
> What are they afraid of?
>   What are they trying to avoid?
>   I want to say that it is absolutely trifling to write about a typical young woman.
>
> Bias, jealousy, and envy—these are three characteristics that are avoided in depicting the woman's nature. But what's so unsightly about this kind of behavior? Hey!
>
> Anyway, I've decided to be the woman pro wrestler of words. I'm going to break to pieces those neatly written, beautifully scripted essays.

Hayashi condemns a homogenized approach to the depiction of women and the writing style that supports such an approach. Her book is a criticism of all of the good-looking men and women portrayed in magazines and television programs since the mid-1970s. Her critique begins with analysis of the world of the media-created woman.

Hayashi is the most prolific of all the popular women writers in Japan today. Since her first book of essays was published in 1982, she has written over one hundred books.[47] In the early years of her career she appeared as a commentator on many television shows and wrote gossip columns that focused on the lives of movie stars and popular singers. She also continued her first career as an advertising copywriter.[48] Her writing took a new direction when she turned to fiction. In contrast to her essays, which covered a wide range of social topics such as the goals and aspirations of the ordinary woman, her fiction was almost entirely autobiographical. Having become a celebrity, she capitalized on the I-novel genre.[49] In 1986 she was nominated for the Naoki Prize for her fictional work, *Budō ga Me ni Shimiru* (Grapes sting my eyes). She is currently considered primarily a novelist, although she contributes articles regularly for *Shūkan Bunshun* magazine and writes book reviews for *Asahi Shimbun*.

Hayashi's writing has evolved into a style that is both reactionary and personal. An iconoclast by nature, she strives to free women from the oppressive values of a culture that tries to turn them into sophisticated Kewpie dolls. Since World War II the fashion magazine has defined women's lifestyles in Japan. Starting in the 1970s a number of magazines were published that catered to the young, fashion-conscious woman. Among the new magazines were *An-An* and *NonNon*. In the latter half of the 1970s there were more entries to the stylish magazine market: *More* and *Croissant*.[50] All of these journals promulgated the stereotypical image of the woman who stood out from the crowd: youthful, cosmopolitan, beautiful, and passionate about creating her own lifestyle and career.

When she first read these magazines, Hayashi became furious. She had come to Tokyo from the countryside and lacked marketable skills. She knew that the dreamy lifestyle these magazines depicted was unattainable for most women.[51] Though many women must have felt angry and inadequate at such glamorized images, none spoke out because they were afraid of being labeled as disgruntled, unfulfilled women. Hayashi Mariko brought these feelings out in the open. She wrote about women's anger, jealousy, and envy. Her critical essays were the beginning of a popular women's movement towards realism in literature. Her work stirred women everywhere who were frustrated with the media's portrayal.

One of the new occupations for women that attracted attention during Hayashi's early years in Tokyo in the 1970s was that of stylist: picking out Western-style clothes for clothing collections. Stylists were the envy of many young women because their job was glamorous and required a flair for fashion. The image of the stylist became so popular that it was regularly featured in mass media such as magazines and television. Hayashi was incensed at the attention these women were receiving. Comparing the stylist to a common clerk, she wrote: "No matter how poorly I get my job done as an advertisement copywriter, I start each task from scratch. I'm nothing like the stylist, who just moves around clothing from the store shelf to the studio."[52] Her attacks on "fashionable" women are both biting and insightful.

Why do I make fun of these women so much? It's because I'm always being made fun of by them.

> You see, I look pretty young, and I am always proper. Anyone in this line of business who acts proper ends up on the short end of the stick. Let's say you're having your first meeting with a director or cameraman. One type of woman will greet him, saying, "Hey, Itoh. How ya doin'? Been out drinking lately?" The other type of woman would greet him with, "How do you do. My name is Hayashi. Nice to meet you." The woman in the latter case is going to lose out. I have often had the unpleasant experience of being snubbed by stylists.[53]

Although Hayashi caricatures these women, she is also self-deprecating, making references to her own ugliness and countryside origins. Such an unflattering self-portrayal has brought Hayashi great praise for her sincerity from women readers. In the early years of her writing career, rather than appearing as a successful, publicly recognized figure, she carefully constructed an image of herself as a disadvantaged member of the working class.[54]

In her commentaries and essays, Hayashi has been particularly critical of the elitist attitude of mass media and the advertising industry. She makes fun of the people who work as directors, producers, and copywriters in the magazine and television industries, ridiculing them for believing that they are the ultimate arbiters of good taste. According to Hayashi, such people seem to think that they are above reproach. She pointed out the case of Yano Akiko, a singer and songwriter who is the wife of the YMO band member Sakamoto Ryūichi. Hayashi taunted the music industry for building Yano into a star and ridiculed Yano for the part she was playing in such a farce. She considered Yano ugly and unworthy of attention and wrote, "One of the reasons that I detest her is that they [members of the industry] have created an atmosphere in which it is impossible for public figures to say that they despise Yano."[55] She felt that Yano was definitely not the type of singer that the public would have picked, given the choice. In Hayashi's words, the music industry's choice of Yano "proved that they were just fooling around, trying to show that their own artistic tastes were the most unique."[56]

Hayashi also vocalizes her disgust with the media's distorted portrayal of career women, complaining that their depictions are limited to the trendy jobs of stylists, fashion consultants, and copyeditors. From this criticism one might mistakenly assume that Hayashi is a staunch feminist. However, her protest against the status quo is not uniformly feminist. She claims that "when it comes to marriage or the workplace, men hold the key to women's happiness."[57] This is intended as a statement of fact about power relations in Japanese society. Yet Hayashi, along with many other women of her generation, has found a compromise that might seem untenable to Western feminists. Despite conceding the dominant position of men in her society, she fervently believes that all women can pursue active careers. Her literature gives her readers free reign to pursue this middle ground in constructing their identities.

Part of the public's fascination with Hayashi is that she does not fit the stereotype of the Japanese "nice girl," a term that conveys the image of a meek working woman. Hayashi has intentionally distanced herself from such values. As a "wrestler with words," she makes sarcastic remarks about people and values and is not afraid to state her opinion openly. Her arguments have prompted many of her readers to question their role and position in society. At the same time, she is careful to stress to her readers that the only means to happiness is through marriage. Hayashi emphasized this point by reiterating her desire to get married. "I would like to pose a question to people who make statements such as 'Marriage may be fun for the first half year, but afterwards it's tedious.' Is there any kind of happiness in this world that stays constant forever? There isn't, is there! Now that I know this fact, I want to get married more than ever."[58] Such declarations ran counter to the trend of popular media in the early 1980s, which portrayed the life of the single woman as beautiful and fashionable. Yet marriage continued to be a theme of Hayashi's essays, even after her own marriage in 1990 at the age of thirty-six. Her candor endears her to her readers.

Hayashi's writing depicts the lives of women who are not beautiful, glamorous, or popular, but who make up for their "failings" with spunk, verve, and determination. These women's stories, steeped in realism, demonstrate the strengths of the protagonist who does not find an easy road to success. Her novel *Budō ga Me ni Shimiru* is the story of Noriko, a young woman born and raised in the grape-producing region of Yamanashi. The first part of the novel depicts her life in junior high school. She has to help out at her family's grape farm in addition to doing her schoolwork, and is exceedingly jealous of the other girls whose fathers are white-collar workers. Though her parents love her, she can tell that they are resigned to her lackluster prospects for a future. She is self-conscious about being overweight and clumsy. The story reveals the cruelty of her classmates and describes her torment: she is alternately sad, jealous, frustrated, and bitter. Hayashi describes the details of her awkward, one-sided crush on Iwanaga, a handsome, athletic student. She eventually accepts that Iwanaga will not fall for someone like her. In a scene that takes place during Noriko's senior year, Hayashi tries to show both the cruel world that such a young woman faces and her need to strike back. When the class draws straws to decide seating, Iwanaga finds himself placed next to her. He yells out to his friend, "This is no joke! Why do I have to sit next to this ugly girl! Hey, Ogawa, I hate to ask, but can you let me draw another straw?"[59] For the first time in her life, Noriko speaks up to defend herself. "Hey you, you're rude! I just became your classmate today, and I haven't ever done anything bad to you. There's no need for you to refer to me the way you just did. Keep your idiotic statements to yourself."[60] Iwanaga apologizes to her with mock sincerity, attracting his classmates' attention and managing to make Noriko look foolish.

Critics regard Hayashi's fiction more for its shock value than for literary merit. Her novels tend to emphasize the trivial aspects of adolescent romance. Of Noriko's crush on Iwanaga, she writes: "She was sure that he was looking at her with the eyes of an accomplice. Noriko never told anyone about it, since she knew she would sound vain, but she felt that Iwanaga had been aware for a long time that she understood him better than anyone else. Otherwise, why would he have looked at her in that way? It was only a little over two months until graduation, and Noriko was certain that he would speak fond words to her in making his farewell."[61] Hayashi intends, through such writing, to show the emotional state of a young woman who is introverted, self-conscious, and lacking in confidence. It is eventually a story of victory for a young woman who lacks the prepossessing qualities of her classmates. Just as her characters bumble along, Hayashi's writing stumbles and falters, enhancing the effect of awkwardness.

Hayashi's characters tend to experience the same frustrations as Yoshimoto Banana's. They are young women who, in their struggle as adolescents, find themselves bewildered and often hurt. However, the course taken by these two novelists in depicting this struggle is very different. Yoshimoto's protagonists, who are orphans or woman in equally atypical situations, look to inner strengths for answers to their frustration. Characters such as Mikage carry on internal dialogues in their attempts to understand their surroundings. Hayashi, however, painstakingly describes details of her characters' daily lives, illustrating the parallels between their fictional experiences and those of her readers. Characters such as Noriko start their lives as ordinary women with roots in settings such as the average conservative country town. Smothered by such an environment, Noriko has experienced rejection since her early childhood and senses that even her own parents pity her. Yet she does not isolate herself. When she is finally accepted at a university in Tokyo, she realizes her dream of moving there. The narrator says, "Noriko believed that someday, somewhere, she would be able to make sense out of her life as a young adult. She would experience many romances. Tokyo is a place where all sorts of people live. She felt certain that she would find someone there who would love her."[62] Unlike Mikage, who looks to the enclosing comfort of the kitchen for relief, Noriko looks out, extrovertedly, to a new beginning in the city.

Hayashi wrote a number of novels following *Budō ga Me ni Shimiru* that were variations on the plot of this story. Each novel involves a woman who pursues a career and escapes the constraints placed on her in early adult-hood. Rather than recreate their identities, these characters reject limita-tions in defining their goals. The novel *Saishūbin ni Ma ni Aeba* (As long as I make the last flight of the day) (1985) is the story of Midori, a woman who, after attaining a degree of success in her career as a well-known commen-tator, gets in touch with Nagahara, her former lover, while on a lecture trip to Sapporo. Because she is now famous, their relationship has changed drastically. Whereas in the past she had paid for their meals to-gether from her meager salary as an office lady, this time Nagahara pays. He had always treated her brusquely and with little affection. Being afraid of losing him, she had overlooked his treatment of her. Now, Midori ex-periences subtle revenge as she shows off her new self. After their dinner together, Nagahara asks her to stay with him, but she refuses, racing her car to make the last flight of the day back to Tokyo. Hayashi describes Mi-dori's feelings of smugness as she takes her seat in the cabin and fixes her makeup.

> Her face was that of a woman beaming with confidence, despite the fact that her makeup was starting to come off. She had flashy facial features. "It wasn't really that bad at all," she thought, deciding that Nagahara had been intimidated by her. In the depth of the dark cabin of the airplane, Midori let slip a small, satisfactory giggle. She thought about what a gluttonous life she and Nagahara were leading. For an instant she felt the dull pain of re-alization. Yet, as she looked into the mirror of her compact case, her face assumed a nonchalant air.[63]

As with all of Hayashi's characters, each conquest serves to boost Midori's confidence.

Hayashi's fiction is inhabited by women who make their fortunes by learning from failure. In the process, they develop a defensive outer core. The women often feel trapped by attachments to men who envy their suc-cessful careers. Desiring release from the tension of the relationships, and angry at the bond that holds them back, they seek revenge.

A book reviewer for *Croissant* magazine links the desire for revenge expressed by one of Hayashi's protagonists with Hayashi's own need for revenge. Commenting on Hayashi's latest novel, *Once a Year* (1992), the re-viewer writes:

> In [the protagonist's] heart, she wanted to take revenge on her former lover, who had made her suffer so much. When a woman succeeds at a ca-reer, she naturally has relationships with men who are of higher status than would formerly have been in her reach, but in this woman's case she found she couldn't leave her lover. He was a sorry excuse for a man, but his pres-ence was comforting because it helped to reaffirm her success. She decided to use the cruelest method possible to take revenge on him. This novel fo-

cuses on the desire and ambition of the protagonist. It is deeply colored by autobiographical material.[64]

Hayashi's desire for revenge can be seen as originating from the need to break out of the passive role that has been imposed on women. However, Hayashi is careful to make a distinction between her message and that of radical feminists. Women should not attempt to put down men. Instead, they should achieve higher social status for themselves, leave their old boyfriends behind, and pursue relationships with more appropriate men. Self image, in such cases, is formed following the individual's decision to create her own identity. The magnetism of novels such as *Once a Year* is generated to a large extent by the glimpses they give of women who exhibit raw power in their searches for advancement.

Traditionally, most Japanese men have felt that women should be soft, gentle, and beautiful.[65] Women did not need to have drive or powerful egos. The internal basis for women's beauty was their ability to persevere. Such values extended from the feudalistic Tokugawa period (1600–1868) to the postwar period.[66] In contrast, Hayashi has taken as her role model the hard woman who has learned to modulate her femininity. Her fictional work focuses on women's rising careers and their romantic attachments. Though Japanese men are responding more favorably in recent years to women pursuing careers, the working woman has found herself caught between the need to be aggressive in the workplace and the need to fulfill men's expectations that women be kind and patient.[67] There is also conflict between women's roles in the public sphere of the workplace and in the private sphere of personal relationships and marriage. Hayashi severely criticized career women for sacrificing everything (including the chance to build a family) in order to pursue career-track positions. Partly as the result of such criticism these roles were deglamorized, and the era of "token" women in the workplace is ending. Japan is now entering the era of the ordinary working woman, who is neither idealized nor forced to choose between career and marriage.

Because Hayashi's work continues to center on her daily experiences, critics set her apart from Yoshimoto Banana and Yamada Emi.[68] Hayashi's readers say that they feel as if they know her from reading descriptions of her personal life. In her collection of essays, *Otona no Jijō* (The circumstances of an adult) (1992), she writes:

> These days I'm usually disturbed by obscene phone calls, or young women calling me.
>
> Woman: Hello. I'm a great fan of Ms. Hayashi's work. I wonder if I could learn from her.
>
> Me: I'm sorry, but she's in the middle of working now.
>
> Woman: Oh, I see. Well please tell her to keep up the good work.

> The woman's tone of voice seemed condescending. But, compared to
> some of the other phone calls I get, this one was rather cute.[69]

Her readers' intense interest in her personal life has helped elevate
Hayashi to celebrity status and turned her into a literary phenomenon.
Though she has stopped making appearances on television shows, her
activities continue to make the news. She appears in countless magazine
interviews with actors, fashion designers, and other famous people. And
over the years, she has continued to announce her desire to marry. Perhaps such tactics are indicative of her wish to be characterized as a "typical" Japanese woman. The Japanese public have come to think of her as
the woman who had a dream. Among her readers are men who read her
works half out of curiosity about why she was so intent on marriage.
Young women readers, many of whom worry about their own impending marriages, sympathize with Hayashi's plight and feel a strong bond
with her. When she reached her mid-thirties, Hayashi requested the services of a marriage broker, and in 1990 negotiated an arranged marriage. She wrote about the relationship in her columns, describing intimate details, such as chaperoned dates with her fiancé. Because her
essays are based so directly on her life, Hayashi's readers relate to her in
a different way from other women writers. When they read the novels of
Yoshimoto Banana, they learn about her and her approach to life
through identification with her characters. But from Hayashi's novels
and essays, her readers learn personal details of her life and identify with
her directly.

Although Hayashi is criticized in literary circles for the autobiographical nature of her essays, she continues to write columns for leading magazines about her married life and maintains her popularity. She has perhaps portrayed women with more honesty and integrity in her direct
approach to examining her life than has any other contemporary woman
writer in Japan. In looking at her overwhelming popularity and at the
"Mariko phenomenon," as it has come to be known, it helps to examine
the context of the era that made her famous. Many more Japanese women
are working than in the past, and more women are living independent
lives. Yet these women rarely have greater access to positions of power in
the workplace than they did in the 1970s and early 1980s. From the stand-
point of some office ladies, the career path is a dead end, and the men they
work for lead uninteresting lives, sacrificing personal satisfaction for their
careers. Women have had few options beyond marriage. An increasing
number of women, however, have chosen to ignore the pleas of their parents and to keep their jobs and forgo marriage. Instead of being trapped
in the cycle of continual self-sacrifice, they use their disposable income to
purchase luxury items and improve their lifestyle.

Such lifestyles are portrayed by the popular press as being self-centered and indulgent. Women in metropolitan areas who remain single and spend money on themselves are known as *Hanakozoku*, a term derived from the name of the most popular women's magazine in Tokyo, *Hanako*, which contains detailed articles about the best restaurants, stores, hotels, and foreign destinations. The success story of Hayashi Mariko inspires women who want to have successful careers and sustain relationships with men. Her writing lends concreteness to their desires. The Mariko phenomenon, conceived single-handedly by this woman who has exploited the power of media exposure to its fullest, continues to evolve. Her readers read her literature for hints of her road to success, happiness, and fame. Just as some readers prefer the unrealistic, symbolic worlds of Yoshimoto Banana's novels, others are content with the world of success that Hayashi Mariko represents. The popularity of both writers speaks to commonalities in the interests of the general reading audience. Women are searching for answers to questions about self-identity and the meaning of life in the work of both of these authors. They are eager for images of success and for knowledge about how to actualize their hopes.

The answers alluded to by Yoshimoto, which point to self-discovery, are in fundamental ways very different from the solutions proposed by Hayashi. Hayashi writes about her life as a writer and celebrity and feeds the dreams of women who would like to be in her position. Both in her early writings, which reveal an anger at a social system that demeans the average woman, and in her later essays, which stress the opportunities available to women, Hayashi demonstrates the belief that fulfillment and empowerment for the Japanese woman require the pursuit of both career and marriage. In the case of Yoshimoto's writings there is no parallel formula. Her novels do not privilege either career or marriage. Instead, she provides the reader with examples of the possibilities for self-growth to be gained through relationships. Rather than provide solutions, she presents allegories.

The similarities in these authors' approaches, although limited, stem from their positions as women of status who grew up in a transitional generation. Their generation is pursuing alternatives to a life of household duties and child rearing. Their popularity with young women readers—high school students, college students, and company employees mostly in their late teens and early twenties—stems from the writers' ability to address women's concerns about their identity and about images they can look to in their search for self-discovery. The readers' thoughts are echoed in the day-to-day concerns of Hayashi Mariko and in the worries of Yoshimoto Banana's characters. In the words of Sakurai Mikage, "All of these things around me that were part of my reality until so recently, seem to have rushed past me with great speed. I'm left here, all on my own, putting all my effort into just trying to cope."[70] Just as Mikage set out on an existential journey, so have the young readers of Hayashi Mariko and Yoshimoto Banana.

NOTES

The authors are grateful to Tokyo Women's Christian University for its support in awarding them with the 1993 Aoyama Nao Research Award. They also thank Dr. Janice Bardsley and other colleagues for their valuable suggestions and contributions.

1. Data from as recently as the mid-1980s, such as Takie Lebra's study *Japanese Women: Constraint and Fulfillment* (Honolulu: University of Hawaii Press, 1984), support the claim that women's career goals are secondary to domestic goals (Lebra, 226–27). However, a number of later English-language ethnographic and sociological studies fail to reflect changes that have taken place since this time. The most recent studies support the notion that few women would like to pursue careers, and a majority, given the choice, would choose marriage over career goals. Jeannie Lo's *Office Ladies/Factory Women: Life and Work at a Japanese Company* (Armonk, New York: M. E. Sharpe, 1990) describes women who "expressed that their life and work choices are limited by the social expectation of marriage" (Lo, 103). And Mary Saso, in *Women in the Japanese Workplace* (London: Hilary Shipman, 1990) comments that "sadly, Japanese women are conditioned to make . . . sacrifices, and historically have always done so, because they have defined their commitments in terms of the family not the workplace" (Saso, 252). However, Anne Imamura, in *Urban Japanese Housewives: At Home and in the Community* (Honolulu: University of Hawaii Press, 1987), provides a contrasting picture for the 1980s, in which the "new woman" who has emerged "believes that she should also be able to engage in activities unrelated to the homemaker role" (Imamura, 14).

2. One of the first novels in this era to use as its theme the topic of childbirth out of wedlock was Tsushima Yūko's *Yama o Hashiru Onna* (Woman running in the mountains), originally published in 1980 by Kodansha Ltd., Tokyo. English translation by Pantheon Books, 1991.

3. See "Increasing Number of Office Ladies in Their Twenties and Thirties Fall Prey to the Foreign Study Syndrome," *Shūkan Bunshun*, April 27, 1989.

4. See Awaya Nobuko, *Onna Kodomo ga Nihon o Kaeru* (Women and children are changing Japan) (P.H.P. Institute, 1991). The author interviews a number of office ladies. Her interview with Keiko-*san* (119–122) reveals a frame of mind that has become more common for young women—the dread of marriage and the restrictions it places on personal freedoms.

5. Since the 1970s, more women have been continuing employment after marriage or postponing marriage. See surveys included in the *Tokyo Josei Hakusho '92* (White paper on the women of Tokyo for 1992), edited by Tōkyō-to Jōhō Renrakushitsu Tosei Jōhō Sentaa Kanri Sentaa Kanrishitsu, published by the city of Tokyo, 1993. Two surveys of 1988 that examined employment rates, Tomin no Shūgyō Kōzō (Sōmukyoku) and Shūgyō Kōzō Chōsa (Sōmuchō), show that nationally 33.9 percent of women were employed full-time, whereas 37.2 percent of

women in Tokyo were employed full-time. For women in the twenty-five to twenty-nine-year-old age bracket, who have passed the age at which a majority of Japanese women get married, 55.6 percent of Tokyo residents were employed, whereas nationally 68.4 percent of women were employed. Marriage rates for this age group, according to the National Census of 1986, showed that over 50 percent of women in Tokyo and over 40 percent of women nationwide were still unmarried.

6. Matsubara Junko, *Onna ga Ie o Kau Toki* (Tokyo: Bunshun Bunko, 1990).

7. Tanimura Shiho, *Kekkon Shinai Ka Mo Shirenai Shōkōgun* (Tokyo: Shufu no Tomo, 1990), 228–229. This translation and all subsequent ones are the work of the authors.

8. Personal interviews such as those conducted by Nobuko Awaya reveal the increasing frequency of such responses. Survey data included in *Tokyo Josei Hakusho '92* also provide evidence of changing views toward work, marriage, and childbearing. In a 1989 survey, the *Josei no Shūrō Pataan ni Kansuru Jikeiretsuteki Kenkyū* (Time series research on trends of women in the workplace) conducted by the *Seikatsu Bunka Kyoku,* 42.1 percent of respondents felt that women's chances for promotion are either lower than for men or nonexistent, and 18.3 percent felt that women are only allowed to assist in the workplace. Dissatisfaction with the workplace, however, is not forcing more women into marriage. According to the *Josei ni Kansuru Yoron Chōsa* (Opinion poll concerning women) of 1990, 54.6 percent of women surveyed nationally and 66.1 percent of women surveyed in Tokyo said that marrying or staying single were equally acceptable options. As for women's attitudes toward leaving the workplace for child rearing, in a 1990 survey of mothers' contributions to the workplace and roles as parents (*Hahaoya no Shūgyō o Chūshin to shita Shakai Sanka to Oya Yakuwari ni Kansuru Chōsa*) conducted by the Seikatsu Bunka Kyoku, only 21 percent of the women surveyed nationally felt it was acceptable for a women who had a child aged three or younger to keep her job. In the 1989 Time Research Series survey, young women in Tokyo in their first year of employment were asked their attitude towards continuing their employment after marriage and childbirth. 32 percent of respondents said they would quit the workplace after marrying; another 40.3 percent said they would leave their jobs after their first child was born.

9. Attitudes to women's pursuit of career-track positions vary from region to region. Despite the relatively liberal attitudes of Tokyo residents, ironically the work environment for the female professional in Tokyo can be more limiting than for women elsewhere in Japan. National surveys of corporate executives by the Ministry of Finance in 1990 revealed that 56.4 percent of the companies interviewed were fostering the support of women in professional, career-track positions, whereas in Tokyo only 35.7 percent of the companies interviewed were pursuing such practices. See *Tokyo Josei Hakusho '92* for survey results.

10. See *Tokyo Josei Hakusho '92.* Responses from a national audience about marriage and women's careers tend to be more conservative than responses in Tokyo. For example, in a 1990 survey conducted by the Prime Minister's Office, men and women were asked if women should have the right to choose whether or not to keep their maiden name after marriage. Nationally, 27.9 percent of the

men and 31.3 percent of the women replied affirmatively. A much higher percentage of Tokyo residents concurred that women should be allowed to keep their maiden name: 34.5 percent of the men who were surveyed and 49.6 percent of the women.

11. Information compiled from *Josei ni Kansuru Yoron Chōsa*, 71.

12. Information compiled from *Fujin Mondai ni Kansuru Yoron Chōsa* (Opinion poll on the problems of married women), *Tokyo Josei Hakusho '92*.

13. See the latest annual edition of *Tokyo Josei Hakusho* for a summary of much of the data that has been collected by various ministries and government offices on women's roles, employment records, goals, and aspirations.

14. Yoshimoto Banana, born in 1964, has chosen "Banana" as her pen name. She graduated from the Arts and Literature Division of Nihon University in 1986. Her father, Yoshimoto Ryūmei, is a prominent social critic and poet.

15. *Kitchen* was an immediate best-seller when first released in 1987. By the end of 1992 it had sold a total of 1.46 million copies. It has won a number of literary prizes, including *Kaien* magazine's *Shinjin Bungakushō* (New writer's prize in literature) in 1987, and the Izumi Kyōka Prize. In 1993, the work was translated into English by Megan Backus for Grove Press.

16. The title for the book is written with the Japanese phonetic equivalent of the English word "kitchen" rather than with the Japanese word for kitchen, *daidokoro*. The use of the word in English rather than Japanese suggests a broader semantic range.

17. For a discussion of the historical development of Japanese women's roles in late nineteenth and early twentieth century, see Sharon Sievers, "The Women's Reform Society," in *Flowers in Salt: The Beginnings of Feminist Consciousness in Modern Japan* (Stanford: Stanford University Press, 1983).

18. This ideology, called *ryōsai kenbo* in Japanese, became part of common parlance after the phrase was introduced in 1875. Drawn in large part from Confucian values, the ideology emphasized the subservience of women to the home and family.

19. Yoshimoto Banana, *Kitchen* (Tokyo: Fukutake Shoten, 1988), 52–54.

20. *Ibid.*, 43.

21. *Ibid.*, 7.

22. *Ibid.*, 70.

23. The publishers at Fukutake Shoten attribute Yoshimoto's popularity to the attractiveness of her novels to young readers. According to their surveys, her novels are most popular with readers in their early twenties. She is also widely read by teenagers. According to the publisher, three factors have contributed to the success of her writing. First, her books are easy to read. Second, readers can empathize with her characters. Third, she is well known for being nominated for the Akutagawa Prize at such a young age.

24. Through high school, junior college, or four-year college, a woman's position in life is defined by her parents' socioeconomic status, by the neighborhood she lives in, by the prestige of the schools she attends, and by her network of friends. After graduation from school, many of these friendships become tenuous. Classmates drift apart as they turn to employment or to marriage.

25. The portion of this novel from pages 71–193, given the separate title of *Mangetsu* (Full moon), was originally published in 1988 as a sequel to *Kitchen*. It was subsequently published in a bound volume with *Kitchen* (Tokyo: Fukutake Shoten, 1988) under the title of *Kitchen*. All references to the novel *Kitchen* in this essay refer to the 1988 edition that includes *Mangetsu*.

26. *Ibid.*, 93.

27. *Ibid.*, 93.

28. James Valentine, "On the Borderlines: The Significance of Marginality in Japanese Society," in *Unwrapping Japan: Society and Culture in Anthropological Perspective*, ed. Eyal Ben-Ari et al. (Honolulu: University of Hawaii Press, 1990), 49.

29. Yoshimoto, *Kitchen*, 42.

30. *Ibid.*, 144.

31. A *maguro* is a fictional character who is manipulated by the author to prove a point or moral. *Maguro* also means tuna fish; Hence Yoshimoto's reference to her character's "flopping around."

32. Yoshimoto Banana, *Pineapprin* (Tokyo: Kadokawa Bunko, 1992), 20.

33. *Ibid.*, 17.

34. *Ibid.*, 19.

35. Like *Kitchen*, *Tsugumi* has met with critical acclaim: it was awarded the Hayamamoto Shūgorō Prize in 1989.

36. Yoshimoto Banana, *Tsugumi* (Tokyo: Chūō Kōronsha, 1989), 31–32.

37. *Ibid.*, 9.

38. *Ibid.*, 236.

39. "Renai Shōsetsu no Yukue: Yamada Emi x Yoshimoto Banana" (The future of the romance novel: a discussion between Yamada Emi and Yoshimoto Banana), in a special edition of *Bungei* devoted to authors who were winners of Bungei literary awards in 1992, the *1992-Nen Bungeishō Tokubetsu-gō* (Tokyo: Kawade Shōbō Shinsha, 1992), 159.

40. Yoshimoto, *Kitchen*, 94.

41. Yoshimoto Banana, "Gekkō," in *Femina* 8 (1990): 82.

42. In one interview with a member of the editorial staff of *Femina*, she was asked to "name the one thing that is most alien to you." She answered, "Office ladies in large corporations." Translated from *Femina*, 8 (1990): xxi.

43. Training in the arts, referred to in Japanese as *hanayome shūgyō*, or "training for the young bride-to-be," traditionally consists of lessons for a year or more in flower arranging, tea ceremony, calligraphy, and how to dress in kimono. In recent years, training has expanded to include the study of foreign languages or Western-style cooking and other aspects of Western culture such as etiquette and table manners.

44. Yoshimoto, *Pineapprin*, 9.

45. Hayashi Mariko was particularly direct in criticizing the male-dominated publishing industry. In the preface to her first book of essays she writes, "I have chosen to write this book because I am enraged at the prejudice I have been subjected to as a woman. Has there ever been a work written by a woman (particularly a young woman), or a journalistic essay in which she actually reveals her true feelings?" Translated from Hayashi Mariko, *Runrun o Katte, Ouchi ni Kaerō* (Tokyo: Kadokawa Bunko, 1985), 3.

46. *Ibid.*, 3–4. Sales for this novel classified it as a major success. Over 720,000 copies were sold by the end of 1992.

47. Hardcover rereleases of earlier paperback editions and serial essays are included in the count of published works.

48. Among her best-sellers in the early years of her writing career were *Hana Yori Kekkon Kibi Dango* (Marriage rice cakes on a stick rather than flowers) (Tokyo: Kadokawa Bunko, 1983), *Yume Miru Koro o Sugite mo* (Even if one is past the age of having dreams) (Tokyo: Shufu no Tomo, 1983), and *Runrun Shōkōgun* (The scooter syndrome) (Tokyo: Kadokawa Shoten, 1983).

49. In 1984 an editor, having read *Runrun o Katte, Ouchi ni Kaerō*, suggested that she start writing fiction. Hayashi promised him on the spot that she would write a novel that would receive the Naoki Prize (a mark of great public recognition that is considered to be the hallmark of any serious fiction writer in Japan). According to Hayashi, the editor told her, "If you keep going on this way, you'll end up known as a woman who writes essays and appears on television as a fake celebrity." Translated from Hayashi Mariko, *Once a Year* (Tokyo: Kadokawa Shoten, 1992), 146.

50. These new journals were aiming for a different group of readers: slightly older working women. The image of the woman projected in these journals was similar, however.

51. Hayashi has mentioned in a number of cases her disgust with the stereotypical images presented in women's magazines. In one example, she writes bitterly, "As a result [of the magazines' glamorization of this type of woman], I will probably end up in the sorry state of having to pour tea for these women." Translation of quote from Hayashi, *Runrun o Katte, Ouchi ni Kaerō*, 114.

52. Hayashi, *Runrun o Katte, Ouchi ni Kaerō*, 113.

53. *Ibid.*, 114.

54. Hayashi came to Tokyo in 1972 at the age of eighteen to attend college. She entered the Arts and Literature Division of Nihon University enrolling in the same creative writing program that Yoshimoto Banana would later attend. Her first novel, *Runrun o Katte, Ouchi ni Kaerō*, was published when she was twenty-eight years old and marks the beginning of her climb to fame.

55. Hayashi, *Runrun o Katte, Ouchi ni Kaerō*, 127.

56. *Ibid.*, 126.

57. Hayashi Mariko, *Hana Yori Kekkon Kibi Dango* (Tokyo: Kadokawa Bunko, 1984), 177. This book was originally published by Sony Magazines in 1983.

58. *Ibid.*, 164.

59. Hayashi Mariko, *Budō ga Me ni Shimiru* (Tokyo: Kadokawa Bunko, 1986), 162. This novel was originally published in 1984 by Kadokawa Shoten.

60. *Ibid.*, 163.

61. *Ibid.*, 184.

62. *Ibid.*, 189–90.

63. Hayashi Mariko, *Saishūbin ni Ma ni Aeba* (Tokyo: Bunshun Bunko, 1985), 64. This novel was first published in 1985 by Bungei Shunjyū.

64. Book review for Hayashi's *Once a Year, Croissant* (November 25, 1992): 139. Like the novel *Kitchen*, the title *Once a Year* is a phonetic transcription into Japanese of the English.

65. The Japanese use the English words "soft" and "hard" to refer to a person's ability to be gentle, kind, and forgiving on the one hand and ruthless, cold, and businesslike on the other.

66. Such feelings are still strong today, as can be judged by the popularity of soap operas such as *Oshin* that recreate the world of the "soft" woman of the early twentieth century.

67. According to the 1988 survey Fujin Mondai ni Kansuru Yoron Chōsa (see footnote 12), 36.4 percent of the male respondents stated that regardless of whether a woman is married or has a family or children, she should have the option to maintain her career.

68. She published collections of essays based on her syndicated work, among which were *Minami Aoyama Monogatari* (The South Aoyama stories) (Tokyo: Shufu no Tomo, 1986) and *Harajuku Nikki* (Harajuku diary) (Tokyo: Asahi Shimbun, 1992).

69. Hayashi Mariko, *Otona no Jijō* (Tokyo: Bungei Shunjyū, 1992), 226.

70. Yoshimoto, *Kitchen,* 52.

TWELVE

Women Legislators in the Postwar Diet

Sally Ann Hastings

The unprecedented number of women elected to the upper house of the Japanese legislature in the summer of 1989 attracted international attention. Twenty-two women were elected, more than twice as many as in any previous election for the upper house. Many were members of the Japan Socialist Party (JSP),[1] and their victories contributed to a major setback for the ruling Liberal Democratic Party (LDP), as it lost its majority in the upper house. The leader of this stunning socialist success was Doi Takako, the first woman to head a Japanese political party. Journalists claimed that a change in women's consciousness was shaking the political order of Japan.[2]

This sudden influx of women into Japanese politics has generated scholarly discussion, most of it based on interviews with the newly elected representatives, about both the present experience of these women and the future effects of their presence in the Diet.[3] It is, of course, in the nature of both headlines and interviews to focus on the present. The purpose of this chapter is to place the events of 1989 in the context of the past, that is, the history of Japanese women as legislators. Doi Takako did not suddenly ascend to power in 1989; she herself had been a member of the Diet for twenty years. When she began her career in 1969, some of her peers were women who had burst upon the political scene in 1946, when the American Occupation forces gave women the right to vote and to hold office.

The history of Japanese women in politics has not been one of simple linear progression, and analogies to land travel—milestones or obstacles in the pathway—cannot express its vicissitudes. It is more accurate to think of it instead as a tributary to the stream of Japanese political life. The elections of 1989, like the ones of 1946 and 1947, constituted a flood of women into politics, a flood that gradually receded, but that left the course of the river irrevocably altered. Events of 1968 and 1969, though they did not significantly increase the flow of women into politics, did alter the currents in the political stream as the number of conservative women decreased and the Japan Communist Party (JCP) co-opted what had been a concern of more moderate politicians: advocacy for women and children. The three elections since 1989—for the lower house in 1990 and 1993 and for the upper house in 1992—provide some sense of how the events of 1989 have permanently affected the pattern of Japanese politics by forcing all of the parties to create at least the illusion that they are inclusive of women.

THE INITIAL FLOOD

It is a peculiarity of Japanese women's history that women received the vote at a time when the entire political system was in disarray and the American Occupation authorities had barred the majority of male incumbents from holding office. The circumstances of Japan in 1946 stand in sharp contrast to those of most countries with parliamentary democracies, where women's suffrage allowed women to compete in a system in which men were already firmly entrenched.

The April 10, 1946, election for representatives to the lower house of the Diet took place only eight months after Japan's unconditional surrender, and the voters were prepared to embark upon a new course. Female political candidates were part of the new order. The old political machinery was in good repair. The last election, that of 1942, had occurred two years after all of the political parties had dissolved themselves. Thus no ordinary election had taken place since 1937.

Occupation policies compounded the difficulties of the old political leadership. A broad purge of undesirables from government office made eighty-two percent of the incumbent members of the Diet ineligible for office. The importance of the purge in opening up the political system is demonstrated by the fact that the few incumbents both eligible and willing to run fared well. The majority (thirty-eight men, or 83 percent) were successful, as were fifty-one others, who had at some time in the past held seats in the Diet. Because the Occupation authorities replaced the medium-sized districts, from which voters of the prewar era had returned four or five representatives to the Diet, with huge, prefecture-wide districts that elected as many as fifteen representatives, even those who survived the purge were not running in exactly the same districts as before. Moreover, election results were difficult to predict because an unprecedented multi-vote system allowed each voter to cast ballots for two or more candidates.

Women were among the newcomers to politics who benefited from the unsettled political atmosphere and the debilitation of the veteran politicians. Of the more than two thousand candidates in the election of 1946, seventy-nine were women, and of those, thirty-nine were elected. In an election in which there were six times as many candidates as there were seats, unusually large districts with many seats, and few incumbents with secure constituencies, any woman who was the only female candidate in her district enjoyed the distinct advantage of being clearly identifiable. Women ran in thirty-nine of the fifty-two election districts. In twenty-two districts only one woman ran, and in seventeen of those she won.[4]

The relatively strong showing by women candidates in the 1946 election cannot simply be explained away as the by-product of postwar confusion. The Japanese women of 1946 were literate, the products of a system of mandatory elementary school education. Those born in the 1880s or earlier had observed a half century of constitutional government, and to a limited extent had participated in it. In the first national election in Japan in 1890, women were members of support groups for candidates. Wives campaigned for their husbands, and women's organizations lobbied for election reform. Prewar Japan could also boast a wide range of women's organizations that promoted, often with the support of the state bureaucracy, women's participation in economic campaigns and mobilization for war.[5]

Moreover, the particular women who entered the political arena in 1946 had a wealth of experience both as professionals in the fields of health and women's education and as social and political activists. The physicians included Nakayama Tama, Takeuchi Shigeyo, and Tomita Fusa. Fujiwara Michiko was a nurse, Tanaka Tatsu a midwife, and Yoshida Sei a dentist. Koshiwara Haru, Matsuo Toshiko, Takeda Kiyo, and Takeuchi Utako were school principals. Other educators included Andō Hatsu, Kondō Tsuruyo, Mogami Hideko, Moriyama Yone, Murashima Kiyo, Niitsuma Ito, Nomura Misu, Sakakibara Chiyo, and Togano Satoko. Among the unsuccessful female candidates were physicians, school principals, teachers, reporters, and Buddhist nuns.[6]

The social and political organizations in which these women had been active included both suffrage groups and highly conventional government-sponsored associations. Sawada Hisa had headed a regional branch of the Suffrage League, and Wazaki Haru had been a prominent member of the league in Akita Prefecture. Katō Shizue had been active in the prewar birth control movement.[7] Niitsuma Ito participated in the Tokyo Women's Federation (Tōkyō rengō fujinkai) in the 1920s.[8] On the more conservative side, Saitō Tei and Tomita Fusa had held office in the Patriotic Women's Association (Aikoku fujinkai), one of the two major government-sponsored organizations.

Though professional concerns and political activism certainly motivated many of the female candidates of 1946, family loyalty was also a factor, especially in a year when many experienced politicians were barred from office. Indeed, on the forms filled out by candidates, approximately half of the women listed "none" as their occupation, thus indicating that their primary identification lay in something other than paid employment, presumably their responsibilities as wives. Kōro Mitsu and Mogami Hideko entered politics when their politician husbands became ineligible for office. Kōro Mitsu's husband, Akira, served in the lower house from 1932 to 1945; when he was barred from office, she ran in his place in 1946. After losing in the 1947 election for the lower house, she secured a seat in the upper house and served for three terms. Kōro Akira attempted to revive his own political career in 1952, but in the election for the lower house he placed tenth in a five-seat district.[9]

Mogami Hideko's career served as a connecting link between that of her husband and that of their adopted son. Her husband, Mogami Masazō, represented Gunma Prefecture in the lower house from 1930 to 1945. In 1946, Mogami Hideko ran in place of her purged husband; she won a seat in 1946 and 1947, but was only the runner-up in 1949. In 1952, Mogami Masazō ran for the lower house, but was not nearly as successful as his wife had been. In 1953 she ran successfully for the upper house, and she was reelected in 1959. In 1974 their adopted son Susumu won a seat in the upper house.[10]

Kōro Mitsu and Mogami Hideko, who are clear-cut cases of women who ran in place of purged politicians, illustrate that there is no simple way to differentiate between women with their own political careers and those running as good wives. Both Kōro and Mogami probably thought that their political involvement was a temporary expedient, but in neither case was the husband able to achieve the same political success in the new Japan as his wife had.

Under the Japanese election laws, which have no residency requirement for candidacy, a woman's political success did not necessarily preclude her husband or her father from winning office. Katō Shizue won a seat from Tokyo in 1946, while her husband Kanjū represented Nagoya. After they both failed to win re-election in 1949, she secured a seat in the upper house in 1950 and was reelected three times; in 1952 he ran successfully in her former Tokyo district. Togano Satoko, who won a Diet seat from Tochigi Prefecture in every election from 1946 until her death in 1971, first entered politics when directives from SCAP (Supreme Commander for the Allied Powers) made her husband Takeshi ineligible. A graduate of Dōshisha Women's College, a Christian university in Kyoto, she had taught English at various schools and worked as a newspaper reporter in Shanghai before the war. In 1946, she was thirty-nine and the mother of two children; her campaign slogan was "Women in politics will bring about better Government for the people."[11] Her husband's election to the upper house in 1953, where he served until his death in 1982, made them a dual-career political couple. Yamaguchi Shizue, who, with only one break, served continuously in the lower house from 1946 to 1980, was joined in the Diet by her father Shigehiko, who won election to the upper house in 1953 and 1959.

Fujiwara Michiko provides an exception to the rule that husbands and wives do not run against each other. In 1946, she ran for the Diet on behalf of her husband Yamazaki Kenji, who had not yet made his way back from military service in Southeast Asia. When he returned home from Borneo a week before the election, bringing with him a new wife and the children she had borne him in Southeast Asia, Fujiwara filed for divorce. (Fujiwara is her family name, to which she reverted after the divorce.) In the 1947 election, Fujiwara, running with the support of the socialist party, defeated her husband, who ran as an independent.[12]

One case in which family loyalty proved to be in conflict with a political career is that of Matsutani Tenkōkō. A graduate of Japan Women's College and the law department of Waseda University, she was well qualified to run on her own as a socialist in 1946. She was reelected in 1947 and 1949, but by the 1952 election, she had married a fellow Diet representative, Sonoda Sunao, a member of the Democratic Party. Although he represented Kumamoto, she continued to run from her Tokyo district, but always for his party. Her political supporters did not make a similar transfer of loyalty, and her repeated candidacies, in 1952, 1953, 1955, and 1958, all met with defeat.[13]

Japanese women were not able to sustain the same level of electoral success in 1947 that they had enjoyed in their first election of 1946. Only fifteen women won election to the lower house and ten to the upper.[14] Although contemporary observers and even some scholars have blamed the confusion and political inexperience of women for the falling number of women in the legislature, women maintained a high degree of interest in politics, and the barriers to their participation were largely imposed on them.[15] In 1947, even more women ran for the Diet than in 1946: eighty-five for the lower house and nineteen for the upper.[16] The veterans of 1946 did not give up easily; of the thirty-nine, all but four ran for re-election, and one of those ran for the upper house.[17]

Despite their interest in politics, women were handicapped as the old political order reasserted itself. By the election of 1947, the districts had been restored to their prewar contours. Each voter was restricted to only one vote in the multimember districts, making it impossible for voters to choose both a man and a woman. Most important, the parties recovered their power to organize support for their approved candidates. The conservative parties did not support female candidates. Of the twenty-five women whose political careers ended abruptly in 1947, seventeen had affiliated themselves with conservative parties.[18]

Although twelve of the fifteen women elected to the lower house in 1947 were incumbents, the sudden reduction in numbers changed the com-

plexion of the female contingent in the Diet. In absolute numbers, socialist strength remained approximately the same (nine in 1946 and eight in
1947), but as a percentage of the total number of women in the Diet, it
jumped from twenty-three percent in 1946 to fifty-three percent in 1947.
The three women newly elected in 1947 reinforced the emerging pattern:
socialist professionals and conservative women whose political activities
were buttressed by powerful male relatives could remain in office, but ordinary conservative women who simply wanted a voice in maintaining the
status quo stood little chance of survival. Fukuda Masako was a socialist
physician. Nakayama Masa's husband Fukuzō, a lawyer, served in the
lower house from 1932 to 1942. Educated at Kassui Girls' Higher School
in Nagasaki and Ohio Wesleyan University, Masa was a mother of four
when she ran for the Diet in 1947. Nakayama ran for office in parallel to
her husband, not in his place; he ran in the Osaka first district in 1947 and
1949 while she ran in the second. He did not immediately meet with the
same success, but eventually secured a seat in the upper house.[19] When
Nakayama Masa retired in 1969, having served in 1960 as Japan's first
woman cabinet minister, her son Masaaki succeeded to her seat.

   The 1947 elections to the upper house, the first to that newly constituted
body, likewise illustrated the advantages enjoyed by socialist women and
conservative women with family support. The constitution provides for
two types of constituency to this body: local and national. The local districts correspond to the prefectures, each of which elects one to four representatives to six-year terms every three years; the local constituencies
elect 152 of the 252 members. The other one hundred members are
elected from the nation at large. Two important ways of winning in this
constituency have been to have a national reputation at the outset or to
have the backing of an organization with a large membership.[20]

   In 1947, as in all subsequent elections, women enjoyed more success in
the national constituency than in the local contests of the upper house.
The women who won in the national constituency in 1947 were distinguished veterans of the women's suffrage movement (Kawasaki Natsu and
Oku Mumeo), the labor movement (Akamatsu Tsuneko), the academic
world (Kiuchi Kyō, Kōra Tomi), social work (Miyagi Tamayo), and the
health professions (Inoue Natsu and Kosugi Ine). Including Kōro Mitsu,
who secured a seat in the upper house by year's end, three women won in
the local constituencies. Two of the three ran in prefectures where their
husbands had a strong political base, Kōro Mitsu in Tokushima and Hirano Shigeko in Yamanashi.[21]

AFTER THE CREST

The flood of women into the legislative process ended in 1947. For the
next twenty years, the number of women in the Diet remained relatively

stable. As some women left office, their places were taken by others of the same generation. The fifty-two women elected in 1946 and 1947 were born over a span of four decades. The oldest member of the group was Takeuchi Shigeyo, a physician born in 1881. The youngest members were Matsutani Tenkōkō and Miki Kiyoko, both born in 1919. Until 1968, when Ogasawara Sadako, born in 1920, won a seat in the upper house, all of the women elected to the Diet fell within these parameters. This generation of Japanese women has been the most influential in shaping women's role in the legislative process. Its influence continued long after 1968; two members of this generation, Nakanishi Tamako and Shinozaki Toshiko, won seats in the upper house in 1989.

Once the political parties reconstituted themselves in connection with the 1947 elections, it became much more difficult for women to break into Diet politics. The women who entered the Diet between 1947 and 1968 were of the same generation as those who won in 1946 and 1947, but their political experience was very different. Whereas fifty-two individual women won election in 1946 and 1947, only fifty served during the approximately twenty years from 1949 to 1968. Of those fifty, nineteen were holdovers from 1946 and 1947. Four-fifths of the first generation of women sat in the lower house, whereas only half of the women in the Diet between 1949 and 1968 did so.

The case of Chiba Chiyose, a socialist, illustrates how the barriers to the lower house had become far more difficult to surmount than those to the upper. Whereas a number of the pioneers of 1946 and 1947 were able to move from the lower to the upper house, Chiba reversed the process. Born in 1907, Chiba graduated from women's higher school and worked as an elementary school teacher until after the war. In 1945, she participated in the organization of a teachers' union and remained active in it for many years thereafter. She won election to the upper house from the national constituency as a socialist in 1959 and 1965. Thus, when she won a new seat in the lower house in 1976, she was a veteran politician. Even so, she finished as the runner-up in Chiba Prefecture, succeeding to office only when one of the successful candidates, Mizuta Mikio of the LDP, died less than a month after the election.[22] The fact that Takada Naoko, likewise a socialist veteran of two terms in the upper house, failed in a similar bid for a lower house seat in 1963 only underscores the difficulty of securing a lower house seat.

One of the few women to break into the lower house without benefit of either family connections or a track record in the legislature was Kamichika Ichiko, a noted writer and veteran of the women's suffrage movement. Born June 6, 1888, in Nagasaki Prefecture, she was educated at Kassui Girls' School and Tsuda College. As a college student, she participated in the feminist literary organization, the Bluestocking Society. In 1914, she became a newspaper reporter, working for the *Tōkyō nichinichi*.

She participated in a study group headed by the anarchist Ōsugi Sakae; in a fit of romantic jealousy, she stabbed him in 1916 and was sentenced to prison. Kamichika thus combined notoriety, potentially useful in establishing name recognition with voters, with a formidable reputation as a writer. She won election from Tokyo to the lower house as a socialist in 1953, 1955, and 1958 and again in 1963 and 1967.[23]

The only other women to enter the lower house on the strength of their convictions rather than loyalty to powerful men were, like Kamichika, members of left-wing parties. Motojima Yuriko, a former reporter and member of the Tokyo Metropolitan Assembly, was elected as a socialist in 1958 and served continuously until 1969. Two other socialists, Hagimoto Takeko and Hirata Hide, served one term each. Two communists, Kanda Asano and Tajima Hide, were both elected in 1949, a banner year for the JCP.

The other eight women who won new seats in the lower house between 1949 and 1967 were all heirs, most of them widows. As in the case of women who entered political life either on their husband's behalf or with him, the succession of heirs was a manifestation of the importance of family in Japanese politics. As Patricia Steinhoff has observed, it is common in Japan for women to reach real positions of political leadership only when the men around them disappear, whether from death, imprisonment, or political purges.[24] Of the women who entered the lower house as political heirs, only two, Momiyama Hide and Matsuyama Chieko, were able to keep their seats for more than two terms. Both inherited LDP constituencies.

Matsuyama Chieko, the mother of three children, succeeded her late husband in politics. Her previous positions included head of the Kawagoe LDP Women's Section and president of the Kawagoe High School PTA. Her father, Education Minister Matsunaga Tō, supported her run for the Diet. In 1967, Matsuyama failed to win re-election despite party endorsement. Her problem was not a decline in LDP popularity but a successful challenge from the son of a late LDP Diet member. She herself blamed her finish as runner-up on her responsibilities as vice-minister of welfare in the Satō cabinet, which prevented her from returning to her election district to campaign. She recovered the seat in 1969, but only for one term.[25] The incident shows that the LDP did endorse female candidates but that the endorsement was not always honored by other party members.

Momiyama Hide also had a family connection to politics. Born in 1907, the second daughter of a Hokkaidō physician, she was adopted as a child by Momiyama Hiroshi, a member of the Diet. Her foster father, a native of Fukushima, was a graduate of Waseda University, the University of California, and the University of North Carolina. Hiroshi served in the Diet from 1920 to 1932, from 1936 to 1942, and from 1952 to 1958; in the

Hamaguchi cabinet, he held the position of parliamentary naval council-lor. Hide graduated from Japan Women's University, where she studied home economics and French. From 1948, she worked as Hiroshi's private secretary. After he died in 1959, Hide stood for the Diet in 1960, but lost by a narrow margin. In her second attempt in 1963, she succeeded and held the seat until 1976, when she retired to make way for a male relative.[26]

Some of the women who succeeded their husbands for only one term did not pursue further political office. For instance, Kōno Takako, widow of the LDP politician Kōno Kinshō, successfully ran in 1958, but retired when the next election was called in 1960. Kaifu Toshiki, Kōno Kinshō's secretary, then succeeded to the constituency, which he held for many years, eventually becoming prime minister.[27] After the socialist Asanuma Inejirō was assassinated in 1960, his widow Kyōko ran successfully in his stead. In her campaign she made clear that her only aim was "to arouse public conscience and sympathy for her husband," and she did not seek re-election.[28] Kobayashi Chizu, also elected as a socialist widow in 1960, likewise declined to run in 1963.

In other cases, widows tried, with party endorsement, to hold their seats, but the party endorsement was no guarantee of success. Hirokawa Kōzen's wife Shizue ran successfully for the LDP in 1967, only to fail in 1969. The socialist women exhibited admirable persistence. It took Kikukawa Kimiko two tries (in 1955 and 1958) to win back her socialist husband's seat, only to lose it again in 1960 when the socialists split into two parties. Itō Yoshiko won her husband's seat in 1958, lost it in 1960, won it in 1963, and lost it again in 1967.[29]

Between 1949 and 1968, about as many new women won seats in the upper house as the lower, but they held the seats longer, and they did so on the basis of different qualifications. The sixteen women who entered the Diet through the upper house in this era divide into two groups along party and occupational lines. The socialists and independents all had ex-perience as teachers. By contrast, the seven affiliated with the LDP were all in other fields, the most important of which was health care.

Several of the women who eventually identified with the LDP first ran for the upper house without any help from the party. All had medical ex-pertise, and they depended for support on the members of their profes-sional associations. Only after they were members of the Diet did they join the LDP. Yokoyama Fuku was chief of the midwives' division of the Japan Nursing Association when she was elected as an independent in 1953.[30] Yamamoto Sugi, who first won a seat in 1959, was a physician and an ac-tivist in Buddhist women's organizations.[31] Hayashi Shio, a nurse, entered the upper house in 1962.[32] Ishimoto Shigeru was an officer of the Japan Nursing Association when she ran successfully as an independent in 1965. All four women ran in the national constituency.

The medical contingent in the Diet reflected the potential of the national constituency to represent special interests. The large metropolitan cities, which each elected several representatives to the upper house, provided the same opportunity.[33] Two leaders of the women's rights movement availed themselves of this system to win seats as independents. Ichikawa Fusae, who was the best-known leader of the prewar women's suffrage movement, won election to the upper house from Tokyo in 1953, 1959, and 1965 almost entirely on the basis of her reputation; she was famous for her very low campaign expenditures. Only after she failed to win election in 1971 did she shift to the national constituency. Yamataka Shigeri, who after the war became president of Japan's largest women's organization, the National Federation of Regional Women's Organizations (Chifuren), won a three-year term in the national constituency in 1962 and was reelected in 1965.

Some women entered the Diet as representatives of their religion. Sōka Gakkai, the most politically active of Japan's "new religions," has used the system to good advantage, eventually developing its own party, the Clean Government Party (CGP). Kashiwabara Yasu was one of the sect's pioneer politicians when she ran for the upper house as an independent from Tokyo in 1959. She received ample support from her fellow religionists, who were particularly concentrated in urban areas. After her initial success, she ran in subsequent elections in the national constituency.

Family ties were not entirely irrelevant to the contests for the upper house. Tanaka Sumiko, who was supremely qualified in her own right for public office, happens to have been married to Tanaka Toshio, a former member of the Diet. With only one break, he represented the third district of Fukuoka in the lower house from 1947 to 1960, but he was no longer in office when his wife ran for the upper house in 1965. Born in 1909, Tanaka Sumiko graduated from Tsuda College and then studied at Bryn Mawr College and Harvard University, specializing in social work. On returning to Japan, she married a young socialist, worked at St. Luke's Hospital, and taught at women's higher schools while bringing up their three children. After the war, she became head of the women's section of the labor bureau. By the time of her election, she had written extensively on women's issues.[34]

Family ties were more salient in the election of Nishioka Haru in the national constituency in 1953. When her husband, Takejirō, who had been a member of the lower house, was deemed unsuitable to retain control of his Nagasaki newspaper company in the postwar political purges, she took over its management. Once the purge ended, he ran for governor of Nagasaki Prefecture, a position he held when she secured her Diet seat in 1953. Five years after her husband's death in 1958, her son was elected to the lower house.[35]

Nishioka Haru's election in 1953 exemplified the paradigm that was operative in the first two decades of women's suffrage: women's role in politics was an extension of their responsibilities in the home. Women belonged in the Diet because they could represent effectively the special interests of women as wives, mothers, and caretakers. The ideal candidate, then, was either an expert on women's responsibilities (physician, nurse, teacher, or social worker) or was someone's wife, usually a politician's. The candidacy of Nakamigawa Aki in the national constituency in 1962 introduced into the political arena a new type of woman, one who exemplified physical beauty, glamour, and forbidden romance, attributes more appropriate to a geisha than a wife.

Nakamigawa was the first of what the Japanese call "talent" candidates: individuals with no formal experience in politics who run for public office on the basis of their celebrity, usually acquired through the mass media.[36] In 1962, Nakamigawa was widely known because of her regular participation, under the name of Fujiwara Aki, on a quiz program on NHK television. Those who were old enough no doubt recalled earlier events in her life. In 1928, as the wife of a prominent Osaka physician, she made national headlines when she ran away to Italy to join the opera star Fujiwara Yoshie. She and Fujiwara had a son and remained together for twenty-six years, but in 1954, he abandoned her for a young prima donna. Nakamigawa (her original family name) went to work for Shiseido cosmetics. Like most talent candidates, Nakamigawa had support from within the LDP; in her case, it came from Fujiyama Aiichirō, a faction leader in contention for the presidency of the LDP and one of the major links between the party and the business community. Nakamigawa's candidacy was a great success; she placed first in the national constituency, winning more votes than any previous candidate.[37]

In 1962, talent candidates were still the exception rather than the rule. Most women entered politics through their own professional or political interests. They were more likely to survive in politics, however, particularly in the conservative parties that became the LDP, if their passion for politics coincided with their husbands'. Some of these husbands and fathers undoubtedly provided concrete support such as campaign funds, party endorsements, and a dependable bloc of voters. Equally important in a society that defined politics as a male activity and assigned women domestic responsibilities, women politicians from political families were less torn by role conflict. The life stories of these women are consistent with Susan Pharr's observation that Japanese women succeed more easily in politics if their political life is an extension of the obligations they owe to a father or a husband.[38]

NEW CURRENTS

Between 1968 and 1989, the legislative activity of Japanese women shifted from being primarily a means of refining and thus preserving the existing order to being part of the opposition to the existing order. This occurred in part because of women's increasing involvement in grassroots movements on behalf of peace, the environment, and women's rights, but it also reflected changes in the political parties, with some parties taking on women's issues as their own and others excluding women and their agenda from the political process.

The arrival of a second generation of women legislators in the Japanese Diet was heralded by the election of Ogasawara Sadako, born in 1920, to the upper house in 1968. On the eve of the 1968 election, the youngest woman in the Diet was Yamaguchi Shizue. At fifty-one, she could anticipate many future years in public life, but as one of the women who had won election in 1946 and one of the few who had served continuously since, she seemed to represent stagnation rather than vitality. The election of Ogasawara, who was a mere forty-eight, was part of the orderly transition to the next generation. This phenomenon cut across gender lines; the percentage of both male and female candidates under age fifty rose in 1969.[39]

A much more significant omen for the political future of Japanese women was the fact that the first woman born in 1920 or later to serve in the Diet was a communist. Ogasawara was the first communist woman to win election to the Diet since 1949, and she heralded a new beginning. With the single exception of the 1971 election for the upper house, communist women have won seats in every election since, sometimes as many as eight at a time. Ogasawara's election occurred just as the JCP was moving away from alignment with China and the Soviet Union towards a more nationalist party, similar to the communist parties in Europe, that had wider appeal in Japan.[40] It also coincided with widespread political disturbances on Japanese college campuses, and it anticipated by only two years the beginnings of the feminist movement in Japan.[41]

Like many of the women who served in the Diet before her, Ogasawara was drawn to politics by her own social and political concerns. Born to devout Christian parents, she was engaged in 1940 to a young man who soon afterward was mobilized into the military. She questioned the necessity of a war that required young men to throw away their lives. After the war Ogasawara worked for the YWCA. and was active in the women's and peace movements. She credits her conversion from Christianity to communism to what she observed of the postwar suffering of the working classes. In 1953 she was chosen as one of the Japanese delegates to the world women's conference, and the next year she was the founding president of the Hokkaidō Women's Peace Association. In 1959 and 1962 she participated in international women's conferences on military disarmament in Sweden and Austria.[42] By 1968 she had compiled an impressive record of activism at the national and international level, and it is not surprising that she emerged a victor from her candidacy in the national constituency.

Six years later, in the 1974 elections to the upper house, communist women won an unprecedented four seats. Ogasawara Sadako was reelected, this time from her native Hokkaidō rather than from the national constituency. Strong local ties, developed through union activities, enabled Yasutake Hiroko to secure one of the seats in the Hyōgo constituency for the upper house.[43] Kutsunugi Takeko, a graduate of Osaka Women's Medical College, won a three-year term from Osaka on the strength of her five terms in the city assembly.[44] The only communist woman to win a seat in the national constituency was Yamanaka Ikuko, a graduate of Waseda University, who had joined the JCP as a student in 1952 and worked for it ever since. She is married to a college professor and has one son, born in 1957. She writes novels under the pen name Akimoto Ikuko.[45]

In 1977, Kutsunugi was reelected to the upper house from Osaka. Shimoda Kyōko, a thirty-seven-year-old junior high school teacher from Fukushima, won a seat in the national constituency. Shimoda had run for the lower house from Fukushima the year before, but her victory in the national constituency was more the result of party strategy than of individual fame. The JCP maximizes the effect of its votes in the national constituency by assigning its organizations in each region to support specific candidates. The party prides itself on supporting female candidates. Shimoda's relative youth was in keeping with the fact that communist members of the Diet are the youngest of any party.[46]

In 1980, all three women incumbents (Ogasawara, Yamanaka, and Yasutake) were reelected, but in 1983 Kutsunugi met with defeat in Osaka, despite winning a respectable 20.5 percent of the vote. The 1983 elections were the first under a new proportional representation system in which citizens chose the one hundred national candidates by casting ballots for a party rather than an individual. Each party seated the number of representatives appropriate to its percentage of the total vote from a list of candidates in ranked order drawn up in advance. The JCP had not supported this reform, but it in fact gained two seats in the upper house in 1983. Kutsunugi's defeat, however, may have been indirectly related to the reform. Yokoyama Nokku, a famous comic performer, who had previously run in the national constituency as an independent, and who was thus forced by

the reform measure to find new political turf, finished first in Osaka, Kutsunugi's district.[47]

Because the JCP had always controlled the choice of party candidates,
the reform made little difference in selection of candidates for the national
seats. In keeping with its principle of fielding both female and male candidates, nine of the twenty-five candidates on its slate were female. The candidates ranked at the top were the incumbents, including Shimoda
Kyōko. The candidate ranked fifth was Yoshikawa Haruko, the mother of
two children. A graduate of the law department of Chūō University,
Yoshikawa had taught junior high school and served in her local city assembly, and had been a candidate for the lower house from Saitama in
1976, 1979, and 1980. The JCP won five seats, thus electing both Shimoda
and Yoshikawa.[48]

In the 1986 election, the JCP maintained its female strength. As an incumbent, Yamanaka was second in the party ranking in the national constituency and thus won re-election, as did Ogasawara in Hokkaidō. Kutsunugi recaptured her Osaka seat, but Yasutake lost in Hyōgo.[49]

This success in placing communist women in the upper house was
paralleled by an even more spectacular increase in the number of JCP
representatives in the lower house, beginning with Kobayashi Masako's
election in 1969, the year after Ogasawara's success in the national constituency had reintroduced communist women to the Diet after a sixteen-
year absence. Both women were part of the rising fortunes of their party,
the JCP. The party's new independent line and the support it now drew
from urban areas because of its assistance in the daily life of citizens combined to win fourteen seats in 1969, a considerable improvement over its
five in 1967.[50]

Kobayashi Masako's victory in 1969, which defied all predictions, was
the product of her intimate involvement as a representative to the metropolitan assembly and as a mother in the life of the community. She had
worked with her neighbors to tackle educational and residential problems
such as day nurseries, drainage ditches, roads, waterways, and a living
wage. First elected to the Adachi Ward Assembly in 1951 and to the Metropolitan Assembly in 1965, she was a politician whose neighbors called
her "The Sun."

Although she was born in Niigata Prefecture, she had lived in Adachi
for most of her life. After finishing elementary school, she worked in a factory and, studying on her own, earned her teaching credentials and joined
the staff of the Yanagiwara Elementary School, where she headed the
women's section of the teachers' union. Right after the war, there were
food shortages. What persuaded her to become a politician was the sight
of children loitering in the school yard and stealing lunches because they
had no money to pay for them.[51]

In the 1972 election to the lower house, two more women directly or indirectly affiliated with the JCP won seats. Tanaka Michiko was one of the two successful candidates of the Progressive Unity Party (Kakushin kyōdōtō), which was supported by the JCP. Born in 1921, Tanaka graduated from the social work department of Japan Women's College; she worked at a child consultation center and taught social work at a university.[52]

Kurita Midori, born in 1932, became a communist as a result of the discrimination she experienced as a female student at Shizuoka High School. Always a top student, she studied labor law at Shizuoka University. After graduating, she taught at a junior high in Numazu. In 1959, she became secretary of the Shizuoka teachers' union. In 1971, when she ran for election to the upper house, her divorce from her activist husband, a member of the city assembly, was used against her, but she nevertheless finished only two places short of victory. In 1972 she won her seat with the slogan "Flowers in the sun and children in peace."[53]

Fujiwara Hiroko, who joined the JCP contingent in the lower house in 1972, ran as a second communist candidate in the Kyoto first district. Born in 1926 in Taiwan, she graduated from a women's higher school in Kyoto in 1944, became a teacher, and joined the teachers' union. As a veteran of the Kyoto City Assembly, she stood a good chance of election, but the strategy of running two candidates in the same district had only limited success for the party. Fujiwara and Umeda Masaru both ran in every election from 1976 to 1990, but only in 1979 did they both win. She won in 1976, 1980, and 1986; he won in 1983, and they both lost in 1990.[54]

From 1979 until 1989, the JCP consistently elected more women to the lower house than any other party did, in part because it had more women candidates than any other party did. The JCP deliberately fields candidates in as many districts as it can, and in every election since 1976 its roster of candidates for the lower house has included at least ten women, usually more.[55] So many women would not have won, however, without the experience and seniority women had already acquired in the party. For instance, when Fujita Sumi ran in 1979 in the fifth Osaka district, which had elected a communist in the previous election, her three victories in previous elections to the Osaka Assembly had already provided her with the voter support she needed to maintain the party's strength in the district.[56]

In 1979, the JCP achieved the impressive total of eight women in the lower house. Besides Fujita, these included three incumbents (Fujiwara, Kobayashi, and Tanaka), a former representative (Kurita), and three newcomers: Iwasa Emi, Nakabayashi Yoshiko, and Yotsuya Mitsuko. An activist in the consumer movement, Iwasa was born in Shanghai in 1939 and graduated from the literature department of Waseda University.[57] Like so many other communist Diet representatives, Nakabayashi and Yotsuya were both teachers.[58] The tenure of JCP Diet representatives, except in a very few secure districts, is uncertain, and several of these women met with defeat in the 1980s. In each of the next three elections, however, additional communist women were elected to the lower house: Minowa Sachiyo in 1980, Fujiki Yoko in 1983, and Ishii Ikuko in 1986.

The seventeen JCP women who served in the Diet in the 1970s and 1980s were models of traditional feminine virtue. Kutsunugi was a physician and Ishii Ikuko a professor, but most of the rest were teachers, wives, and mothers. They were advocates of peace, consumerism, environmentalism, and child welfare. None of the other parties could match them in either numbers or rhetoric.

At the beginning of this era, on the eve of the 1968 election, the LDP still had by far the strongest representation of women. It could claim fourteen, more than half of the twenty-four women in the Diet. The other women legislators were five socialists, two Democratic Socialists, two independents, and one member of the CGP. The elections of 1968 and 1967 sharply reduced the number of LDP women in the Diet, leaving the party with only five: Yamashita Harue and Yokoyama Fuku in the upper house and Matsuyama Chieko, Momiyama Hide, and Yamaguchi Shizue in the lower. Two of these five, Yamashita and Yamaguchi, were survivors from the original thirty-nine women elected in 1946. Yamaguchi, at the age of fifty-two in 1969, was the youngest of the five. With only six years of parliamentary experience, the sixty-two-year-old Momiyama Hide was the political neophyte.

By 1980, none of these experienced politicians remained in the Diet, and a majority of the women representing the LDP in the Diet had entered politics as talent candidates. In her first election in 1971, Shimura Aiko, a singer, finished second in the entire national constituency.[59] In 1974, the only LDP women elected from the national constituency were two talent candidates, Ōtaka Yoshiko and Santō Akiko. Under her stage name, Yamaguchi Yoshiko, Ōtaka entered movies in 1937 and appeared in many films during World War II. After her second marriage, she retired. Her husband, Ōtaka Hiroshi, graduated from the law department of Tokyo University and has close ties with the ruling government; he served as ambassador to Fiji, Sri Lanka, and Singapore in the 1980s.[60] Santō Akiko, a television model, entered politics at the relatively young age of thirty-two as the sponsored candidate of Hitachi, the giant electronics company. (Corporate sponsorship of candidates was a concept developed in preparation for the upper house elections of 1974 as a way of obtaining assistance from the business community for the huge expenses that the LDP always incurred in the elections for the national constituency.)[61] In the 1977 election, Hayashi Hiroko, an actress and television star known by her stage name of Ōgi Chikage, provided the LDP with an additional seat from the national constituency. Her husband and her sons are well-known kabuki actors.[62]

The LDP continued to receive some support in the upper house from health care professionals and the female relatives of LDP politicians. The health care contingent consisted of the nurse, Ishimoto Shigeru, who returned to the Diet in 1971 and served continuously until 1989, and the pediatrician Kawanobe Shizu, also elected in 1971. Ishimoto ran in the national constituency, depending upon the nurses' association for support. By contrast, Kawanobe ran in Shizuoka Prefecture where she had been a doctor, served in the Shizuoka city assembly from 1951 to 1955, and could depend upon support from the strong LDP women's organization.[63] Both Ishimoto and Kawanobe were single career-women.

Not surprisingly, the two women who ran as a result of their husbands' careers each had strong backing in one of the prefectural constituencies for the upper house. When Nakamura Tomi's husband, Kishirō, died in 1971 shortly after his election to the upper house as an LDP candidate from Ibaraki, she ran in the by-election for his seat and won, despite the fact that she lacked the party endorsement.[64] In the next upper house election in 1974, Iwakami Taeko, the wife of the governor, ran successfully as an independent in the prefectural constituency. She resigned in 1977, after her husband was no longer governor, and he then ran successfully in the by-election for her seat.[65]

The fate of the LDP women in the lower house was a product of the same mixture of occasional support and overall indifference to the presence of women in politics displayed by the party in the contests for the upper house. After the 1980 election, there were no LDP women in the lower house. Momiyama retired to make way for a male relative and Matsuyama and Yamaguchi met with defeat. Matsuyama lost in 1972, despite the party endorsement; when the LDP could hold only two of its three seats in the district, she lost out. The Fukuda faction secured the party endorsement for Yamaguchi's candidacy in 1980 and again in 1983, but the endorsement did not stop a member of the Nakasone faction from running as an independent and taking the seat. Takahashi Chizu, the only additional LDP woman to serve in the lower house, met with a fate similar to Matsuyama's. When her husband died suddenly in 1972, the party endorsed her for his seat from Niigata, which she won. The LDP endorsed her for re-election in 1976, but the party was unable to hold onto its two seats, losing one to a Democratic Socialist, and Takahashi was the candidate who lost.[66]

The kindest possible reading of the LDP policy on women prior to 1980 would be to term it merely benign neglect. What all of the female LDP candidates for the upper house had in common was a support base of some kind—corporate sponsorship, national reputation, family or organizational support in a prefecture, or institutional support from a professional organization—that would save the party campaign expenses. By 1980, the LDP was in danger of having its female contingent composed entirely of women who had chosen it, rather than of women they chose to represent their ideal of a public woman. The message implicitly conveyed by their self-selected representatives was that political women should be entertainers, unmarried nurses, or doctors.

In 1980, when Moriyama Mayumi was elected to the upper house from Tochigi Prefecture, the LDP had a candidate whom they could hold up as an ideal of modern womanhood. Her distinguished career would have been impossible in the prewar era. Shortly after the war, she entered Tokyo University, and upon graduation she became the first female career officer in the government bureaucracy. She chose this career because jobs in private industry were closed to women, but her limited options meant that some thirty years later when she ran for the Diet, her degree from Tokyo University and twenty years of experience in the Labor Ministry made her remarkably similar in background to many of the male candidates. Moreover, Moriyama had married at the appropriate age of twenty-two and was the mother of three grown children.

Moriyama relates in public interviews how Prime Minister Ōhira Masayoshi persuaded her to enter politics, despite her great reluctance. The fact that Moriyama's husband, Kinji, served thirteen terms in the lower house, beginning in 1949, explains both why, as a wife loyal to her husband's party, she would agree to run and how, as a newcomer to politics, she was able to win.[67]

With the introduction of proportional voting in the 1983 election, the LDP had control over which women it would slate for the national constituency. The party respected the seniority of the three incumbents, Ishimoto, Shimura, and Hayashi, and slated them thirteenth, fifteenth, and sixteenth. Given that the party won nineteen seats, all were elected.[68]

The re-election of the three incumbents retained the character of the LDP as a party of entertainers and unmarried career women. The party had slated two women as the next candidates on the LDP ranked list. The choice of Ishii Michiko as one of them suggests that the party was making some effort to recruit women with professional expertise, legislative experience, and companionate marriages. A pharmacist and vice president of her professional organization, she gave promise of the same type of professional support that Ishimoto had always been able to draw. Ishii had also served two terms in the Saitama prefectural assembly, a body in which both her father and her physician husband had served. When one member of the upper house died in 1984, Ishii Michiko succeeded to the seat.[69]

In 1986, the LDP again slated the two incumbent women entertainers from the national constituency towards the bottom of the ranked list; Hayashi Hiroko and Santō Akiko were fourteenth and fifteenth respectively. The runner-up candidate was once again a woman. Shimizu Kayoko was a nurse and an officer of the nursing association.[70] In the local constituencies, Moriyama was reelected from Tochigi, and the LDP secured one more female member in the upper house when Ono Kiyoko, a wife and mother and former Olympic star, won in Tokyo.

As had the communists, the JSP incorporated some new women into its ranks as a result of the political turmoil of 1969. Doi Takako, who won international renown during her five-year term as chair of the JSP from 1986 to 1991, and Kaneko Mitsu, who with Doi represented the party in the lower house for the better part of the next two decades, first ran in that election.

Although the socialist party had in the past incorporated professionally competent women such as Fukuda Masako and Kamichika Ichiko into its ranks, Doi's election nevertheless marked the beginning of a new era. As a faculty member in law, she had professional expertise in a field that in the prewar era had been almost entirely closed to women.[71] Born in 1928, she belonged to the generation that came of age after the war, and she was the first of that cohort of women to win election as a socialist.

Doi's academic specialty was constitutional law, and after completing her master's degree at Dōshisha University in Kyoto she joined the faculty. As a child, Doi imagined that she would follow in her father's footsteps as a physician, but Abraham Lincoln, or at least Henry Fonda's film portrayal of him, inspired her to study law instead. As a junior college student in Kyoto, she was moved to tears by Fonda's performance.[72]

Doi had attracted the attention of the JSP through her position as executive secretary of the Hyōgo Prefecture Society for Protection of the Constitution. Reluctant as she was to abandon her scholarly life, she felt that, given the violent protests on Japanese college campuses over the military alliance with the United States, she had to do whatever she could to bring the principles of the constitution into actual politics.[73] Looking back on those times, she reflected that as a scholar she could only question why laws existed as they did. She entered politics to reform bad laws and introduce new ones.[74]

Although Doi was neither an incumbent nor a political heir when she stood for election in 1969, her candidacy was considered a serious one. Her opponents in the election included five incumbent males. Her victory was at the expense of Yamashita Eiji of the smaller Democratic Socialist Party.[75]

Born in 1914, Kaneko Mitsu was half a generation older than Doi, but she too was an academic and a newcomer to politics. After graduating from St. Luke's Girls' School in Tokyo, she studied in Toronto. Upon her return to Japan, she entered the Welfare Ministry, where she rose to become head of the nursing section. She later became an assistant professor at Tokyo University and president of the Japan Nursing Association. In her first campaign for the Diet in 1969, she finished as a runner-up, but in 1972 she met with success, inaugurating her seventeen-year career as a legislator.[76]

The socialist party maintained a modest representation of capable women in the upper house, although the absolute numbers fell from five to two in the late 1970s as the first generation of women in politics retired. With the exception of one talent candidate, the women elected to the upper house resembled Doi and Kaneko in that they were well-educated career women. The one talent candidate was Suzuki Mieko, a movie actress who finished right behind the LDP singer Shimura Aiko in the national constituency in 1971.[77] Of the others, Kasuya Terumi and Itohisa Yaeko were teachers, Sasaki Shizuko and Chiba Keiko were lawyers, and Kubota Manae, a law graduate of Keiō University, was an experienced government bureaucrat.

The Democratic Socialist Party, which shared a common history with the JSP until 1960, elected three women to the upper house, all three from the Hyōgo prefectural constituency: Nakazawa Itoko (1965 and 1971), Hagiwara Yukako (1968), and Nukiyama Eiko (1983).

The unprecedented success of the CGP in the election of 1969—eleven percent of the vote and forty-seven seats, twice its 1967 total—drew international attention. The fact that two of those forty-seven seats were won by women went largely unnoticed.[78] Although Kashiwabara Yasu was a member of the upper house from 1979 to 1983, the 1969 election was the first in which the CGP was able to elect women to the lower house. Tada Tokiko and Watanabe Michiko, born in 1925 and 1932 respectively, were part of the transition to a new generation. Tada left women's higher school to go to Mongolia to work, returning to Japan in 1944. Watanabe, who was only thirteen when the war ended, graduated from the prestigious Waseda University, an option that would most likely not have been open to her had she entered college before the war. Both women were married to prominent CGP politicians, and both touted the welfare of women in their campaign rhetoric; Tada pledged herself to build a society for mothers and children, and Watanabe called for an environment in which women could be happy from youth to old age.[79] Neither woman won re-election to the lower house, nor did any other woman from their party until 1990. Watanabe won a seat in the upper house in the Hyōgo prefectural constituency in 1977.

In the 1980s, the CGP made good use of the national constituency to elect women. In 1983, the party slated three women among its seventeen candidates, two of them in ranked in the top six, both of whom were elected when the party took eight seats. Nakanishi Tamako had decades of experience as an employee of the International Labor Organization, and Karita Teiko came to politics from the consumer movement.[80] In 1986, the party included only two women on the slate, but because one, Hironaka Wakako, was at the head of the list, she was assured of winning. After graduating from Ochanomizu Women's College in 1957, Hironaka went to the United States, where she received a master's degree from Brandeis University and studied further at Harvard and Columbia. The wife of a college professor and the mother of two grown children, she has translated novels into English.[81]

Proportional representation, in which votes are cast for parties rather than for individuals, instituted in 1983 for the national seats for the upper house, closed one means by which political outsiders had been able to enter the Diet without the support of a party—that of running as an independent in the national constituency. It was still possible to run as an independent for the lower house or for the prefectural seats for the upper house, but those types of elections required huge campaign funds. A number of noted women had run as independents in the past, including the pioneer suffragist, Ichikawa Fusae, who died not long after her election to the national constituency in 1980. Had Ichikawa lived, she would have had to choose between shifting to a local constituency or founding her own party. Nakayama Chinatsu, a television star and writer who also won a seat in the national constituency in 1980, did not survive the transition to proportional representation. When she came up for re-election in 1986, she ran in Tokyo, but finished as the runner-up.[82]

THE DELUGE OF 1989

In the 1989 elections for the upper house, the LDP was unusually vulnerable to attack on three issues: the unpopularity of its recently imposed consumption tax, the Recruit Scandal, in which numerous politicians had accepted gifts of stock, and indecorous revelations about Prime Minister Uno's treatment of a former mistress.

All of these were issues in which women had a stake. As the managers of family finances, they were acutely aware of the consumption tax. In light of the small economies they were planning to make in their budgets, the huge windfalls of politicians in the Recruit Scandal rankled. On March 3, the traditional Japanese date for Girls' Day, over two thousand women rallied in Hibiya Park to call for the cancellation of the consumption tax and the thorough investigation of the Recruit Scandal.[83] Shufuren, the national housewives' organization, opened a hotline on the consumption tax at the end of January, and by April they had been so flooded with calls that they decided to shut it down.[84] When the complaints of Uno's former mistress appeared in a weekly magazine, it was Kubota Manae, a socialist woman in the upper house, who confronted the prime minister at a plenary session of the Diet and castigated him for embarrassing Japan in the eyes of the world.[85]

With a stalwart woman, Doi Takako, as their party leader, the JSP was in a strong position to link discontent with the LDP and confidence in the incorruptibility of women with votes for the socialist party. When the election results came in, both the JSP and the women of Japan had achieved unprecedented results. For the first time in thirty-four years, the LDP lost its majority in the upper house. Twenty-two women won seats in the upper house, more than twice the number in any other election. There were now forty women in the Diet, and for the first time, the women of Japan had equaled their initial victory in 1946.

In the main arena of Japanese politics, this victory was a JSP blow against the LDP; for Japanese women in politics, it represented a victory of the JSP over the JCP. The JCP maintained its large representation of women, and in fact added one to their number, but given that the JSP tripled the number of women it had in the Diet, the JCP was no longer the party with the most women in the Diet. Of the two incumbents in the national constituency, only Yoshikawa Haruko ran for re-election. (The other, Shimoda Kyōko, ran the next year in the lower house elections but lost.) Yoshikawa and Hayashi Toshiko, a newcomer, were third and fourth on the party slate and thus got half of the four seats the JCP won in the national constituency. In addition, Takasaki Yūko secured victory in the local constituency in Hokkaidō. Since the JCP only won five seats in this election, the communist women did very well indeed within their party.

The LDP emerged from this election with six women in the Diet, two fewer than after the 1986 elections. It slated three women for the national constituency, placing Shimizu Kayoko, the nurse who was the runner-up in the previous election, at the top of the list. Ishii Michiko, the pharmacist, also won a seat, so this time the medical personnel emerged victorious, and Hayashi Hiroko, the entertainer, was the runner-up.[86] Ishimoto Shigeru and Shimura Aiko, whose terms both expired in 1989, were rendered ineligible by the party's policy of mandatory retirement from the national constituency at age seventy.[87]

The women of the CGP maintained the status quo in this election. Two incumbent women were up for re-election in the national constituency, and the party slated them high enough so that they both won.

There were several minor changes in configuration. For the first time since the death of Ichikawa Fusae in 1981, a representative of the women's movement won as an independent candidate. Kihira Teiko finished first in the Kumamoto local constituency. Two women, Inui Harumi and Sasano

Teiko, were successful candidates of the newly formed Japan Trade Union Confederation. The Democratic Socialist Party failed to elect any women, as Nukiyama Eiko met defeat in Hyōgo.

In neither of the next two elections after 1989, one for the lower house in 1990 and one for the upper house in 1992, did women do as spectacularly well as in 1989, although they did better in these elections than in any since 1949. The JSP added more women to its delegation, and the CGP doubled the number of its representatives from three to six. The fact that the number of women in the JCP dropped from eleven to six was an indication of the fortunes of the party, not of any reversal of party policy toward women.

Although the LDP still did not elect any women to the lower house and its total number of women dropped, it began phasing out the blatant examples of talent candidates from the entertainment world. In the 1992 election, the only woman on the LDP slate for the national constituency was Nōno Chieko, a nurse-midwife and an officer of the nursing association.[88] With her election, the LDP had five women in the Diet, three of them health care professionals. Former bureaucrat and sometime cabinet minister Moriyama Mayumi, a woman who combined marriage, motherhood, and success in the formerly all male bureaucracy, remained an anomaly. The closest that the party came to having a talent candidate was Ono Kiyoko, the former Olympic star. As a wife and mother and recently appointed member of the Japan Olympic Committee, she certainly presented a more wholesome image than the television personality who had run off with an opera singer or the singer sponsored by a corporate giant. Ono herself flaunts her motherhood as a political asset, telling an interviewer, "A female candidate for office has a tremendous advantage having a family and the experience of childbirth; she understands things better."[89]

Will women continue to participate in politics in the numbers recently achieved, or will the flood subside? One major determinant of whether the flood of women into politics of 1989 becomes part of the mainstream of Japanese politics will be the number of women elected in 1995 when the terms begun in 1989 come to an end. Whether these particular women win re-election will be determined in large part by the JSP. Skeptics argue that the JSP supported women in 1989 only because it did not have enough men available and that it has not built a support structure either to assist these women in office or to bring more women into politics.[90] However, the reasonably strong record of the JSP in promoting women such as Tanaka Sumiko, Doi Takako, and Kubota Manae into positions of leadership suggests that party policy is not as serious a problem in the JSP as in the LDP. What may well prove to be more detrimental to socialist women is the eroding strength of the JSP, which is threatened by competition from newly formed parties recently broken away from the LDP.

The election of 1989 marked an important generational transition as well. Women born in 1940 or later do not remember a time when women could not vote, and although strong social pressures have often deterred them from taking advantage of opportunities, they have had access to the best education Japan has to offer. Eight women of this generation served in the Diet before 1989. Five of them were communists, who are typically younger than candidates of other parties. Two were talent candidates, more attractive for their relative youth. The harbinger of the future was Chiba Keiko, the socialist lawyer elected in 1986. At the end of 1992, this generation accounted for more than one third of the forty-eight women in the Diet.

The flood of women candidates in 1989 established firmly across all party lines that women have a legitimate place in politics. By various gestures, the LDP has grudgingly acknowledged that even the ruling party must include women in the political order. Two prime ministers, Kaifu Toshiki and Miyazawa Kiichi, have called upon Moriyama Mayumi to serve in their cabinets. In group photographs, her feminine attire stands out as a striking, albeit somewhat deceptive, sign that the LDP is including women in its ruling circle. In contrast to the 1970s, when the New Liberal Club presented its challenge to the LDP and passed from the scene without ever electing a woman to the Diet, the New Japan Party, one of the latest challenges to the LDP, included Koike Yuriko, a television newscaster, among its two top candidates in the 1992 elections for the national constituency, and thus elected her.[91]

At the end of the 1992 elections, there were more women in the Diet than ever before in Japanese history. That group of women, however, was more weighted towards the opposition parties than any previous women's caucus. Japanese women have established their place in the loyal opposition; in 1989, women were an important part of the challenge to the ruling party. This history of women in the legislature shows how women have been progressively marginalized by the ruling party, first disappearing as respectable heirs to family members in the lower house and then losing the opportunity to win as individual independents in the national constituency for the upper house. Moreover, the LDP has been much slower than the other parties to guarantee the election of women by placing them high on the proportional list of candidates. The political needs of women were trivialized when the majority of the women elected as representatives of the ruling party were put forward for their charm and beauty rather than their ability or experience. It remains to be seen whether political women can transform Japanese society into one that allocates power as well as votes to women.

EPILOGUE

The election of July 18, 1993, for seats in the lower house, which denied the LDP control over the lower house for the first time since its founding in 1955 and thus permitted the establishment of a coalition cabinet, altered the political framework in which women's politics had become opposition politics. In the spring of 1995, it is still difficult to discern the shape that Japanese party coalitions will finally take, but it is possible to make a few remarks about how women fared in the election of 1993 and about what electoral reform promises for women's participation in the political process.

First, the number of women in the Diet continued to increase. Fourteen women won seats in the lower house, more than in any other lower house election since 1947. In addition, their number in the upper house increased by one as a result of individuals resigning to run in the lower house election. The two men and one woman who resigned were replaced by two women and one man.[92]

Second, although the total number of women in elected office remained more or less constant, the women's contingent in the lower house became considerably more conservative. The five socialist incumbents and one communist who went down in defeat were replaced largely by independents and representatives of parties such as the LDP, the CGP, and the New Japan Party. The election of Noda Seiko, a member of the Gifu prefectural assembly and the head of the party prefectural women's organization, to the seat which her grandfather had held marked the first time since 1979 that a woman had been elected as an LDP member of the lower house. Her candidacy in 1993, with the party endorsement and the support of a faction, was in contrast to her unsuccessful candidacy in 1990 as an independent.[93]

One of the independent candidates was Tanaka Makiko, daughter of a former prime minister. Running for the seat in Niigata that her father had held for forty-four years, she defeated three veteran LDP members whom the party had endorsed, but soon afterward, on August 4, 1993, she joined the LDP.[94] Her husband, Naoki, a former official of a steel company who was adopted into the Tanaka family when he married Makiko in 1969, also won a seat in the Diet, running from the third district of Fukushima from which he had been elected in 1983 and 1986.[95] In contrast to Makiko's status as an independent maverick, Naoki enjoyed the support of Prime Minister Miyazawa's faction.

Third, under Prime Minister Hosokawa Morihiro, who came to office with the backing of a seven-party coalition, women held high office in unprecedented numbers. Hosokawa appointed three women to his cabinet, more than had ever before served at one time. In addition, he recommended Doi Takako to be speaker of the house and, on February 9, 1994, named Takahashi Hisako to the Japanese Supreme Court, thus incorporating women into all three branches of the government.[96] Hosokawa's policies on behalf of women have not been continued by his successors with quite the same vigor. In summer 1994, Prime Minister Murayama Tomiichi included only one woman, Tanaka Makiko, in his cabinet.

Finally, on January 29, 1994, the Diet passed the electoral reform that Hosokawa had promised when he came to office. Under the new system, some seats for the lower house will now be elected from large districts in a proportional system in which votes will be cast for parties rather than individuals. Although some analysts have predicted that the new proportional districts will make it easier for parties to put women up for election, the history recounted here shows that women have often had to launch their own political careers as independents in defiance of party policy, as Tanaka Makiko did in 1993. Under the new law, there will be many fewer seats in the lower house for which it will be possible to run, unless one is a member of a recognized party.[97]

NOTES

1. The party has now changed its English name to Social Democratic Party Japan, but for the sake of consistency, I refer to it as the Japan Socialist Party (JSP) throughout.

2. Sawachi Hisae, "The Political Awakening of Women," *Japan Quarterly* 36 (1989): 383.

3. See for instance Yuriko Ling and Azusa Matsuno, "Women's Struggle for Empowerment in Japan," in *Women Transforming Politics: Worldwide Strategies for Empowerment*, ed. Jill M. Bystydzienski (Bloomington, Indiana: Indiana University Press, 1992), 50–64 and Iwai Tomoaki, "'The Madonna Boom': Women in the Japanese Diet," *Journal of Japanese Studies* 19, no. 1 (winter 1993): 103–120.

4. A list of candidates by district, with vote totals for each, is provided in Kōmei senkyo renmei, *Shūgiin giin senkyo no jisseki* (Record of elections to the lower house) (Tokyo: Kōmei senkyo renmai, 1967). Of those seventeen, all but four met defeat in the next election. One other secured a seat in the upper house. The surviving five were Fujiwara (Yamazaki) Michiko, Kondō Tsuruyo, Mogami Hideko, Togano Satoko, and Kōro Mitsu. All had male relatives in politics.

5. A woman who ran a hairdressing business was part of the support group for one of the candidates in Tokyo's Kyōbashi Ward. R. H. P. Mason, *Japan's First General Election, 1890* (London: Cambridge University Press, 1969), 154. For Yosano Akiko's campaigning for her husband in 1915, see Laurel Rasplica Rodd, "Yosano Akiko and the Taishō Debate over the 'New Woman'," in *Recreating Japanese Women, 1600–1945*, ed. Gail Lee Bernstein (Berkeley: University of California Press, 1991), 185–187. Miyazaki Ryūkichi's wife spoke on his behalf in 1928 and Pak Ch'un-kum's for his candidacy in 1932. Sally A. Hastings, *Neighborhood and Nation in Tokyo, 1905–1937* (Pittsburgh: University of Pittsburgh Press, 1995),

182, 186. On women's organizations, see Sheldon Garon, "Women's Groups and the Japanese State: Contending Approaches to Political Integration, 1890–1945," *Journal of Japanese Studies* 19, no. 1 (winter 1993): 5–41.

6. Kōmei senkyo renmei, *Shūgiin giin senkyo no jisseki*, gives occupations for the candidates. Kokkai shūgiin sangiin, *Gikai seido shichijūnen* (Seventy-year history of the Diet system), 12 vols. (Tokyo: Ōkurashō, 1960–1963) gives brief biographies in volume eight. Unless otherwise noted, information on profession and activism are taken from these two sources. Dorothy Robins-Mowry says Murashima taught in a finishing school; *The Hidden Sun: Women of Modern Japan* (Boulder, Colorado: Westview Press, 1983), 93. Yoshida Sei is listed as a dentist by *Seijika jinmei jiten* (Biographical dictionary of politicians) (Tokyo: Nichigai asoshietsu kabushiki kaisha, 1990), 579.

7. Katō Shizue's memoirs have been published in English. Shidzue Ishimoto, *Facing Two Ways: The Story of My Life* (Stanford, Calif.: Stanford University Press, 1984).

8. Chino Yōichi, *Kindai Nihon kyōiku shi* (History of education in modern Japan) (Tokyo: Domesu shuppan, 1979), 242.

9. *Seijika jinmei jiten*, 202, and Steven R. Reed, *Japan Election Data: The House of Representatives, 1947–1990* (Ann Arbor, Michigan: The Center for Japanese Studies, The University of Michigan, 1992), 416.

10. *Seijika jinmei jiten*, 530, and Reed, *Japan Election Data*, 108.

11. *Nippon Times*, April 12, 1946 and Kokkai shūgiin sangiin. *Gikai seido shichijūnen*, 8:325.

12. *Nippon Times*, April 13, 1946. This incident is mentioned in Robins-Mowry, *The Hidden Sun*, 96.

13. Kokkai shūgiin sangiin. *Gikai seido shichijūnen*, 8:467 and Reed, *Japan Election Data*, 181–183.

14. Fourteen of the original thirty-nine returned to the Diet, either in 1947 or 1949 (twelve to the lower house in 1947, one to the lower house in 1949, and one to the upper house in 1947).

15. Russell Brines, *MacArthur's Japan* (Philadelphia: J. B. Lippincott, 1948), 206, describes the "pioneer feminine legislators" as "too completely in a man's world and too thoroughly shunted to the background." For a more scholarly instance of blaming the women themselves for their reduced numbers in politics, see Yanaga Chitoshi, *Japanese People and Politics* (New York: John Wiley & Sons, 1956), 19.

16. The number of female candidates is given in Nakamichi Minoru, "Fujin giin; tarento giin" (Women Diet members; talent Diet members), in *Kokkai giin no kōsei to henka* (Change and the makeup of the Diet), ed. Naka Hisao (Tokyo: Seiji kohō sentaa, 1980), 174.

17. Based on Reed, *Japan Election Data*. The four were Koshiwara Haru, Moriyama Yone, Nomura Misu, and Takeuchi Shigeyo. Nomura Misu ran for the upper house and Takeuchi Shigeyo was purged from politics.

18. Lists of party affiliations are given in Kokkai shūgiin sangiin, *Gikai seido shichijūnen*, vol. 6.

19. Kokkai shūgiin sangiin. *Gikai seido shichijūnen*, vol. 8, 355, and Reed, *Japan Election Data*, 322. Narushima Noriko, the third woman newly elected to the lower

house in 1947, was a political wife or sister. Her husband, Narushima Isamu, a veteran of three terms in the lower house from the same prefecture, was elected in 1946. Since she ran in 1947 and 1949, only to have him run again in 1953, I suspect that he was purged. Kokkai shūgiin sangiin, *Gikai seido shichijūnen*, vol. 8, 364, and Reed, *Japan Election Data*, 128–129.

20. Ronald J. Hrebenar, *The Japanese Party System* (Boulder, Colorado: Westview Press, 1992), 37–38, and Nathaniel B. Thayer, *How the Conservatives Rule Japan* (Princeton, New Jersey: Princeton University Press, 1969), 50.

21. On Hirano Shigeko and her husband Hirano Rikizō, see *Seijika jinmei jiten*, 443.

22. Nihon minsei kenkyūkai, *Kokkai giin sōran* (Register of Diet members) (Tokyo: Nihon minsei kenkyūkai, 1970), 330, and *Japan Times*, December 26, 1976. Women's higher schools were the institutions for secondary level education for women in the prewar Japanese system. They were roughly equivalent to middle schools for men or to high schools.

23. *Konsaisu jinmei jiten* (Concise biographical dictionary) (Tokyo: Sanseido, 1976).

24. See Steinhoff, this volume.

25. Nihon minsei kenkyūkai, *Kokkai giin sōran* for 1970, 221, and Thayer, *Conservatives*, 131–132.

26. Nihon minsei kenkyūkai, *Kokkai giin sōran* for 1970, 235; Kokkai shūgin sangiin, *Gikai seido shichijūnen*, vol. 8, 504. The relative was Momiyama Akira.

27. Reed, *Japan Election Data*, 29.

28. *Asian Recorder* 6 (1960): 3679.

29. Reed, *Japan Election Data*, 159, 162, 294.

30. *Who's Who in Japan*, No. 2, (Winter 1958–1959): 110–111.

31. *Seijika jinmei jiten*, 567.

32. Shiratori Rei, *Gekidō no Nihon seiji-shi* (Activists in Japan's political history) (Tokyo: Asaka shobō, 1979), 1:1195.

33. Hrebenar, *Japanese Party System*, 35–37, shows that the LDP has its greatest success in districts with a small number of seats; conversely, minor parties and independent candidates do better if there are more seats per district. In contests for the upper house, the minor parties win most of their local constituency seats in three- and four-seat districts.

34. Nihon minsei kenkyūkai, *Kokkai giin sōran* for 1974, 325.

35. *Seijika jinmei jiten*, 393.

36. Nakamichi, "Fujin giin; tarento giin," 180.

37. Tatamiya Eitarō, *Nihon no seijikatachi* (Japan's politicians) (Tokyo: Michi shobō, 1965), 209–214.

38. Susan J. Pharr, *Political Women in Japan: The Search for a Place in Political Life* (Berkeley: University of California Press, 1981), 104.

39. Jung-suk Youn, "Candidates and Party Images: Recruitment to the Japanese House of Representatives, 1958–1972," in *Parties, Candidates, and Voters in Japan: Six Quantitative Studies*, ed. John Creighton Campbell (Ann Arbor, Michigan: Center for Japanese Studies, University of Michigan, 1972), 105.

40. Peter Berton, "The Japan Communist Party: The 'Lovable' Party," in Hrebenar, *The Japanese Party System*, 120.

41. On the feminist movement, see Ehara Yumiko, "Japanese Feminism in the 1970s and 1980s," *U.S.–Japan Women's Journal English Supplement* 4 (1993): 50–51.

42. Nihon minsei kenkyūkai, *Kokkai giin sōran* for 1970, 277, and *Nihon fujin mondai shiryō shūsei* (Materials on the women's problem in Japan) (Tokyo: Domesu, 1980), 10:267, 275, 302, and 315.

43. *Seijika jinmei jiten*, 546.

44. *Japan Almanac* (Tokyo: Tokyo Mainichi Newspapers, 1976) and *Jinji kōshin-roku* (Biographical dictionary) (Tokyo: Jinji Kōshinjo) vol. 37 (1993).

45. *Seijika jinmei jiten*, 562, and Kokumin shinbunsha, *Nihon gendai shukujoroku* (Record of modern Japanese women) (Tokyo: Kokumin shinbunsha, 1987).

46. Hrebenar, *The Japanese Party System*, 38, and Berton, "The Japan Communist Party," 128, 137. On Shimoda, see *Yomiuri shinbun*, June 28, 1983, and Reed, *Japan Election Data*, 73.

47. On Yokoyama Nokku, see Nakamichi, "Fujin giin; tarento giin," 181.

48. *Yomiuri shinbun*, June 28, 1983. On Yoshikawa, see also *Seijika jinmei jiten*, 577, and Reed, *Japan Election Data*, 127.

49. *Yomiuri shinbun*, July 8, 1986.

50. Berton, "The Japan Communist Party," 123.

51. Nihon minsei kenkyūkai, *Kokkai giin sōran* for 1973, 105.

52. Ibid., 152.

53. Ibid., 97.

54. Kojunsha, *Nihon shinshiroku* (Japan who's who) (Tokyo: Kojunsha, 1982), and Reed, *Japan Election Data*, 315–317.

55. There was a shift in practice in the late 1970s. For the period 1958 to 1972, Youn found no difference among the parties, including the JCP, in their propensity to nominate women ("Candidates and Party Images," 105).

56. *Nihon shinshiroku* (1982).

57. *Nihon shinshiroku* (1982).

58. *Jinji koshinroku*, vol. 37, (1993).

59. Nakamichi, "Fujin giin; tarento giin," 181.

60. *Nihon gendai shukujoroku*. On Ōtaka Hiroshi, see Nichigai asoshietsu, *Gendai Nihon jinmei roku* (Biographical dictionary of modern Japan) (Tokyo: Nichigai asoshietsu, 1990).

61. Hrebenar, *The Japanese Party System*, 66.

62. *Seijika jinmei jiten*, 427.

63. Nihon minsei kenkyūkai, *Kokkai giin sōran* for 1973, 288.

64. Ibid., 342.

65. *Seijika jinmei jiten*, 68.

66. Reed, *Japan Election Data*, 177, 210.

67. *Chicago Tribune*, June 19, 1988.

68. *Yomiuri shinbun*, June 28, 1983.

69. *Seijika jinmei jiten*, 36.

70. *Yomiuri shinbun*, July 8, 1986. On Shimizu, see *Seijika jinmei jiten*, 262.

71. On the few exceptions, see Yoko Hayashi, "Women in the Legal Profession in Japan," *U.S.–Japan Women's Journal English Supplement* 2 (1992): 16–27.

72. Doi Takako, "Nichibei kankei kaizen no tame no mitsu no hoto," *Gekkan shakaitō*, no. 383 (December 1987), 94–95; and Susanne Fowler, "The New Face of Japanese Politics," *Chicago Tribune*, July 28, 1991.

73. Nihon minsei kenkyūkai, *Kokkai giin sōran* for 1970, 150.

74. Nohara Kazuhiko and Kouji Hoshino, "First Lady Comes," *Waseda Guardian* 54, no. 2 (October 1988): 19.

75. *Tōkyō shinbun* (Tokyo newspaper), November 30, 1969, translated in Department of State, Tokyo Embassy, Political Section, Translation Services Branch, *Daily Summary of Japanese Press*, and Reed, *Japan Election Data*, 351.

76. Nihon minsei kenkyūkai, *Kokkai giin sōran* for 1973, 77.

77. Nakamichi, "Fujin giin; tarento giin," 181, and Nihon minsei kenkyūkai, *Kokkai giin sōran* for 1973, 321.

78. "Lotus Power," *Newsweek* 75 (January 19, 1970): 46.

79. Nihon minsei kenkyūkai, *Kokkai giin sōran* for 1970, 137 and 256.

80. *Yomiuri shinbun*, June 28, 1983.

81. *Jinji kōshinroku* (1993).

82. *Nihon gendai shukujoroku* and *Yomiuri shinbun*, July 8, 1986.

83. *Japan Times*, March 4, 1989.

84. *Japan Times*, April 16, 1989.

85. *Japan Times*, June 10, 1989.

86. *Yomiuri shinbun*, July 25, 1989.

87. Shimura was not happy about the policy. *Japan Times*, May 20, 1989.

88. *Yomiuri shinbun*, July 27, 1992.

89. Quoted in Iwai, "'The Madonna Boom,'" 110.

90. Ibid., 113–114, 116.

91. For an account of the New Liberal Club, see Susan J. Pharr, *Losing Face: Status Politics in Japan* (Berkeley: University of California Press, 1990), 44–58. On Koike Yuriko, see *Jinji kōshinroku* (1993).

92. A list of the candidates and the votes they secured can be found in *Gekkan shakaitō*, September 1993, 84–94. For a list of candidates and brief descriptions of each, see *Yomiuri shinbun*, July 5, 1993. For the resignations and replacements in the upper house, see *Yomiuri shinbun*, July 16, 1993.

93. Reed, *Japan Election Data*, 260.

94. *Yomiuri shinbun*, August 5, 1993. Earlier, on July 21, the LDP had endorsed five other candidates who had run as independents. *Yomiuri shinbun*, July 23, 1993.

95. Chalmers Johnson, "Tanaka Kakuei, Structural Corruption, and the Advent of Machine Politics in Japan," *Journal of Japanese Studies* 12, no. 1 (1986): 17, and Reed, *Japan Election Data*, 77.

96. *Chicago Tribune*, "Womanews," February 6, 1994, and *Yomiuri shinbun*, January 14 and 15, 1994. When Hosokawa announced to a group of women leaders on January 13 his intention to nominate Takahashi, he made explicit his satisfaction in drawing women into all three branches of government.

97. For an analysis of the electoral reforms, see Raymond V. Christensen, "Electoral Reform in Japan: How It Was Enacted and Changes It May Bring," *Asian Survey* 34 (1994): 589–605.

THIRTEEN

Three Women Who Loved the Left
Radical Woman Leaders in the Japanese Red Army Movement

Patricia G. Steinhoff

Hibiya Outdoor Amphitheater buzzed with activity on September 5, 1969, as 26,000 students from 178 universities passed through a heavy ring of fully equipped riot police and entered the gates to attend the first national convention of Zenkyōtō, the student movement organizations responsible for most of the on-campus student protests that rocked Japanese college campuses in 1968 and 1969.[1] Somewhere in the crowd outside the amphitheater were two young women selling the first edition of *Sekigun*, the newspaper of the Red Army Faction (Sekigunha), a new radical student sect that threatened to escalate the off-campus violence against the Japanese state to new levels with guns and explosives. Shigenobu Fusako and Shiomi Kazuko were doing what women routinely did in the Japanese New Left: performing the support functions that kept the movement going.[2]

That same day another young woman, Nagata Hiroko, was performing a different kind of support service for yet another obscure New Left group that called itself the Japan Communist Party Revolutionary Left Faction (Nihon Kyōsantō Kakumei Saha).[3] The previous day, September 4, several thousand massed riot police had blocked a huge demonstration from marching on Haneda Airport. A few of Revolutionary Left Faction's male members had outmaneuvered the police by swimming from a nearby pier and coming ashore at the airport. After a brief moment of glory running around the terminal building, they had promptly been arrested. Nagata Hiroko's job was to organize legal, social, and financial support for their defense.

The year 1969 was a key turning point in a decade of postwar Japanese student conflict that affected a whole generation of young people, and Shigenobu Fusako, Shiomi Kazuko, and Nagata Hiroko were right in the center of it. In the previous two years, a multilayered New Left student movement of highly organized political sects had expanded rapidly, energized by a confluence of interrelated political issues including the Japan–U.S. Joint Security Treaty, Japan's secondary involvement in the Vietnam

War, and the return of Okinawa. The sects emerged regularly from their safe campus bases to engage in violent clashes with the riot police. Simultaneously with the growth of the sects, the Zenkyōtō movement had spread rapidly across Japan as an ecumenical, campus-based movement that organized local protests against school administrations. Although Zenkyōtō cut across the sects and incorporated many "nonsect" students, often the same people were heavily involved in both types of organization.[4] At Hibiya Amphitheater on September 5, the main event was the organizing meeting of a national federation of the campus-based Zenkyōtō groups, but the side events were clashes between sects.

Conflicts also erupted frequently within sects and quickly turned into factional divisions. The Red Army Faction, led by Shiomi Kazuko's husband Shiomi Takaya, emerged from one such internal factional breach within the sect called the Communist League (Kyōsanshugisha Dōmei) and nicknamed Bund. Kazuko had met her husband through her independent involvement as assistant to the leader of another Bund faction. An elementary school teacher and the mother of a six-month-old son, she was now a working adult and semiretired from the student movement but participated in special events like the big Zenkyōtō convention at Hibiya Amphitheater.

If Shiomi Kazuko was present at the Hibiya gathering largely as the chairman's wife, Shigenobu Fusako was there as a central player in her own right. From participating in a student strike at Meiji University, she had risen to become the only woman on the Central Committee of the newly independent Red Army Faction.

Nagata Hiroko represented another trend within the New Left in 1969: the involvement of students and former students in organizing young workers into New Left unions and other interest groups. Nagata Hiroko had become involved in a series of New Left sects and breakaway factions as a pharmacy student in Yokohama, and after graduation she became an effective organizer of women workers, promoting her group's strong Marxist-feminist message among pharmacists, nurses, and female factory workers.

Born in 1945, these three women were among the first children of postwar Japan. They shared with their families the hope and hardships of the early postwar years and the rising living standards of the 1950s and 1960s. As bright little girls they surely benefited from the postwar reorganization of the education system, absorbing new aspirations of democracy and equality. By 1969, through their own talents and sheer chance, they had gravitated as young adult women to the center of the radical New Left student movement. They had made choices that were not traditional, but they were still more or less within the alternative mainstream of their generation. And they had achieved their positions of prominence by performing distinctly female roles in male-dominated organizations.

If anyone had told these three young women their futures in 1969, they would have laughed. Who could possibly believe that in 1995 Shigenobu Fusako would be living in the Middle East under the protection of various Arab governments as the internationally known leader of the Japanese Red Army, her name and description regularly distributed on Interpol wanted lists; that Shiomi Kazuko would still be an elementary school teacher but, having raised her son as a single parent, would be coping with the return of her husband after twenty years in prison; or that having led her group into a disastrous merger with the Red Army, Nagata Hiroko would be in Tokyo House of Detention, awaiting a death sentence for her leadership role in a bloody internal organizational purge, her final appeal denied by the Japanese Supreme Court?

Because of their intimate involvement in the radical New Left, Shigenobu Fusako, Shiomi Kazuko, and Nagata Hiroko have all led remarkable lives. They were not typical even for New Left women, but a close examination of their experiences reveals the abilities, opportunities, and choices that shaped their unique life courses. Yet woven through these unusual lives are also common threads of experience shared by most women in postwar Japan. In important ways, these three women are not unique, but rather reflect patterns common to their generation, social circumstances, and culture.

Finally, all three of these women who loved the left are public figures whose lives have been stylized, by other people and the mass media, into powerful cautionary images for young women in Japan.[5] These stylized images and their distance from the private and personal reality of the three women's lives highlight the external social pressures that shape and inform the life choices every Japanese woman makes.

SHIOMI KAZUKO

Shiomi Kazuko was a student at Shizuoka University in the mid-1960s, preparing to become a social studies teacher. Her social science interests led her to the student movement, where she became the aide-de-camp of the leader of the Marxist Front Faction (Marusenha). This group was trying to resurrect the New Left organization Bund, which had played a leading role in the 1960 Anti-Security Treaty protests and later had broken into factions over its failure to stop the treaty.

Through this involvement, she met Shiomi Takaya, an intense, intellectual philosophy dropout from Kyoto University who was a rising star in the Kansai Bund, another faction that was trying to resurrect Bund to its former glory. At that time the movement was a completely legal, above-board activity that attracted bright, committed students with political interests and good organizational skills. During the brief period when their respective groups were brought together in the reunited second Bund, Kazuko graduated from college, began teaching in the Tokyo public schools, and married Shiomi in 1968. She knew when she married him that they would not have an ordinary life. Shiomi was a professional organizer on the payroll of the fledgling national Bund organization, being groomed for the leadership role of party theorist. Shiomi's family had reservations about the marriage because of their son's inadequacies as a breadwinner, but Kazuko's family was quite supportive.[6]

Kazuko believes her own life would have been radically different if she had entered college a year or two later. Instead of passing smoothly through college and leaving the student movement upon graduation to join the adult world of work, she would have been in the thick of the student movement when it became violent, and she would have been on the front lines herself. As it was, she had left school, married, gone to work, and had a baby by the time the movement reached that critical stage. She lived with Shiomi very little after their marriage, since he was off organizing or participating in various campaigns and came home only about once a week. When her son was born, she put him in day care and kept on teaching to support the family.[7]

In the mid-1960s in Japan, as in the United States in earlier decades, being a schoolteacher was one of only a handful of occupations in which a woman could expect to maintain a career. As a government employee, Shiomi Kazuko could keep her job despite marriage and motherhood, could earn enough to support her family independent of her husband's income, and could enjoy a respected social position in her own right. Shiomi Kazuko had prepared herself for such a position by entering a four-year course at a competitive prefectural coed university. Though some young women with education degrees joined the ranks of office ladies instead of teaching and many more planned to quit teaching when they married, the teaching credential offered an extra measure of personal economic security and independence. Her choice was thus not radical, but she was certainly more ambitious than most Japanese women of that time, even if her aspirations were conventionally feminine.

By the time their child was born, Shiomi Kazuko's husband was in the thick of a factional dispute at the center of Bund and had become the chief theorist for the emerging Red Army Faction, which advocated more violent tactics, a guerrilla army to fight the state, and international links to other revolutionary movements to overcome the stalemate between the state and the movement inside Japan. These ideas, emerging from long group discussions but transformed by Shiomi into arresting verbal images of violence and power, were deeply divisive within Bund. Over the next six months the Red Army Faction was formally ousted from Bund and organized itself as an independent radical group.

By the fall of 1969, her husband's activities as the leader of a radical group engaged in increasingly serious illegal activities had driven him underground.[8] Shiomi Kazuko was under constant surveillance by the police as well, so they could rarely meet. Then in late March of 1970, on their son's first birthday, Shiomi Takaya was arrested on an outstanding warrant charging him with violation of the 1952 Anti-Subversive Activities Law.[9] A week later, nine Red Army members caused a sensation by successfully hijacking a domestic Japanese airliner to North Korea, the first airline hijacking Japan had ever experienced.

Shiomi Kazuko was suddenly the wife of a famous political prisoner. Her husband was held incommunicado for the next eighteen months while he was interrogated on one charge after another. His wife was permitted a few carefully controlled visits; all other communication came through his lawyers, who also had very limited contact with him.

Despite postwar reforms, the Japanese criminal justice system is heavily oriented toward confession. Arrestees can be held for extended periods of interrogation without any outside contact, although Shiomi's eighteen months of incommunicado interrogation was a record that did not fall until the late 1980s. Lawyers are not permitted to be present during interrogations and can only see their clients for about thirty minutes once a week. Under these pressures over 99 percent of those arrested break down and confess to a crime, then plead guilty and receive only a summary trial, at which expressions of remorse tend to lighten the sentence. Most criminal defense lawyers are only brought into the case after the police have obtained a confession, at which point they encourage a guilty plea and a display of remorse in hopes of reducing the sentence, rather than defending the client as innocent until proven guilty by the prosecution's evidence. Consequently, some people even confess and are convicted of crimes they did not commit. An individual has little hope of defending himself or herself under these conditions even with a private lawyer.

Within the Japanese left there is a well-developed voluntary system to provide support for members of political organizations who are arrested for politically based offenses and wish to mount a strong political defense. Lawyers provide their services at low cost, and a voluntary organization created by the prisoners' families and associates provides both paralegal services to the defense lawyers and support to the prisoners during the long trial period. They help the arrested person resist the pressure to confess, enter a plea of not guilty, and force the state to try its case in court. This ensures that all the political as well as legal issues will be aired in a full trial before a panel of three judges and that all avenues of appeal will be exhausted. A political defense rarely results in reduction of sentence, and in serious cases the defendant remains in detention through years of trial and appeals. Political defendants are generally kept in solitary confinement, but since they are technically in "unconvicted detention" they have greater communications privileges than a prisoner serving a criminal sentence in a regular prison, and much of the detention time may later be counted as time served. Shiomi Kazuko kept on teaching school and raising her small son, but she also became a central figure in the support group organized to manage her husband's defense. She was thus pulled back into the political arena by her husband's arrest, even though he was now totally cut off from both his political and private life.

In the fall of 1971 the severe communications restrictions were lifted, and for the next twelve years, until 1983, Shiomi Takaya lived in unconvicted detention in a solitary cell in Tokyo House of Detention, where he could have one visitor a day and could communicate freely by letter both with people outside and with other prisoners inside Tokyo House of Detention. During that time he was convicted and given a twenty-year sentence, but remained in Tokyo House of Detention while his case was appealed twice and finally decided by the Supreme Court. He served the remaining eight years of his sentence in Fuchū Prison, allowed one visit a month from his wife and teenage son.

By the mid-1970s, Shiomi's support group had become an independent faction of the Red Army with Kazuko as one of its several leaders. The group had its own political agenda shaped by Shiomi Takaya from prison, but by then neither he nor the faction advocated the use of violence. Because of her own continuing political activity, Shiomi Kazuko remained under constant police surveillance for many years. At one time the plainclothes police waiting for her to come out of school became such a nuisance that the principal, although sympathetic to her situation, asked if she would leave by the rear door. On another occasion, a squabble within her faction put Shiomi Kazuko's name prominently in the newspapers. Neither the school administration nor the parents were upset, but the local school committee (Kyōiku Iinkai) pressured her to resign. When she refused, they backed off, knowing that she would sue and probably win if they tried to fire her for her private political activity. Instead, they gave her a year's sabbatical, which she spent reading books at the school committee's office.

The following year she took a position at a school on the other side of Tokyo. She chose, however, to keep living in her friendly community in the old downtown (*shitamachi*) area of the city, where the neighbors would look after her son if she had to stay late at school. It is difficult for a woman to raise a son alone in Japan under any circumstances, but the fact that the boy's father was a famous prisoner complicated matters further. When Shiomi's name was in the newspapers, other children would sometimes harass the boy, but sympathetic New Left teachers who respected his father gave him some protection, and he learned to handle his situation very early.[10]

When I first met Shiomi Kazuko in 1983, she expressed considerable apprehension about what would happen when her husband was released from prison and returned to live with his family. They had barely lived together as newlyweds, and in the years since she had made a comfortable, independent life for herself and her son. She wondered what his expectations would be and whether she could fit him back into her life.[11]

At the end of 1989, Shiomi Takaya completed his prison term and returned home to his wife and twenty-one-year-old son. Since then, his wife and friends have been engaged in Shiomi's rehabilitation. The first step was physical, repairing the damage done to his back by several years of forced kneeling for hours at a time as he made paper bags in solitary confinement at Fuchū Prison (a punishment designed to break him that provoked protests from Amnesty International).

His social *rehabiri* has taken longer. The difficulties seem not to be the ones Kazuko expected, because Shiomi has tried to be very cooperative at home. Still, it has not been easy. In a series of articles in the support group newsletter, Kazuko has written perceptively of the little troubles of living with someone who has spent the past twenty years in prison. In one issue, she talks about how he kept leaving the refrigerator door open and defensively denying that he was the only one doing it, until finally the open refrigerator broke from the strain when he was alone at home. Their son complained that he was always leaving the bathroom door open as well. She observes that for twenty years he was never permitted to close a door; the doors were locked and unlocked on the other side, closed and opened by a guard, and the toilet stood doorless in the corner of his cell.[12] These little vignettes reveal not only the myriad details of everyday life that have to be relearned by an ex-prisoner, but the tremendous friction and frustration involved in the process.

The larger difficulties have concerned Shiomi's readjustment to the world outside his front door. He is a Rip Van Winkle or Urashima Tarō, returned to a fundamentally different Japan. The New Left is no longer a relevant force, and his place in the world is not at all clear.[13] When his social expectations no longer fit the situation, the person who most often has to tell him he can't do something inappropriate or downright dangerous is his wife.

Shiomi has a circle of loyal supporters, but the faction his wife helped to lead is not really a political organization anymore, and she no longer holds a leadership role. At public events where he is the featured attraction, I have marveled at how easily she slips into the support roles: manning the registration table, cleaning up the tea cups, dividing the flower arrangements to give to the guests. She is very much her own person, with her own warm relationships to people in the group, yet she seems happy to be a wife again rather than a political leader.

Despite her own political activity, Shiomi Kazuko's public image is as the good and loyal wife who stuck by her husband throughout his long time in prison. Shiomi says that the prisoners from organized crime groups (*yakuza*) he knew at Fuchū Prison were envious of him and deeply admired her.[14] Even the security police admired her. In a recent book documenting his own lengthy interrogation, Japanese Red Army member Maruoka Osamu recounts that one of his police interrogators spoke admiringly of how Shiomi Kazuko had raised her son alone and taken care of her elderly father during Shiomi's long absence.[15] The police, of course, know these details of Shiomi Kazuko's life because they have kept her under close surveillance during the past twenty years. That surveillance was clearly prompted by her own political activities, since Shiomi Takaya was safely under lock and key the whole time.

NAGATA HIROKO

Although she began her political activities in an entirely different group, Nagata Hiroko's life course was affected indirectly by the arrest of Shiomi Takaya. During the eighteen months immediately after his arrest, the Red Army was decimated by other arrests and defections. It was partially rebuilt under the leadership of a young man named Mori Tsuneo, who saw himself as a loyal follower of Shiomi's ideas but in fact led the organization in a different direction, under very different operating conditions. Mori rebuilt the underground army, and by the spring of 1971 its squads were engaged in a successful series of bank and payroll robberies and an unsuccessful quest for guns. It was that combination that led to Nagata Hiroko's association with Mori's Red Army.

Nagata had grown up in Yokohama as the daughter of a factory worker at a large electrical company, but her mother, a nurse, had sent her daughter to a private girls' high school to improve her academic and social future. Nagata then entered a pharmacy college in Yokohama, again at her mother's urging.[16] Like teaching, pharmacy was a career open to women that offered the possibility of long-term economic security and independence. It was a safe, respectable choice for a young woman who was good at math and science but did not want to become a teacher.

Through involvement in political demonstrations, Nagata Hiroko gradually was drawn into a Bund faction called the Marxist Leninist Faction (ML Ha). By following a particular leader through a series of factional splits, she ended up in the Revolutionary Left Faction, a small group with ideological ties to a Maoist group that had been ousted from the Japan

Communist Party. After graduation from college she remained politically involved, organizing women's groups and eventually quitting her job in a pharmacy lab to become a full-time activist. Her group took the Marxist-feminist position that women could only be liberated by revolution, and therefore women who sought to be liberated ought to work first for the revolution.

That position conveniently permitted the leader of the organization, Kawashima Tsuyoshi, to maintain the rather paternalistic practice of arranging marriages for his followers. Nagata was asked to marry a member of the group, but she refused because she did not like him. Then in late August of 1969, Nagata was called to Kawashima's apartment while his wife was away. They worked until it was too late to return home, and he offered to let her stay for the night, a common enough occurrence in a city where the trains stop running shortly after midnight. Before she knew what was happening, he raped her. Nagata was shaken by the experience, but blamed it on Kawashima as an individual. She remained faithful to the organization and its ideology. Having no way to take up the problem within the organization, she tried having sex with a couple of other men, then suppressed her confused feelings and threw herself into her work, continuing to take orders from Kawashima.[17]

In December 1969, Kawashima was arrested on explosives charges and held incommunicado for a month, after which he awaited trial in Yokohama Prison with regular communications and visitor privileges. Kawashima's wife was a member of the Revolutionary Left Faction engaged in legal activities such as political organizing, but she was under heavy surveillance. Kawashima ordered Nagata to visit him and began using her as his courier while he tried to run the Revolutionary Left Faction from prison. Her visible link to Kawashima soon put her under heavy police surveillance as well, but Nagata developed great skill at eluding her tail by disguising her looks, sometimes slipping into public restrooms to change clothes and put on a wig.

At about the same time, the Revolutionary Left Faction "swimmers" who had been arrested in September 1969 for entering Haneda Airport from the bay were released from jail pending the completion of their trials.[18] One of them, Sakaguchi Hiroshi, asked Nagata to marry him. Recognizing that they felt neither love nor any particular sexual attraction for each other, Nagata at first refused. Sakaguchi persisted, asking her how she could refuse someone who was facing a seven-year prison term. She agreed to have sex with him once and then decided to accept his offer of marriage after all. In May 1970, they began living together in a communal apartment (*ajitto*) that served as meeting place for the faction.[19]

By this time Nagata, Sakaguchi, and three other people were acting de facto as the collective leadership of the Revolutionary Left Faction. A persuasive speaker and writer, Nagata wrote the group's theoretical statements and put out its publications. Sakaguchi was reluctant to hold a formal position of authority because he was still in the middle of a trial, so Nagata ended up as official head and spokesperson of the organization. In the midst of this, Nagata discovered that she was pregnant. She and Sakaguchi decided that she could not have a baby under their current circumstances and would have to get an abortion.[20] Sakaguchi was supportive at the time of the abortion, but became irritated by her need for emotional support later and hit her, only to become immediately chagrined at this lapse in his stance as a supporter of women's liberation.[21]

Despite these personal matters, their mutual focus was on the pressing needs of their tiny movement. Kawashima was still trying to run it from jail, and the group still tried to follow his direction. After his request for release was denied by the court, Kawashima suddenly ordered the group to get him out of jail by some other means. They worked out a plan to free Kawashima that required guns, so their energy became diverted into efforts to obtain some. Guns were rare commodities in Japan until recently, most often found in police holsters. After an unsuccessful knife attack on a police box that left one of their own members killed and two others seriously injured, they succeeded in robbing a gun shop in the country town of Mōka in the winter of 1971, just as Mori's Red Army was beginning to rob banks. Nagata, Sakaguchi, and several other members fled to Hokkaido and later retreated into the mountains west of Tokyo, where they set up housekeeping in an abandoned cabin and invited their followers to join them for an idyllic experiment in revolutionary communal living.

At this point Mori's Red Army had money but no guns, and Nagata's group had guns but no money. The imperatives of supply and demand gradually brought the two groups together in a disastrous marriage of convenience. They met at a mountain cabin in December 1971 to form a new group called the United Red Army, hoping to strengthen their revolutionary capability by working together. Instead, they tumbled step-by-step into a bloody internal purge in which twelve members were beaten and tortured to death under the joint leadership of Mori and Nagata.[22]

Nagata is not a very insightful person, and she readily follows dominant male authority. However, she is a powerful speaker who was accepted as a leader, particularly by the many women in her organization. In her dealings with Mori, she was a strong spokesperson for her group, and he appeared to treat her as his equal. In fact, however, Mori dominated the merger, and she deferred to him—so much so that in mid-February she told Sakaguchi she was leaving him for Mori, because Mori thought the two leaders of the revolutionary movement ought to be married.[23] Just days later the police tracked the group to their mountain hideouts, and

Mori and Nagata were arrested on February 19, 1972. The United Red Army purge came to light a few weeks later during the interrogations of other arrested members of the group. As the gory details emerged, the entire nation recoiled in shock, and the New Left movement was shattered.[24]

For the first ten months after her arrest, Nagata was a prominent figure, but Mori was generally acknowledged to be the leader of the United Red Army. Then on New Year's Eve of 1972, on the anniversary of the death of the first purge victim, Mori committed suicide in his cell at Tokyo Prison. In his long prison writings and his suicide notes Mori tried to take responsibility for what had happened but he also continued to describe Nagata as his co-leader. After Mori's death, attention shifted to Nagata as the top leader responsible for the terrible purge. Though both the court and the public have treated Mori as a political leader whose plans went astray, they have treated Nagata as a menacing crazy-woman motivated by spite and jealousy. The standard file photos of Nagata used by the media date from her arrest and early court appearances. They usually show her either helmeted and shouting slogans or struggling in the grip of police officers. Her eyes bulge from Grave's disease, which contributes to the image of wild defiance.

The court's official decision in the first United Red Army trial, issued in 1982 by Judge Nakano Takeo, contains the following astonishing passage: "Defendant Nagata has a flourishing desire for self-exposure and along with an emotional, aggressive personality, she is suspicious and jealous, and to these are added the female characteristics of obstinacy, spitefulness, and cruel sadism; she harbors a variety of problems in her temperament."[25]

The judge's misogynous opinion of Nagata as an *onibaba* (witch) was based in part on her aberrant behavior in court during the late 1970s, when she would sometimes shout out inappropriately, faint, or otherwise disrupt the proceedings. When she complained of headaches, nausea, vision problems, and vertigo in the early 1980s, the prison doctors prescribed tranquilizers and said it was only natural that she should have headaches after what she had done. It was only when an alert eye doctor from outside the prison examined her in 1984 that it was discovered Nagata had a brain tumor.[26] Since then she and her lawyers and supporters have fought continuously to get her appropriate medical treatment, but the prison administration refuses even to tell her what is wrong. The tumor itself cannot be removed, but she was taken to a university hospital for an operation to insert a shunt that helps relieve the pressure. She has already lived several years longer than most others with her condition.

More amazing still, during the 1980s Nagata wrote and published six books from her isolation cell in Tokyo House of Detention. Although often in severe pain, she remains lucid and determined. Her first book, a two-volume autobiography that covers her life until her arrest, attracted the attention of many women because of her frank, feminist analysis of her relationships with men. Her later books have focused on more recent periods in her life. One is a collection of her correspondence with the well-known author and Buddhist nun Setouchi Harumi, whom she met after requesting that Setouchi write a preface for one of her books. In her preface Setouchi comments, "I came to know Hiroko as a very normal woman, intelligent, frank, with a strong sense of justice, incapable of self-deception, and honest to a fault."[27] Setouchi's impression corresponds much more than Judge Nakano's with my own experience of Nagata, except that I think she remains quite capable of self-deception. She also embodies, as much as any Japanese person I know, the quality of *gambaru* (dogged perseverance).

After Mori's death, Nagata had an extended prison correspondence with Shiomi, who was struggling to come to terms with the United Red Army purge and his own sense of responsibility for it. She subsequently developed a prison romance with Uegaki Yasunari, another of the United Red Army defendants. Nagata has thus had a full social and literary life despite severe illness and physical isolation.

Nagata Hiroko was able to publish and correspond freely from her prison cell because, despite being given a death sentence in 1982, she remained technically in unconvicted detention in Tokyo House of Detention during another decade of appeals. Then on the twenty-first anniversary of the day of her arrest, February 19, 1993, the Supreme Court handed down its decision in her final appeal and upheld the death penalty. No one knows if or when the execution will be carried out, but in the meantime Nagata Hiroko remains in Tokyo House of Detention, now restricted to monthly visits from family members and prohibited from corresponding with anyone else.

Since Nagata no longer has regular contact with her family, before her death sentence was finally confirmed she entered into a legal marriage with one of the most loyal members of her support group, who took her family name. Such marriages, and sometimes family adoptions, are undertaken on behalf of New Left prisoners awaiting the death penalty to ensure that someone can continue to visit the prisoner regularly and will be notified as next of kin when the death sentence is quietly carried out. These relationships are awesome testimony to the dedication of New Left support group members.

SHIGENOBU FUSAKO

The events that led to Nagata Hiroko's death sentence had an indirect but profound effect on the life of Shigenobu Fusako. Shigenobu was one of the few members of the original leadership group of the Red Army Faction who remained active a year after Shiomi Takaya's arrest. Shigenobu had grown up in the outskirts of Tokyo, the daughter of an educated man who had become bitter and poor after the war and ran a small grocery store. Shigenobu was bright, lively, and beautiful, but she could not afford to go to college. After high school graduation, she went to work as an office lady, doing clerical work and pouring tea at the Kikkōman Shōyū company. This was the most normal, proper course for a young woman to take at the time. She was considered successful in that she was hired by a good company for a downtown Tokyo office job where she would be likely to meet an eligible young salaryman.

But Shigenobu was restless and inquisitive. As soon as she had earned enough money, she decided to go back to school and entered the evening division of Meiji University. As Japan began its economic boom during the 1960s, there was a growing demand for higher education that could not be met in the established national and public universities. Private institutions stepped into the breach, taking in thousands of new students whose needs they could not really meet. This failure sparked some of the most serious campus disputes of the late 1960s.

On the day that Shigenobu went to enroll at Meiji University, there was a sit-in against a tuition increase and poor instructional conditions. Shigenobu listened to the protesters' arguments and promptly sat down and joined the protest herself. The group Shigenobu joined happened to be affiliated with the newly reorganized Bund, and Shigenobu soon was in the thick of the movement. Although she fit in easily as a student and student activist, from her work at Kikkōman she had a more practical sense of the real world than did other students.

Shigenobu did what other young women in the New Left did: made the arrangements for meetings and rallies; hand-cut stencils for endless handbills (a task for which she was much in demand because of her beautiful handwriting); and went to violent demonstrations with a backpack full of emergency supplies to tend to anyone from her group who got hurt. Because she was very competent, she was soon organizing these support operations and supervising other people. She also took a part-time hostess job in the Ginza and began political organizing there.[28] As Bund began to break apart, her Meiji University group sided with Shiomi, and Shigenobu's role became even more central. The new faction needed money, and Shigenobu proved to be adept at soliciting contributions from her well-heeled Ginza associates.

When the Red Army Faction became an independent organization and some of its key members began working underground, Shigenobu and her friend Toyama Mieko, the fiancée of another Central Committee member, organized a sophisticated telephone contact system using women stationed in coffee shops to maintain communications. Shigenobu had a boyfriend in the movement as well; by all accounts he was madly in love with her, whereas she was more committed to the cause than to him. In contrast to her closest friends, who became regular prison visitors and support-group participants when their husbands or lovers were arrested, Shigenobu never visited her erstwhile boyfriend after his arrest, perhaps fearing that it would place her under closer surveillance and make it more difficult to keep working in the movement.

As the Red Army tried to rebuild after Shiomi's arrest and the North Korean hijacking, Shigenobu was assigned to a committee to develop additional international links for the group. The other committee members soon dropped out or were arrested, but Shigenobu quietly pursued the problem. By early 1971 Shigenobu had developed ties with the Popular Front for the Liberation of Palestine (PFLP), a new faction of the Palestine Liberation Organization (PLO) that had a philosophy similar to the Red Army's and was inviting foreigners to undertake guerrilla training at its facilities in Lebanon. However, by that time Mori Tsuneo had reorganized the Red Army's underground for a series of domestic attacks, and he was no longer interested in international links.

Shigenobu had had enough of the increasingly autocratic Mori, and when he ordered her not to go to the Middle East, she simply went ahead on her own. Knowing that she would have difficulty getting a passport in her own name because of her previous arrests and her association with the Red Army, Shigenobu arranged a formal marriage to a young activist at Kyoto University, Okudaira Takeshi, who wanted to go to the Middle East with her for guerrilla training. As Okudaira was not a known member of the Red Army and had no police record, he could easily leave the country. Posing as a newly married couple on their honeymoon, Okudaira Takeshi and the new Mrs. Okudaira obtained their passports and slipped out of Japan. Shiomi Kazuko and Toyama Mieko saw her off at the airport.

In Lebanon, Shigenobu began working in the PFLP offices in Beirut while Okudaira went off for guerrilla training. Shigenobu circulated freely in the tiny Japanese community of businessmen, journalists, and embassy officials, even as she widened her contacts in the PLO. She quickly produced both a book and a film depicting the Red Army's role in working alongside the PLO to liberate Palestine. The images they portrayed, of Japanese Red Army guerrillas casually leaning on their Kalashnikov rifles, were a New Left fantasy come true. Her friend Toyama Mieko arranged for the film to be shown on college campuses all over Japan, often with a PFLP representative in attendance. From the group of students who worked with Toyama to arrange the film showings, new recruits were gradually sent to Lebanon for guerrilla training under Okudaira's supervision.

Then, in the early spring of 1972, Shigenobu received a series of telephone calls from Japan informing her of the death of Toyama Mieko and another of her friends in the United Red Army purge. No fans of Mori Tsuneo, Shigenobu and Okudaira issued a statement condemning the purge and dissociating their group from the United Red Army. In response to the purge, the group conducted a direct revolutionary attack that courted death in support of the Palestinian cause.[29]

In the deadly attack, carried out at Israel's Lod Airport on May 30, 1972, twenty-six people were killed and another seventy-five wounded. Okudaira Takeshi and one other Japanese participant died. The third member of the attack team, Okamoto Kōzo, survived and was immediately arrested by the Israeli authorities and tried for terrorism. Although the attack was condemned throughout most of the world, within much of the Arab world it was regarded as a major achievement for the Palestinian cause and its Japanese perpetrators were treated as heroes. In Beirut, Shigenobu Fusako became an instant celebrity, and her responsibilities as leader of the Japanese Red Army broadened. The Lod airport attack was also treated as a victory within radical left circles in Japan, and a steady trickle of young recruits made their way to the Japanese Red Army group in Lebanon.

During the 1970s the group carried out a number of spectacular hostage-taking attacks and airplane hijackings throughout the world, usually negotiating with governments to obtain the release of specific prisoners. Shigenobu's name has been on Interpol wanted lists since that time, although she has not been directly linked to most of the incidents. After 1977 the group withdrew to integrate its new members and rethink its political positions, surfacing again during the 1982 Israeli invasion of Lebanon as fighters who retreated with the PLO to Tripoli. They have since returned to the Bekâa valley, but the press reports occasional sightings elsewhere of Shigenobu and other members of the group.

Little is known of the inner workings of the Japanese Red Army, and from time to time there are reports in the media that one or another of the men who joined the group through prisoner releases has become its leader. Following the original Red Army model, from the outset the group in the Middle East has had both a more or less aboveground wing that concentrates on publications, political analysis, and public relations and an "army" trained for various kinds of direct action whose members have also served in combat units with PFLP. Shigenobu has always worked with the former wing of the organization, while at various times other male members have headed the army. Despite this leadership bifurcation, the evidence suggests that Shigenobu Fusako retains her position as the official spokesperson and senior leader of the Japanese Red Army. She is personally acquainted with most of the radical leaders in the Arab world, and her name is a household word in Lebanon. An outside observer who visited the group in the 1980s reported that all of the members stood up when Shigenobu entered the room, a gesture of respect toward this particular woman that is not common custom either in Japan or in the Middle East.[30]

Shigenobu has written several books, including personal accounts of her experiences in the Middle East, general reportage about Middle Eastern current events and their political and historical background, and theoretical discussions issued in the name of the organization and reflecting their extensive group study and discussions. As a result of these writings, the Japanese Red Army has grudgingly become recognized as containing some of Japan's most knowledgeable experts on the Middle East, and the Foreign Ministry maintained six subscriptions to the group's monthly published report on Middle East conditions.[31]

During the 1970s Shigenobu Fusako married and had a daughter, but her private life is shielded from public view for her safety. Although she occasionally gives interviews to carefully screened Japanese journalists, photographs never reveal her face. Magazine photos generally show her in shadowy silhouette inside an unidentifiable room, always with long, flowing hair. On a wanted poster of the Japanese Red Army circulated worldwide by the Japanese government in the late 1980s, Shigenobu's picture dates from her school days in Japan two decades earlier. Sometime after the poster circulated, the Italian government suddenly charged Shigenobu with participation in the 1988 bombing of a USO club in Rome, claiming that eyewitnesses had identified her at the scene, presumably from very old pictures of a young Japanese woman with long hair. Shigenobu wrote an open letter to the Italian government, denying any involvement and offering to answer any questions in writing. She was subsequently tried in absentia and acquitted, but another Japanese Red Army member, also tried in absentia, was found guilty.

The public image of Shigenobu Fusako, mirrored in her elusive photographs, evokes a mysterious and beautiful woman of great power. Whatever the reality may be inside the Japanese Red Army, in the public image she is the group's leader and the architect of its activities, a cool and competent Mata Hari who glides secretly around the world and is never captured. Credited with intelligence, political astuteness, and leadership, she is nevertheless depicted in the media as completely feminine, an unattainable erotic fantasy. Achieving an interview with her is treated by journalists almost like eating dinner with the Sun Goddess.[32]

THREE WOMEN, THREE LIVES, THREE IMAGES

What can we learn from these three women? All three began their involvement in the New Left in quite ordinary ways for young women of their era. They did the feminine jobs that keep a political movement going, and they had significant personal relationships with men in leadership positions. The women received recognition for their abilities, but were only thrust into externally visible positions of leadership when the men around them disappeared for one reason or another. In this respect they resemble the wives who help run small family businesses all over Japan. Their competence and value to the business are tacitly acknowledged daily, but they only ascend to formal authority at the highest level if their husbands die.

All three of these women displayed a characteristically feminine style of leadership, relying on collegiality and collective decisionmaking rather than an assertive, authoritarian style, yet they were capable of speaking and acting with great personal authority. In large measure these women rose to positions of leadership because of their skill in organizing people and activities through collegial, voluntary approaches. Although this feminine style of leadership is used widely in Japan and has been heralded in America as one of the secrets of Japanese corporate success, it must be emphasized that families and smaller businesses often feature much more unilateral and authoritarian leadership by a single head, usually male. The New Left organizations in which these three women exercised leadership were in scale and structure more like a family business led by its founder than like a large bureaucratic corporation. In that context, their personal leadership styles were distinctively feminine.

It could be argued that the three women were not true leaders but simply surrogates for male leaders who were temporarily unavailable. In this view, Shiomi Kazuko was simply a stand-in for her imprisoned husband, Nagata for a whole string of males (Kawashima, Sakaguchi, and then Mori), and Shigenobu for the deceased Okudaira until other males were brought to the organization who could take over. Such views are sometimes implied in the Japanese mass media. They reflect both a desire on the part of Japanese male journalists to discount female leadership and a lack of understanding of the spaces created for female leadership within their particular New Left organizations.

The Japanese New Left was generally male-dominated, with women playing supporting roles. Frustration with that arrangement led many New Left women into the feminist movement in the 1970s. Yet because of the organizational complexity of New Left organizations of the late 1960s the support activities in which women participated also became leadership training grounds for those women. With respect to the three women studied here, the combination of their own abilities, leadership training within the New Left, and personal relationships with male leaders engaged in high-risk behaviors produced capable women who could step into visible positions of leadership when the male leaders suddenly vanished from the organizational scene. Yet it is clear that all three women acted as independent leaders and managers within their organizations well before they were thrust into the public eye.

The parallel with Japanese women who participate in the management of small family businesses must be underscored again. When there is a male head of household present, it is presumed that he runs the business, even though the wife may be an equal partner and the sole manager of particular parts of the organization. In the absence of a male head of household, outsiders may be reluctant to let women perform certain leadership functions publicly, but the women work around these constraints and run their businesses nonetheless. In either case, the external demand for public male leadership makes the actual leadership activities of women less visible, perpetuating the myth that women cannot and do not hold positions of authority outside the home.

In the private realm, the experiences of these three women with men and marriage are in some respects emblematic of the New Left's flouting of convention, but there are revealing glimpses here of traditional Japanese conventions regarding marriage. In a society with nearly universal marriage and strong institutions for arranging matches for convenience rather than love, it should not be too surprising that a radical leader arranges marriages to provide housekeeping services for his male followers or that a woman activist who can't get a passport in her own name arranges a legal marriage to get out of the country—or even that a loyal supporter enters a legal marriage to a person on death row not out of love, but to maintain essential support services. All three of these women have experienced both romantic love and legal marriage, but the two did not necessarily coincide.

Although none of the three women has been a conventional housewife, none was ever forced to make the sharp choice between marriage and career that faces so many bright and ambitious young Japanese women. They were thrust into doing both, and in retrospect, would not have wanted it any other way. Consequently, the three women's lives reflect the complex interweaving of public and private that confronts every women who is active outside her home. Each has had to make significant choices in her private life that were contingent upon the demands of her public life. Nagata had to cope with rape by her superior on the job and an abortion to terminate an ill-timed pregnancy. Shigenobu must take special precautions to protect her child's privacy. Shiomi Kazuko commuted hours each day to keep her son in safe and familiar surroundings, after she was effectively forced out of her school because of her political activity.

Despite their similarities with each other and with much larger categories of women, these three women who loved the left are also individuals with very different lives. There are real differences in personality, temperament, and style among them that belie any stereotyping of "the kind of women" who join the New Left. About the only thing they have in common is the personal honesty and openness that the New Left attracted and encouraged in its participants. The differences between these three women are revealed most sharply in their mass media images. Although all three came out of the same social movement and have been associated with more or less the same tiny part of it, their public images in the mass media reflect three fundamentally different stereotyped roles for women in Japan. As such, they reveal a great deal about the limits and trade-offs of the public roles permitted to contemporary Japanese women.

Shiomi Kazuko, despite being the wife of the leader of what was surely at one time the most feared radical group in Japan, comes across as an object lesson in *ryōsai kenbo* (good wife, wise mother) for our time. The message seems to be that no matter who you are married to and what happens to him, you can be a virtuous and loyal wife. Moreover, a virtuous and loyal wife will be respected and honored even by those who stand diametrically opposed to her husband's politics. What gets lost in this image is the fact that the virtuous and loyal wife is also a strong political actor in her own right; or perhaps it is simply that her political behavior, however distasteful, can be ignored so long as she shines in her wifely role.

Nagata Hiroko, in contrast, stands as the negative image of everything women are not supposed to be—aggressive, selfish, malicious, jealous, and cruel—even if most of these characteristics have nothing to do with Nagata's real personality. This negative characterization explains away the United Red Army's strange and incomprehensible purge as something that could not be carried out by ordinary people and deflects the blame away from males and politics. It produces an object lesson about the dangers of verbal aggression and sexual freedom for women. The characterization of Nagata as an evil person consumed by hideous private emotions negates her role as conscious political actor and leader in much the same way that Shiomi Kazuko's wifely virtuosity obscures her political leadership.

The mass media characterization of Shigenobu Fusako places both of these alternative images into better perspective. Though Shigenobu's role as wife and mother is downplayed, even hidden from public view, she is seen favorably both as leader and as sex object. Why is her image not negative like Nagata's? Precisely because she remains both feminine and elusive. Because she remains feminine, she can be permitted even political leadership, and because she remains unattainable, the political acts associated with her enhance her erotic power rather than devalue her as a madwoman. On both counts, her image sets a standard that is impossible for most women to attain. Lesser mortals like Shiomi Kazuko and Nagata Hiroko can be either good wives whose political and economic achievements are obscured and excused or she-devils whose warped emotions and sexual transgressions lead straight to the gallows.

These media images reflect a distinctly male view but may convey rather different, unintended messages to Japanese women. In addition, the relative balance of media coverage among the three women, combined with their own writings and other achievements, further subverts the messages.

Shiomi Kazuko is the least known of the three, as perhaps befits a model wife. She still turns up occasionally in media stories related to her husband, but she is not front-page news on her own account. The media image that is supposed to be the most positive is thus the least visible. Her own writings about life with Shiomi are humorous and insightful, but they circulate only within the narrow confines of the support group, and it seems unlikely that she will write for a wider audience. Shiomi is very protective of her privacy, but I have wondered if it is not his own domestic privacy that is really at issue. Consequently, despite her political past and her famous husband, nowadays Shiomi Kazuko is probably as widely known for being a schoolteacher, where she serves as a model of the working wife and mother with a serious professional career instead of just a part-time job. That image says you can have it all, without visible compromise.

Shigenobu Fusako's glamorous media image may seem remote and unattainable, but it may serve nonetheless as a highly attractive fantasy for both men and women. Though Shigenobu as media fantasy may titillate the male reader, to women she may appear as both free and powerful: a woman who has successfully defied convention in pursuit of her own goals. Women who read Shigenobu's autobiographical writings find not an exotic fantasy woman, but a real, down-to-earth person who writes about her unusual personal experiences with clarity and humor. Though Shigenobu does not reveal details that the police would like to know, she still offers the reader vivid glimpses of a likable, independent woman leading a life of genuine adventure. Few readers want to follow her to Beirut, but her example opens up a vast range of possibilities to dream about.

Even Nagata Hiroko has been able to subvert her negative media image through her own writings. The thousands of women who have read her books may not condone her involvement in the United Red Army purge, but they see her as a very different person from the crazed she-devil of her media caricature. Readers of her first books met a young woman of average circumstances with whom they could readily identify, talking openly about her relationships with men and describing how she was drawn into an increasingly bizarre series of experiences. Readers of her later books, including those readers introduced to her through Setouchi Harumi, found a woman courageously battling for her life and sustaining herself in the most unpromising of circumstances.

Thus, although mass media images are an important part of what these three women stand for in contemporary Japan, they themselves stubbornly resist being reduced to mere images. Through their own autobiographical writings, they present alternative personae to be set against the mass media images. Yet I want to resist the notion that the significance of these women can be reduced to a battle of competing texts. They are not media creations after all, nor even their own literary creations. At bottom, these three women who loved the left are real people whose choices and personal relationships intersected with chance and historical circumstance to produce uncommon lives. Their significance lies in those real lives and what they reveal about the constraints and opportunities that frame the choices other Japanese women make daily in their own, equally real, lives.

NOTES

My thanks to the Fulbright program, the Harry Frank Guggenheim Foundation, and the University of Hawaii Japanese Studies Endowment for the research support that has made this work possible.

1. Zenkyōtō is an acronym for Zengaku Kyōtō Kaigi, or All-Campus Joint Struggle Committee. These all-campus groups arose suddenly in 1968 and 1969. They represented a new form of student movement organization, created for the purpose of confronting the school administration over campus grievances and open to all students on an individual, voluntary basis. They differed deliberately from the existing New Left student sects, which had a campus base but were organized nationally and engaged heavily in protests over national political issues.

2. When eighty Red Army members in their shiny new red helmets were refused entry into the amphitheater and a fight broke out, someone came over to warn the two women that there was going to be trouble. Instructed to wait at a nearby coffee shop, the two friends chatted over their coffee until a call came that the coast was clear. They returned to the amphitheater, went inside without incident, and sold their entire stock of 1,000 copies of *Sekigun* at ¥100 apiece. Shiomi Kazuko, interviewed by the author, Tokyo April 30, 1983.

3. The group was better known by the name of its mass organization, Keihin Anpo Kyōtō, an acronym that translates as Tokyo-Yokohama Anti-Security Treaty Joint Struggle Committee.

4. The leadership of the Red Army Faction, for example, in their previous incarnation as members of Bund, had been heavily involved in the Tokyo University student movement and the formation of the Tōdai Zenkyōtō.

5. Ihara Saikaku's famous novel depicts *Kōshoku Gonin Onna* or *Five Women Who Loved Love* in William deBary's translation (Charles E. Tuttle Co., 1963), but I could only fit three women who loved the left into the space of this chapter.

6. Shiomi Kazuko, interview.

7. *Ibid.*

8. The Red Army had begun manufacturing crude pipe bombs, and fifty-three associates of the group had been arrested while engaging in guerrilla train-

ing in the mountains near Tokyo. After their arrest, it was discovered that they had been planning to kidnap the prime minister and hold him hostage to prevent him from traveling to the United States. Shiomi had not attended the guerrilla training, but there was a warrant out for his arrest because he had helped organize a banned demonstration several months earlier.

9. These were very serious felony charges, since the effect of the rarely applied law was to increase the penalty for various ordinary crimes when they were carried out for certain political purposes. Shiomi was one of only a handful of individuals against whom the law had ever been used.

10. Shiomi Kazuko, interview.

11. *Ibid.*

12. Shiomi Kazuko, "Rihabiri Tenmatsu Ki, 2" (Rehabilitation report number 2), *Fūsetsu* (Blizzard), no. 54 (August 15, 1992): 9–10.

13. The Japanese version of the Rip Van Winkle story is the tale of Urashima Tarō, a young fisherman who is lured out to a kingdom beneath the sea by a mermaid. When he returns to his home beach he discovers that generations have passed and his own drowning is only dimly remembered by the village.

14. Shiomi Takaya, " 'Myōnichi no Jō wa shinazu' saishūkai" ("Tomorrow's Joe isn't dead," final segment) *Shūkan Post* (Weekly post), April 27, 1990, 84.

15. Maruoka Osamu, *Kōan Keisatsu Nan'bo na Mon'ja?* (The security police, just who are they?) (Tokyo: Shinchōsha, 1990).

16. Nagata, Hiroko, *Jūroku no Bohyō* (Sixteen tombstones), vol. 1 (Tokyo: Sairyūsha, 1982), 15–24.

17. *Jūroku no Bohyō*, 64–72.

18. Criminal trials in Japan do not run continuously once they begin, but instead meet on a schedule of one or two half-day sessions a month. Defendants may be released at the discretion of the prosecutors, which in relatively minor political cases sometimes occurs after the prosecution has completed its case and argued for a particular sentence.

19. *Jūroku no Bohyō*, 114.

20. Nagata has Grave's disease, a hyperthyroid condition that she had thought would make pregnancy unlikely, but which also increased the risk of a difficult birth. Nagata's later interpretation of the situation is that at the time she justified the abortion for medical reasons because she was not sufficiently liberated to understand that she had a right to make the decision on other grounds.

21. Nagata, *Jūroku no Bohyō*, 160–162.

22. For a full account of the purge, see Steinhoff, P. G., "Death by Defeatism and Other Fables: The Psychosocial Dynamics of the Rengō Sekigun Purge" in *Japanese Social Organization*, ed. Takie Sugiyama Lebra (Honolulu: University of Hawaii Press, 1992).

23. Nagata consistently refers to her relationships with Sakaguchi and Mori as marriages, though it is doubtful that they were ever legally registered. Mori already had a wife and child in Tokyo when he proposed this arrangement.

24. In addition to the murder charges resulting from the United Red Army purge, Nagata was charged with complicity in the murders of two defecting members of her group who had been killed months earlier at Mori's casual suggestion.

25. Decision of the Tokyo District Court against Nagata Hiroko, Sakaguchi Hiroshi, and Uegaki Yasunari (United Red Army united trial), 223.

26. Medical experts with whom I have consulted feel that neither the Grave's disease nor the particular type of brain tumor she has would have been a causal factor in the purge, and neither condition would create mental abnormality. From numerous personal conversations over a ten-year period and reading her voluminous writings, I can attest that she is a lucid, intelligent woman whose thinking is not disordered and whose emotions appear to be well under control.

27. Setouchi Harumi, preface to *Watashi Ikitemasu* (I'm still alive), by Nagata Hiroko (Tokyo: Sairyūsha, 1986), ii.

28. Tamiya Takamaro, a seasoned political activist from Osaka who later led the Red Army hijacking to North Korea, came to Tokyo in 1968 to work as a labor organizer and was assigned to work with Shigenobu in the Ginza district. He was shocked to discover that his teammate was a beautiful, smartly dressed "bourgeois" young woman and their territory was office buildings full of middle-class salarymen; he went off in disgust to find some "real" laborers to organize. When they later worked together in the Red Army, Tamiya confessed to Shigenobu that he had misjudged her in their initial meeting. She replied that she hadn't thought much of him either and wondered "what the country bumpkin from Kansai was so stuck-up about." Tamiya Takamaro, "Rōdōsha no Naka e" (Among the workers), in *Hishō Nijuunen—"Yodogo" de Choson e* (Twenty years after the flight—to North Korea on the "Yodogo") eds. Tamiya Takamaro et al. (Tokyo: Shinchōsha, 1990), 47.

29. See Maruoka Osamu, "*Nihon Sekigunha* ni Tsuite" (Concerning *The Japanese Red Army Factions*) in *Za Pasupōto* (The Passport), no. 28, (September 18, 1992): 16. This statement by a member of the group who is now in jail in Japan was made in response to my published assertion based on other sources that the Red Army group in Lebanon had lost face because of the purge and felt impelled to carry out the attack when it was suggested by PFLP. See P. Steinhoff, *Nihon Sekigunha: Sono Shakaigakuteki Monogatari* (The Japanese Red Army Factions: A sociological tale) (Tokyo: Kawade Shobō Shinsha, 1991). Maruoka says the Japanese group chose a suicidal attack, and PFLP asked them to be taken prisoner instead. Whichever version is correct (and both may be true), it is clear that the attack was a direct response to the purge.

30. M. M., interviewed by the author, Tokyo, July 30, 1990.

31. This is according to the publisher in Japan, Endo Tadao, interviewed by the author, Tokyo, December 1990. This publication, *Chūtō Repōto*, (Middle East report) was available only by private subscription and ceased publication in 1994 following the Middle East peace accords between Israel and the Palestine Liberation Organization.

32. See Takagi Kikuro, *Nihon Sekigun o Mukae* (Going to meet the Japanese Red Army) (Tokyo: Gendai Hyōronsha, 1986).

Afterword

Gail Lee Bernstein

When I first drafted the introduction to *Recreating Japanese Women, 1600–1945*, I considered bringing readers up to date about changes in Japanese women's lives since 1945, but these were too great for me to tackle on my own and in the time allotted for publication. *Re-Imaging Japanese Women* confirms the wisdom of my decision not to address the lives of contemporary Japanese women, for, as we see, it has required the combined efforts of numerous scholars from several disciplines to document the multiplicity of female roles, goals, work, and lifestyles that characterizes Japanese society on the eve of the twenty-first century.

Although the composite portrait that emerged from the authors' "re-imaging" belies any lingering myth of the monolithic Japanese woman, the starting point for any discussion of Japanese women remains the ideal of the "good wife, wise mother," however embattled that ideal may be. A dichotomy remains, in society and in people's minds, between the public realm, defined generally as male, and the domestic realm, perceived as female, with separate gender socialization for each.

Furthermore, in the largely urban society of present-day Japan, the increase in prosperity has expanded opportunities for achieving a clear-cut gendered division of labor. In Meiji society, far fewer women could hope to approximate the ideal enviously described by contemporary farm women as being "just a housewife." In postwar society, not only can more women hope (or be expected) to follow this domestic ideal, but the job description for the homemaker has expanded to include management of considerable sums of household money, major consumer decisions, and extensive involvement in children's education. At the same time, the homemaker role continues to include the more traditional filial obligation of caring for the elderly, whose longevity (among Japanese women, the greatest in the world) can require middle-aged women to devote many years to nursing their elderly parents.

Woman's nurturing role is deemed so natural that, despite the demographic handwriting on the wall, the Japanese government continues to rely on female family members to solve the staggering problems caused by the combination of a large population of old people and a declining birthrate. In this sense, political leaders still expect the family (read: wife and mother) to serve the public function, first articulated in the Meiji period, of guardians of the nation's progress and social well-being. The expression "professional housewife," which captures not only women's devotion to hearth and home but the kind of vocational élan with which they perform their household obligations, helps explain in part why at least until recently, lacking assistance from overworked husbands, few women have attempted to combine marriage and career.

Nevertheless, the postwar changes charted in this book are significant. First, continued prosperity has eased the physical burdens of women even in rural areas and on remote islands. Second, the nuclear family is predominant, at least in the early years of a couple's marriage. Third, more married women have entered the workforce, even those who are the mothers of grade-school children. Finally, leisure activity for middle-aged and older women and for younger working women before marriage is the norm. Indeed, their fashionable clothes, overseas travel, diverse hobbies, and expanded educational opportunities have created more jobs for women, because eighty percent of the consumer market is female. These factors may explain the common perception in Japan, according to Lock, that middle-aged Japanese women live in "women's heaven."

Japanese women have several ways to modify or bypass the societal norm of the full-time, professional housewife without mobilizing an outright assault on it. They can marry late, as they have been doing in recent years: Japan's age of first marriage for women is the highest in the world. They can choose to have fewer children: Japan's fertility rate is among the lowest in the world. Women can experience either work or leisure or a combination of both before and after their child-rearing years. If they also choose to (or must) work while their children are young, as do thirty-four percent of women between the ages of twenty-four and thirty-four, then among their possible options is to live with parents or in-laws and turn child care largely over to them, a traditional practice among Japanese families that, as several chapters here attest, may serve the needs of all concerned.

Although family obligations, from one point of view, may appear to weigh down contemporary women, viewed from another perspective the Japanese family remains a flexible institution that cares for members of all ages and accommodates a variety of living arrangements. Rather than seeing women as totally constrained by societal expectations that define a managerial role for them within the household and therefore force them to flee the family in order to fulfill themselves, it may be more accurate to say that contemporary Japanese women can negotiate their role much the way one rearranges physical space within the traditional Japanese house, by sliding open certain walls at certain times and keeping others closed. By manipulating age at marriage, fertility, and marital residence patterns and by managing the household budget, women can create space (education, hobbies, travel, leisure, part-time work, and even careers) for themselves in the course of their life.

The Japanese woman's answer to the late twentieth-century American woman's dilemma about how to "have it all" may be to have at least some of it sequentially, rather than simultaneously, and to take advantage of options rather than engage in open revolt. In present-day Japanese society, independence (including romance) is permissible before marriage and children.[1] In later years there is time again for travel, study (of the tea ceremony or a foreign language or French cooking or piano), friendships, and other activities that permit self-development and self-expression. Self-fulfillment and autonomy thus become not issues forming an ideological manifesto or feminist agenda but experiences in certain stages of life, tried on like the several wedding dresses worn by a Japanese bride.

Opportunities for self-expression, self-development, a modicum of autonomy, and discretionary power are more numerous for women of high status with husbands who have good incomes; indeed, alternatives to the status quo ironically accrue to precisely those women who marry well and stay married. Such women tend to be more highly educated: as in the past, parents invest in their daughters' education to enhance their marriage prospects, and once married, the highly educated woman tends to stay home after child rearing. But what about those who do not marry at all or who want to advance in the world of business, government, or the professions—the "man's world"? Authors in this volume found that such paths are not encouraged: women's magazines equate freedom, individual choice, and fulfillment of personal desire with leisure and consumption, not with full-time, skilled, professional work or a political career. Although this volume presents evidence that marriage and child rearing as universal goals for all women are being questioned in popular magazines geared to young women and in books with such titles as *The "Maybe I Won't Marry" Syndrome*, the small percentage of women who never marry, Creighton concludes, "evoke pity at best and social rebuke at worst." Women in managerial positions tend not to marry, but rather than serving as professional role models, they discourage the career aspirations of younger women workers, who consider them pathetic.

Another group of women avoiding the norm of marriage and motherhood consists of bar hostesses, who work in one of the very few arenas, Mock argues, "where Japanese women can gain economic and social independence." Among poorly educated women, who cannot enter the white-collar world, hostessing may be the only way to achieve "even a modicum of individual independence."

This is not to say that all women crave professional careers or even full-time, paid employment. Over fifty percent of housewives polled in 1994 endorsed the sexual division of labor that placed women exclusively in the home.[2] Not all women want to function in the public sphere, "exposed", as Mori's tea ceremony teachers put it, to criticism, nor do they wish to turn over their children to their parents' care, work the long hours of men, or have the problems and responsibilities of managerial-level workers. Presumably they also prefer to avoid the sexual harassment, marginalization, and trivialization experienced by many of the women workers described in this book. For them, not resistance but flexible adjustment seems a more attractive route to the fulfillment of both family obligations and personal needs, a route promising more rewards and less conflict, stress, and frustration.

If demography becomes destiny, however, the homemaker role, even a "modified" one with a part-time job on the side, may prove to be a luxury. With fewer young people, Japan will need their well-educated women both to ease the labor shortage and to support the elderly. Unlike prewar and wartime government efforts to manipulate reproduction rates, policymakers' attempts in the early 1990s to encourage women to bear more children fell on deaf ears. Joking references to the homemaker's life as "three meals and a nap" may signal a perceived need for change in the domestic norm for women.

The availability of "multiple and competing sets of ideas and practices," as Rosenberger writes, means that women in the 1990s were already prepared to "switch between alternative positions." However, in the absence of another, more persuasive model, it remains to be seen exactly how (and by whom) the primacy of Japanese women's "housewife-breeder-feeder role" will be questioned and what new definition of womanhood will replace it.[3] One possibility is a return to the more cooperative family ideal observed among commoners in the Tokugawa period and described in *Recreating Japanese Women*, when the gendered division of labor was not yet well rooted and husbands and wives shared productive and reproductive work.[4]

This volume presents ample evidence of such distinctively gendered concerns as unequal pay, glass ceilings, assigned nurturing roles, paternalistic male bosses and bureaucrats, and barricaded political power circles. Yet the conflicting images also described in this book demonstrate the opportunities Imamura sees for expanding women's behavioral choices. These choices extend to political activity of various kinds, including mainstream politics, radical engagement, and various movements to promote women's rights and chart new courses.[5] Choice might also mean "refusing to play the game"—the theme of certain popular literature writers whose female protagonists' expression of anger and discontent is itself a form of rebellion that reminds us of the potential pain inherent in both accepting received notions of womanhood and in contesting them.

The varied images and viewpoints presented in these essays will, I hope, help track alterations in contemporary Japanese women's lives through the eyes of the women themselves. Certainly what we have repeatedly seen from our historical as well as contemporary studies of Japanese women is that, despite notions of innate gender roles, gender has been continuously recreated and re-imaged.

NOTES

1. Contemporary literature and pornography depict women engaging in extramarital sexual liaisons as well, but it is hard to measure the extent to which these represent actual fulfillment of desire rather than fantasy.

2. The poll results, released by the Health and Welfare Ministry and reported in the *Japan Times*, weekly international edition, January 2–15, 1995, also found that almost seventy percent of housewives "would prefer their husbands to share equally household chores and child-rearing duties."

3. This term is used by Gerda Lerner, in *The Majority Finds Its Past: Placing Women in History* (New York: Oxford University Press, 1979), p. 114. Lerner argues that the confinement of woman to a sex-linked domestic role "has been the key element in her subordination in all her other societal roles."

4. I am grateful to Matsui Machiko for articulating this point in "Changes and Continuity in Gender Role Perceptions of Japanese Women," unpublished ms.

5. See Kathleen S. Uno, "The Death of 'Good Wife, Wise Mother'?" in Andrew Gordon, ed., *Postwar Japan as History* (Berkeley: University of California Press, 1993), 293–322.

NOTES ON CONTRIBUTORS

Anne Allison, assistant professor in the Department of Cultural Anthropology at Duke University, works on issues of sex and gender in contemporary Japan. Among her publications are: *Nightwork: Sexuality, Pleasure, and Corporate Masculinity in a Tokyo Hostess Club* (University of Chicago Press, 1994), which examines corporate entertainment in hostess clubs, and a collection of essays on parents and children in Japan, which is forthcoming from Westview Press.

Nobuko Awaya, lecturer at Tokai University, is also a translator, interpreter, and freelance journalist in Japan and the United States. Her publications include numerous articles on women's issues, men's issues, and cross-cultural understanding between Japan and Western Cultures. She is the author of *Onna Kodomo Ga Nihon o Kaeru* (Women and children are changing Japan) (PHP Institute, 1991), a book that explores the changing social roles of women and children, and translations of John Lee's *The Flying Boy*, a book about men's issues, and *Shy-Man Syndrome*, by Dr. Brian G. Gilmartin.

Gail Lee Bernstein, professor of history at the University of Arizona, is the author of *Haruko's World: A Japanese Farm Woman and Her Community* (Stanford University Press, 1983) and the editor of *Recreating Japanese Women, 1600–1945* (University of California Press, 1991). She is currently writing the history of a Japanese family, centered on six sisters.

Millie R. Creighton, associate professor of anthropology at the University of British Columbia, specializes in the study of Japanese society. She lived in Japan for four years while conducting research on Japanese department stores.

Sally Ann Hastings, associate professor of history at Purdue University, is the author of *Neighborhood and Nation in Tokyo, 1905–1937* (University of Pittsburgh Press, 1995) and of several articles on women's history.

Anne E. Imamura, chair of Asian Studies, Foreign Service Institute, United States Department of State, is a sociologist who has taught at Georgetown University, the University of Maryland, Sophia University in Tokyo, and the University of Malaya. She is the author of *Urban Japanese Housewives: At Home and in the Community* (University of Hawaii Press, 1987) and articles on Japanese women, urban community, and international marriage in Japan and in Nigeria.

Margaret Lock, professor in the departments of anthropology and social studies of medicine at McGill University, is the author of *East Asian Medicine in Urban Japan: Varieties of Medical Experience* (University of California Press, 1980), translated into Japanese as *Toshi Bunka to Toyoigaku* (Shibunkaku, 1990), and *Encounters with Aging: Mythologies of Menopause in Japan and North America* (University of California Press, 1993), which won the Eileen Basker Memorial Prize and the Canada-Japan Book award and was a finalist for the Hiromi Arisawa Award. Lock has edited three other books and written over ninety scholarly articles. Her present research is a comparative study in Japan and North America on changing concepts of life and death as a result of new medical technologies.

Susan Orpett Long teaches anthropology and East Asian Studies at John Carroll University, where she also coordinates the East Asian Studies Program. She has done research on the Japanese medical system and issues of women and family. Her publications include *Family Change and the Life Course in Japan* (Cornell University East Asia Papers, 1987) and articles on attitudes toward cancer, physician-nurse relationships, and home caregiving for the frail elderly in Japan. She is currently conducting research on bioethics and culture in Japan and the United States.

Robert J. Marra is executive director of the National Association of Japan-America Societies, Inc. He previously served as associate executive director for the Japan–U.S. Friendship Commission and taught at the University of Maryland. He lived for several years in Japan while completing his dissertation research for the University of Pittsburgh.

John Mock, associate professor and chair, department of Japan Area Studies, Minnesota State University—Akita, Japan, has done fieldwork in Hokkaido and the Tohoku and Kansai areas of Japan and taught at a variety of institutions in Japan and the United States. His publications include articles on Hokkaido, the significance of the Japanese castle town, and Japanese neighborhoods.

Barbara Lynne Rowland Mori, associate professor of sociology at California Polytechnic State University—San Luis Obispo, conducted her research on *chadō* in Japan from 1983 through 1985. She is the author of *Americans Learning the Japanese Tea Ceremony: The Internationalization of a Traditional Art* (Mellen Research University Press, 1992)

Andrew A. Painter teaches anthropology at Mukogawa Women's University—Kyoto, Japan. He is currently doing research on Japanese television audiences and working on documentary and experimental video production.

David P. Phillips, assistant professor in the East Asian Languages and Literatures department at Wake Forest University, has a background in urban planning, Asian studies, and anthropology. He spent several years in Japan, first with the JET program and later at the Inter-University Center and a private consulting firm, and he has conducted research on Japanese architectural history at Kyoto University. His current research includes work on the use of film in Asian education, gender roles in the workplace, and Japanese urban history.

Glenda S. Roberts is associate professor of anthropology at the University of Hawaii at Manoa. After holding research positions at the University of Hawaii at Manoa and at the East West Center, she undertook a study of Japan's Silver Human Resource Centers under the auspices of a Japan Foundation Professional Fellowship. She is the author of *Staying on the Line: Blue-Collar Women in Contemporary Japan* (University of Hawaii Press, 1994). Her latest research concerns the role of nongovernmental organizations in addressing the problems of undocumented immigrant workers in Japan.

Nancy R. Rosenberger, associate professor of anthropology at Oregon State University, is the editor of *The Japanese Sense of Self* and the author of numerous articles on Japanese women. She is writing a book on meaning and empowerment in the lives of Japanese women within the framework of state policies and women's magazines. Her current research is on young single women above marriage age in Japan and Korea.

Patricia G. Steinhoff is professor of sociology at the University of Hawaii, where she was formerly director of the Center for Japanese Studies. She is the author of *Tenko: Ideology and Societal Integration in Prewar Japan* (Garland, 1991) and *Nihon Sekingunha: Sono Shakaigakuteki Monogatari* (Kawade Shobo Shinsha, 1991). She is coeditor (with Ellis Krauss and Thomas Rohlen) of *Conflict in Japan* (University of Hawaii Press, 1984).

FURTHER READING

Adlercreutz, Herman, Esa Hämäläinen, Sherwood Gorback, and Barry Goldin. "Dietary phyto-oestrogens and the menopause in Japan." *The Lancet* 339 (1992): 1233.

Allison, Anne. "Japanese Mothers and *Obentōs:* The LunchBox as Ideological State Apparatus." *Anthropological Quarterly* 64, no. 1 (1991): 41–66.

Anderson, Jennifer. *An Introduction to the Tea Ceremony.* New York: State University of New York Press, 1991.

Anderson, Stephen. "Beyond the Developmental State: Welfare, Wage-earners, and Public Pensions in Japan." Paper presented at the Association for Asian Studies, New Orleans, April 12, 1991.

Bachnik, Jane M. "Recruitment Strategies for Household Succession: Rethinking Japanese Household Organization." *Man* 18 (1983): 160–182.

Befu, Harumi. *Japan: An Anthropological Introduction.* San Francisco: Chandler, 1971.

Benedict, Ruth. *The Chrysanthemum and the Sword.* New York: Meridian, 1946.

Bernstein, Gail Lee. *Recreating Japanese Women, 1600–1945.* Berkeley: University of California Press, 1991.

Berton, Peter. "The Japan Communist Party: The 'Lovable' Party." In *The Japanese Party System.* 2nd ed. Edited by Ronald J. Hrebenar. Boulder, Colorado: Westview Press, 1992.

Bestor, Theodore C. *Neighborhood Tokyo.* Stanford: Stanford University Press, 1989.
———— "Tradition and Japanese Social Organization: Institutional Development in a Tokyo Neighborhood." *Ethnology* 24 (1985): 121–135.

Boocock, Sarane Spence. "Controlled Diversity: An Overview of the Japanese Preschool System." *The Journal of Japanese Studies* 15, no. 1 (winter 1989): 41–66.

Bornoff, Nicholas. *Pink Samurai: Love, Marriage & Sex in Contemporary Japan.* New York: Pocket Books. 1991.

Brines, Russell. *MacArthur's Japan.* Philadelphia: J. B. Lippincott, 1948.

Brinton, Mary C. "Christmas Cakes and Wedding Cakes: The Social Organization of Japanese Women's Life Course." In *Japanese Social Organization.* Edited by Takie Sugiyama Lebra. Honolulu: University of Hawaii Press, 1992.

———— "The Socio-Institutional Bases of Gender Stratification: Japan as an Illustrative Case." *American Journal of Sociology* 94, no. 2 (1988): 300–334.

———— *Women and the Economic Miracle: Gender and Work in Postwar Japan.* Berkeley: University of California Press, 1993.

Brown, Keith. "The Content of *Dozoku* Relationships in Japan." *Ethnology* 7 (1968): 113–38.

———— "*Dozoku* and the Ideology of Descent in Rural Japan." *American Anthropologist* 68 (1966): 1129–1148.

Calder, Kent. *Crisis and Compensation.* Princeton: Princeton University Press, 1988.

Campbell, Ruth. "Nursing Homes and Long-term Care in Japan." *Pacific Affairs* 57 (1983): 78–79.

Campbell, Ruth and E. M. Brody. "Women's Changing Roles and Help to the Elderly: Attitudes of Women in the United States and Japan." *The Gerontologist* 25 (1985): 584–592.

Castile, Rand. *The Way of Tea.* Tokyo: Charles Tuttle, 1976.

Caudill, William. "The Cultural and Interpersonal Context of Everyday Health and Illness in Japan and America." In *Asian Medical Systems: A Comparative Study.* Edited by Charles Leslie. Berkeley: University of California Press, 1976.

Caudill, William and Helen Weinstein. "Maternal Care and Infant Behavior in Japan and America." *Psychiatry* 32 (1969): 12–43.

Christensen, Raymond V. "Electoral Reform in Japan: How It Was Enacted and Changes It May Bring." *Asian Survey* 34 (1994): 589–605.

Clark, Rodney. *The Japanese Company.* New Haven: Yale University Press, 1979.

Coleman, Samuel. *Family Planning in Japanese Society: Traditional Birth Control in a Modern Urban Culture.* Princeton: Princeton University Press, 1983.

Creighton, Millie R. "Contemporary Japanese Women: Employment and Consumer Roles." In *Canadian Perspectives on Modern Japan.* Edited by T. G. McGee, Kate Elliot, and Bev Lee. Vancouver: University of British Columbia Institute of Asian Research, 1990.

Deal, William. "Japan as an Aging Society." Presentation in panel discussion at the conference on Dementia: Moral Values and Policy Choices in an Aging Society. University Hospital of Cleveland Alzheimers Center, April 27, 1990.

De Becker, J. E. *The Nightless City.* Tokyo, Charles E. Tuttle Co., 1971.

Doi, Takeo. *The Anatomy of Dependence.* Tokyo: Kodansha, 1973.

Duke, Benjamin. *The Japanese School: Lessons for Industrial America.* New York: Praeger, 1986.

Edwards, Walter. *Modern Japan through Its Weddings: Gender, Person, and Society in Ritual Portrayal.* Stanford: Stanford University Press, 1989.

Ehara, Yumiko. "Japanese Feminism in the 1970s and 1980s." *U.S.–Japan Women's Journal English Supplement* 4 (1993): 50–51.

Eto, Jun. "The Breakdown of Motherhood is Wrecking our Children." *Japan Echo* 6 (1979): 102–109.

Fallows, Deborah. "Japanese Women." *National Geographic* 177, no. 4 (1990): 52–83.

Field, Norma. "Child Labor in Prosperity: The Implications of the Japanese Schooling Crisis." Paper presented at the Children at Risk conference in Bergen, Norway, May, 1992.

Fujita, Mariko. " 'It's All Mother's Fault': Childcare and Socialization of Working Mothers in Japan." *Journal of Japanese Studies* 15, no. 1 (1989): 67–91.

Garon, Sheldon. "Women's Groups and the Japanese State: Contending Approaches to Political Integration, 1890–1945." *Journal of Japanese Studies* 19, no. 1 (winter 1993): 5–41.

Gluck, Carol. *Japan's Modern Myths: Ideology in the Late Meiji Period.* Princeton: Princeton University Press, 1985.

——— "The Meaning of Ideology in Modern Japan." In *Rethinking Japan.* Edited by A. Boscaro, F. Gatti, and M. Raveri. Folkestone: Japan Library Ltd., 1990.

Hakuhodo Institute of Life and Living. *Japanese Women in Turmoil: Changing Lifestyles in Japan.* Tokyo: Hakuhodo Institute of Life and Living, 1984.

Hamabata, Matthews Masayuki. *Crested Kimono: Power and Love in the Japanese Business Family.* Ithaca: Cornell University Press, 1990.

Hane, Mikiso. *Peasants, Rebels, and Outcasts: The Underside of Modern Japan.* New York: Pantheon Books, 1982.

Harootunian, H. D. "Visible Discourses/Invisible Ideologies." In *Postmodernism and Japan.* Edited by M. Miyoshi and H. D. Harootunian. Durham: Duke University Press, 1989.

Harris, Phyllis Braudy and Susan O. Long. "Daughter-in-Law's Burden: An Exploratory Study of Caregiving in Japan." *Journal of Cross-Cultural Gerontology* 8 (June 1993): 97–118.

Hastings, Sally A. *Neighborhood and Nation in Tokyo, 1905–1937.* Pittsburgh: University of Pittsburgh Press, 1995.

Hayashi, Mariko. *Once a Year.* Tokyo: Kadokawa Shoten, 1992.

Hayashi, Yoko. "Women in the Legal Profession in Japan." *U.S.–Japan Women's Journal English Supplement* 2 (1992): 16–27.

Hendry, Joy. *Becoming Japanese: The World of the Preschool Child.* Honolulu: University of Hawaii Press, 1986.

Hibbitt, Howard. *The Floating World in Japanese Fiction.* Oxford: Oxford University Press, 1959.

Higuchi, Keiko. "The PTA—A Channel for Political Activism." *Japan Interpreter* 11 (1975): 56–67.

——— "Women at Home." *Japan Echo* 12 (1985): 51–57.

Horio, Teruhisa. *Educational Thought and Ideology in Modern Japan: State Authority and Intellectual Freedom.* Translated by Steven Platzer. Tokyo: University of Tokyo Press, 1988.

Hrebenar, Ronald J. *The Japanese Party System.* Boulder, Colorado: Westview Press, 1992.

Ihara, Saikaku. *Five Women Who Loved Love.* Translated by William de Bary. Tokyo: Charles E. Tuttle Co., 1963.

——— *The Life of an Amorous Woman and Other Writings.* Translated and edited by Ivan Morris. New York: New Directions, 1963.

Imamura, Anne E. "The Active Urban Housewife: Structurally Induced Motivation for Increased Community Participation." In *Proceedings of the Tokyo Symposium on Women.* Edited by Merry White and Barbara Malony. Tokyo: International Group for the Study of Women, 1978.

———— *Urban Japanese Housewives: At Home and in the Community*. Honolulu, University of Hawaii Press, 1987.

Ishimoto, Shidzue. *Facing Two Ways: The Story of My Life*. Stanford: Stanford University Press, 1984.

Iwai, Tomoaki. " 'The Madonna Boom': Women in the Japanese Diet." *Journal of Japanese Studies* 19 (winter 1993): 103–120.

Iwao, Sumiko. *The Japanese Woman: Traditional Image and Changing Reality*. New York: The Free Press, 1993.

Jackson, Laura. "Bar Hostesses." In *Women in Changing Japan*. Edited by Joyce Lebra, Joy Paulson, and Elizabeth Powers. Stanford: Stanford University Press, 1976.

Johnson, Chalmers. "Tanaka Kakuei, Structural Corruption, and the Advent of Machine Politics in Japan." *Journal of Japanese Studies* 12, no. 1 (1986): 17.

Kato Shūichi. "Notes on Tea Ceremony." In *Form, Style, Tradition: Reflections on Japanese Art and Society*. Translated by John Bester. Tokyo: Kodansha International, 1975.

Kawai, Hayao. "Violence in the Home: Conflict between Two Principles—Maternal and Paternal." *Japan Quarterly* 28 (1981): 370–378.

Kelly, William. "Rationalization and Nostalgia: Cultural Dynamics of New Middle-Class Japan." *American Ethnologist* 13 (1986): 603–618.

Kiefer, Christie W. "The Elderly in Modern Japan: Elite, Victims, or Plural Players?" In *The Cultural Context of Aging*. Edited by J. Sokolovsky. New York: Bergin and Garvey Publishers, 1990.

Kline, Stephen, "The Theatre of Consumption: On Comparing American and Japanese Advertising." *Canadian Journal of Political and Social Theory* 12, no. 3 (1988): 101–120.

Kondo, Dorinne. *Crafting Selves: Power, Gender, and Discourses of Identity in a Japanese Workplace*. Chicago: University of Chicago Press, 1990.

———— "Symbolic Analysis of the 'Way of Tea.' " *Man*, n.s., 20, no. 2 (1985): 287–306.

Krauss, Ellis S., Thomas P. Rohlen, and Patricia G. Steinhoff, eds. *Conflict in Japan*. Honolulu: University of Hawaii Press, 1984.

Kumagai, Fumie. "Filial violence: A Peculiar Parent-Child Relationship in the Japanese Family Today." *Journal of Comparative Family Studies* 12, Special Issue (summer 1981): 337–350.

Kuzume, Yoshi. "Images of Japanese Women in U.S. Writings and Scholarly Works, 1860–1990." *U.S.-Japan Women's Journal English Supplement* 1 (August 1991): 6–50.

Lebra, Takie Sugiyama. *Above the Clouds: Status Culture of the Modern Japanese Nobility*. Berkeley: University of California Press, 1992.

———— "Gender and Culture in the Japanese Political Economy: Self-Portrayals of Prominent Businesswomen." In *Cultural and Social Dynamics*. vol. 3 of *The Political Economy of Japan*. Edited by S. Kumon and H. Rosovsky. Stanford: Stanford University Press, 1992.

———— *Japanese Women: Constraint and Fulfillment*. Honolulu: University of Hawaii Press, 1984.

———— "Japanese Women in Male-dominant Careers." *Ethnology* 20, no. 4 (1981): 291–306.

Lebra, Takie Sugiyama and William P. Lebra. *Japanese Culture and Behavior*. Rev. ed. Honolulu: University of Hawaii Press, 1986.

Ling, Yuriko and Azusa Matsuno. "Women's Struggle for Empowerment in Japan." In *Women Transforming Politics: Worldwide Strategies for Empowerment*. Edited by Jill M. Bystydzienski. Bloomington, Indiana: Indiana University Press, 1992.

Lo, Jeannie. *Office Ladies/Factory Women: Life and Work at a Japanese Company*. Armonk, New York: M. E. Sharpe, 1990.

Lock, Margaret. "Ambiguities of Aging: Japanese Experience and Perceptions of Menopause." In *Culture, Medicine, and Psychiatry*. Edited by A. Kleinman. Dordrecht, Netherlands: D. Reidel Publishing Company, 1986.

———— *Encounters with Aging: Mythologies of Menopause in Japan and North America*. Berkeley: University of California Press, 1993.

———— "Flawed Jewels and National Dis/Order: Narratives on Adolescent Dissent in Japan." *The Journal of Psychohistory* 18 (1991): 507–531.

———— "A Nation at Risk: Interpretations of School Refusal in Japan." In *Biomedicine Examined*. Edited by Margaret Lock and Deborah A. Gordon. Dordrecht, Netherlands: Kluwer Academic Publishers, 1988.

———— "New Japanese Mythologies: Faltering Discipline and the Ailing Housewife in Japan." *American Ethnologist* 15 (1988): 43–61.

———— "Protests of a Good Wife and Wise Mother: The Medicalization of Distress in Japan." In *Health, Illness, and Medical Care in Japan*. Edited by Edward Norbeck and Margaret Lock. Honolulu: University of Hawaii Press, 1987.

Lock, Margaret, Patricia Neiland Kaufert, and Penny Gilbert. "Cultural Construction of the Menopausal Syndrome: The Japanese Case." *Maturitas* 10 (1988): 317–332.

Long, Susan O. "Roles, Careers, and Femininity in Biomedicine: Women Physicians and Nurses in Japan." *Social Science and Medicine* 22 (1986): 81–90.

———— *Family Change and the Life Course in Japan*. Ithaca: Cornell University East Asia Papers, No. 44, 1987.

Long, Susan O. and Phyllis Braudy Harris. "Festival for a Cause: Culture and Participant Mobilization in a Japanese Social Welfare Movement." *Sociological Focus* 26, 1993, 47–63.

Long, Susan O. and Noriko Iwai. "Personal Patriarchies: Women's Employment and Marital Relations in Japan." Paper presented at the annual meeting of the American Anthropological Association, New Orleans, December 2, 1990.

Maeda, D. "Family Care in Japan." *The Gerontologist* 23 (1983): 579–583.

Maeda, D., K. Teshima, H. Sugisawa, and Y. S. Asakura. "Aging and Health in Japan." *Journal of Cross-Cultural Gerontology* 4 (1989): 143–162.

Martin, Linda G. "The Graying of Japan." *Population Bulletin* 44, no. 12 (1989): 1–41.

Mason, R. H. P. *Japan's First General Election, 1890*. London: Cambridge University Press, 1969.

Mayer, Adrian C. "The Significance of Quasi-Groups in the Study of Complex Societies." In *Social Networks in Urban Situations*. Edited by J. C. Mitchell. Manchester: Manchester University Press, 1969.

Matsumoto, Nancy. "Women Who Don't Need Men." *PHP Intersect* 4 (October 1988): 42–43.

Miyake, Yoshiko. "Doubling Expectations: Motherhood and Women's Factory Work under State Management in Japan in the 1930s and 1940s." In *Recreating Japanese Women, 1600–1945*. Edited by Gail Lee Bernstein. Berkeley: University of California Press, 1991.

Mochida, Takeshi. "Focus on the Family" Editorial Comment. *Japan Echo* 3 (1980): 75–76.

Mock, John. *Social Change in an Urban Neighborhood: A Case Study in Sapporo, Japan.* Ph.D. dissertation, Michigan State University, 1980.

Moeran, Brian. "Individual, Group, and Seishin: Japan's Internal Cultural Debate." *Man* 19 (1984): 252–266.

Mori, Barbara Lynne Rowland. *Chadō: A Symbolic Interactionist Analysis of Transmission, Adaptation, and Change.* Ph.D. dissertation, University of Hawaii, August 1988.

——— "The Tea Ceremony: A Transformed Japanese Ritual." *Gender & Society* 5, no. 1 (March 1991): 86–97.

Nagy, Margit. "Middle Class Working Women during the Interwar Years." In *Recreating Japanese Women, 1600–1945*. Edited by Gail Lee Bernstein. Berkeley: University of California Press, 1991.

Nakane, Chie. *Japanese Society.* Los Angeles: University of California Press, 1970.

Nolte, Sharon and Sally Ann Hastings. "The Meiji State's Policy toward Women, 1890–1910." In *Recreating Japanese Women, 1600–1945*. Edited by Gail Lee Bernstein. Berkeley: University of California Press, 1991.

Ogawa, Naohiro. "Population Aging and Medical Demand: The Case of Japan." In *Economic and Social Implications of Population Aging. Proceedings of the International Symposium on Population Structure and Development, Tokyo.* New York: United Nations, 1988.

Ohnuki-Tierney, Emiko. *Illness and Culture in Contemporary Japan: An Anthropological View.* Cambridge: Cambridge University Press, 1984.

Okakura, Kakuzo. *The Book of Tea.* New York: Dover Publications, 1964.

Okamura, Masu. *Changing Japan: Women's Status.* Tokyo: The International Society for Educational Information, 1973.

Painter, Andrew. "Japanese Daytime Television, Popular Culture, and Ideology." *The Journal of Japanese Studies* 19, no. 2 (1993): 26–67.

Peak, Lois. *Learning to Go to School in Japan: The Transition from Home to Preschool Life.* Berkeley: University of California Press, 1991.

Perry, Linda. "Being Socially Anomalous: Wives and Mothers without Husbands." In *Adult Episodes in Japan.* Edited by David W. Plath. Leiden: E. J. Brill, 1975.

Pharr, Susan J. *Losing Face: Status Politics in Japan.* Berkeley: University of California Press, 1990.

——— *Political Women in Japan: The Search for a Place in Political Life.* Berkeley: University of California Press, 1981.

Plath, David W. *The After Hours: Modern Japan and the Search for Enjoyment.* Berkeley: University of California Press, 1964.

——— *Long Engagements.* Stanford: Stanford University Press, 1980.

———— "My-Car-Isma: Motorizing the Showa Self." *Daedalus,* Special Issue, *Showa: the Japan of Hirohito.* (summer, 1990): 229–244.

Porter, Hal. *The Actors: An Image of the New Japan.* London: Angus and Robertson, Ltd., 1968.

Prestowitz, Clyde. *Trading Places: How We Allowed Japan to Take the Lead.* New York: Basic Books, 1988.

Ramsey, S. "To Hear One and Understand Ten: Nonverbal Behavior in Japan." In *Intercultural Communication.* 4th ed. Edited by L. A. Samovar and R. E. Porter. Belmont, Calif.: Wadsworth Publishing Co. 1985.

Reed, Steven R. *Japan Election Data: The House of Representatives, 1947–1990.* Ann Arbor, Michigan: The Center for Japanese Studies, The University of Michigan, 1992.

Reischauer, Edwin O. *The Japanese Today: Continuity and Change.* Cambridge: Belknap Press of Harvard University Press, 1988.

Richie, Donald and Kenkichi Ito. *The Erotic Gods.* Tokyo: Zufushinsha, 1967.

Roberts, Glenda S. *Staying on the Line: Blue-Collar Women in Contemporary Japan.* Honolulu: University of Hawaii Press, 1994.

Robins-Mowry, Dorothy. *The Hidden Sun: Women of Modern Japan.* Boulder: Westview Press, 1983.

Rodd, Laurel Rasplica. "Yosano Akiko and the Taishō Debate over the 'New Woman.' " In *Recreating Japanese Women, 1600–1945.* Edited by Gail Lee Bernstein. Berkeley: University of California Press, 1991.

Rohlen, Thomas P. *For Harmony and Strength: Japanese White-Collar Organization in Anthropological Perspective.* Los Angeles: University of California Press, 1974.

———— "Order in Japanese Society: Attachment, Authority, and Routine." *The Journal of Japanese Studies* 15, no. 1 (1989): 5–40.

———— " 'Permanent Employment' Faces Recession, Slow Growth, and an Aging Work Force." *Journal of Japanese Studies* 5, no. 2 (1979): 235–272.

Rosenberger, Nancy. "Gender and the Japanese State: Pension Benefits Creating Difference." *Anthropological Quarterly* 64, no. 4 (1991): 178–94.

———— "Japan's Youth Economy: Messages about Freedom and Status in the Mass Media." Paper given at the Association for Asian Studies, New Orleans, La., 1991.

———— "Status, Individuality, and Leisure: Messages of Western Styles in Japanese Home Magazines." In *Remade in Japan.* Edited by J. Tobin. New Haven, Conn.: Yale University Press, 1992.

Ross, Philip D., Hiromichi Norimatsu, James W. Davis, Katsuhiko Yano, Richard D. Wasnick, Saeko Fukiwara, Yutaka Hosoda, and L. Joseph Melton. "A Comparison of Hip Fracture Incidence among Native Japanese, Japanese Americans, and American Caucasians." *American Journal of Epidemiology* 133 (1991): 801–809.

Sadler, A. L. *Cha-No-Yu: The Japanese Tea Ceremony.* Tokyo: Charles Tuttle and Castile Rand, 1962.

Salamon, Sonya. " 'Male Chauvinism' as a Manifestation of Love in Marriage." In *Adult Episodes in Japan.* Edited by David W. Plath. Leiden: Brill, 1975.

Saso, Mary. *Women in the Japanese Workplace.* London: Hilary Shipman, 1990.

Sawachi, Hisae. "The Political Awakening of Women." *Japan Quarterly.* 36 (1989): 381–385.

Sen Sōshitsu, ed. *Chanōyu: The Urasenke Tradition of Tea.* Translated by Alfred Birnbaum. Kyoto and New York: Weatherhill, 1989.

Serizawa, Motoko. "Aspects of an Aging Society." In *Review of Japanese Culture and Society.* 3 (1989): 37–46.

Sievers, Sharon. *Flowers in Salt: The Beginnings of Feminist Consciousness in Modern Japan.* Stanford: Stanford University Press, 1983.

Smith, Robert J. *Ancestor Worship in Contemporary Japan.* Stanford: Stanford University Press, 1974.

————— "Gender Inequality in Contemporary Japan." *The Journal of Japanese Studies* 13, no. 1 (winter 1987): 1–25.

————— *Japanese Society: Tradition, Self, and the Social Order.* Cambridge: Cambridge University Press, 1983.

Smith, Robert J. and Ella Lury Wiswell. *The Women of Suye Mura.* Chicago: University of Chicago Press, 1982.

Smith, Stephen R. "For the Sake of Sake: Negotiating a Drinking Role in Japan." Presented at the annual meeting of the American Anthropological Association, Chicago, November 22, 1987.

Steinhoff, Patricia G. "Death by Defeatism and Other Fables: The Psychosocial Dynamics of the Rengō Sekigun Purge." In *Japanese Social Organization.* Edited by Takie Sugiyama Lebra. Honolulu: University of Hawaii Press, 1992.

Steven, Rob. *Japan's New Imperialism.* Armonk, N.Y.: M. E. Sharpe, 1990.

Sussman, Marvin B. and James C. Romeis. "Willingness to Assist One's Elderly Parents: Responses from the United States and Japan." *Human Organization* 41 (1982): 256–259.

Takenaka, Emiko. *Sengo Joshi Rōdō Shiron* (A History of Postwar Women's Labor.) Tokyo: Yūhikaku, 1989.

Tamanoi, Mariko. "Songs as Weapons: The Culture and History of Komori (Nursemaids) in Modern Japan." *Journal of Asian Studies* 50, no. 4 (1991): 793–817.

Tanaka, Keiko. "Intelligent Elegance: Women in Japanese Advertising." In *Unwrapping Japan.* Edited by E. Ben-ari, B. Moeran, and J. Valentine. Honolulu: University of Hawaii Press, 1990.

Tanaka, Sen-O. *The Tea Ceremony.* Tokyo: Kodansha International, 1983.

Thayer, Nathaniel B. *How the Conservatives Rule Japan.* Princeton: Princeton University Press, 1969.

Tobin, Joseph J. "The American Idealization of Old Age in Japan." *The Gerontologist* 27 (1987): 53–57.

————— "Komatsudani: A Japanese Preschool." In *Preschool in Three Cultures: Japan, China, and the United States.* Edited by Joseph J. Tobin, David Y. H. Wu, Dana H. Davidson. New Haven: Yale University Press, 1989.

Tsuya, Noriko and Karen Mason. "Changing Gender Roles and Below-Replacement Fertility in Japan." Paper presented at the IUSSP Seminar on Gender and Family Change in Industrialized Countries, Rome, Italy, January 26–30, 1992.

Ueno, Chizuko. "The Japanese Women's Movement: The Counter-values to Industrialism." In *The Japanese Trajectory: Modernization and Beyond*. Edited by G. McCormack and Y. Sugimoto. Cambridge: Cambridge University Press, 1988.

———— "The Position of Women Reconsidered." *Current Anthropology* 28, no. 4 (supplement) (1987): 75.

Uno, Kathleen S. "The Death of 'Good Wife, Wise Mother'?" In *Postwar Japan as History*. Edited by Andrew Gordon. Berkeley: University of California Press, 1993.

———— "Good Wives and Wise Mothers in Early Twentieth Century Japan." Paper presented at panel on Women in Prewar Japan, Pacific Coast Branch of the American Historical Association and Western Association of Women Historians joint meeting, San Francisco, 1988.

———— "Women and Changes in the Household Division of Labor." In *Recreating Japanese Women, 1600–1945*. Edited by Gail Lee Bernstein. Berkeley: University of California Press, 1991.

Valentine, James, "On the Borderlines: The Significance of Marginality in Japanese Society." In *Unwrapping Japan: Society and Culture in Anthropological Perspective*. Edited by Eyal Ben-Ari, Brian Moeran, and James Valentine. Honolulu: University of Hawaii Press, 1990.

Vogel, Ezra F. *Japan's New Middle Class*. Berkeley: University of California Press, 1971.

Vogel, Suzanne H. "Professional Housewife: The Career of Urban Middle Class Japanese Women." *Japan Interpreter* 12, no. 1 (1978): 16–43.

Whittaker, D. H. "The End of Japanese-Style Employment?" *Work, Employment, and Society* 4, no. 3 (1990): 321–347.

Yanaga, Chitoshi. *Japanese People and Politics*. New York: John Wiley and Sons, 1956.

Yoshimoto, Banana. *Kitchen*. Tokyo: Fukutake Shoten, 1988.

Youn, Jung-suk. "Candidates and Party Images: Recruitment to the Japanese House of Representatives, 1958–1972." In *Parties, Candidates, and Voters in Japan: Six Quantitative Studies*. Edited by John Creighton Campbell. Ann Arbor, Michigan: Center for Japanese Studies, University of Michigan, 1972.

INDEX

Age: of bar hostesses, 183; employment policy on, 194; marital, 4, 14, 29, 44n62, 205–6, 208, 210, 326; of married blue-collar workers, 223; of women managers, 209. *See also* Life span

Aging Well Club (Tokyo), 73

Aida Yuji, 144–45, 154nn16,17

Akamatsu Tsuneko, 276

Akimoto Ikuko, 283, 284

Akutagawa Prize, 267n23

Allied Occupation, 110, 159, 271, 272

Allison, Anne, 7

Amae (passive dependent relationship), 63–64, 137

An-An, 22, 45n70, 257

Andō Hatsu, 273

Anti-Security Treaty protests (1960), 303

Anti-Subversive Activities Law (1952), 305, 322n9

Asahi Shimbun, 257

Asanuma Inejirō, 279

Asanuma Kyōko, 279

As Long As I Make the Last Flight of the Day (Hayashi), 261, 269n63

Autonomic nervous system, 98

Awaya, Nobuko, 6, 265n4, 266n8

Banana. *See* Yoshimoto Banana

Bar hostesses (*hosutesu-san*): dress/living arrangements of, 182–84; education of, 180, 190–91n2–4; geographic origins of, 179; income/tenure of, 177, 178, 181–82, 191n6; in-

teraction skills of, 180–81, 188; marriage of, 189; nurturing role of, 8; physical harassment of, 186; prostitution by, 187–88, 191n10; social networks of, 183–85, 186–87, 191n8–9; work motivations of, 189–90, 327

Bathing, 168

Benson, Susan, 192

Bentō (lunch boxes), 145–46, 155n21

Bernstein, Gail Lee, 1, 6, 9, 241

Biomedicines, 74–75. See also *Kōnenki;* Menopause

Birthrate: by age-specific groups, 29, 44n64; decrease in, 4, 159, 194; government position on, 17, 41n16, 171; of married working women, 226

Block, Fred, 39n5

Blue-collar women: age/tenure of, 223, 242n3; career commitment of, 233–36; combined work/home roles of, 224–26, 241; on elder care, 88; four careers of, 230–40, 243n9–12; as lifetime regular workers, 222; mothers-in-law's interaction with, 236, 237, 238; physical stress of, 232; promotion reluctance of, 228–29, 242n7; social networks of, 191n7; work motivations of, 9, 226–28, 242n6. *See also* Employment

Bluestocking Society, 277

Boocock, Sarane Spence, 153n6

Boseishugi (doctrine of motherhood). *See* Motherhood

Bourdieu, Pierre, 41–42n24

Bowing, 202

Branch families, 108, 110

Brines, Russell, 297n15

Brinton, Mary C., 205–6, 212, 213, 217

Brody, E. M., 167, 170

Brother Corporation, 201–2

Budō ga Me ni Shimiru (Grapes sting my eyes) (Hayashi), 257, 259–60

Bund (Communist League), 302, 303, 304–5, 313, 321n4. *See also* New Left

Campbell, Ruth, 167, 170

Canada, 196

Caregivers. *See* Nurturing role

Castile, Rand, 130n1

Caudill, William, 161, 163

CGP (Clean Government Party), 280, 286, 290–91, 292, 293

Chadō (tea ceremony), 117–18, 121–22, 127–28, 130nn1,2; female membership/participation in, 124–25, 128, 133–34n29; interactive creativity of, 126–27, 129–30; lessons in, 118, 126, 130–31n3, 131n8, 131–32n10; reasons for studying, 7, 117, 120–21, 123–24, 125, 127, 132n13, 133n17; research methodology on, 119, 131–32n9–10, 132n12

Chanoyū (in tea ceremony), 130n1. *See also Chadō*

Chiba Chiyose, 277

Chiba Keiko, 290, 294

Chifuren (National Federation of Regional Women's Organizations), 280

Childcare: at day-care centers, 17, 41n15, 142–43, 153n6; employment policies on, 15, 16, 40n10, 230, 237, 242n5, 243n9; husbands' participation in, 159, 165–66, 175n35; in-company provision of, 200, 218n22; Japanese versus American style of, 160, 161, 163; maternity/paternity leave for, 198–99, 200; by mothers-in-law, 236, 237, 326. See also *Kyōiku mama*

Children: government allowances for, 17, 29–30, 41n16, 44n65; identity of, in school, 144, 145, 154n18; mother's socialization of, 137, 141–42, 153n7; performance pressures on, 137–38, 148–49, 150, 152; pre-school skills of, 154n12; school uniforms for, 145, 154n14, 154n20; summer discipline strategies for, 135–36, 139–41, 146–47, 155n25. *See also* Nursery school

Chūtō Repōto (Middle East report), 323n31

The Circumstances of an Adult (Hayashi), 262–63

Civil service positions, 182

Clark, Rodney, 194, 219n42

Clean Government Party. *See* CGP

Climacterium, 97

Cole, Robert, 242n7

Communist League (Kyōsanshugisha Dōmei). *See* Bund

Conservative parties, 275. *See also* LDP

Consumption: and employment options, 213–14, 326; female sexuality and, 25, 43n54–55; media stimulation of, 20, 21–22, 37; state's encouragement of, 18–19; status and, 20, 25, 41n23. *See also* Leisure

Consumption tax, 291–92

Cosmopolitan, 32

Cost of living, 225, 226–27

Crea, 23

Creativity: individual versus group, 125–27. See also *Chadō*

Creighton, Millie R., 8, 9, 327

Criminal justice system, 305, 322n18

Croissant, 257, 261

Cultural ideals: versus lived experience, 156–58, 172–73. *See also* Nurturing role

Danjo kōyō kikai kintōhō (1985). *See* EEOL

Day-care centers (*hoikuen*), 17, 41n15, 153n6, 200, 218n22

Democratic Socialist Party, 286, 289, 290, 293

Dentsū, 26, 214

Department store employees: appearance regulations for, 202–3, 218n30; on career employment system, 207–8, 213; on women managers' single status, 212, 215, 327; senior-junior relationships of, 206–7, 215, 220n59; work-marriage ambivalence of, 208–11, 219n45, 220n46. *See also* Employment

Department stores: boring routines in, 202; counter culture of, 193; day-care facilities at, 200, 218n22; as female-oriented industry, 196, 197–98, 214, 218n17; field research in, 193; gender-differentiated tasks in, 204–5; lifestyle requirements of, 201–2, 218n27; maternity/paternity leave at, 198–99, 200; promotion/rehiring policies of, 9, 199, 200–201, 203–4, 208, 219n33

Diet: CGP members of, 290–91; communist women in, 282–86, 299n55; JSP representation in, 289–90, 292; LDP candidates for, 286–89, 292; lower house membership in, 277–79, 285–86; 1947 party affiliations in, 275–76; 1989 elections to, 271, 291–94; Occupation's purge of, 272; party coalitions in, 295; under proportional representation system, 283–84, 288, 291, 296; upper house membership in, 279–81

Dietwomen. *See* Women politicians

Discipline (*shitsuke*): as motherhood requirement, 139–42

Distinctions (Bourdieu), 41–42n24

Divorce, 3–4, 16, 29–30, 44n65, 160

Doi Takako, 4, 271, 289, 292, 293, 296

Dōki (same year entrants), 50

Dress: of bar hostesses, 182–83; role-defined, 51, 59, 66; stores' regulations on, 202–3, 218n30

Duke, Benjamin, 190n2

Edo period, 179

Education: of bar hostesses, 180, 190–91n2–4; as employment/promotion criterion, 180, 194, 198, 203–4, 218n18, 219n33; formal intervals of, 118, 131n7; hiring policies on, 194, 198, 218n18; legal requirements on, 180, 190n2, 191n4; mothers' role in, 3, 7–8, 14, 17; prewar secondary, 298n22; rising cost of, 226–27. *See also* Kindergarten; *Kyōiku mama;* Nursery school

Education mother. See *Kyōiku mama*

EEOL (Equal Employment Opportunity Law, 1986), 4, 196, 198–99; employer requirements under, 15, 174n19, 195, 203; gender role distinctions in, 200, 215; international motivation for, 8–9, 192–93

Elder care: as accepted responsibility, 88; in films and television, 58, 62, 63, 66–67, 164–65; government policy on, 79–80, 171, 325–26; life span's effect on, 78–79; opinion polls on, 167; physical comfort as goal of, 168; state-individual tension over, 8; in Tokugawa period, 159; as totalizing experience, 163, 169; women's responsibility for, 17–18, 66, 76, 91, 167–68, 171, 176n42. *See also* Nurturing role

Elections: in 1946, 272–74, 296n4; in 1947, 275–76, 297n15, 297n17; in 1968, 282–83; 286; in 1969, 290; in 1972, 285; in 1979, 285–86; in 1983, 283–84, 288, 290–91; in 1989, 271, 291–94; in 1993, 295. *See also* Diet; Women politicians

Elementary school, 137. *See also* Kindergarten; Nursery school

Employment: career versus noncareer-track, 195; *chadō* opportunities for, 123, 133–34n29;

demanding work ethic of, 207–8, 213, 220n53; demographic/attitude surveys on, 265–66n5, 266–67n8–10; and departmental transfers, 231–32, 238–39; education as criterion of, 180, 194, 198, 218n18; female consumer identity and, 213–14, 216, 226–27; female participation in, 4, 8–9, 11n6, 153n18, 192, 193, 213–14, 265–66n5, 271n6; gender discrimination in, 47–48, 49, 70n2, 160, 174n19, 182, 193–94, 204; of late twenties age group, 30, 44n66; legislation on, 4, 8–9; life expectancy and, 194–95, 217n11; male career model of, 226, 242n5; marriage's conflict with, 16–17, 208–12, 215, 219n45, 220n46, 224; of married women, 221, 224–26; M-curve pattern of, 224–25, 226; of middle-aged women, 34, 45n71, 84, 92, 171, 194; nonagricultural female share of, 222, 226; nurturer role's intersection with, 8–9; and pensions, 14–16, 18, 39n8, 40n12; and pregnancy, 15, 16, 40n10, 230, 234–35, 242n5, 243n9, 243n11; and promotion policies, 9, 194, 200–201, 203–4, 208, 219n33, 228–29, 266n8; and rehiring programs, 15, 40n10, 199, 208; and senior-junior relationships, 206–7; social constraints on, 192, 213. *See also* Bar hostesses; Blue-collar women; Department store employees; EEOL; Part-time employees; *Shain* women; Women managers

Entertainment industries, 178–79. *See also* Bar hostesses

Equal Employment Opportunity Law. *See* EEOL

Etiquette training, 121, 127. See also *Chadō; Shitsuke*

Europe. *See* West, the

Even If One Is Past the Age of Having Dreams (Hayashi), 269n48

Expo '85, 218n30

Extended family: flexible arrangements of, 326–27; as home drama resolution, 62–63, 64–66; middle-aged women's role in, 77–78, 81, 89–90; nurturer ideology's link to, 94–95, 159; state's promotion of, 78, 79–81. *See also* Nuclear family

Family budget, 213, 216, 220n54

Family Game, 164

Fashion magazines. *See* Women's magazines

Fathers. *See* Japanese men

Femina, 268n42

Feminists, 158, 248, 258–59

Fertility rate. *See* Birthrate

Field, Norma, 137–38, 152

Firstborn sons (*chōnan*), 58, 71n10

Fishing households, 107–8

Fishing industry, 110, 112, 113, 114

Five Women Who Loved Love (Ihara), 321n5

"Floating World" (prints), 179

Flower arrangement (*ikebana*), 117, 119

Fonda, Henry, 289

Foucault, Michel, 38n3, 144

Freedom (*jiyū*) image, 24, 30, 31, 43n53, 115

Free time. *See* Leisure

Fuchū Prison, 306, 307

Fujiki Yoko, 286

Fujin Mondai ni Kansuru Yoron Chōsa (Opinion poll on the problems of married women), 270n67

Fujita Mariko, 205

Fujita Sumi, 285

Fujiwara Aki, 281

Fujiwara Hiroko, 285

Fujiwara Michiko, 273, 275, 296n4

Fujiwara Yoshie, 281

Fujiyama Aiichirō, 281

Fukuda faction, 287

Fukuda Masako, 276, 289

Fukutake Shoten, 267n23

Full Moon (Yoshimoto). See *Mangetsu*

Full-time employees. See *Shain* women

Furoshiki (wrapping cloth), 145, 155n22

Gakureki shakai (academic pedigree society), 138

"Gekkō" (Moonlight, Yoshimoto), 255

Genba sections, 50, 71n4–5

Gendaibyō (diseases of modernization), 81–82. See also Menopause

Gender: dominant ideology of, 47–48, 50, 70n2, 71n3; media's relationship with, 46, 70n1; organizational ranking by, 49, 50–51; parodied notions of, 54; telerepresentations of, 57–58, 66–68, 69

Germany, 40n14, 97

Girls' Day (March 3), 205, 291

Gluck, Carol, 84

Gold Plan, 79–80

Good wife, wise mother role. See *Ryōsai kenbo*

Grapes Sting My Eyes (Hayashi), 257, 259–60

Grave's disease, 311, 322n20, 323n26

Gray Sunset, 164, 170

Grounded theory concept, 119

Gynecology, 74–75. See also *Kōnenki;* Menopause

Hacking, Ian, 73

Hagimoto Takeko, 278

Hagiwara Yukako, 290

Hahaoya no Shūgyō o Chūshin to shita Shakai Sanka to Oya Yakuwari ni Kansuru Chōsa (1990 survey), 266n8

Hakuhodo Institute of Life and Living (Tokyo), 86

Hamabata, Matthews Masayuki, 157

Hamaguchi cabinet, 279

Hamamoto Sojun Sensei, 128

Hanako, 45n70, 264

Hanakozoku, 264. *See also* Single women

Hanayama neighborhood, 179, 183–85, 191n7–8. *See also* Bar hostesses

Hana Yori Kekkon Kibi Dango (Marriage rice cakes on a stick rather than flowers) (Hayashi), 269n48

Hanchō (supervisor), 223

Haneda Airport demonstration, 301, 309

Hannaichimonme (*Gray Sunset*), 164, 170

Harajuku Nikki (Harajuku diary) (Hayashi), 270n68

Harris, Phyllis Braudy, 161

Hastings, Sally A., 9, 10

Hayamamoto Shūgorō Prize, 268n35

Hayashi Hiroko (pseud. Ōgi Chikage), 286–87, 288, 289, 292

Hayashi Mariko: audience of, 246; autobiographical fiction of, 257, 263, 269n49; career woman in works of, 261, 262; compromised feminism of, 258–59; education of, 269n54; marriage interest of, 259, 263; on media-created woman, 256, 257–58, 268n45, 269n51; personal essays of, 262–63, 270n68; published works of, 256, 269n47, 269n48; revenge desires of, 261–62; Yoshimoto's writing versus, 260, 264

Hayashi Shio, 279

Hayashi Toshiko, 292

Herbal medicine (*kanpō*), 98

Hibiya Outdoor Amphitheater, 301, 302

Higuchi Keiko, 80

Hirano Shigeko, 276

Hirokawa Kōzen, 279

Hirokawa Shizue, 279

Hironaka Wakako, 291

Hitachi, 286

Hokkaidō Women's Peace Association, 283
Home drama (*hōmu dorama*), 57–58. *See also* Tele-representations; *Wife, Mother-in-Law, and a Complicated Engagement*
Homemakers. *See* Housewives
Hormone replacement therapy, 98
Hosokawa Morihiro, 295–96, 300n96
Hosoya, Tsugiko, 80
Hosutesu-san. *See* Bar hostesses
Houses, 105, 115–16n1, 141, 326–27
Housewives (*shufu*): care of husbands by, 161–62, 176n42; conflict avoidance by, 166, 175n37; contemporary alternatives to, 326–27, 328–29; control of family budget by, 213, 216, 220n54; education of, 175n34; elder care responsibilities of, 17–18, 66, 325–26; Hanayama social networks of, 184; house-work/childcare role of, 45n71, 165–66; ironic idealization of, 84; *kōnenki* ideology of, 87–88; leisure time for, 119–20, 123, 124, 228; of modern nuclear family, 2–3, 82, 158; mothers-in-law's relationship with, 58–60, 62, 63–64, 69, 90–91, 93; pension status of, 15–16; postwar role of, 325; prostitution by, 188; television's focus on, 54, 55–56. See also *Kyōiku mama;* Middle-aged women
Housework, 34, 45n71, 165–66
Hyogo Institute for the Study of Family Issues, 165
Hyōgo Prefecture Society for Protection of the Constitution, 289

Ichikawa Fusae, 280, 291, 292
Identity: Yoshimoto's focus on, 247–48, 249, 250–51, 254–55. *See also* Individualism
Ideology: resistance to, 84–85. *See also* House-wives; *Kyōiku mama;* Middle-aged women; Motherhood
Idobatakaigi (conferences by the well), 184
Iemoto system, 128. See also *Chadō*
Ie (three-generation household), 77, 79, 159. *See also* Extended family
Ihara Saikaku, 32n5
Iibuka Masaru, 138
Ikuyo (stage name), 54
"The Image of Women in Canadian Maga-zines" (Wilson), 41–42n24
Images: age-targeted presentation of, 21–24; in American studies of Japan, 10–11n1; institu-tions' contradictory presentations of, 6, 12–13, 21, 37; to legitimize behavior, 5–6, 7;

postwar expansion of, 2–4; of radical women leaders, 10, 319–20, 321; of resis-tance, 24–27, 37–38; roles versus, 1–2; in women's magazines, 24–26, 43n53–55, 256, 257–58, 268n45, 269n50–51; women's re-constitution of, 13, 27–28, 29–31, 38n3. *See also* Roles
Imamura, Anne E., 162, 228, 265n1, 328
Imported Goods Catalog (*Yūnyū Zakka Katarogu*), 18–19
Income: of bar hostesses, 177, 178, 181–82; male versus female, 16, 40n13, 217n8; as pension determinant, 14–15, 39n8; from prostitution, 187; tax policy on, 18
Independence (*jiritsu*) concept, 139, 141
Individualism (*kojinshugi*): creativity's association with, 125–26; and diseases of modernization, 7, 81–82; independence versus, 7–8, 139; and individuality, 24; nurturing's tension with, 8–9
Individuality (*kosei*) image, 24, 29, 30, 31, 43n53
Inoue Natsu, 276
I-novel (*shishōsetsu*), 252, 253–54
Institute for Advancement of Women in Em-ployment, 192
Internationalism: status and, 24–25, 29, 31
Inui Harumi, 292–93
Isetan department store, 199, 201, 202, 204, 206, 208
Ishihara Ichiko, 197, 216
Ishii Ikuko, 286
Ishii Michiko, 288, 292
Ishimoto Shigeru, 279, 287, 288, 292
Isshin denshin (heart to heart communication), 63
Italian government, 316
Itohisa Yaeko, 290
Itō Yoshiko, 279
Ito-*san* (pseud.), 31, 45n70
Iwakami Taeko, 287
Iwao Sumiko, 4–5
Iwasa Emi, 285
Izumi Kyōka Prize, 267n15

Jackson, Laura, 179
Japan: age demographics of, 78–79, 171, 328; Al-lied Occupation of, 110, 159, 271, 272; cele-brated life transitions in, 95–96; consumer base in, 20, 42n25; corporate leadership style in, 317; cost of living in, 225, 226–27; crimi-nal justice system in, 305, 322n18; economic policy of, 13, 19, 39n5; educational require-

Japan (*continued*)
ments in, 138, 180, 190n2, 191n4; entertainment industries of, 178–79; female nurturer ideal of, 156–59, 158; feudal women in, 77; household registration in, 15; ideological awareness in, 84–85; labor market shortage in, 171, 180; leisure time in, 119–20; maturation perspective in, 73–74, 75–76, 95–96, 99; postwar societal changes in, 2–4, 81, 158, 325, 326; social networks in, 105–7, 185–86; status images in, 24–25; traditional versus modern houses in, 105, 115–16n1; as vertical society, 202; women's magazines in, 19–20, 41n22; work hours in, 17, 40n14. *See also* State, the

Japan Communist Party. *See* JCP

Japan Communist Party Revolutionary Left Faction (Nihon Kyōsantō Kakumei Saha), 301, 308–9, 321n3

Japan Consumer Association, 214

Japan Department Store Association (*Nihon Hyakkaten Kyōkai*), 196, 197, 219n33

Japanese Blue Collar: The Changing Tradition (Cole), 242n7

The Japanese Company (Clark), 194

Japanese family: postwar changes in, 2–4. *See also* Extended family; Nuclear family

Japanese men: *chadō* practice of, 127–28, 133n17, 133–34n29; elder care by, 167–68, 176n42; housework/childcare by, 159, 165–66, 175n35; leisure enjoyment by, 44n67, 45n73; on menopausal wives, 83; noncareer track exclusion of, 195; paternity leave for, 200; patriarchal perspective of, 47–48; physical care of, 161–62, 176n42; politician wives of, 274, 279, 280–81, 287; wives' interaction with, 166, 175n37; on women's career status, 262, 270n67; work and identity of, 144–45

Japanese Red Army: as Bund faction, 302, 304–5, 321n4; illegal activities of, 305, 321–22n8–9; as Middle East experts, 316, 323n31; Mori's rebuilding of, 308; and Palestinian cause, 314, 315, 323n29; Shigenobu's role in, 313–14, 315–16; and United Red Army purge, 310–11, 315, 323n29; at Zenkyōtō convention, 301

Japanese women; acceptance of gendered roles by, 104–5, 115, 119, 123, 148, 155n27, 219n34, 328, 329n2; age-defined marketing to, 21–24; *chadō* participation by, 117–18, 119, 128, 133–34n29; college age, 28–29; as consumer market, 213–14; control of family budget by,

213, 216, 220n54; elder care responsibility of, 17–18, 66, 76, 91, 167–68, 171, 176n42; home/work dichotomy of, 13, 14, 26–27, 33–34, 162; "housewife-breeder-feeder role" of, 328, 329n3; and housework, 34, 45n71, 165–66; and images of resistance, 13, 24–27, 37–38, 38n3; in labor force, 4, 8–9, 11n6, 192, 193, 213–14, 265–66n5, 271n6; in late twenties age group, 29–30, 44n66; life span of, 194, 217n11; marital urgency for, 205–6, 210, 211, 212, 243n12, 248, 327; M-curve employment pattern of, 224–25; nurturing's association with, 6–8, 77–78, 157–58, 159, 172; pension status of, 15–16; postwar images of, 2–4; role options for, 4–6, 326–29, 329n1; state-determined roles for, 13–19; state versus media images of, 6, 12–13, 21, 37; traditional image of, 262, 270n65, 270n66; Western images of, 10–11n1, 156–57; work attitudes of, 207, 219n42. *See also* Employment; Housewives; *Kyōiku mama;* Middle-aged women; Women politicians; Women radical leaders

Japanese Women: Constraint and Fulfillment (Lebra), 265n1

Japan New Party, 295

Japan Socialist Party. *See* JSP

Japan Times, 329n2

Japan Trade Union Confederation, 293

JCP (Japan Communist Party), 271–72, 282–86, 292, 293, 299n55

JNR (National Railways), 185, 186

Josei ni Kansuru Yoron Chōsa (Opinion poll concerning women, 1990), 266n8

Josei no Shūrō Pataan ni Kansuru Jikeiretsuteki Kenkyū (Time series research on trends of women in the workplace, 1989), 266n8

JSP (Japan Socialist Party), 271, 289–90, 293–94

Kaban (school bag), 144, 145, 154n13

Kaien, 267n15

Kaifu Toshiki, 279, 294

Kakarichō (subsection chief), 223

Kamichika Ichiko, 277–78, 289

Kanda Asano, 278

Kaneko Mitsu, 289–90

Kansai Bund, 303

Kanshin na mono (admirable) designation, 113

Karaoke, 181

Karita Teiko, 291

Kashima Takashi, 200

Kashiwabara Yasu, 280, 290

Kasuya Terumi, 290
Kateinai bōyoku (violence in the home), 72n14
Katō Kanjū, 274
Katō Shizue, 273
Kato Shūichi, 127
Kawanobe Shizu, 287
Kawasaki Natsu, 276
Kawashima Tsuyoshi, 309, 310
Kazoku Gēmu (Family game), 164
Keiō department store, 206
Kekkon shinai kamoshiranai shōkōgun (Tanimura).
   See *The "Maybe I Won't Marry" Syndrome*
Kekkon-tekireiki (suitable marriage period), 208,
   209, 210. *See also* Marriage
Kelly, William, 81
Kihira Teiko, 292
Kikukawa Kimiko, 279
Kindergarten (*yōchien*), 142-43
Kitchen (Yoshimoto), 247, 248-49, 251,
   267n15-16, 268n25, 268n31
Kiuchi Kyō, 276
Kline, Stephen, 42n27
Kobayashi Chizu, 279
Kobayashi Masako, 284, 285
Kobe public schools, 165
Koike Yuriko, 294
Kokumin nenkin (pension type), 14, 40n12. *See also*
   Pension system
Kokumin Seikatsu Center (Center for the study of
   national living conditions), 73
Kōdansha publishing house, 21
Kōnenki: leisured housewife myth and, 87-88,
   99; medical profession on, 83-84, 102n46;
   versus menopause, 75, 97-98;
   symptoms/treatment of, 96-97, 98
Kōno Kinshō, 279
Kōno Takako, 279
Kōra Tomi, 276
Kōro Akira, 274
Kōro Mitsu, 274, 276, 296n4
Kōsei nenkin (pension type), 14, 40n12. *See also* Pen-
   sion system
Kōshoku Gonin Onna (Five women who loved love)
   (Ihara), 321n5
Kondo, Dorinne K., 157, 241
Kondō Tsuruyo, 273, 296n4
Koshiwara Haru, 273, 297n17
Kosugi Ine, 276
Kubota Manae, 290, 292, 293
Kurita Midori, 285
Kuruyo (stage name), 54
Kutsunugi Takeko, 283, 284, 286

Kuzume, Yoshi, 10-11n1, 156
Kyōiku mama (education mother): contradictory
   roles of, 138-39, 148, 152; interviews with,
   142, 147, 154n9; preparatory tasks of,
   143-44, 145-46; respect and reprobation
   for, 136; scholarly positions on, 137-38;
   schools' criticism of, 150, 155n29; on schools'
   demands, 147-52, 155n27; schools' expectations of, 3, 7-8, 17, 139-41. *See also* Nursery
   school
Kyōsanshugisha Dōmei (Communist League). *See*
   Bund

Labor unions, 49
LDP (Liberal Democratic Party): economic policy of, 13; endorsements by, 278; medical
   contingent of, 279, 287, 293; 1989 election
   defeat of, 271, 291-92; in 1993 election, 295;
   proportional voting system and, 288; talent
   candidates of, 10, 281, 286-87, 289, 290,
   294; welfare policy of, 79
Lebra, Takie Sugiyama, 132n14, 157, 219n44-45,
   220, 236, 265n1
Leisure: as extended domestic role, 162-63; increased time for, 119-20; and kōnenki distress, 87-88; media's presentation of, 25-26;
   for middle-aged women, 34, 45n73, 73, 94,
   326; for single women, 30, 44n67; as social
   value, 118; state discourse on, 18-19, 20; tra-
   ditional arts as, 117. *See also* Chadō; Con-
   sumption
Lerner, Gerda, 329n3
Let's Buy a Scooter and Return Home (Hayashi). *See*
   Runrun o Katte Ouchi ni Kaerō
Life span, 78-79, 171, 194, 217n11, 328
Lingerie companies, 242n2. *See also* Azumi Cor-
   poration
Lo, Jeannie, 201-2, 206, 265n1
Lock, Margaret, 7, 162, 326
Lod Airport (Israel), 315
Long, Susan, 8
Long-Term Outlook Committee, 79
Lunch boxes (*obentō*). *See* Obentō

MacArthur's Japan (Brines), 297n15
McCracken, Grant, 27
Maeda, D., 176n47
The Majority Finds Its Past: Placing Women in History
   (Lerner), 329n3
Mamagon (mother godzilla), 136
Mangetsu (Full moon, Yoshimoto), 249, 251,
   268n25

Manitoba, 96–97

Manufacturers: rationalization drive by, 221–22. *See also* Azumi Corporation

Marginalization: of *shain* women, 50, 71n3; of women managers, 214–15; Yoshimoto's theme of, 247–48, 249–51, 253

Mariko phenomenon. *See* Hayashi Mariko

Marra, Robert J., 7

Marriage: age at, 4, 14, 29, 44n62, 326; of bar hostesses, 189; chosen alternatives to, 245–46, 263–64, 265–66n4–5; cultural urgency of, 205–6, 210, 211, 212, 243n12, 248, 327; declining rate of, 160; demographic/attitude surveys on, 265–66n5, 266–67n8–10; employment's interference with, 208–12, 215, 219–20n45–46, 224; governmental encouragement of, 15; Hayashi on, 259, 263; of New Left activists, 312, 318; into stem family, 110; traditional arts training for, 117–18, 268n43

Marriage Consultation Centers, 15

Marriage Rice Cakes on a Stick Rather Than Flowers (Hayashi), 269n48

Married women: blue-collar careers of, 230–40, 243n9–12; home/work ambivalence of, 229; increased employment of, 221, 224–26; in nonagricultural workforce, 222–23, 226; work motivations of, 226–28, 242n6. *See also* Housewives; *Kyōiku mama;* Middle-aged women

Maruoka Osamu, 308, 323n29

Marxist Front Faction (Marusenha), 303

Marxist Leninist Faction, 308

Massachusetts, 96–97

Maternity leave, 15, 16, 40n10, 198–99, 230, 242n5, 243n9

Matsubara Junko, 245

Matsunaga Tō, 278

Matsuo Toshiko, 273

Matsutani Tenkōkō, 275, 277

Matsuyama Chieko, 278, 286, 287

Matsuzakaya department store, 209

Maturation, 73–74, 75–76, 95–96, 99. See also *Kōnenki*

The *"Maybe I Won't Marry" Syndrome* (Tanimura), 212, 245–46, 327

Mayer, Adrian, 187

M-curve employment pattern, 224–25, 226

Media: alternative female images in, 4, 21, 245; on education mothers' role, 139–41; and gender, 46, 70n1; Hayashi's criticism of, 256,

257–58, 268n45, 269n51; nurturer image of, 8, 164–65; on radical women leaders, 317, 319–20, 321; versus state-fostered images, 6, 12–13, 21, 37. *See also* Women's magazines; Telerepresentations

Medical profession: on *kōnenki*, 83–84, 97–98, 102n46; pharmacist employees of, 35, 45n76; political candidates from, 273, 279–80, 287; rehabilitative services of, 168

Meiji period (1868–1912), 73, 77, 85, 159, 325

Meiji University, 313

Menopause, 7, 74, 75, 82, 97–99. See also *Kōnenki*

Middle-aged women: elder care responsibility of, 76, 80, 88, 91, 325; employment availability of, 34, 45n71, 84, 92, 171, 194; fragile resistance by, 33–34; interviews with, 89–95, 96–97, 102n46; *kōnenki* experience of, 75, 82–83, 87–88, 96–97; leisured image of, 34, 45n73, 73, 94, 326; magazine images of, 23–24; marriage urgency of, 240, 243n12; medicalized focus on, 74, 75, 76–77; 1984 survey of, 102–3n54; productive household role of, 159; reality versus stereotype of, 94–95; in *shōwa hitokeka* generation, 85–86, 95–96; status-specific case studies of, 34–37

Middle class, 81, 158

Middle East, 314–16

Mihara-*san* (pseud.), 36

Miki Kiyoko, 277

Miller, Gale, 193

Minami Aoyama Monogatari (The south Aoyama stories) (Hayashi), 270n68

Ministry of Education Statistical Handbook, 190n2

Ministry of Finance, 266n9

Ministry of Health and Welfare, 329n2

Ministry of Labor, 18, 80, 192, 198, 199, 200, 215, 218n18, 225

Minowa Sachiyo, 286

Mitsukoshi department store, 198, 199, 202, 209, 218n7

Miyagi Tamayo, 276

Miyazawa Kiichi, 294, 295

Mizunoya Etsuko, 44n66

Mizu shōbai (water trades), 178–79. *See also* Bar hostesses

Mizuta Mikio, 277

Mock, John, 8, 327

Modernity: diseases of, 81–82. See also *Kōnenki;* Menopause

Moeran, Brian, 43n53
Mogami Hideko, 273, 274, 296n4
Mogami Masazō, 274
Mogami Susumu, 274
Momiyama Hide, 278, 279, 286, 287
Momiyama Hiroshi, 278–79
"Moonlight" (Yoshimoto), 255
More, 257
Mori, Barbara Lynne Rowland, 7, 328
Mori Tsuneo, 308, 310, 311, 314, 315
Moriyama Kinji, 288
Moriyama Mayumi, 288, 289, 293, 294
Moriyama Yone, 273
Motherhood: doctrine of, 77; education respon-
    sibilities of, 3, 7–8, 14, 17; employer's accom-
    modations of, 15, 16, 40n10, 198–99, 230,
    234–35, 242n5, 243n9, 243n11; self-sacrifice
    criteria of, 120, 132n14; state's encourage-
    ment of, 16, 17, 41n16. See also *Kyōiku mama*
Mothers-in-law: career-women's reliance on,
    236, 237, 238, 326; wives' relationship with,
    58–60, 62, 63–64, 69, 90–91, 93
Motojima Yuriko, 278
Murashima Kiyo, 273
Murayama Tomiichi, 296

Nagata Hiroko: death sentence for, 303, 312; ed-
    ucation of, 308; media image of, 10, 319;
    medical condition of, 311, 323n26; Mori's
    dominance of, 310–11, 322n23–24; New Left
    role of, 301, 302; political position of, 309;
    pregnancy of, 310, 318, 322n20; published
    books of, 311–12, 320
Nakabayashi Yoshiko, 285–86
Nakamigawa Aki (pseud. Fujiwara Aki), 281
Nakamura Kishirō, 287
Nakamura Tomi, 287
Nakane Chie, 202
Nakanishi Tamako, 277, 291
Nakano Takeo, 311, 312
Nakasone faction, 287
Nakayama Chinatsu, 291
Nakayama Fukuzō, 276
Nakayama Masa, 276
Nakayama Masaaki, 276
Nakayama Tama, 273
Nakazawa Itoko, 290
Naoki Prize, 257, 269n49
Narushima Isamu, 297–98n19

Narushima Noriko, 297–98n19
National Council of Social Welfare, 176n42
National Federation of Regional Women's Or-
    ganizations (Chifuren), 280
National Railways (JNR), 185, 186
Natsuko (*Wife, Mother-in-Law, and a Complicated
    Engagement*), 60, 62, 64, 66–67
Neighborhoods: as political body, 105–7; social
    relationships of, 105, 109, 110–11, 183–85,
    191n7–9
Net fishing, 107
New family, 3–4. See also Extended family; Nu-
    clear family
New Japan Party, 294
New Left: as leadership training ground,
    317–18; marriage of prisoners in, 312; Revo-
    lutionary Left Faction of, 301, 308–9, 321n3;
    and United Red Army purge, 310–11; volun-
    tary legal system of, 305–6; women's role in,
    301, 302–3, 313; Zenkyōtō and, 321n1. See
    also Japanese Red Army; Women radical
    leaders
New Liberal Club, 294
New middle class, 81, 158
New residence system (*atarashii jūtaku shisutemu*),
    79. See also Extended family
Nihon Keizai Shinbun, 5
Niitsuma Ito, 273
Nikkei Woman, 23
Nishioka Haru, 280–81
Nishioka Takejirō, 280–81
Nobuko Matsubara, 11n6
Noda Seiko, 295
Nōno Chieko, 293
Nomura Misu, 273, 297n17
Nonagricultural workforce, 222, 226
NonNon, 45n70, 257
Non-*shain* women. See Temporary employees
Nuclear family, 2–3, 81–82, 83, 120, 158, 326.
    See also Extended family
Nukiyama Eiko, 290, 293
Nursery school (*yōchien*): annual events at, 146,
    155n24; child/parent interview at, 143,
    154n11; versus day-care centers, 142–43,
    153n6; home-prepared necessities for,
    143–44, 145–46; performance pressures in,
    148–49, 150; summer vacation discipline
    and, 135–36, 139–41, 146–47, 155n25; uni-
    forms at, 145, 154n14, 154n20; weekly sched-
    ule of, 154n19. See also Day-care centers;
    Kyōiku mama

Nursing homes, 167, 171
Nurturing role: alternative choices to, 169–70; of bar hostesses, 8; caregiving responsibilities of, 7–8, 167–70, 176n42; conflict avoidance in, 162, 166, 175n37; contemporary modification of, 326–27, 328–29; contradictory images of, 6; as cultural ideal, 156, 164–65; departure from ideal of, 8, 165–66, 167, 170, 175n34–35, 175n37; and employment, 8–9; and femininity, 157–58, 159, 172; labor discrimination and, 160–61, 174n19; Meiji ideology of, 77–78, 85; physical comfort aspect of, 161–62, 163, 168; physical/mental stress of, 80, 168, 176n47; state's fostering of, 8, 80–81, 171, 325–26; women's acceptance of, 88, 94–95. *See also* Elder care; *Kyōiku mama;* Middle-aged women; Motherhood

Obentō (lunch boxes), 140, 145–46, 155n21
Odakyū department store, 199
Oda Nobunaga, 132n13
Office flowers (*shokuba no hana*), 194
Office Ladies/Factory Women: Life and Work at a Japanese Company (Lo), 265n1
Ogasawara Sadako, 277, 282–83, 284
Ogawa, Naohira, 79
Ōgi Chikage. *See* Hayashi Hiroko
Ōhira Masayoshi, 78, 288
Okamoto Kōzo, 315
Okamoto Takako, 176n47
Okudaira Takeshi, 314, 315
Oku Mumeo, 276
Once a Year (Hayashi), 261–62
Onna ga Ie o Kau Toki (When women buy homes) (Matsubara), 245
Ono Mikinori, 73
Ono Kiyoko, 289, 293
Opinion Poll Concerning Women (1990), 266n8
Opinion Poll on the Problems of Married Women, 270n67
Orange Page, 45n70
Osawa Mari, 241
Oshin (soap opera), 270n66
Ōsugi Sakae, 278
Ōtaka Hiroshi, 286
Ōtaka Yoshiko (pseud. Yamaguchi Yoshiko), 286
Otona no Jijō (The circumstances of an adult) (Hayashi), 262–63

Painter, Andrew A., 6, 164
Pāto employees, 221–22, 242n1. *See also* Part-time employees; Temporary employees

Part-time employees: government incentives for, 18; instability for, 45n75; middle-aged women as, 34, 45n71, 84, 92, 194; *pato* workers versus, 242n1; as share of female workers, 153n8. *See also* Temporary employees
Paternity leave, 200
Patriarchal ideology, 47–48, 49–50, 70n2–3
Patriotic Women's Association (Aikoku fujinkai), 273
Peak, Lois, 137, 138
Pension system, 14–16, 18, 39n8, 40n12
Perry, Linda, 182
PFLP (Popular Front for the Liberation of Palestine), 314, 315, 323n29
Pharmacists, 35, 45n76
Pharr, Susan, 281–82
Phillips, David P., 6
Physicians. *See* Medical profession
"Planning and Promotion of Policies for Women" committee, 192
Plath, David, 78
PLO (Palestine Liberation Organization), 314
Political prisoners, 305–6
Political sphere. *See* Women politicians
Popular Front for the Liberation of Palestine. *See* PFLP
Popular literature: alternative female roles in, 6, 244, 245–46, 249–51, 255, 265n2, 327, 329n1; realist movement in, 257. *See also* Hayashi Mariko; Yoshimoto Banana
Pregnancy: employers' accommodations for, 198–99, 230, 234–35, 243n9, 243n11; labor laws and, 15, 16, 40n10, 242n5
Progressive Unity Party (Kakushin kyōdō), 285
"Promises for Summer Vacation," 146
Promotion policies, 200–201, 203–4, 208, 219n33, 228–29, 242n7, 266n8
Prostitution, 187–88, 191n10

Que Sera, 23

Rape, 186
Recreating Japanese Women, 1600–1945 (Bernstein), 1, 325, 328
Recruit Scandal, 291
Red Army Faction (Sekigunha). *See* Japanese Red Army
Rehiring policies, 15, 40n10, 199, 208
Resistance: and status, 28, 31, 33, 34, 36–38, 327; case studies of, 30–32, 33–35; to everyday practices, 84–85; reconstituted images

of, 24–27, 37–38, 38n3; socioeconomic models of, 28–30. *See also* Images; Roles

Revolutionary Left Faction. *See* Japan Communist Party Revolutionary Left Faction

Roberts, Glenda S., 9; women's interviews with, 230–40

Robins-Mowry, Dorothy, 219n45

Rohlen, Thomas P., 71n4, 153n7, 219n40, 223

Rōjin byōin (hospitals for the elderly), 168

Roles: acceptance of gendered, 104–5, 115, 119, 123, 148, 155n27, 219n34, 328, 329n2; age-appropriate, 66; and dress, 59, 66; expanded choice of, 4–6; image versus, 1–2; legitimized by images, 5–6, 7; in popular literature, 244, 245–46, 249–51, 253, 254, 255, 265n2, 327, 329n1; social versus personal, 122–23; switched versus combined, 214–15. *See also* Housewives; *Kyōiku mama;* Middle-aged women; Motherhood; Nurturing role

Romance novel genre (*renai shōsetsu*), 247, 254

Rosenberger, Nancy R., 6, 170–71, 328

Runrun o Katte Ouchi ni Kaerō (Let's buy a scooter and return home) (Hayashi), 256, 269n46, 269n54

Runrun Shōkōgun (The scooter syndrome) (Hayashi), 269n48

Rural women, 104–5, 112–15

Ryōsai kenbo (good wife, wise mother), 77, 224, 228, 267n18, 325. *See also* Housewives; *Kyōiku mama;* Middle-aged women; Motherhood

Sadō (tea ceremony). See *Chadō*

Saishūbin ni Ma ni Aeba (As long as I make the last flight of the day) (Hayashi), 261, 269n63

Saitō Tei, 273

Sakaguchi Hiroshi, 309, 310

Sakakibara Chiyo, 273

Sakamoto Ryūichi, 258

Salary. *See* Income

Salaryman family. *See* Nuclear family

Sales clerks, 202

Samurai customs, 25

San shoku hirune tsuki (three meals and a nap), 228. *See also* Housewives

Santō Akiko, 286, 289

Sapporo, 179

Sasaki Shizuko, 290

Sasano Teiko, 292–93

Saso, Mary, 265n1

Sawada Hisa, 273

School. *See* Day-care centers; Education; Kindergarten; *Kyōiku mama;* Nursery school

The Scooter Syndrome (Hayashi), 269n48

Seibu department store, 198, 199, 200, 206, 210

Seikatsu Bunka Kyoku, 266n8

Seiyu Stores, 200

Sekigun, 301, 321n2

Self-employment, 165–66

Selfishness (*waganama*), 208, 219n44

Selfish Women (*Wagamama na Onnatachi*), 69

Sen family, 117, 130n1–2, 132n12

Senile dementia, 79

Senior-junior relationships (*senpai-kōhai*), 50–51, 206–7, 215, 223

Sen Sōshitsu XV Hounsai, 126, 130n2, 131n9

Setouchi Harumi, 312, 320

Sexuality: consumption and, 21–22, 25, 43n54; state's position on, 25, 43n55

Shain women: discriminatory treatment of, 47–48, 49, 70n2, 71n5; dress of, 51; versus non-*shain* stereotypes, 51–52; numeric minimalization of, 46–47; pension/health benefits for, 14–15, 39n8; seniority/gender rankings of, 50–51; as special cases, 50, 71n3; union struggles of, 49. *See also* Employment

Shiba-*san* (pseud.), 89–90

Shiga survey, 167, 169, 170

Shigenobu Fusako: media image of, 10, 316, 319–20; and Palestinian cause, 303, 314–15, 323n29; Red Army role of, 301, 302, 313–14, 321n2; Tamiya Takamaro and, 323n28

Shimizu Kayoko, 289, 292

Shimoda Kyōko, 283, 284, 292

Shimura Aiko, 286, 288, 290, 292

Shinjin Bungakushō (New writer's prize in literature), 267n15

Shinozaki Toshiko, 277

Shiomi Kazuko, 314; on husband's rehabilitation, 307, 320; media image of, 10, 319, 320; motherhood responsibilities of, 304, 306–7, 318; New Left role of, 301, 302, 303, 321n2; police surveillance of, 305, 306, 308

Shiomi Takaya, 302, 303–4, 305, 306, 307, 308, 312, 321–22n8

Shiotsuki Yaeko, 130n2

Shokuba no hana (office flowers), 194

Shōwa hitoketa generation, 85–86, 95–96. *See also* Middle-aged women

Shufuren (national housewives' organization), 291–92

Shūdan seikatsu (group life), 137, 140

Shūkan Bunshun, 257

Sievers, Sharon, 218n7

Sign, 22

Single women, 244, 245, 263–64, 265–66n4–5; corporate paternalism toward, 201–2, 218n27; as household heads, 30; as managers, 211, 212, 220n46; as media niche, 23

Smith, Robert J., 127

Smith, Steven, 162

Social Democratic Party Japan, 296n1. See also JSP

Social institutions: contradictory messages of, 6, 12, 37; reconstituted images of, 13, 27–28, 38n3; role model impact of, 1, 142, 152. See also Media; Nursery school; State, the; Telerepresentations; Women's magazines

Sōka Gakkai, 280

Sonoda Sunao, 275

The South Aoyama Stories (Hayashi), 270n68

State, the: contradictory role messages of, 16–17, 19; on diseases of modernization, 81–82; economic goals of, 13, 19, 39n5; on elder care, 17–18, 76, 79–81, 171, 325–26; extended family system of, 78, 79, 159; female nurturer image of, 12, 13, 159, 164, 171; leisure/consumption position of, 18–19, 20; on maternity leave, 15, 16, 40n10, 242n5; media-fostered images versus, 6, 12–13, 21, 37; pension/rehiring policies of, 14–16, 18, 39n8, 40n10, 40n12; on sexual imagery, 25, 43n55

Status: chadō's provision of, 7, 117, 125; consumption and, 20, 25, 41n23; internationalism and, 24–25, 29, 31; public versus private, 112; and resistance, 28, 31, 33, 34, 36–38, 327

Steinhoff, Patricia G., 10, 278

Stem families, 108, 110

Student movement. See New Left

Students. See Children

Stylist occupation, 257–58

Suffrage League, 273

"Summer Discipline Strategies for Hurrying a Child's Independence," 139–41

Suzuki government, 79

Suzuki Mieko, 290

Symbolic interactionist analysis, 119

Tada Tokiko, 290

Tajima Hide, 278

Takada Naoko, 277

Takahashi Chizu, 287

Takahashi Hisako, 296, 300n96

Takasaki Yūko, 292

Takashimaya department store, 197

Takeda Kiyo, 273

Takenaka, Emiko, 226

Takeuchi Shigeyo, 273, 277, 297n17

Takeuchi Utako, 273

Talent candidates, 10, 281, 286–87, 289, 290, 293, 294. See also Women politicians

Tamiya Takamaro, 323n28

Tanaka Keiko, 43n53

Tanaka Makiko, 295, 296

Tanaka Michiko, 285

Tanaka Naoki, 295

Tanaka Sen-O, 126

Tanaka Sumiko, 280, 293

Tanaka Tatsu, 273

Tanaka Toshio, 280

Tanimura Shiho, 245–46

Tax policy, 18, 291–92

Tea ceremony. See Chadō

Teachers, 148–49, 182, 273, 304. See also Kindergarten; Nursery school

Telerepresentations: alternative female images in, 69, 245; audience reaction to, 70; domestic conflict in, 69, 72n14; ideological transparency of, 57–58, 66; nurturer role in, 6, 58, 164–65; subverted hierarchies in, 54; valid cultural themes of, 69–70. See also Wife, Mother-in-Law, and a Complicated Engagement

Television industry: genba sections in, 51, 71n4, 71n5; housewife research by, 55–56; male/female employees in, 46–47; organizational structure of, 48–49; patriarchal ideology of, 47–48, 49–50, 70n2; programming and production roles in, 71n8; seniority/gender rankings in, 50–51; subverted hierarchies of, 52–54; union efforts in, 49; women's employment by, 46–47

Temae (ways of preparing tea), 120–21. See also Chadō

Temporary employees, 47, 51–53, 194. See also Part-time employees

Tenki (reproductive cycle quality), 97

Thompson, John B., 38n3, 68

Three-generation household. See Ie

Time Series Research on Trends of Women in the Workplace (1989), 266n8

Tobin, Joseph J., 153n6

Togano Satoko, 273, 274, 296n4

Togano Takeshi, 274

Tokugawa period (1600–1868), 159, 220n54, 262, 328

Tokyo: marriage/employment surveys in, 265–66n5, 266–67n8–10

Tokyo House of Detention, 306, 312
Tokyo Josei Hakusho '92, 266n8
Tokyo Women's Federation (Tōkyo rengō fu-jinkai), 273
Tokyo-Yokohama Anti-Security Treaty Joint Struggle Committee (Keihin Anpo Kyōtō), 321n3
Tokyū department store, 214
Tōbu department store, 199, 208
Tomita Fusa, 273
Tōkyō nichinichi, 277
Toyama Mieko, 314, 315
Toyotomi Hideyoshi, 132n13
Traditional arts, 117, 120, 268n43. See also *Chadō*
Tsugumi (Yoshimoto), 247, 253–54, 268n35
Tsushima Yūko, 265n2
TV Station, 58
"Two O'Clock Wideshow" (talk show), 50, 55

Uegaki Yasunari, 312
Ueno Chizuko, 15, 218n22
Umeda Masaru, 285
UNESCO survey, 127
Uniforms, 145, 154n14, 154n20, 203
United Nations Decade for Women (1975–1985), 192
United Nations Resolution on Elimination of All Forms of Discrimination against Women, 4, 192
United Red Army purge, 310–11, 312, 315, 319, 320, 322n24, 323n29
United States, 40n14, 42n27, 156, 158, 160. *See also* West, the
University graduates, in labor force, 194, 198, 203–4, 218n18
Uno, Prime Minister, 291, 292
Urasenke Senmon Gakkō (Urasenke training school): employment opportunities at, 123; male presence at, 133–34n29; membership/branches of, 119, 130n1; research study at, 119, 131n9, 131–32n10; Sen family of, 130n2; teacher-student network at, 128; Zen Buddhism at, 121–22
Urashima Tarō, 307, 322n13
Urban Japanese Housewives: At Home and in the Community (Imamura), 265n1

Valentine, James, 214, 250
Vinsancans, 32, 45n70

Wages. *See* Income
Watanabe Michiko, 290

Water trades. See *Mizu shōbai*
The Way of Tea (Castile), 130n1
"The Way to Spend [*sugoshikata*] Summer Vacation," 146–47
Wazaki Haru, 273
West, the: biological maturation focus in, 74, 75, 76; creative process in, 125–26; economic race with, 13, 39n5; female Japanese stereotypes of, 10–11n1, 156–57; menopausal symptoms in, 96–97
When Women Buy Homes (Matsubara), 245
Whittaker, D. H., 196
Widows, 16, 124–25, 278, 279
Wife, Mother-in-Law, and a Complicated Engagement (*Yome, Shūto, Kekkon Sōdō*): eating festivities scene in, 60–61, 71n111; elder care theme of, 58, 63–64; reified domestic role in, 66–68; tradition-based resolution of, 62–63, 64–66; wife/mother-in-law relationship in, 58–60, 62
Wilson, Susannah, 41–42n24
Wives. *See* Housewives
Women in the Japanese Workplace (Saso), 265n1
Women managers: age of, 209; career-marriage ambivalence of, 208–11, 219n45, 220n46, 262; education of, 44n66; marginalization of, 214–15; and morale, 197; perceived domestic failure of, 212, 215, 327; post-EEOL resistance to, 196, 201; questioned capabilities of, 206, 219n40; television's exclusion of, 47; Tokyo opportunities for, 266n9. *See also* Employment
Women politicians: cabinet positions for, 294, 295–96, 300n96; family connections of, 9, 273–75, 278–79, 280–81, 287; as JCP candidates, 282–86; JSP's support of, 271, 289–90, 292, 293–94; as LDP talent candidates, 10, 281, 286–89, 290, 293; lower house election of, 277–79; national constituency success of, 276, 279–80, 281; in 1946 election, 272–73, 296n4; in 1947 election, 275–76, 297n15, 297–98n19; 1969 CPG success of, 290; 1989 electoral success of, 291–93, 294; in 1993 election, 295; in opposition parties, 282, 294
Women radical leaders: autobiographical writings of, 320–21; leadership style of, 317; marriage/career complexities for, 318; media images of, 303, 319–20, 321; traditional support functions of, 301, 302–3, 313, 321n2. *See also* Nagata Hiroko; Shigenobu Fusako; Shiomi Kazuko

Women's Bureau of the Ministry of Labor, 15, 225

Women's magazines: alternative female images in, 24–27, 43n53–55, 257, 264, 269n50; contradictory discourse of, 20–21, 41–42n24, 42n27; growth of, 19–20, 41n22; Hayashi's criticism of, 256, 257–58, 268n45, 269n51; readers' response to, 28–29; versus state-fostered images, 6, 12–13, 21, 37; targeted age groups of, 21–24

Women's suffrage, 272

Wrapping cloth (*furoshiki*), 145, 155n22

Yakusoku (A Promise), 164, 170

Yakuza, 186

Yamada Emi, 254, 262

Yamaguchi Shizue, 274–75, 282, 286, 287

Yamaguchi Yoshiko, 286

Yamamoto Sugi, 279

Yamanaka Ikuko (pseud. Akimoto Ikuko), 283, 284

Yama o Hashiru Onna (Tsushima), 265n2

Yamashita Eiji, 289

Yamashita Harue, 286

Yamataka Shigeri, 280

Yamazaki Kenji, 275

Yano Akiko, 258

Yasutake Hiroko, 283, 284

Yokohama Prison, 309

Yokohama survey, 168

Yokoyama Fuku, 279, 286

Yokoyama Nokku, 283–84

Yōiku (nurture), 158. *See also* Nurturing role

Yoshida Sei, 273

Yoshikawa Haruko, 284, 292

Yoshiko (*Wife, Mother-in-Law, and a Complicated Engagement*), 58, 60, 62–64, 66, 67

Yoshimoto Banana (pseud. Banana): education of, 267n14; Hayashi's writings versus, 260, 264; I-novel identification and, 252, 253–54; on *Kitchen*, 251, 268n31; marginalized characters of, 247–48, 249–51, 253; on office ladies, 268n42; as public persona, 247, 252; reading audience of, 246, 249, 255–56, 267n23; self-discovery theme of, 247–49, 250–51, 254–55, 264, 267n24; success of, 267n15

Yoshimoto Ryūmei, 267n14

Yotsuya Mitsuko, 285–86

Youn, Jung-suk, 299n55

Young Childcare Leave Law (*Ikuji kyūgyōhō*, 1991), 200

Yukako Shinseiin, 130n2

Yume Miru Koro o Sugite mo (Even if one is past the age of having dreams) (Hayashi), 269n48

Zen Buddhism, 121–22, 164

Zenkyōtō (Zengaku Kyōtō Kaigi, All-Campus Joint Struggle Committee) movement, 301, 302, 321n1

ZTV (pseud.). *See* Television industry

Compositor: Impressions Book and Journal Services, Inc.
Text: 10/12 Baskerville
Display: Baskerville
Printer and Binder: Edwards Brothers, Inc.